What Would Jesus Read?

What Would Jesus Read?

Popular Religious Books and Everyday Life

in Twentieth-Century America

ERIN A. SMITH

The University of North Carolina Press
CHAPEL HILL

Published with the assistance of the Authors Fund
of the University of North Carolina Press.

© 2015 The University of North Carolina Press

Library of Congress Cataloging-in-Publication Data
Smith, Erin A. (Erin Ann), 1970–
What would Jesus read? : popular religious books and everyday
life in twentieth-century America / Erin A. Smith.
pages cm
Includes bibliographical references and index.
ISBN 978-1-4696-2132-6 (pbk : alk. paper) — ISBN 978-1-4696-2133-3 (ebook)
1. Christian literature, American—History and criticism. 2. Religious literature,
American—History and criticism. 3. United States—Church history—20th century.
4. Literature and society—United States—History—20th century. I. Title.
BR117.S55 2015
261.5'8—dc23
2014040580

An earlier version of chapter 1 appeared as "'What Would Jesus Do?' The Social
Gospel and the Literary Marketplace," *Book History* 10 (2007): 193–221. An
earlier, shorter version of chapter 2 appeared as "Melodrama, Popular Religion, and
Literary Value: The Case of Harold Bell Wright," *American Literary History* 17, no. 2
(Summer 2005): 217–43. An earlier version of the second half of chapter 3 appeared
as "The Religious Book Club: Print Culture, Consumerism, and the Spiritual Life
of American Protestants between the Wars," in *Religion and the Culture of Print in
America*, edited by Charles L. Cohen and Paul S. Boyer (Madison: University of
Wisconsin Press, 2008), 217–42. An earlier version of chapter 4 appeared as "'Jesus,
My Pal': Reading and Religion in Middlebrow America," *Canadian Review of
American Studies* 37, no. 2 (2007): 147–81.

For the UUs

CONTENTS

FIGURES

ACKNOWLEDGMENTS

I have incurred many debts during the writing of this book. First, I benefited from generous early funding for the project—summer stipends from the National Endowment for the Humanities and the Louisville Institute and a year-in-residence at the National Humanities Center in Research Triangle Park, North Carolina, in 2002–3. The University of Texas at Dallas provided a yearlong leave from teaching in 2009 for me to finish archival research and begin transforming these pieces into a book.

Archivists and librarians at many institutions have been extraordinarily generous. I am grateful to the staff at the Wisconsin Historical Society, Special Collections at the University of Arizona, Kansas State Historical Society, Lilly Library at Indiana University, Howard Gotlieb Research Center at Boston University, Burke Library at Union Theological Seminary, Special Collections at Syracuse University, and the Library of Congress. I spent a lot of time at the libraries at Duke University reading *Publishers Weekly*, and I am grateful for the hospitality and generosity of their off-site librarians. The University of Texas at Dallas interlibrary loan service kept a steady stream of popular religious books coming my way.

When I began this project, my best sources were studies of American popular books from the 1940s, 1950s, and 1960s. By the time I finished it, I was in conversation with a whole class of smart scholars who had begun to map the field of religious print culture—Candy Gunther Brown, Amy Johnson Frykholm, Paul Gutjahr, Matt Hedstrom, Gregory Jackson, Lynn Neal, and David Paul Nord, among them. I am grateful for their feedback at conferences, their collegiality, and their own scholarly work.

Audiences and panel members at the annual meetings of the American Studies Association, the Society for the History of Authorship, Reading, and Publishing, the Modern Language Association, the American Academy of Religion, the Reception Studies Society, and numerous smaller conferences were helpful interlocutors. I am especially grateful to Jan Radway, Joan Shelley Rubin, Amanda Porterfield, John Corrigan, and Michael Winship, who offered wise comments and encouragement along the way. Matt Hedstrom and Danielle Brune-Sigler began the Religion and American Culture Caucus at the American Studies Association, which provided my orientation to the field. Matt and Bob Orsi were generous guides to the American Academy of Religion and the field more generally. I benefited immensely from a series of seminars on religion and American culture organized by Andy Delbanco and Charlie Capper at the National Humanities Center. The biennial conferences on Religion and American Culture at Indiana University–Purdue University Indianapolis similarly mapped the field for me.

Audiences at numerous invited talks offered feedback as well. Christine Pawley invited me to speak at a daylong conference on religion and print culture at the University of Wisconsin Center for Print Culture in 2009. I am grateful for her hospitality, and to Jim Danky and Wayne Wiegand, who made my research and conference trips to Madison over the years a genuine pleasure. Wendy Griswold at Northwestern University invited me to present work to her Culture and Society workshop of dissertation students, an immensely energizing experience. I am grateful to Dan Raff at the University of Pennsylvania, who invited me to be part of a series, The Book in America: Economic Aspects of the Material Text, in 2006. Barbara Hochman and the members of her research workshop, Literature, Book History, and the Anxiety of Disciplinarity, provided a rich intellectual environment for interdisciplinary exchange at Ben-Gurion University in Israel in 2008. I was particularly energized by the passionate interest of community audiences at the Duke Institute for Learning in Retirement in 2003 and at Arizona State University in 2006.

Many colleagues offered feedback on the book proposal or read and commented on chapters or articles on which they are based. They include Julia Ehrhardt, Ellen Gruber Garvey, Jaime Harker, Natalie Houston, Alexis McCrossen, Jennifer Parchesky, Trysh Travis, Cathy Turner, Liz Turner, and Dan Wickberg. I have benefited from the feedback of the Dallas Area Social History Circle (DASH) on many occasions, and from writing groups at the National Humanities Center and the Southern Methodist University English Department. I got excellent feedback at the book proposal stage from Candy Gunther Brown, Amy Johnson Frykholm, and other anonymous press readers.

Graduate and undergraduate students—who read *The Man Nobody Knows*, *The Power of Positive Thinking*, and *Left Behind* in various courses with me—helped clarify my thinking about religion and popular culture. I am most grateful to the religious readers who welcomed me into their book clubs, talked to me about their reading and spiritual lives, responded to my queries, and offered feedback on my work.

At the University of Texas at Dallas, Dean George Fair at the School of Interdisciplinary Studies did his best to get me the time and resources I needed to get this project done. Sanaz Okhovat, who handles the Internal Review Board, helped me navigate that process on several occasions. Her genuine interest in the project came at a time when my own energy and enthusiasm for it were in short supply.

The University of Wisconsin Press, *Book History*, the *Canadian Review of American Studies*, and *American Literary History* granted permission to reprint revised versions of material published in article or essay form. I am especially grateful to Ezra Greenspan, Jonathan Rose, and Gordon Hutner— all truly generous editors.

I have been assisted by many people at the University of North Carolina Press. Sian Hunter signed the book and was its early champion. Mark Simpson-Vos inherited the project and hung in there patiently with me during its final years. I am also grateful to his assistants, Zachary Read, Caitlin Bell-Butterfield, and Lucas Church, and to my copyeditor, Dorothea Anderson, and production guru, Paul Betz. I received capable advice on the logistics of turning a manuscript into a book from everyone there. In particular, they found me wise and generous readers to vet the book proposal and the manuscript. I am grateful to Barbara Hochman and those anonymous readers.

Finally, friends and family took care of me during the long and sometimes miserable process of writing this book, which was interrupted by almost three years of cancer treatment. I am deeply touched by their encouragement and their tireless enthusiasm for its ultimate appearance. The dogs (quite rightly) insisted that research and writing required regular interruptions to take walks, throw tennis balls, and tug on rope toys.

What Would Jesus Read?

Introduction

One of the first tasks of a history of reading that hopes to understand the
varieties of the paradigmatic figure of the reader as poacher is . . . to ascertain the
networks of reading practices and the rules for reading proper to the various
communities of readers—spiritual, intellectual, professional and so forth.
—ROGER CHARTIER

Any attempt to clarify the value of literature must surely engage the diverse
motives of readers and ponder the mysterious event of reading, yet
contemporary theories give us poor guidance on such questions. We are
sorely in need of richer and deeper accounts of how selves interact with texts.
—RITA FELSKI

What Would Jesus Read? had its origins in a course I have taught at the University of Texas at Dallas for the last sixteen years on the history of American popular culture. The final project for this course is an ethnography, an opportunity for students to apply the critical terms and approaches from the course to their contemporary popular cultures. Over the years, my students have taught me about all kinds of Christian popular media—music, books, movies, television—and what it means to be part of these fan communities.

Inspired by these projects, I assigned the first of the *Left Behind* books, best-selling novels about the end times, with Amy Johnson Frykholm's scholarly study of their readers, *Rapture Culture: Left Behind in Evangelical America* (2004), to a graduate seminar on American popular books. I am a compulsive note-taker, but at the end of *Left Behind* I had not made a single mark in the book. This became *the* topic of classroom discussion—how resistant this book was to our literary ways of reading, how its interpretive community and its mission/goals were distinct from those of literary fiction, and how we might describe the cultural work of this popular book in contemporary America. These questions were the seeds of the project that became *What Would Jesus Read?*, a historical examination of selected

1

twentieth-century popular religious books and the communities of readers and writers for whom they were important.

At its most basic level, *What Would Jesus Read?* makes the case for the enduring importance of religious reading and writing in twentieth-century America. Fifty years ago, historian of religion Martin Marty argued that religious publishing was "a largely invisible phenomenon," and—until recent years—it continued to be a conspicuous absence in scholarship. However, religious publishing holds a central place in the history of print culture in America, and it continues to flourish.[1] Religious books were the backbone of most antebellum publishers' lists, and the number of religion titles published annually was exceeded only by fiction until after World War II.[2] In the 1920s, popular religion titles often outsold popular novels by a wide margin. Moreover, sales of religion titles were notoriously underreported, because—until Bookscan in 2002—bestseller lists did not track books sold through mail order, book clubs, specialty bookshops, or other nontraditional channels. For example, although it never appeared on any bestseller list, the best-selling nonfiction book of the 1970s was Hal Lindsey's *The Late Great Planet Earth*, a layperson's guide to end-times prophecy. Since 1945, religious publishing has grown at a faster rate than the overall book industry.[3] Nevertheless, scholars of American religion and literature have only recently turned their attention to religious publishing, and studies of historical and contemporary reading groups often begin by bracketing off religious reading.[4]

Although religion is a central concern of literary historical studies of colonial and nineteenth-century America by David Hall, Matthew J. Brown, Jane Tompkins, David Reynolds, Gregory S. Jackson, and others, the critical consensus is that the process of "secularization" was so complete by the late nineteenth century that religion ceased to be central to American literature.[5] *What Would Jesus Read?* challenges that critical commonplace by demonstrating how religious reading continues to shape the ideas and assumptions of millions of modern and contemporary Americans. The book spans a long twentieth century from Social Gospel novels like Charles Sheldon's *In His Steps: What Would Jesus Do?* from the 1880s and 1890s through ethnographic work with a contemporary religious reading group discussing such bestsellers as Dan Brown's *The Da Vinci Code* (2003), Kathleen Norris's *The Cloister Walk* (1996), and Thomas Moore's *Care of the Soul* (1992). I reconstruct the readers of Bruce Barton's 1925 *The Man Nobody Knows* (a portrait of Jesus as the father of modern advertising); describe the cultural work of Norman Vincent Peale's 1952 *The Power of Positive Thinking* and other religious self-help books by ministers, priests, and rabbis promising Cold War

Americans peace of mind; and situate the evangelical blockbuster of the 1970s, Lindsey's *The Late Great Planet Earth*, in its literary field.

These books have two things in common. First, they were immensely popular. They appear on lists of all-time bestsellers, and many have stayed in print into the present day. Second, most of them were dismissed by scholars and intellectuals as "bad books." Theologians and ministers filled the pages of newspapers and magazines with invective about the theological incorrectness of these dangerously popular books. Literary scholars deplored (and continue to deplore) their aesthetic and stylistic failings. Why would so many Americans spend their time reading such irredeemably bad books? Instead of dismissing these texts as unworthy of scholarly attention and their readers as stupid or lacking in taste or suffering from false consciousness, I re-create what Jane Tompkins calls the "cultural work" of these texts in readers' lives, cultural work that is largely independent of their theological claims and aesthetic qualities.

What Would Jesus Read? is located at the intersection of three fields of scholarship—the history of the book, lived religion, and consumer culture. As a book historian, my goal is to contribute to a more representative history of reading in America, one that includes the entire reading public, not just self-consciously literary readers and writers. I argue that these much-loved (and much-maligned) religious books illuminate *nonliterary* ways of reading that assume that literature and life are connected and that the right kind of reading can inspire the faithful to build a better world. Dismissing aesthetic concerns and ideas about art for art's sake, these religious writers considered writing to be a form of ministry, and they used popular allegory and contemporary, colloquial language to ensure that these texts were useful to modern readers and that they engaged readers' daily lives in immediate, material ways.

These modes of religious reading were not just nonliterary, they were often explicitly antiliterary. The New Critical ways of reading that began in universities in the early twentieth century made heresies of religious ways with words. New Criticism's indictment of the "intentional fallacy" and the "affective fallacy" insisted that a book's value had nothing to do with its writer's desire to make the world a better place or the powerful transformation of the reader's heart that resulted from reading it. In turn, many Social Gospel novels indicted the self-contained intellectual gamesmanship of scholars and intellectuals, offering instead a model of literacy that moved readers straight from reading to social action.

What Would Jesus Read? also engages what David D. Hall calls "lived religion." This field, which coalesced in the 1990s, privileges the everyday religious practices of laypeople over theology and church history. That is, it emphasizes what people do rather than what they are urged to think by religious leaders. For Robert Orsi, what lived religion scholarship does is transform the disciplinary structures of religious studies, interrogating the founding distinction between sacred and profane by investigating the religious dimensions of everyday life, the ways in which the material is always already interwoven with the divine.[6]

One of the goals of lived religion scholarship is to establish the importance of formerly trivialized texts and practices that traditional religion scholarship has ignored or dismissed. Church leaders and theologians indicted these immensely popular books as misguided, inaccurate, or even heretical. The unprecedented popularity of Norman Vincent Peale's *The Power of Positive Thinking* drew such a vitriolic response that Peale's biographer called it "the rage of the intellectuals."[7] Readers' letters to Bruce Barton are filled with accounts of laypeople trying to convince their disapproving ministers that *The Man Nobody Knows*—theological failings aside—helped ordinary people to live better, more Christian lives. Many church leaders got busy in 2003 running programs debunking *The Da Vinci Code* when it became clear that countless lay readers found that its claim to be based on truth profoundly challenged their relationship to organized religion.

Finally, *What Would Jesus Read?* engages with studies of consumer culture, highlighting what Leigh Eric Schmidt has called "the interplay of commerce, Christianity, and consumption."[8] These books were commodities—often remarkably successful ones—and they were turned into bestsellers in part through enormous advertising budgets, innovative mail-order and book-club marketing, and film tie-ins. For example, the advertising budgets for Harold Bell Wright's Social Gospel novels were staggering, and their success revolutionized bookselling. One 1921 sales gimmick—a free promotional phonograph record of Wright reading a passage from his latest novel—won first prize from the National Convention of the Direct Advertising Association for "the most original and result-getting stunt."[9]

These books were commodities, but they were also sacred books. One reader praised Barton for his mass-marketed life of Jesus: "You have written the Fifth Gospel."[10] Although we are accustomed to separating the sacred from the profane, culture from commerce, these much-loved religious bestsellers illustrate the ways people create and maintain religious meaning in part through their consumer choices. As Schmidt, Colleen McDannell, and David Morgan have argued, people construct their lived religion from the materials mass culture makes available.[11] I argue that buying and reading these popular books was a way to participate in a transdenominational imagined community of Christians (or Judeo-Christians) that sometimes overlapped with and sometimes conflicted with readers' institutional religious identities. Moreover, the engagement of these texts with the consumer economy is complicated and contradictory. These very successful commodities often offer spiritually inflected critiques of materialism and the consumerist ways of being in the world that come with it.

Because religious print culture is an enormous and largely uncharted field, this book is not a comprehensive study. I have structured *What Would Jesus Read?* as a series of case studies of important religious books, the communities of readers for whom they were important, and the literary and religious institutions that made them available to audiences. The chapters that follow are essays, examples of how particular communities of readers have appropriated popular books to actively make sense of the world and their place in it. They are also essays in the sense that they are attempts to describe a poorly charted world of popular religious reading. I have divided the book into five chronological sections that focus on specific kinds of religious books and readers—the Social Gospel novel (1880s–1910s), a bestselling life of Jesus from the 1920s "religious renaissance," religious self-help books of the post–World War II religious revival, a popular account of the apocalypse from the 1970s and early 1980s, and books for the seeker in the 1990s' "decade of the soul" and beyond. All are periods when the size and rapid growth of the religious literary marketplace garnered a great deal of attention in popular magazines and newspapers. I selected popular religious texts to represent a range of genres—novels, biography, nonfiction, self-help, history. I have reconstructed the religious and literary cultures from which these books emerged through scenes of reading and writing in the texts themselves, letters from readers, author and publisher archives, *Publishers Weekly* coverage, advertising and reviews in mainstream and religious media and on Amazon.com, reader interviews, and participant-observation of contemporary reading groups. My goal is to bring together these diverse kinds of evidence to illuminate larger patterns of religious reading, mostly—although not exclusively—among white Protestants.

Although *What Would Jesus Read?* briefly discusses Catholic and Jewish readers in Parts II and III, most of the distinct reading communities around these popular texts are white, Protestant, and nondenominational. The books themselves and the coverage of them in popular periodicals often feature slippage among Protestantism, Christianity, and religiosity. That is, they often take for granted that religious people are all Christians and/or that all Christians are Protestants. Scholars like Tracy Fessenden and John Lardas Modern have traced the construction of a secular, nominally neutral public sphere in America that is implicitly Protestant from the Puritans forward.[12] Fessenden details the real and symbolic violence that went into creating secularism as a ruling idea and the ways it privileged Protestantism and Protestants. Modern traces a common logic, what he calls a "metaphysics of secularism," which appears across a wide variety of Protestant subcultures in nineteenth-century America—evangelicals, Unitarians, spiritualists, early anthropologists, prison reformers, and others. I see these twentieth-century popular religious texts as engaged in the grassroots work of creating an idea of American religiosity that is implicitly white and Protestant (or that can be articulated through a kind of Protestant "common sense"). This is to say that—among other things—these popular books continue the symbolic work detailed by Fessenden and Modern for earlier periods. There are many stories about religious reading in the United States to be told—liberal and conservative, Protestant, Catholic, Jewish, Muslim, Hindu, Buddhist, and "spiritual but not religious" among them. *What Would Jesus Read?* is an examination of some of the most popular, best-loved religious books of the twentieth century and an invitation to scholars from many disciplines to contribute by telling the stories of more.

Theorizing Popular Reading

This is a book about popular reading. I was motivated by the desire to participate in writing the history of reading called for by Roger Chartier and in taking up Rita Felski's call to better theorize the value of literature—all kinds of literature—alluded to in the epigraphs to this chapter.[13] "What are the networks of reading practices and rules for reading characteristic of various religious communities," I asked myself, as I ventured into the archives, read primary texts, and examined conversations about religious reading in religious and secular periodicals in an attempt to answer that question.

As the chapters that follow make clear, readers emerge as what Michel de Certeau calls "poachers," readers whose own concerns and preoccupations shaped which texts they read, which aspects of texts they privileged, and how they read them. "Popular," for me, then, refers not to a fixed body of texts, but to a way of reading, what Roger Chartier describes as "a kind of relation, a way of using cultural products."[14] This popular way of reading or appropriating cultural artifacts is like de Certeau's poaching in that cultural consumption becomes an active production of meaning that is useful given one's situation, goals, and personal history. The social and political implications of these readings depend entirely on specific circumstances; I am not suggesting that these popular readings are—ipso facto—transgressive or conservative. Although cultural commentators of the time privileged the readings/interpretations of scholars and intellectuals over those of ordinary or popular readers (which is to say, readers who do not read and write for a living),[15] I do not. Ordinary readers did not seem to care much about theological correctness or historical accuracy in their texts, issues of great importance to scholarly readers.[16] Quite pragmatically, popular readers cared if these texts *worked*—that is, made them better people, managed their fears and anxieties, and made them feel as if their lives mattered in the larger scheme of things. I am not primarily concerned with which readings are "right" or better or more politically efficacious, although these questions—of course—come up. My concern is to describe these religious reading and writing communities and place these ways of reading in dialogue with the other "cultures of letters" in modern and contemporary America—which they were from its beginnings.[17]

These "readings"—however individualistic and idiosyncratic—are always shaped by the structure of the social institutions readers inhabit and by the rules for reading in their interpretive communities, which guide what readers should read, how they should read, and what kinds of interpretations are acceptable or defensible. That is, meaning emerges from the interaction of the text (the words on the page), the material book (with its price, packaging, and promotional materials), and the needs and desires of socially situated readers.[18] This is to say that the *ways* readers poach have everything to do with their social locations, their historical moment, and the rules and networks for reading in their specific communities. Thus, *What Would Jesus Read?* has both large and small claims to make. My larger claim is that popular religious reading involves aggressively personal appropriations of religious texts, bringing them close to make them over into our own image, to make them "useful" in our daily lives. *How* we do that, however, is historically and culturally specific. That is, it requires a kind of fine-grained "thick description" to elucidate the contours of specific reading communities and specific ways of making sense of texts.[19]

Because all reading is socially situated, I should make clear the subject positions from which I have conducted this research. I hold an interdisciplinary Ph.D. in literature/literary theory and women's studies, and I have worked in an American Studies department for the last sixteen years teaching courses in nineteenth- and twentieth-century American literatures and cultures and gender studies. I consider my disciplinary home to be American Studies, although I attend book history, literature, and religion conferences as well. My primary scholarly concern is reconstructing popular reading in nineteenth- and twentieth-century America. I was raised in Presbyterian churches in the Midwest (including a stint teaching Sunday school to early childhood and elementary grades) and have attended a number of mainline interdenominational and Unitarian Universalist churches off and on in my adult life. Although I do not find the religious bestsellers in *What Would Jesus Read?* compelling as aesthetic objects or (at least some of them) especially helpful or moving personally, I do think they are immensely important cultural documents. Popular reading matters—morally, socially, politically, and psychologically—and we would be bad scholars, indeed, if we did not investigate these best-selling books and these immense and sometimes powerful communities of readers.

Although these are historically specific case studies of popular religious reading, they are connected by a number of through-lines. The relationship between consumer culture and religious reading is the most important connecting thread. In Part I, Social Gospel novelists clearly distinguished Christian uses of literacy from commercial ones. Nevertheless, writers like Harold Bell Wright succeeded because of immense and unprecedented advertising of their books and innovative marketing to those outside regular book-trade channels. In the 1920s, Bruce Barton embraced advertising without ambivalence, making common cause between popular reading and commercial culture against the organized church, which—he argued—offered believers only unappealing, dry-as-dust versions of Jesus. Cold War writers of religious self-help books fully embraced the transition from "salvation" to "self-realization" (the terms are Jackson Lears's),[20] emphasizing the cultivation and perfection of the self over traditional religious doctrines or faith communities. In addition, these books emphasized the practical benefits of religion for this life, a reduction of faith to a means to worldly ends. This emphasis connects sometimes warring authors from diverse faiths—liberal and conservative Protestantism, Catholicism, Judaism. Lindsey's 1970 *The Late Great Planet Earth* was a more sophisticated commodity, a single text niche marketed as two different books for distinct audiences—evangelical and trade. By the 1990s, "books for the seeker" modeled how readers/consumers could custom-make a religious faith to meet their desires from the raw materials these texts provided and offered them the warrant to do so. Nonetheless—in every case—the status of these books as successful commodities and their embrace of consumerist ways of being in the world in no way undermined their status as sacred texts. These books are all examples of the promiscuous mingling of sacred and secular, spiritual and commercial.

The relationship of religious reading to the academy similarly connects these case studies. The Social Gospel novelists described in Part I distinguished their own brand of literacy, with its mingling of literature and life, from the self-contained, abstract literacy of the academy. What I trace in Part I is the "boundary work" that both self-consciously literary writers and explicitly evangelical writers did to differentiate their authorial missions. That mutual disdain continued—from the appalled theologians reviewing Barton's *The Man Nobody Knows* in the 1920s, to the *Partisan Review* intellectuals during the Cold War criticizing the bad thinking of new religious converts, to the theologians publishing indictments of *The Late Great Planet Earth*, to the scandal over truth claims in *The Da Vinci Code*. I suggest that these debates and controversies involve scholarly readers and nonprofessional readers talking past each other about what books are good *for,* discussions with implications for contemporary debates about the humanities in public life.

Finally, these popular books are connected by their relationships to organized religion. Although Social Gospel writers were often ministers/ authors who saw their callings as connected, the most popular of these books put forward an "untheological Christianity" that would appeal to the largest ecumenical Protestant audience possible.[21] Many of these popular books either challenged church leaders or attempted to fill spiritual vacuums left by them. Barton thought his 1925 *The Man Nobody Knows* could "save" Jesus from the irrelevance and effeminacy imposed on him by churches. Barton's brand of popular religion sidestepped modernist/fundamentalist controversies by focusing on practical Christianity. According to critics, Cold War religious self-help books trafficked in "the cult of reassurance," a bastardized faith (which came in Protestant, Catholic, and Jewish varieties) that substituted positive thinking for the real thing. *The Late Great Planet Earth* was countercultural in its energies, dismissing liberal and conservative churches alike as "religious county clubs" irrelevant to the salvation of individual, youthful souls. The heresies in *The Da Vinci Code* and *The Gnostic Gospels* challenged both church doctrine and the patriarchal structures of many readers' church homes. Popular religious reading, then, meets spiritual needs not met by organized religion and emphasizes usefulness for everyday life over doctrine. What emerges is a surprising family resemblance among the uses made of popular religious books—conservative and liberal, Catholic, Protestant, and Jewish. Whatever their significant differences, Americans of all faiths and no faith share and have shared a set of assumptions about religious reading based on inherited traditions of scripture reading, a therapeutic worldview, beliefs about the power and efficacy of literacy, and commodity culture.

Popular Religious Reading and the Middlebrow

"Middlebrow" is a term I use throughout *What Would Jesus Read?* to describe some of these ways of reading. As Joan Shelley Rubin argues in *The Making of Middlebrow Culture*, a number of cultural entrepreneurs sought to harness the machinery of mass production to make elite culture accessible and appealing to a general audience between the two world wars. The Book-of-the-Month Club, the Great Books program, and various efforts to popularize high culture for radio and newspapers earned the dubious label of "middlebrow," locating them between the highbrow culture of elites and the lowbrow, commercial culture of the masses.[22] Janice Radway argues that the middlebrow Book-of-the-Month Club was scandalous to cultural critics between the world wars, because it imagined literature as a means to the end of achieving social and professional status rather than as an end in itself.[23] Radway's thinking, like that of many scholars of popular culture (including my own), is indebted to the work of French sociologist Pierre Bourdieu in *Distinction*. Bourdieu insists that culture is the terrain on which social class is (re)created. He distinguishes between the "pure aesthetic" and the "popular aesthetic" or ethos. The pure aesthetic—a bourgeois aesthetic—insists on art for art's sake, severs the link between literature and life, and requires a distanced, aesthetic contemplation that privileges form over function. This is the appropriate disposition for approaching legitimate works of art. Conversely, the popular ethos—a working-class aesthetic—insists on the connection between literature and life, on the usefulness of texts for daily living, and on the engagement of one's emotions in reading.[24] The scandal of the middlebrow was the promiscuous mingling of "popular" ways of reading with texts that were or aspired to be legitimate art. Radway argues that the firestorm of debate in the early and mid–twentieth century over the middlebrow is related to its violation of cultural boundaries, "its failure to maintain the fences cordoning off culture from commerce, the sacred from the profane, and the low from the high."[25]

Like many debates about cultural hierarchy, the mid-twentieth-century controversies over middlebrow culture were articulated through the categories of gender, social class, and race/ethnicity, although they were by no means reducible to them. Legitimate culture was that of educated elites, and its aesthetic merit and intellectual heft were implicitly masculine. Popular culture belonged to the uneducated throngs, and it was usually associated with the feminine masses. Moreover, the terms themselves were shot through with racist assumptions. "Highbrow" culture was that of northern Europeans, who reputedly possessed high foreheads. The "lowbrow" belonged to blacks and swarthy immigrants, whose less lofty foreheads were allegedly a physical marker of their lack of intellect.

"Middlebrow" captures several characteristics of the popular religious ways with words that interest me: (1) their emphasis on the *usefulness* and immediate applicability of religion to everyday life; (2) their erasure of history and historical context; and (3) their scandalous intermingling of sacred and profane, culture and commerce. Religious readers tended to read these books as if they were written explicitly to address their personal concerns. These books were not abstract or theoretical, but *practical*, offering clear guidance for everyday life. Their lack of aesthetic beauty or (often) theological orthodoxy was immensely less important to most readers than that they *worked*—brought people closer to God; made them feel less empty, anxious, and sad; or offered clear instructions for practical action to take in the world. For example, advertising executive Bruce Barton wrote about a Jesus who was "the father of modern advertising" and offered practical pointers on running a business to white-collar Christian men in the 1920s. Contemporary Unitarian Universalists see lessons for themselves as an embattled liberal religious minority in the lives of second-century Christians we now know as the Gnostics. Bible prophecy like that in *The Late Great Planet Earth* involved reading words written thousands of years ago as being about the contemporary moment, that is, about *us*. In this way, these readings are like those encouraged by the Great Books program between the world wars discussed by Rubin, in which readers were encouraged to read all of the Western literary tradition as though it contained lessons for daily life in contemporary America.[26] Often, critics alleged, these books reduced faith to a means to an end—to business success, to peace of mind, to political or social positions about worldly issues.

Middlebrow reading practices sound remarkably similar to what Amy Johnson Frykholm calls the "life-application method" of religious reading.[27] I discuss this mode of reading in detail in Chapter 1. Suffice it to say here that life-application reading has its roots in Calvinist methods of reading scripture, and it involves seeking a "take-home lesson" for everyday life rather than placing passages of scripture in their historical context or examining competing interpretations. I want to suggest that middlebrow reading emerges from Calvinist modes of reading scripture that have been taken out of their explicitly religious context and remade for modern life. For life-application method readers, the Bible is both an ancient text and a how-to manual (more credible because of its ancient, supernatural origins). Great Books curricula were the secularization of this principle. "Classics," whose credibility/usefulness comes from their endurance over time, can be read as if they were advice manuals for contemporary readers. Middlebrow reading wrenches texts out of original contexts and interpretive communities and recontextualizes them as part of contemporary conversations about the good life, just as life-application method readers of scripture do. Middlebrow reading, then, is a secularization of these religious ways with words.[28] If nineteenth-century evangelical leaders thought you needed to sit down and read in a focused, prayerful way, taking notes and returning again and again to study key passages of scripture in order to sanctify your life, secular authorities similarly embraced the idea that one must do serious reading of the right books in a serious, focused way in order to build character, to develop one's mind, and to be worthy of the social and economic mobility that would follow.

The intellectual genealogy offered by Rubin in *The Making of Middlebrow Culture* offers some support for this claim. Rubin argues that the middlebrow represents the persistence of the "genteel tradition" into the 1920s, 1930s, and 1940s. "Genteel tradition," a phrase coined by George Santayana in 1911, was an epithet for him and other critics of the period. It denoted a repressive past—"an attenuated Calvinist strain in nineteenth-century American literature and philosophy"—that artists needed to escape in order to achieve greatness.[29] Although most historians insist that the genteel tradition disappeared after World War I, replaced by avant-garde artistic movements and commercial, mass-cultural entertainments, Rubin argues that "the terrain of middlebrow culture proved solid ground on which the genteel outlook could be reconstituted."[30] Her history of self-culture in America connects the middlebrow and the genteel tradition to notions of character developed by Harvard moral philosophers—Joseph Stevens Buckminster, Andrew Norton, and William Ellery Channing. For these thinkers, individuals had a divine obligation to develop their character. "To them," Rubin argues, "attainment of a cultured sensibility was part of larger task: the achievement of salvation."[31] For their more secular descendants in the 1920s, 1930s, and 1940s, middlebrow reading and study offered a kind of secularized salvation.

The similarities between Frykholm's "life-application method" readers of scripture and Rubin's middlebrow readers are no coincidence; this is a family resemblance. Life-application method readers have adapted Calvinist modes of scripture reading to the modern world; middlebrow readers are the descendants of the "genteel tradition"—that "attenuated strain of Calvinism" that has also been reconstituted for the modern world. These ways of reading have common intellectual ancestors and suggest that much "popular reading" is always already "religious reading," even if the religious ground out of which it emerged has eroded. This is to say that religious ways with words shape modes of literacy and ways of thinking about literature, even in a secular context. It is no coincidence that much of the language of modern literary studies was borrowed from the study of sacred texts.[32]

In his masterful study, *The Rise of Liberal Religion: Book Culture and American Spirituality in the Twentieth Century*, Matthew Hedstrom makes the case that although liberal Protestant institutions were in decline for much of the twentieth century, liberal Protestant ideas maintained immense and growing influence, in part through massive popular reading and book campaigns in the 1920s, 1930s, and 1940s. Middlebrow religious readers read for self-improvement and to be better, more tolerant, more inclusive citizens of the modern world, Hedstrom argues. Moreover, the focus on mysticism and psychological approaches to religion in these books created the conditions of possibility for the generation of "spiritual seekers" that preoccupy contemporary sociologists of religion.[33] Hedstrom's "middlebrow religion" is liberal and Protestant and tied to specific institutional locations—the Religious Book Club, the Religious Books Roundtable of the American Library Association, Harper's religious books division, and the National Conference of Christians and Jews. Although middlebrow ways of reading are characteristic of the liberal Protestant establishment Hedstrom describes, they do not seem to be limited to them. One of my goals is to ask why "middlebrow" ways of reading and therapeutic religion transcend this institutional matrix and to look across political and theological divides for common ground.

WHAT WOULD JESUS READ? presents a series of linked case studies of religious reading cultures. Part I, "The Social Gospel and the Literary Marketplace," looks at selected popular novels from the 1880s through the 1910s that imagined how a liberal Christian faith could transform modern social institutions and bring about the kingdom of God here on earth. Chapter 1, "What Would Jesus Do? Reading and Social Action," examines three of the most popular: Mrs. Humphry Ward's *Robert Elsmere* (1888), Charles Sheldon's *In*

His Steps: What Would Jesus Do? (1897), and Winston Churchill's *Inside of the Cup* (1913). I analyze representations of reading and of writing in these novels and historical examples of how readers were inspired to take social action by them. All were self-consciously about print culture, making clear that founding the kingdom of God here on earth depended on making appropriate use of books and literacy. The library is cast as hero in *Robert Elsmere* and *Inside of the Cup,* and all three novels feature the juxtaposition of artist/writer figures whose fates illustrate that the right kind of reading and writing invariably moves readers to work for social justice, while the wrong kinds are either strictly academic or blatantly commercial. Chapter 2, "The Dickens of the Rural Route: Harold Bell Wright and Christian Melodrama," looks closely at the career of one Social Gospel novelist who achieved immense popularity but is almost entirely absent from American literary history. Wright's *That Printer of Udell's* (1903), *The Shepherd of the Hills* (1907), *The Calling of Dan Matthews* (1909), *The Winning of Barbara Worth* (1911), and *The Eyes of the World* (1914) outsold almost every other novel published before World War I. However, Wright's blatantly commercial and blatantly evangelical model of authorship left him outside the literary mainstream. I consider the role of mail-order distribution, advertising, and film tie-ins in reaching a large, nonliterary audience and argue that these books succeeded not as aesthetic objects, but as popular melodramas for white, Protestant, predominantly rural and small-town readers.

Part II, "The 1920s Religious Renaissance," looks at the religious revival and growth in sales of religious books that followed the end of World War I. Chapter 3, "Good Books Build Character: Promoting Religious Reading in the 1920s," examines efforts to better market religious books to a general audience, including the nearly decade-long, industry-wide "Religious Book Week" promotional campaign organized in 1921 and the founding of the mail-order Religious Book Club in 1927. Drawing on the newsletters of the Religious Book Club, a decade's worth of book advertising and editorial coverage related to religion in *Publishers Weekly*, and scholarship on middlebrow institutions making high culture available to a mass audience, I argue that these efforts created a nonsectarian, mass-marketable religion that reframed theological controversies as matters of consumer choice. Chapter 4, "Jesus, My Pal: Reading Bruce Barton's Jesus," looks closely at letters readers wrote to Bruce Barton, president of the New York advertising agency Batten, Barton, Durstine, and Osborn (BBD&O) and author of a best-selling life of Christ, *The Man Nobody Knows* (1925), its sequel about the Bible, *The Book Nobody Knows* (1926), and a practical guide to religion, *What Can a*

Man Believe? (1928). Scholars have dismissed Barton's books as theologically empty justifications for consumer capitalism. Whatever their intellectual or theological failings, however, ordinary Christians found in them a religion that was newly accessible, relevant, and compelling. Barton offered readers a Jesus who was a personal friend in a world in which people were increasingly imagined as undifferentiated masses or placeholders in bureaucratic structures. His books gave readers a way to negotiate profound splits in Protestant America between modernism and fundamentalism, between religion and science, not by settling these controversies, but by reframing faith as a matter of practice rather than belief.

In Part III, "America's God and Cold War Religious Reading," I examine a group of best-selling religious self-help books by ministers, priests, and rabbis that promised Americans better living through the union of faith and psychology. They include Rev. Harry Emerson Fosdick's *On Being a Real Person* (1943), Rabbi Joshua Loth Liebman's *Peace of Mind* (1946), Bishop Fulton Sheen's *Peace of Soul* (1949), Rev. Norman Vincent Peale's *The Power of Positive Thinking* (1952), and Rev. Billy Graham's *Peace with God* (1953). Chapter 5, "Pealeism and Its Discontents: Cold War Religion, Intellectuals, and the Middlebrow," discusses the bitter divisions about the proper place of religion in American public life that filled the pages of mass-market magazines and elite intellectual journals, a debate with profound consequences for the reception of religious self-help books. Galvanized in part by a number of high-profile conversions to Christianity, *Partisan Review* ran a symposium on "Religion and the Intellectuals" in 1950, a symposium *Saturday Review* subsequently dismissed as intellectual posturing irrelevant to the rising religious fervor of ordinary people, many of whom wrote fan letters to the authors of these religious self-help books. Although writers for these magazines disagreed over the desirability of the revival and the proper relationship between religion and art, both located the moral high ground with the autonomy of the individual soul or intellect, casting their position as the truly "American" position to take. Chapter 6, "The Cult of Reassurance: Religion, Therapy, and Containment Culture," places popular religious self-help books in the context of what Will Herberg called the "triple melting pot" of Protestant-Catholic-Jew that shaped post–World War II society. Based on reader letters and business archives, I argue that these books engaged readers at home and abroad as part of the global war on communism. Although the threat of nuclear war loomed, these books promised Americans the happiness, prosperity, and optimism that were their birthright, and these texts were also translated and exported to the developing world as propaganda for the "American way of life."

In Part IV, "Reading the Apocalypse: Christian Bookselling in the 1970s and 1980s," I look specifically at evangelical Christian publishing and its relationship to trade bookselling through the lens of Hal Lindsey's *The Late Great Planet Earth* (1970), a layperson's guide to end-times prophecies. Chapter 7, "*The Late Great Planet Earth* and Evangelical Cultures of Letters in the 1970s and 1980s," uses coverage of religious books in *Publishers Weekly* and in the religious periodicals *Christian Century* (liberal Protestant) and *Christianity Today* (evangelical) to argue that *The Late Great Planet Earth* became a blockbuster bestseller because it offered an accessible, engaging presentation free of esoteric theology and difficult religious jargon; because it appealed to a new, nondenominational youth audience in an affordable paperback edition; and because it was marketed in innovative ways. Zondervan sold it alongside other books on Bible prophecy in Christian bookstores; Bantam issued an edition with a New Age/science fiction cover to capture the attention of secular readers in trade bookstores. Chapter 8, "End-Times Prophecy for Dummies: *The Late Great Planet Earth*," uses reviews on Amazon.com and other accounts from readers to challenge the idea that the politics of *The Late Great Planet Earth* can be deduced from the words on the page. Although readers encountered *The Late Great Planet Earth* through the lens of millennial anxieties about the nuclear arms race and environmental degradation, they also read for personal reasons—to create a sense of belonging at church or Sunday school, to please a counter-cultural girlfriend, or to imagine an escape from an awkward adolescence. Though the book was widely condemned by scholars for its unorthodox theology and undermining of religious institutions, ordinary readers preferred to focus pragmatically on its positive influence in saving individual souls.

Part V, "The Decade of the Soul: The 1990s and Beyond," focuses on a group of popular texts with particular appeal to "spiritual seekers" and self-proclaimed heretics. Chapter 9, "Books for the Seeker: Liberal Religion and the Literary Marketplace in the 1990s," considers Thomas Moore's *Care of the Soul* (1992), Karen Armstrong's *A History of God* (1993), Kathleen Norris's *The Cloister Walk* (1996), Jack Miles's Pulitzer Prize–winning *God: A Biography* (1996), and reviews by their readers on Amazon.com. These books model the formation of alternative, individual spiritual faiths outside formal religious institutions. They respond to the ills of consumer culture by promising that dedicated spiritual practice, deliberate cultivation of a sense of the sacred, and the adoption of new ways with words will re-enchant everyday life. Ironically, these critiques of consumer capitalist life embrace postmodern notions of subjectivity and history, suggesting that both can be imagined as consumer choices. Chapter 10, "The New Gnosticism: Gender, Heresy, and Religious Community," discusses ethnographic work with one contemporary Unitarian Universalist (UU) religious reading group, investigating how discussion of popular titles related to "the new Gnosticism"— Elaine Pagels's *Beyond Belief* (2003) and Dan Brown's *The Da Vinci Code* (2003)—allows readers to fashion religious identity narratives. The reading group emerges as both a spiritual community and a support group, a place where readers explore what it means to be women in patriarchal religious institutions and what it means to be embattled religious liberals in the Bible Belt. Although these UUs define themselves against an evangelical Christian "other," whose unquestioning embrace of orthodoxy serves as a foil for their own spiritual seeking, their ways of reading, the therapeutic worldview that structures their conversations, and the ways they create religious communities overlap significantly.

The Conclusion considers the relationship between religious reading and other forms of popular reading and foregrounds the threads connecting these texts and readers over the long twentieth century. I ask why these books and these readers matter—to religious studies, to American literary history, and, ultimately, to the fate of the humanities.

PART I

The Social Gospel and
the Literary Marketplace

ONE

What Would Jesus Do?

Reading and Social Action

—◆◇◆—

This library is my church, and men and women of
all creeds come here by the thousands.
—*Inside of the Cup* (1913)

Hegemonizing is hard work.
—STUART HALL

Frank Luther Mott, esteemed scholar of bestsellers in America, argues that "one cannot dip into the popular literature of the first two decades of the twentieth century without being impressed by the emphasis on the church and its problems."[1] Much of this literature was part of the Social Gospel, an ecumenical Protestant movement in North America in the late nineteenth and early twentieth centuries seeking to transform social institutions according to Christian principles. Sometimes called the "Third Great Awakening," the Social Gospel was a response by liberal Protestants to the problems caused by industrialization, massive immigration, and urbanization. The religious expression of the Progressive movement, the Social Gospel had a major influence on the policies of Theodore Roosevelt and Woodrow Wilson, advocating for workers' rights to collective bargaining; federal regulation of wages, hours, and working conditions; protective labor legislation for women and children; and the formation of a welfare state to mitigate the negative effects of unbridled capitalism. In part, Social Gospel leaders wished to bring working men and women into the church, but they also intended to bring about the kingdom of God (that is, a just social order) here on earth.[2]

Although the Social Gospel is usually discussed through the nonfiction writings of its most prominent leaders, liberal Protestant ministers Washington Gladden, Richard Ely, and Walter Rauschenbusch, there is a sizable body of Social Gospel fiction that popularized the doctrines of these more learned writers. About one hundred Social Gospel novels were published around the turn of the twentieth century. Between 1886 and 1914, roughly three or four Social Gospel novels appeared every year.[3] The most popular American novels include Charles Sheldon's *In His Steps* (1897), Harold Bell Wright's *That Printer of Udell's* (1903), and Winston Churchill's *Inside of the Cup* (1913). All of these novels are self-consciously *about* print culture, making clear that founding the kingdom of God here on earth depends on making appropriate use of books and literacy. These novels are rich resources, then, for uncovering the rules of reading and the networks of reading practices authors, ministers, and publishers urged on their Social Gospel readers in turn-of-the-century America. Moreover, the commentary and controversy they engendered offer testimony to some of the ways Social Gospel readers appropriated these texts as "equipment for living" their everyday lives.[4]

In these texts, appropriate use of books invariably moves readers to social action. That is, one reads not in order to contemplate abstract ideas or to improve oneself, but in order to change the world. In Social Gospel fiction, poverty, drunkenness, crime, and urban blight are no match for the right kind of books in the hands and minds of the right kind of readers. Although many popular Social Gospel novels engage deeply with the theological divisions of their day—embracing modern biblical criticism and the extensive reading of new books bringing faith to bear on the problems of contemporary life—perhaps the best-known Social Gospel novel, Sheldon's *In His Steps: What Would Jesus Do?*, sidesteps theological controversy and critiques the modern, mass-literary marketplace. Although Sheldon's book is also self-consciously engaged with questions about reading, writing, and social action, his brand of "untheological Christianity" makes his work appropriable to new generations of believers in ways most Social Gospel novels are not.[5]

This chapter looks closely at three of the most popular Social Gospel novels, Mrs. Humphry Ward's *Robert Elsmere* (1888), Sheldon's *In His Steps*, and Winston Churchill's *Inside of the Cup*, all of which self-consciously represent different models of reading and writing in order to demonstrate the porousness of the boundaries between literature and life for good Christian readers. Although the hundred or so Social Gospel novels can by no means be reduced to a single formula or plot, I chose to investigate these novels specifically for four reasons. First, they were bestsellers, suggesting that the particular version of social salvation through Christian action these novels offered was especially compelling to ordinary readers. Second, the public attention and controversy they generated created a paper trail of testimony about what ministers, reviewers, and other social commentators thought religious books ought to do. Third, the texts themselves deliberately consider different ways of reading to an extraordinary degree. Fourth, in the scholarly discussions about Social Gospel fiction, these novels are often granted emblematic status.[6]

I am concerned not only with representations of reading and writing *in* the novels, but also with Social Gospel readers. Sheldon wrote about himself as a reader in his 1925 autobiography, and these books motivated many ordinary readers to take social action. The interplay between Social Gospel literature and life is striking. Sheldon was inspired to dress up as a tramp and inhabit the underworld of his own city of Topeka, Kansas by reading Ward's *Robert Elsmere*, and his tramping, in turn, inspired him to write *In His Steps*. The representation of a Christian daily newspaper in *In His Steps* motivated one Kansas editor to make his own periodical a Christian newspaper for one week in 1900. That newspaper offered specific recommendations on the social action Christian readers should take after perusing the news. Literature in Social Gospel novels is not a self-contained, intertextual world of ideas, but a series of concrete transactions with the material world undertaken by readers who understand books and literacy differently than contemporary scholars do.

The Library as Savior: *Robert Elsmere* and *Inside of the Cup*

Henry James hailed the 1888 publication of Mrs. Humphry Ward's *Robert Elsmere* as a "momentous public event." Called "the publishing sensation of the century," it was an immediate and enduring bestseller on both sides of the Atlantic, selling over 40,000 copies in the United Kingdom and over 200,000 (mostly in pirated editions) in the United States in its first year. One American distributor gave away a free copy of the novel with each purchase of a bar of Balsam Fir Soap. Its phenomenal American sales hastened the passage of the 1891 International Copyright Act. In June 1899, the *Ladies' Home Journal* books columnist complained about the novel's ubiquity: "Everybody from the silliest miss to the learned Divine has something to say of it, until the subject has been worn thread-bare."[7]

The novel narrates a young Oxford-educated minister's loss of faith caused by reading historical biblical criticism and his rebirth as a settlement house worker in London. Once Elsmere takes up residence in his rural parish with his devout, evangelical wife, he struggles to finish the book he is writing in the absence of intellectual companionship. He strikes up a friendship with an infamous squire whose legendary library is described at length. Reading and discussion with the squire make Elsmere's orthodox faith seem untenable. He resigns his pastorate and takes up social settlement work in the slums of London, struggling to live peaceably with his devout—but closed-mindedly orthodox—wife. The books in the squire's library drive the action of the novel and profoundly reshape the characters' relationships to each other. Orthodoxy has been replaced at the close by a celebration of the power of stories (true and untrue)—from across history and throughout the world—to move the human heart.

Ward offers several different models of the scholar/intellectual in *Robert Elsmere*, so as to more clearly illustrate the appropriate uses of reading and writing. Elsmere has two formative influences at Oxford: Edward Langham (his tutor) and Mr. Grey (a mentor). Langham is a brilliant scholar, and he instills intellectual discipline in the flighty Elsmere, but Ward clearly condemns Langham's uses of literacy. Although he wrote some passionate position pieces in his early career, alienating him from his family and his conservative Oxford College, he has long since sunk into melancholy and intellectual inertia. "So he wrote no more, he quarreled no more, he meddled with the great passionate things of life and expression no more," Ward explains.[8] Although offered a prestigious chair at a university in Scotland, Langham declines, imagining only more failure. He falls in love with Elsmere's sister-in-law but ultimately reneges on his pledge of love and marriage, since he believes himself incapable of abandoning his soul-deadening scholarly routines to rejoin the living.

Grey captivates Elsmere from the first words of a lay sermon he preaches on some select words of St. Paul. Much of the address is cast in metaphysical terms that are intellectually beyond the young Elsmere, but he is bewitched by the passion of the speaker and by the occasional passage addressing the practical, spiritual needs of his listeners: "He put before them the claims and conditions of the higher life with a pregnant simplicity and rugged beauty of phrase."[9] Grey becomes Elsmere's longtime friend and mentor, instilling in him a love of both scholarship and practical, life-affirming work on behalf of others. When Elsmere goes to take up his ministry in rural Surrey, Grey urges him to continue cultivating a life of the mind (writing a book about the making of France), dedicating half his day to the service of society and half his day to scholarship. Elsmere quotes his mentor: "*The decisive events of the world take place in the intellect*. It is the mission of books that they help one to remember it."[10] Elsmere was particularly impressed by these words because they came from Grey, who was also passionately engaged with practical work.

Elsmere's intellectual interlocutor in Surrey is the neighboring squire Roger Wendover, a Ph.D. from the University of Berlin and a celebrated hermit who has been at work for over thirty years on a magnum opus about Christian witnessing throughout history. In the interim, he has published two books that scandalized conventionally religious English readers. Although it is Wendover's books and his relentlessly brilliant arguments that precipitate the loss of Elsmere's orthodox faith, the squire is devastated by Elsmere's determination to leave the ministry because he cannot stand the hypocrisy of preaching what he no longer believes.

After the clearly suffering Elsmere takes his leave, the squire sits in his magnificent library, dumbfounded: "So Elsmere was going! In a few weeks the rectory would be once more tenanted by one of those nonentities the squire had either patronized or scorned all his life. The park, the lanes, the room in which he sits, will know that spare young figure, that animated voice, no more. The outlet which had brought so much relief and stimulus to his own mental powers is closed; the friendship on which he had unconsciously come to depend so much is broken before it had well begun."[11] This loss of his intellectual protégé awakens in the squire an awareness of all the other loving relationships he has sacrificed for his scholarship—the wife he did not marry, the children he never had. "He had never, like Augustine, 'loved to love'; he had only loved to know," Ward explains.[12] Nevertheless, the squire had begun to feel he possessed a spiritual son in the attentive, intelligent Elsmere, but this relationship, too, is a casualty of his scholarship. The suffering etched into Elsmere's face brings the squire to an epiphany about the real human consequences of intellectual gamesmanship, however brilliant: "He had been thinking and writing of religion, of the history of ideas, all his life. Had he ever yet grasped the meaning of religion *to the religious man*? *God* and *faith*—what have these venerable ideas ever mattered to him personally, except as the subject of the most ingenious analysis, the most dedicated historical inductions? Not only skeptical to the core, but constitutionally indifferent, the squire had always found enough to make life amply worth living in the mere dissection of other men's beliefs."[13] Although an incontestable genius and an immensely learned man, the squire has clearly misused books and reading, to his own detriment and that of the world. Ward clearly thinks there are better uses for a magnificent library and a magnificent mind, uses that men like Grey might have made.

The ending to the novel bears this out. The squire comes to call on Elsmere, once Elsmere has become known for both his historical scholarship and his firsthand knowledge of the squalid social conditions that challenge urban missions. The squire is clearly in failing health and has abandoned his magnum opus two-thirds done. "If you had stayed, I should have finished it, I suppose," the squire tells Elsmere, "but after a certain age the toil of spinning cobwebs entirely out of his brain becomes too much for a man."[14] Inspired by a recent article of Elsmere's, the squire bequeaths him his unfinished manuscript. Their conflicting uses of literacy become clear when the squire castigates Elsmere for allowing his preaching and social work to impede his scholarly work. Elsmere explains: "There is the great difference between us, Squire. You look upon knowledge as an end in itself. It may be so. But to me knowledge has always been valuable first and foremost for its bearing on life."[15] Not long after, the squire succumbs to hereditary insanity and dies in his magnificent library.

That literacy and the library (appropriately put to use in the world) are the ultimate heroes of the book becomes additionally clear. Although Elsmere has lost his orthodox faith—he no longer believes in Jesus' divinity and in the literal truth of his miracles—he does have faith in *stories*. His most successful programs as a London social worker and rural minister are evenings of storytelling. None of these stories are religious stories per se—they are merely gripping accounts of the history of London, realistic narratives about working-class life, dialect stories of rural life, sea stories, fairy tales, Icelandic sagas and Greek myths, biographies of famous men of the people. His goal here was simple: "The rousing of moral sympathy and the awakening of the imaginative power."[16] His audiences are captivated—laughing, crying, sighing with relief as they come to imaginatively inhabit these other worlds—but they do not know what to make of Elsmere. "What is he, d'ye know?" one mechanic in the audience asks another: "Seems like a parson somehow. But he ain't a parson."[17] Since these two have had enough of hypocritical, self-serving ministers who periodically appear to save souls, this is probably a good thing. Having impressed them with his open-mindedness, genuine love, and willingness to listen, Elsmere is able to deliver his working-class audience from atheism and cynicism on Easter Sunday by telling them stories about the historical Jesus—*a man*—stories that call them as human beings to lives of love and service.

Elsmere's religion of humanity is affirmed in the dying words of one of those mechanics, who becomes his assistant in teaching and preaching to working men throughout the city. He tells Elsmere, "I cared about nothing . . . when you came. You've been–God—to me—I've seen Him—in you."[18] Elsmere comforts him by reciting from the Psalms, the Gospels, and the letters of St. Paul. The function of books and stories, then, is not to fuel self-contained intellectual endeavors and hone the minds of scholars, but to inspire passions, bring comfort, and build relationships between people. One reads not in order to read, write, and think, but in order to change the world.

Similarly, Winston Churchill's 1913 *Inside of the Cup* is a story about a young minister who loses his orthodox faith through reading historical biblical criticism and is reborn as a social reformer, although the women in this case are all quite modern and liberated and hasten our hero on his journey toward disillusionment. It was published serially in 1912 and 1913 in *Hearst's Magazine*, before topping the bestseller list of 1913 and coming in at number three in 1914.[19] The replacement of orthodox religion with extensive reading of modern books is even more transparent in this case. John Hodder, the minister/protagonist, has his crisis of faith on the steps of the library: "Had he the courage now, to submit the beliefs which had sustained him all these years to Truth's inexorable inspection? Did he dare to turn and open those books . . . ,—the new philosophies, the historical criticisms which he had neglected and condemned, which he had flattered himself he could do without,—and read of the fruit of Knowledge? Twice, thrice he had hesitated on the steps of the big library, and turned away with a wildly beating heart."[20] Once he enters the library, he is taken under the wing of the librarian, a former minister named Mr. Engel (German for "angel") who immediately fills the vacuum left by Hodder's crumbling orthodox faith with modern books on religion and religious philosophy: "Ah, my friend, if you could only see, as I do, the yearning for a satisfying religion which exists in this big city! It is like a vacuum, and those books are rushing to supply it. I little thought . . . when I renounced the ministry in so much sorrow that one day I should have a church of my own. This library is my church, and men and women of all creeds come here by the thousands."[21] Engel describes the contemporary moment as "a reading age" and insists that many people who used to get their religious instruction in church now get it from books.[22]

Even this superficial summary makes clear the family resemblance of these popular Social Gospel novels. Modern books and libraries play a starring role in replacing the untenable orthodoxy of the past with a new liberal faith centered on Christian social work. But Charles Sheldon did not buy it. Although he ends up in the canonical place—with social settlement work in the ghetto—there is no critique of orthodox religious belief in Sheldon's work. Although broadly liberal in his positions on the virgin birth and other issues of doctrine, Sheldon studiously avoided taking a position on the modernist/fundamentalist controversies of the period, although he was a prolific writer and speaker on almost every other issue. His biographer calls his brand of faith "untheological Christianity," suggesting the irrelevance of doctrine to his practice-based religion and perhaps explaining his enduring popularity.[23]

Sheldon on Modern Literature and Publishing

Charles Sheldon's 1925 autobiography embraces a model of traditional literacy—the intensive, careful reading and rereading of a small body of classic works, especially the Bible—dismissing the mass-produced print and extensive reading practices of his own day.[24] He writes, "I have thought often in the flood of books and book sellers that have laid siege to my time and my salary that if all the books ever printed were destroyed except the Bible I would not weep over it."[25] Further, he maintains that extensive reading undertaken by many modern ministers does a massive disservice to their congregations. "May I be allowed to express my heretical views on the habit of book reading indulged in by many ministers?" he asks rhetorically. Indicting such reading as a waste of time and intellectual energies, he maintains that these modern sermons "are nothing but diluted reviews of diluted books" and that they are a "tragedy."[26]

Sheldon's small library contained only books "that minister to life." Citing the widely publicized five-foot shelf of classics then being marketed by Charles Eliot Norton of Harvard, Sheldon asserts that the library of books genuinely useful for teaching and preaching "can be stood up within a space measured by the minister's outstretched arms held parallel with each other."[27] These few volumes are not valued for practical purposes only, but thought of as "old friends" by the old man who has been a lifelong reader: "There is a fine sifting out of titles and authors, and the reliable and the classic and the enduring sort of arrange themselves on his shelves in the proper order, and he loves them as if they were indeed alive, and as he takes them down for an evening or a stormy afternoon he pats them gently and affectionately, as a lover of a horse pats neck or side."[28] Reading then, is both an intellectual and a sensual exercise, and these favorite volumes promise both companionship and a shared history with the reader, who requires no help from critics to tell him which of these volumes have enduring value.[29] Moreover, Sheldon believed that reading other good books was very much like reading the Bible. Rather than a desultory reading or skimming of a work, it was probably best to study it. "No book is worth reading once that is not worth reading twice," argued Sheldon, "and most books that are worth reading at all ought to be worth reading once every year."[30] This model of reading is very much like the serious, reflective, prayerful reading that religious and missionary periodicals advocated in the early nineteenth century.[31]

Sheldon was not so traditional as to distrust fiction, however. His claim to fame was the writing of what he called "sermon stories," which he read from the pulpit at Sunday evening services in lieu of a more traditional sermon. He would tell the story in installments, stopping at a cliff-hanger to bring congregants back the next week to hear what happened. Between 1891 and 1919, he wrote and read to Sunday evening audiences almost thirty stories, of which *In His Steps* was the seventh. Many were serialized at the same time in the popular Chicago Congregational periodical, *The Advance*, which paid him a flat fee and did not bother to seek copyright protection.[32]

Like the nineteenth-century wives and daughters of ministers who wrote best-selling sentimental or domestic fiction discussed by Jane Tompkins, Sheldon considered his stories to be extensions of the soul-saving work of the pulpit. Writing stories, he explained, was a way to "enlarge his parish," although he maintained it also gave his mind a break from the more traditional and constrained work of sermon writing. Moreover, sermon stories were in some ways superior to sermons, since they allowed the speaker more freedom in choosing illustrative incidents, enabled him to treat a larger range of subjects, and kept his listeners captivated with details for which they would have had no patience in an ordinary sermon.[33] Sheldon himself distinguished between literary fiction and his own writings in the preface to his 1925 autobiography: "There has been no attempt on my part to write a literary treatise. If literature is what the dictionary says,—'the productions of a country or of a period, specially [*sic*] those that are notable for beauty or force of style,' the reader will not find it in this book. But may I hope that what is told will be of interest to the reader, and add to his happiness and his good will towards all mankind."[34] As an author, Sheldon did not imagine his work as part of a self-contained aesthetic world or as a finely wrought stylistic artifact, but instead as having what Tompkins called "designs on the world." A successful work, then, was one that transformed the world by eliciting powerful emotions, changing people's hearts and minds.

Gregory S. Jackson calls novels like Sheldon's "homiletic novels" and traces their formal and rhetorical devices back to Puritan sermon conventions,

conventions Sheldon learned while at seminary at Andover.[35] The goal of such novels was to place readers imaginatively *in* the world of the novel, merging fiction and readers' everyday lives in ways that motivated social action. Even some of their titles suggest as much—William Stead, *If Christ Came to Chicago* (1895), Milford Howard, *If Christ Came to Congress* (1894), Edward Hale, *If Jesus Came to Boston* (1894), to name a few. In imaginatively transporting Jesus to late nineteenth-century America, these books implicitly asked readers Sheldon's question—"What would Jesus do?"—and urged them to take that action. For Jackson, then, the homiletic novel created "a practical link between reading and doing, knowledge and action, representation and reality."[36]

Sheldon did not think most authors met their obligations to make the world a better place, one Christian heart at a time. In an 1899 interview for the religious periodical *Our Day*, Sheldon singled out *Quo Vadis*, the novel of early Christianity then at the top of the bestseller list, for particular criticism. Although Sheldon's own novels were appropriate for reading on a Sunday either privately or from the pulpit, the author of *Quo Vadis* did not hold himself to similar standards: "He has brought in a great mass of sensational, blood and thunder material that might far better have been omitted. There are passages in the book that one would be ashamed to read before the family circle. I do not think there is any necessity for dragging into religious fiction—or any other for that matter—details that would bring a blush to a young girl's face."[37]

In His Steps as a Critique of the Literary Marketplace

Sheldon's most searing indictment of the modern republic of letters, however, is *In His Steps*. Because it was not protected by copyright, at least twenty-six American publishers and thirty more in Britain brought out more than 8 million copies, and the story was translated into twenty-three different languages, inspiring comic book, stage, and screen versions. Although there is significant controversy about exactly how many copies it sold, it is likely the best-selling novel of the nineteenth century, and it has a great deal to teach us about religion and print culture at the turn of the twentieth century.[38]

Critics in the past have explicated this novel as an insightful psychological portrait of the new urban middle class—beset on one side by the passionate, violent immigrant workers in the ghetto and on the other by the decadent, useless, overcivilized aristocracy. "What would Jesus do?" is then a reminder of the role of the native-born, white, middle class in saving

Christian civilization from these two extremes.[39] Conversely, Gregory S. Jackson argues that the novel called readers to identify personally across lines of gender, class, and race, suffering with the downtrodden as Christ did and being moved to take social action on their behalf. For Jackson, then, the novel invites readers to transcend social divisions, taking up instead their common identities as struggling Christian pilgrims.[40]

Although the class narrative (whatever its implications) is unmistakably central, *In His Steps* is also a specific meditation on religion and print culture in turn-of-the-century America. The action of the novel is launched by the appearance of a Christ figure in the city of Raymond. John Manning, a thirty-three-year-old tramp, spends a week going door-to-door seeking honorable work from the owners and managers of the city. After a rousing Sunday sermon about the importance of patterning lives of suffering and self-sacrifice after Jesus' example from Rev. Henry Maxwell, Manning stands up in the aisle at the close of services demanding to know just what these wealthy, self-satisfied citizens mean by this and narrating his own story of unemployment, homelessness, and struggle. Weakened by grief and hunger, he collapses before he can finish. Taken to the minister's home to be cared for, he dies several days later. Manning, the stand-in for Jesus here, was—significantly—a skilled printer put out of work by the arrival of linotype machines.[41] Dick Falkner, the Christ figure/homeless tramp at the start of Harold Bell Wright's 1903 *That Printer of Udell's*, is also an unemployed printer (whose later Christian service includes superintending a reading room for working men).

In Sheldon's novel, the contact of complacent, self-satisfied members of the congregation with this Christ figure fundamentally transforms their lives. We hear in detail about the transformations of twelve characters, who pledge to take no action for a year without first asking what Jesus would do: (1) Rev. Henry Maxwell, pastor of the First Church of Raymond; (2) Edward Norman, who almost bankrupts the Raymond daily newspaper by editing it as Jesus would; (3) Rachel Winslow, a gifted soprano who gives up a career in opera to sing at revivals and teach music in the Rectangle ghetto district; (4) Virginia Page, a wealthy heiress who endows both Norman's Christian newspaper and the social settlement they begin in the Rectangle; (5) Rollin Page, Virginia's wealthy playboy brother who dedicates his life to reclaiming the souls of dissolute young rich men; (6) Alexander Powers, a railroad executive who turns in his company for taking illegal rebates, losing his job and his social position and alienating his family in the process; (7) Milton Wright, who transforms his empire of shops into a profit-sharing enterprise characterized by loving concern between workers and owners; (8) Professor Donald Marsh, the president of nearby Lincoln College, who leaves behind his idyllic world of books and ideas to do battle for control of Raymond with the liquor interests; (9) Jasper Chase, a popular novelist (more on him later); (10) Rev. Calvin Bruce, minister of Nazareth Avenue Church in Chicago, who resigns his post to live among the poor in a social settlement; (11) his bishop, who follows suit; and (12) Felicia Sterling, a once-wealthy young woman who teaches housekeeping and pure food preparation to immigrant women at the Chicago social settlement, after her father has bankrupted the family with shady business dealings and killed himself. These twelve major characters are intended to be latter-day apostles of Jesus, and various commentators in the novel link the late nineteenth-century world of Raymond and Chicago to the early church of Jesus' followers in its fellowship and commitment to mutual financial, spiritual, and emotional support.[42]

The Judas in the bunch is the popular novelist Jasper Chase, who is the only major character who reneges on his promise. He has carried on a long-term flirtation with Rachel Winslow, the beautiful soprano. In fact, his first novel's heroine was an idealized Rachel and its hero an idealized version of himself. In giving Rachel a copy of the novel, he made his love clear to her.[43] After a powerful night of saving souls with her bewitching voice, Rachel is irritated to be called back from her possession by the Holy Spirit to deal with Jasper's professions of romantic love, so she tells him that she does not love him and that her heart is entirely engaged by her Christian mission. Jasper ceases coming to the weekly meetings of those who took the WWJD (What Would Jesus Do?) pledge and falls into a profound isolation that contrasts sharply with the deep fellowship of the group. He struggles over what to do about his second novel, which is ready to go to the publisher:

> He had not forgotten his pledge made with the other church members at the First Church. It had forced itself upon his notice all through his writing, and ever since Rachel had said no to him, he had asked a thousand times, "Would Jesus do this? Would He write this story?" It was a social novel, written in a style that had proved popular. It had no purpose except to amuse. Its moral teaching was not bad, but neither was it Christian in any positive way. Jasper Chase knew that such a story would probably sell. He was conscious of powers in this way that the social world petted and admired. "What would Jesus do?" He felt that Jesus would never write such a book. The question obtruded on him at the most inopportune times. He

became irascible over it. The standard of Jesus for an author was too ideal. Of course, Jesus would use His powers to produce something useful or helpful, or with a purpose. What was he, Jasper Chase, writing this novel for? Why, what nearly every writer wrote for—money, money, and fame as a writer. There was no secret with him that he was writing this new story with that object. He was not poor, and so had no great temptation to write for money. But he was urged on by his desire for fame as much as anything. He must write this kind of matter. But what would Jesus do? The question plagued him even more than Rachel's refusal. Was he going to break his promise? Did the promise mean much after all?[44]

After he looks out his window to see handsome young Rollin Page walking with Rachel, both of them dedicated to winning souls for Christ, Jasper resolves the dilemma "by denying his Lord." Sheldon glosses the moment: "It grew darker in his room. He had deliberately chosen his course, urged on by his disappointment and loss." Sheldon drops in some scripture for good measure: "But Jesus said unto him, no man having put his hand to the plow, and looking back, is fit for the Kingdom of God."[45]

Not only is our Judas a popular novelist, but he is uniquely condemned for his backsliding. The drunks, prostitutes, and hold-up men from the wrong side of the tracks are saved again and again by ministers, settlement house workers, and the bishop, who never tire of rescuing and re-rescuing these sinners from demon rum and lives of violence and dissolution. Although Rev. Maxwell has noticed on several occasions Jasper's absence from the after-service Sunday meetings of the WWJD crowd, nobody comes looking for him. Virginia and Rachel notice his absence, but Virginia is just glad Rachel turned his proposal down, since she never liked him very much. Note that Jasper is not writing pornography or salacious crime fiction, but merely useless light entertainment for bored society men and women. Oddly, this is the only unforgivable sin in the book.

Moreover, the other artist/writer figures in the novel serve as foils to the backsliding Jasper. Rachel could make lots of money and be a famous opera singer, but she chooses not to: "There was a fortune in her voice . . . and she was obliged to acknowledge that until two weeks ago she had purposed to use her voice to make money and win admiration and applause." Instead, she proposes other, better work, for herself: "To use my voice in some way so as to satisfy my own soul that I am doing something better than pleasing fashionable audiences, or making money, or even gratifying my own love of singing."[46] Jasper, however, cannot imagine life without critical esteem and large royalties, however financially unnecessary. Edward Norman, editor of the daily paper, also makes great sacrifices. He thinks that the primary purpose of his paper is not to make money but to further the kingdom of God, printing what news people *ought* to read rather than the prize fights, sensational crime news, and ads for liquor and tobacco that pay for the paper. He cancels the (very profitable) Sunday edition, renounces partisan politics, attacks the liquor interests, refuses to run dishonorable ads, and does not report on sinful entertainments or scandal. He would have gone bankrupt had Virginia Page not bailed the financially failing paper out with a $500,000 endowment. Writers and artists *can* follow Jesus, Sheldon wants us to know; it is just that popular novelists *choose* not to.

As in *Robert Elsmere*, the free and unencumbered pursuit of knowledge for its own sake is *not* a noble pursuit for Sheldon but a shameful abdication of one's responsibilities as a citizen. Professor Marsh, the president of Lincoln College, resolves to enter politics in an attempt to free Raymond from the damaging influence of corrupt politicians on the payroll of big liquor. "Jesus would not hide in his books and his study," Marsh insists. The indictment applies to Rev. Maxwell also, the other man of letters in Raymond. "We have lived in a little world of literature and scholarly seclusion, doing work we have enjoyed and shrinking from the disagreeable duties that belong to the life of the citizen," Marsh tells him. The suffering and self-sacrifice here is the loss of that protected academic bubble of "scholarly, intellectual, self-contained habits," when one feels called by Jesus to an "open, coarse, public fight."[47]

Unlike other Social Gospel novelists, Sheldon did not replace the church with the library or scripture with books of modern, historical criticism. Modern print culture is not the savior of an embattled minister's soul but a temptation to sin and a waste of time and intellect. In his most famous work, the one unredeemed sin is not drinking, prostitution, or a life of crime, but instead the writing of conventional, popular society novels. Although men and women from all walks of life do not hesitate to make personal sacrifices to bring about the kingdom of God here on earth, the popular novelist is unable to forgo royalties, social status, and critical acclaim. Sheldon's condemnation of modern publishing seems prescient, given what happened once the industry realized the copyright on *In His Steps* was defective. Lots of publishers made fortunes with editions of *In His Steps*, but few paid Sheldon any royalties. Although he reported himself delighted that the error placing the story in the public domain had allowed millions to read it and move closer to God as a consequence, he also wrote an article about the many versions of his book he had encountered in his travels, his lack of royalties from the vast majority of them, and the lack of honor among publishers he believed fueled it, in an article entitled, "The Ethics of Some Publishers."[48]

The Life-Application Method of Reading and the Sheldon Edition

Having explored representations of reading and writing in Social Gospel novels, I turn now to a consideration of readers, asking what kinds of traces they left in the historical record. In every case, these traces suggest that readers embraced ways with words that arise from nineteenth-century evangelical cultures of letters and that continue (adapted for new contexts) into the present day. As Gregory Jackson argues, these ways of reading had their roots in practices of biblical exegesis he calls "typological hermeneutics." Readers of homiletic novels applied these texts to their daily lives, just as they had been taught to read and interpret scripture as having immediate relevance for the present day.[49]

In the context of contemporary evangelicalism, Amy Johnson Frykholm explains a way of reading scripture that she calls the "life-application method." In accordance with Calvinist traditions, one reads the Bible in order to apply it directly and immediately to daily life, finding there instructions for taking action in the contemporary world. Frykholm explains: "The purpose of the Bible study then is not to explore the Bible, not to contemplate the various meanings or to look into the historical context of the passage, as it might be in liberal or mainline churches. Rather, the purpose is to focus the reading through the lens of one's own life and then determine how the reading can be directly and somewhat immediately applied."[50] What readers are seeking is a "take-home message" rather than fine points of theology or differing historical interpretations to contemplate. Although Sheldon's readers lived a century earlier, they, too, were life-application method readers. The difference here is that the lives they applied religious reading *to* looked a good deal different than those of contemporary readers.

Sheldon himself was inspired to dress up as a tramp and go seeking honorable work in Topeka (an experience that became the kernel of *In His Steps*), after reading Mrs. Humphry Ward's *Robert Elsmere*, described above.[51] Similarly, he spent a week in the 1890s shadowing eight representative classes of people (doctors, lawyers, businessmen, railroad men, streetcar men, college students, newspaper men, Negroes) in Topeka to better equip himself for Christian service (that is, to *be* Topeka's Robert Elsmere). Instead of writing up a critique of Ward's theology or hunting down the historical criticism of the Bible that fatally undermines Elsmere's faith, Sheldon found in the novel a take-home message—a model for Christian living and an invitation to take action to change the *unchristian* social order. Others were similarly inspired to act in the world by Sheldon's book. For example, David Popenoe, the new editor of the *Topeka Daily Capital*, handed over his newspaper to Sheldon for one week in March 1900, so that (like Edward Norman of *In His Steps*) he could edit it as Jesus would.[52]

It was a media circus, what fellow editor William Allen White called "the best advertising scheme that ever struck Kansas."[53] The "experiment" got national and international press coverage (at least nineteen national and international correspondents were in Topeka to cover the story), and the daily circulation went from 11,000 or 12,000 copies to over 350,000. "Sheldon week" was announced in huge block letters on the front page of the *Topeka Daily Capital* on 23 January. It was front-page news throughout the Midwest and appeared in the front sections of major papers in the East as an Associated Press wire story. Without Sheldon's knowledge, the *Capital*'s owner had hired undercover press agent Auguste Babize to publicize Sheldon's week of editing the Jesus newspaper (13 March–20 March). The *Capital* promised to run a symposium of opinions on the newspaper before and after its run. Almost every day's paper between the 23 January announcement and the first Sheldon edition on 13 March advertised Sheldon in some way—opinions from ministers or reporters about the experiment, reports on Sheldon's intentions and preparations for the week, and so on. Every clergyman in Kansas received a letter from the *Capital* announcing the experiment and urging the recipient to subscribe and interest his congregants in the great experiment. Christian Endeavor Societies (an interdenominational Protestant youth group of over 3 million members worldwide) were hired as de facto subscription agents, having been promised that for every twenty-five-cent subscription they sold they could keep a dime for their local society. Many papers chose to run secular sermons that week to compete with Sheldon's much-ballyhooed Jesus newspaper. H. H. Brookes, the editor of the *Atchison (Kansas) Champion* announced that he would run his paper that week as the Devil would.[54]

Sheldon replaced the Sunday edition with a Saturday evening issue made up entirely of reading appropriate for the Sabbath. The lead story, for example, was the Sermon on the Mount. He insisted on no swearing, smoking, or slang in the newsroom. He did not cover immoral entertainments or sports, and he refused to run ads for alcohol, tobacco, patent medicines, or women's hosiery and corsets (too suggestive). The paper was nonpartisan. All contributions were signed, so that each writer was held accountable for his own work. Everyone from Sheldon to the janitor appeared on the masthead as contributors, with the notable exceptions of Popenoe and Babize, whom he held responsible for turning this noble religious experiment into a publicity stunt. The society reporter gave the week over to adding up how much money was wasted on frivolous parties and entertainments in one week in Topeka that might otherwise have been donated to charity. Sheldon devoted a lot of copy to protesting the twin evils of drink and militarism.

Perhaps most interesting was the way Sheldon wove together editorial copy and news, so that the "take-home message" for action in the world was readily apparent to even the dimmest readers. For example, a news item about the attorney general's interpretation of the new canteen law to allow sales of liquor to overseas servicemen appeared on page two of the first day's edition. Directly under this news item, the prohibitionist Sheldon included a signed editorial directive (with a form letter and instructions to write to congressional representatives): "Let every Christian Endeavor Society in the United States take action at once in regard to this matter. Here is an opportunity for us to show what we mean by 'Christian Citizenship.' "[55] There are explicit lessons about appropriate reading practices here. As soon as one reads about a moral wrong, one organizes to correct it as Jesus would (or—at least—as Sheldon *thought* Jesus would). No research or analysis of similar events in history were necessary; no investigation of the author's background or social location was called for; such dilly-dallying was to be discouraged, since the boundary between print and life was perfectly fluid.

Most striking was the lead story on page one of the first day's edition, coverage of the ongoing famine in India with eyewitness reports from several of Sheldon's missionary friends. "*The Capital* knows of no more important matter of news the world over this morning than the pitiable condition of famine-stricken India. We give the latest and fullest available information of the progress of the scourge." Sheldon followed this up with a directive for action: "If every reader of this paper will give ten cents to a relief fund for this terrible Indian famine, we may be able to save thousands of lives. Will you do it? Let us all have a share in helping our brother man. For these starving creatures are a part of the human family which Jesus taught us to love, when He taught us to say 'Our Father'—Charles M. Sheldon."[56] Not only was over $200,000 raised, but Kansas farmers donated a trainload of grain to be shipped to the famine-stricken region. In Sheldon's autobiography, he remembers this famine assistance as the single most important outcome of his week editing the newspaper, an experiment widely judged to be a complete failure.[57]

What is most striking about this very directed way of reading, this effort to pin down a single meaning so as to delineate clearly the action to be taken, is the fact that both Sheldon's editorials and the characters of *In His Steps* endlessly rehearse and urge tolerance for differences of opinion about what Jesus might do. Sheldon himself stated in his first *Capital* editorial: "If a thousand different Christian men who wished to edit Christian dailies should make an honest attempt to do so, the result might be a thousand different papers in very many particulars." Stating explicitly that he was in no way seeking to speak *for* Jesus or to dictate correct action for anyone else, Sheldon laid out the contours of his humble project in his first editorial: "The only thing I or any other Christian man can do in the interpretation of what is Christian in the conduct of this paper is to define the term Christian the best that can be done after asking for divine wisdom and not judge others who might with equal desire and sincerity interpret the probable action of Jesus in a different manner."[58] However tolerant he may have been of differences of editorial opinion, Sheldon was pretty clear about what *readers* of his newspaper ought to do—and drinking their morning coffee and doing nothing was not it.

Although the Jesus newspaper was a particularly vivid illustration of the fluid boundary between literature and life for Social Gospel readers and writers, there is evidence that a similar fluidity characterized the reading of other texts. For example, Mrs. Humphry Ward engaged in a war of words with W. E. Gladstone, former Liberal prime minister and staunch believer in religious orthodoxy, about *Robert Elsmere* in the pages of the British periodical *Nineteenth Century*. His passionate, negative review in May 1888 was as celebrated as the controversial novel itself, and Ward responded to the critique in the periodical's March 1889 issue.[59] Neither was slowed in the least by the fact that they were (at least nominally) arguing over the religious beliefs and practices of fictional characters. Similarly, the character of Mr. Grey in the novel is modeled on Oxford don T. H. Green, to whom Ward also dedicated the novel. The lines of Grey's speeches quoted in the novel are, in fact, from speeches Green delivered at Oxford. Although Green had a small following, his fame among the general public was *created* by *Robert Elsmere* and Gladstone's detailed refutations of his positions in his review of the novel.[60] When Ward herself was instrumental in founding the Passmore Edwards Settlement in Bloomsbury in 1897, the press recognized that this was literature coming to life; the headline in the *Daily News* of London at its formal opening was "Robert Elsmere's Scheme at Work."[61] Although a novel, *Robert Elsmere* was clearly understood as continuous with life—real people argued over the theological positions of its characters and real, material consequences resulted from the minds changed by its reading and writing.

Gendered Reading: Patriarchy and Orthodoxy in Social Gospel Novels

Social Gospel novels are not only books about literacy and social action, about the power of words and libraries to transform souls and to remake the world; they are also love stories. Moreover, the fates of patriarchy and orthodoxy are linked in these novels. The reading that destroys traditional religious faith also undermines patriarchal marriages, and the remaking of relationships between God and men always remakes relationships between men and women as well.[62]

In His Steps, the most conservative of the novels about modern print culture, is also the most conservative about marriage.[63] For women, marriages and lives of Christian service are inextricable. Rachel has no romantic interest in Rollin Page the wealthy playboy, but falls deeply in love with Rollin Page the missionary for Christ. Rachel and Rollin appear in Maxwell's waking vision of the future of Christianity at the end of *In His Steps* as a married couple "both fully consecrated to the Master's use, both following His steps with an eagerness intensified and purified by their love for each other." The same is true for Felicia (a cook) and Stephen (a carpenter), the Chicago settlement's resident romance.[64]

Love and faith are not so easily reconciled in *Robert Elsmere*. Elsmere's loss of orthodox faith estranges him from his devout, evangelical wife. They struggle to live together peaceably and love each other, although Elsmere finds Catherine's heart and mind willfully closed to his vision of the kingdom of God, and Catherine finds his reconstructed faith abhorrent and fears such ideas will contaminate her and her daughter's immortal souls. The years of tension, suffering, and estrangement are enacted, in part, over Elsmere's reading. Catherine reads the Bible or devotionals like *The Christian Year*. She is so "shocked" by the single page she reads of one of the squire's borrowed books she finds in Elsmere's study that she drops it as if the touch of it burned her fingers. "Was it right for Robert to have such books! Was it wise, was it prudent, for the Christian to measure himself against such antagonism as this," she asks herself.[65]

Elsmere's liberal colleagues and fellow philanthropists (who are not so liberal on gender issues) all assume that Catherine is a subordinate wife, a disciple of her husband who believes—as one colleague puts it—that "the husband is the wife's pope."[66] Catherine suffers countless indignities and aspersions on her faith before simply withdrawing from Elsmere's society. The resolution of the novel not only reconciles scholarship and practical Christianity, but also restores the proper relationship between Elsmere and his wife. They are reconciled, once Elsmere's colleague tells Catherine about Elsmere's selfless service to the poor and working people and recounts his loving ministry to his dying assistant. She comes to recognize Elsmere's faith *as a faith*. Regardless of what he believes, he is doing God's work. She tearfully explains: "I have seen things as they are, Robert. . . . You were right—I *would* not understand. And, in a sense, I shall never understand. I cannot change. . . . My Lord is my Lord always, but He is yours too. Oh, I know it, say what you will! That is what has been hidden from me; that is what my trouble has taught me; the powerlessness, the worthlessness, of words. *It is the spirit that quickeneth*. I should never have felt it so, but for this fiery furnace of pain. But I have been wandering in strange places through strange thoughts. God has not one language, but many. I have dared to think He had but one, the one I knew."[67] That very same evening, Elsmere rededicates himself to his marriage and to his wife, after a woman (unsuccessfully) propositions him at a dinner party, criticizing his wife for her failure to support him and his work. Elsmere dies not long after the reconciliation, but Catherine—who remains an orthodox churchgoer—dedicates herself to continuing his work at the various charities, missions, and institutes for working men in London. Although Catherine's religious faith and her ultimate destiny are hers to work out alone, her acknowledgment of the *many* languages of God makes it possible for her to carry on her husband's work without embracing his beliefs.

Literacy and love are even more intimately enmeshed in *Inside of the Cup*. Throughout, the inadequacy of orthodox faith and the inadequacy of traditional ideas about women's appropriate place are linked. Churchill opens the novel by describing a once conservative, provincial city—"existence was decorous, marriage an irrevocable step, wives were wives, and the Authorized Version of the Bible was true from cover to cover."[68] As liberal faith transforms belief in the Bible's literal truth, it also calls into question the role of wives and the status of marriage. The modern young people in this city hunger for something more than traditional faith can offer. They have been educated to apply their reason to problems of theology, and as their (unreasonable) orthodox faith crumbles, so does their faith in the (unreasonable) social system based on it—traditional marriage, women's subordination.[69] One young congregant desires that her minister be a "man of modern ideas," "somebody who will present Christianity to me in such a manner that it will appeal to my reason, and enable me to assimilate it into my life."[70] Hodder is—at least initially—not that person.

He is called to ministry at St. John's by the church leaders—all wealthy pillars of the community—because of his reputation for orthodoxy. Once his beliefs about divorce, womanly self-sacrifice, and the efficacy of the church are challenged by various women of the city, Hodder decides he must work harder to meet the needs of his flock. First, Eleanor Goodrich, troubled by the doctrine of the virgin birth, seeks clarity from Hodder, who dismisses her concerns and adamantly holds the orthodox line. Then Mrs. Constable appears, requesting that Hodder conduct the ceremony for her divorced daughter's second wedding. He refuses, but is troubled by his meeting with the daughter, who "looks pure," and by the story Mrs. Constable tells him of her own miserable, mismatched marriage. A weeping woman appears at the church praying for her dying son, whose father had been ruined and driven to suicide by Eldon Parr (a wealthy deacon of the church). While helping to care for the dying child, Hodder encounters an alcoholic prostitute (also ruined by Parr) who gives him a stern talking-to about the distinctly unchristian behavior of his parishioners and the irrelevance of religion to people like her.[71] Most important, Hodder's introduction to the seductions and dangers of historical biblical criticism is not extricable from his sexual attraction to Alison Parr, a beautiful, liberated young woman who left the Midwest against her father's wishes to go to New York to become a famous landscape architect and an unapologetically single woman. Alison does not mince words with Hodder, naming the hypocrisy of his church and the moral bankruptcy of his ideas about women. She thinks her wealthy father (a corrupt financier and deacon of the church) is a Pharisee, and she indicts him and his class for maintaining an exploitative social system fundamentally at odds with the true spirit of Christianity. Hodder's crisis of faith and his attraction to Alison are one and the same:

> Day by day the storm increased, until from a cloud on the horizon
> it grew into a soul-shaking tempest. Profoundly moved as he had
> been . . . he had resolutely resolved to thrust the woman and the
> incident from his mind, to defer the consideration of the questions
> she had raised—grave though they were—to a calmer period. For
> now he was unable to separate *her*, to eliminate the emotion—he
> was forced to acknowledge—the thought of her aroused, from the

problems themselves. Who was she? At moments he seemed to see her shining, accusing, as Truth herself, and again as a Circe who had drawn him by subtle arts from his wanderings, luring him to his death; or, at other times, as the mutinous daughter in revolt. But when he felt, in memory the warm touch of her hand, the old wildness of his nature responded, he ceased to speculate or care, and he longed only to crush and subdue her by the brute power of the man in him. For good or bad, she had woven her spell.[72]

Ultimately, her challenge sends him to the library (discussed above), where he finds new truth. At the close of the novel, Hodder is put on trial for heresy before the bishop, and he can only be furious at the triviality of these charges that take him away from the work God has called him to do among the poor and unemployed. He defies his wealthy, nominally Christian congregants to embrace a life of community service and comes to believe that it is sinful to keep people in loveless marriages. Alison proposes to *him*, and her previous indictments of his hypocritical flock are transformed into a this-worldly theology that makes the love of men and women for each other part of the larger human community and a life of service to God: "Do you remember saying to me once that faith comes to us in some human form we love? You are my faith. And faith in you is my faith in humanity, and faith in God."[73]

Nevertheless, the feminism of *Inside of the Cup* is qualified. Alison Parr is a disobedient daughter, an unmarried woman, and a celebrated professional landscape architect. However, when they first openly declare their love for each other, Alison tells our hero the truth: that she had become "contaminated" in New York by trailing her art and herself "in the dust," that she was miserable, had been wooed by a man only interested in her father's money (who seduced her in part with feminist rhetoric), and had finally come to the brink of marrying a man she did not love, simply because she wanted to feel safe and protected and could no longer stand the life she had been living.[74]

Alison and Hodder are undoubtedly soul mates, and Hodder comes to believe that men and women of spiritual necessity must work out their own salvations as autonomous beings, but one cannot help suspecting that part of Alison's appeal for Hodder is the idea that this formidable, independent woman *needs* him. Their moment of spiritual communion does not sound particularly transcendent to the modern reader: "He took her in his arms, crushing her to him in his strength in one ineffable brief moment finding her lips, inhaling the faint perfume of her smooth skin. Her lithe figure lay passively against him, in marvelous, unbelievable surrender."[75]

The Social Gospel and the Literary Canon

Churchill suffered such damning criticism of this embrace of liberalism and settlement work when it ran in magazine serialization that he added an afterword to the book publication. In it, he defended himself against charges of heresy by declaring that he was not a theologian, and that Hodder's solution to his crisis of faith was only one solution among many (and not even one Churchill necessarily endorsed). *Robert Elsmere* was similarly condemned for its heretical content. Ward and Gladstone engaged in a "battle royal" about its theological claims, and Henry James took up the cause of defending Ward in the American press. Nobody accused Charles Sheldon of heresy, and the theological emptiness of *In His Steps* no doubt made it more acceptable to liberal and conservative Christians alike.[76]

Nobody reads *Inside of the Cup* anymore, and almost nobody besides Victorian novel scholars reads *Robert Elsmere* (neither stays consistently in print). *In His Steps*, however, continues to crowd the shelves of Christian bookstores and to hold an iconic status in evangelical Christian circles. Evangelical teenagers wear WWJD bracelets to remind themselves of their Christian faith and advertise it to others. Holy Bears, a Texas-based manufacturer of scripture-bearing stuffed bears for every occasion, makes a "Sheldon Bear" with "WWJD" emblazoned across his chest.

In part, *In His Steps* survived because—unlike the theologically dense *Robert Elsmere* and *Inside of the Cup*—it fit so well into the world of nineteenth-century evangelical popular print culture. David Paul Nord describes the characteristics that American Tract Society colporteurs claimed made a good tract: it was "simple, striking, entertaining, nonsectarian" and had lots of narrative and dialogue, a description that fits *In His Steps* equally well.[77] Moreover, the American Tract Society missionaries—who had a good deal to say about religion and reading—shared the faith in the power of reading to save souls and the power of bad books to poison the reader. American Tract Society colporteurs, like Sheldon, were fans of a small group of English dissenting books (*Pilgrim's Progress*, *Call to the Unconverted*) and suspicious of the commercial world of mass publishing, even though they pioneered its systems of mass production and distribution.

Candy Gunther Brown describes an evangelical print culture from 1789 to 1880 as a "distinctive set of writing, publishing, and reading practices centered on the power of the Word to transform the World," assumptions shared by later Social Gospel writers. Brown claims that evangelical readers had a "functionalist" view of sacred language—that is, the beauty or register of language was less important than its usefulness in allowing readers to make connections between scripture and life.[78] Moreover, books that were bad by literary standards were not necessarily bad by religious ones. Brown argues: "Rules for evaluating evangelical texts differed from the standards of secular literature. New publications gained entrance to the canon if they shared certain marks of membership, in other words, if they reinforced the same values as texts previously recognized as canonical. Usefulness, rather than genre or form, was the primary characteristic that marked texts as evangelical."[79] *In His Steps* was the story of a pilgrim community's sanctification (that is, lifelong progress toward holiness), one of many widely shared story structures in evangelical literature. Readers of *In His Steps* were always already *re*reading it, since it merely put a familiar narrative in modern garb.[80]

Although a disaster by conventional literary standards, *In His Steps* was immensely powerful for communities of nonliterary readers.[81] Sheldon made the case for traditional literacy—the intensive reading of a small set of classic texts—at the same time that his own mass-produced fiction urged reading godly novels as one read the Bible, with an eye toward immediate application to one's daily life. By valuing what texts *do* in readers' lives over style, form, aesthetics, or understanding them in their historical context, *In His Steps* challenges literary historians to resituate their own professional practices as one among many possible ways with words.

In His Steps and other similar works are not merely aesthetically bad books; they are books that seek to succeed on entirely different terms—the transformation of individual and social life. In this way, they find their place in evangelical traditions of reading and writing in America, rather than in the self-consciously literary traditions which emerged just after the Social Gospel heyday. This is a familiar story.[82] However, Social Gospel novels also provide a new way of understanding the establishment and maintenance of *literary* ways with words as dominant. These novels enact a contest over competing models of reading and writing in order to embrace one that engages the soul and inspires readers to social action. *In His Steps*, *Robert Elsmere*, and *Inside of the Cup* are as much documents in the history of reading in America as they are documents in religious history. Sheldon, Ward, and Churchill were aware of the emergence of *literary* ways with words, and they dismissed them as deficient. That is to say that we should not think of these writers as failed T. S. Eliots and Ezra Pounds, but instead as writers who understood what self-consciously literary writers like Pound and Eliot were doing and decided the world needed other kinds of reading and writing instead. Ward demonstrates the spiritual bankruptcy of scholars like Langham and the squire, who pursue ideas as pure abstractions. Sheldon recognizes the devil in two competing ways with words: (1) the professorial detachment of Donald Marsh; and (2) the commercial engagement of Jasper Chase. Churchill sees the library as a savior only because people come pouring through its doors seeking guidance for everyday life and take their transformed thinking out into the world to effect social change. What we witness in these Social Gospel novels is the battle of words over which of the many "cultures of letters" would be privileged in early twentieth-century America.[83] Although Sheldon, Churchill, Harold Bell Wright, and others clearly lost that battle (at least in the academy), this was by no means a foregone conclusion at the time. In part, we can see these books as dispatches in the struggle for literary hegemony and evidence of the hard work modernists and their New Critical interpreters had to do institutionalizing a particular kind of literary study at universities and colleges. New Critical modes of reading preoccupied with rhetoric and form and a set of canonical texts that rewarded this kind of reading could function as cultural capital only if other ways of reading were understood as deficient or naive and other kinds of books were written out of literary history.[84]

The battle over ways with words also had religious overtones. If modernists and the New Critics for whom their work was foundational found transcendence in a self-contained realm of aesthetics and form, Social Gospel writers insisted that we could achieve our own salvation here and now through passionate engagement with the material world. If Eliot's individual talent located himself in relation to the works of the past and intended his own works to transform that tradition,[85] Social Gospel writers located themselves in the contemporary social and political world and intended their works to transform its people and institutions instead. The creation of literary orthodoxy made heretics of writers with a mission and heresies of their most fundamental assumptions about how texts worked (the intentional fallacy, the affective fallacy). It canonized a small class of texts, installed a priestly aristocracy (literary critics) charged with interpreting them, and began the work of writing literary history from a specific point of view.[86]

What if—in reading books like these much-loved Social Gospel novels— we are not just reading *bad* books, but reading heretical ones? Why did scholars spend so much energy discrediting books like these and the kinds of reading they encourage, unless there was something potentially revolutionary about these ways with words? Why are battles over the literary canon (not only what we read, but often *how* we read) so often waged like holy wars? In part, books like *Robert Elsmere*, *Inside of the Cup*, and *In His Steps* offer alternative histories that invite us to imagine how literature, literary studies, and humanistic inquiry might be different, if we imagined books and reading as engaged in the work of transforming us and the world in material ways. Even if we no longer find their challenges to religious orthodoxy (or even just conventional churchgoing) compelling, we ought to read these books for their challenges to literary orthodoxy. For those of us engaged in advocacy for the humanities in public life, these books remind us of historical models that promiscuously mingled literature and life and of the fact that books can matter deeply to people who do not necessarily imagine themselves as intellectuals. In Chapter 2, I turn to the career of best-selling Social Gospel writer Harold Bell Wright, whose adamantly evangelical, adamantly commercial notion of authorship left him and his readers outside of mainstream American literary culture.

TWO

The Dickens of the Rural Route

Harold Bell Wright and Christian Melodrama

I write for those who cannot read.

—RENÉ CHARLES GUILBERT DE PIXERÉCOURT,

melodramatist

I came to my work, not by way of the graded highways of literature

but by the rough trails and rutted roads of desperate living.

—HAROLD BELL WRIGHT

In 1984, President Ronald Reagan wrote to Harold Bell Wright's daughter-in-law to tell her what one of Wright's books had meant to him in his boyhood. Several days after finishing *That Printer of Udell's*, Reagan declared himself saved and was baptized at the Christian church in his home town of Dixon, Illinois. Reagan claimed that Dick Falkner, the printer/protagonist of the book's title, was a role model for him, and that the character continued to shape the course of his life into the present day.[1]

In spite of his influence on Ronald Reagan and millions of other readers, Wright is almost entirely absent from American literary history. In this chapter, I examine some reasons for his exclusion from the literary canon and argue that his novels were useful to nonliterary audiences as popular melodramas. Unlike his fellow Social Gospel writers, Wright did not see faith and commerce as opposed; he thought a savvy book-marketing plan would both make money and bring readers closer to God. Moreover, Wright's audience was disproportionately made up of rural and small-town readers who were outsiders to literary culture. Wright's "sermon" and his ideas about gender, race, and progress were far more compelling to them than his aesthetics.

Authorship, Manliness, and Ministry

Wright (1872–1944) was a household name in the early twentieth century. He wrote nineteen books between 1903 and 1942, six of which appeared on bestseller lists. *That Printer of Udell's* (1903), *The Shepherd of the Hills* (1907), *The Calling of Dan Matthews* (1909), *The Winning of Barbara Worth* (1911), *The Eyes of the World* (1914), and *When a Man's a Man* (1916) outsold almost every other novel published before World War I. Literary historian Russell Nye lists Wright as one of the five best-selling novelists in the first quarter of the twentieth century. Wright was the third most popular writer between 1895 and 1926, and he held the top spot between 1909 and 1921.[2] His absence from literary history can be explained—in large part—because he embraced a model of authorship that was both blatantly commercial and blatantly evangelical, a model at odds with the modernist vision of authorship that became dominant in the early twentieth century.

In some ways, Wright's model of authorship was a nineteenth-century model. Like the wives and daughters of liberal Protestant ministers such as Harriet Beecher Stowe, Susan Warner, and Maria Cummins, who dominated the literary marketplace with pious, domestic novels that were continuous with the ubiquitous evangelical Christian tracts of nineteenth-century America, Wright intended his books to transform readers' lives and bring them closer to God.[3] A pastor at several churches in Missouri, Kansas, and later California, Wright read his first novel in installments to his congregation in place of a more conventional sermon, much as Charles Sheldon did. Writing novels, Wright maintained, was merely an alternate ministry, one with a much bigger congregation.[4]

Highbrow literary critics used Wright's evangelical fervor as a way to discredit his artistry. H. L. Mencken described the work of writers like Wright as being "on the plane of letters, precisely what evangelical Christianity is on the plane of religion, to wit, the product of ill-informed, emotional and more or less pushing and oafish folk." One article in *Bookman* criticized Wright's "Salvation Army methods," which involved both a literary style lacking in subtlety and a simplistic worldview that cast characters as purely good or purely evil.[5]

Wright knew that this model of authorship was out of fashion by the early twentieth century. He saw writers and publishers as an unsympathetic "fraternity" hell-bent on exposing the unspeakable and immoral for profit.[6] In a paragraph of the draft copy of his autobiography deleted from the published version, Wright explains, "Dare to speak of an author as a servant or to suggest that it is a writer's job to add something to the fullness of all life, that the glory and honor of writing is the measure of the contribution to the more abundant living of those who read, and you will very quickly see what the fraternity will do to you."[7]

Although he shared their evangelical mission, Wright eschewed the domesticity of popular, sentimental fiction writers of the nineteenth century. Wright's books were often Westerns. In *The Winning of Barbara Worth*, well-educated, wealthy, effeminate easterner Willard Holmes conquers the burning California desert and the raging Colorado River to prove himself a real man, winning the hand of Barbara Worth in the process. In *When a Man's a Man*, wealthy, well-educated, effeminate Lawrence Knight leaves his namby-pamby eastern life behind to prove himself in the Arizona desert as Patches—nameless cowboy, ranch hand, and, ultimately, real man.

Wright was part of a larger turn-of-the-century movement intended to shore up embattled white American manhood, weakened by the "overcivilization" of modern, middle-class life. This movement included Theodore Roosevelt's advocacy of "the strenuous life," the growth of high school and college athletics, and the founding of the Boy Scouts, among others. The Christian wing of this movement advocated for "muscular Christianity." Billy Sunday, a professional baseball player turned evangelist, told Christian men that their bodies were temples and that athletic training was not a waste of time better spent in studying the scriptures but rather preparation to be Christian soldiers in a world that needed their courage and manly leadership.[8]

Although Protestant churches in America had been two-thirds female since the 1660s, between 1880 and 1920 a number of church leaders identified this as a "crisis." There were interdenominational efforts to "find" those missing men and bring them into the pews to do manly work for the church. Most visibly, the 1911–12 Men and Religion Forward Movement held rallies in major cities across the country, placed ads in newspapers and magazines targeting those missing men, and reimagined the church in terms of manly metaphors of sports and business.[9] The Men and Religion Forward Movement was allied with the Social Gospel, discussed in Chapter 1. Wright was among the most popular Social Gospel novelists, reimagining in fiction the transformation of social institutions according to Christian principles.

Wright addressed the masculinization of Christianity in two novels: *That Printer of Udell's* and *The Calling of Dan Matthews*. *Printer* is about the fundamental transformation of a western town by the founding of an institutional church that provided for the material needs of all, rather than just sponsoring Sunday worship. In the early pages, the men on the church board argue about how to raise additional money for the church. Although many are ready to let the church women hold bazaars and bake sales, others insist that Christ would not run a church on a "lemonade and ice cream basis" but would run it like a business.[10] The feminization of the organized church is a central problem of *The Calling of Dan Matthews*, a book about how Matthews leaves the ministry to do God's *real* work—becoming an industrialist and the developer of a mine on his family's property. A fine, manly man, born and bred in the Ozarks, Matthews finds that the effeminate role of minister chafes him: "He was already conscious of being somewhat out of place with the regular work of the church: the pastoral calls, which mean visiting, day after day, in the homes of the members to talk with the women about nothing at all, at hours when the men of the household are away laboring, with brain or hand, for the necessities of life; the meetings of the various women's societies, where the minister himself is the only man present, and the talk is all women's talk; the committee meetings, where hours are spent in discussing the most trivial matters with the most ponderous gravity—as though the salvation of the world depends upon the color of the pulpit carpet, or who should bake a cake for the next social."[11] If Wright's ministry of print is descended from the female writers of sentimental fiction, he is at pains to distinguish himself from them here, dismissing as trivial all of the sacred domestic rituals they invested with transcendent importance.[12]

Wright imagined books as the products of a manly, skilled craft worker. The early pages of his 1934 autobiography, *To My Sons*, included a meditation on the family name. A "wright" was a skilled workman, and Wright prided himself on his craftsmanship: "I look upon writing as my job. My study, to me, is a workshop. Paper, pencils, pens, ink, thesaurus, dictionary—these are the tools of my craft."[13] Wright contributed to *The Editor: A Journal of Information for Literary Workers* and *Writer's Monthly* in the mid-1920s, offering training to would-be literary apprentices. The principles for building a book, he argued, were identical to the principles for constructing a building. "I am not an artist, but a carpenter," he wrote. "I build books."[14] Writing was not set apart in a pristine, aesthetic realm inhabited by inspiration and genius but was continuous with ordinary, everyday work for Wright. "I have never in my work looked toward a place in literature," he insisted. "But I *have* hoped for some small part in the life of the people for whom I have written."[15]

Wright and the Popular Aesthetic

Critics excoriated Wright from almost his first appearance in print. He was widely held to be an illiterate hack whose sentimental, overblown plots were an insult to self-respecting writers everywhere. Waldo Frank called Wright's work "pseudo-literature." Irving Harlow Hart surveyed the first fifty years of bestseller lists in a 1946 article for *Publishers Weekly*. Wright got special mention: "To the student of the phenomena of the popularity of fiction, Harold Bell Wright supplies more negative data on the literary quality of the taste of the fiction reading public than any other author."[16] The literati developed an entire industry of defaming Wright in witty and erudite ways. H. L Mencken called a whole class of writers—including Wright—from the "middle layer" of American letters "liberated yokels" from the "cow and hog States." He dismissed their literature for its lack of culture and sophistication: "The worse [*sic*] of it is not that it is addressed primarily to shoe-drummers and shop-girls; the worst of it is that it is written by authors who *are*, to all intellectual intents and purposes, shoe-drummers and shop-girls."[17]

Wright got tired of defending himself against those who claimed his work was not Literature. He did not intend it to be. He wrote, "As God is my Judge, I have never claimed . . . so much as a single literary pin-feather. I have felt too keenly my lack of schooling in literature ever to dream of winning a place among the world's accredited authors."[18] Wright admitted that although he had tried to read Balzac, Dostoyevsky, and James, he had gotten little from the effort. This did not make them bad books, however ("this is not a criticism or denial of their greatness"), merely not the right books for him, a nonscholarly reader who left school in eighth grade. Rather than sorting writers along a single scale of aesthetic merit, Wright recognized different kinds of equally valid narrative pleasures.[19] His own were distinctly nonliterary. As he patiently explained in a 1921 interview: "If I entered a library of the man of scholarly-intellectual type I should not expect to find my books upon his shelves. But it gives me great joy to find them, as I often do, upon the desk of a superintendent of a great power company—to find them appreciated by ranch owners and cowboys and equally by men who are leaders in business and public affairs."[20]

Thus, Wright thought he was being judged by the wrong criteria. Repeatedly taken to task by critics for his melodramatic, sentimental plots and flowery language, Wright steadfastly maintained that his books were first and foremost arguments for Christian virtue, arguments requiring clear delineations of good and evil and poetic descriptions of nature that exposed the designing hand of God. The *Wichita Eagle* got it: "The author makes no attempt at fine writing. He drives at his sermon in every sentence. He wants to reach humanity with human lessons. And he succeeds."[21] Wright started every book with an "argument," which he developed as one would develop a legal brief. Only then did characters, settings, scenes, and dialogue come into view. He had completed the manuscript of *The Eyes of the World* before giving any of the characters a name. Each was known, as in morality plays, by the characteristics she or he represented: Greed, Lust, Art, and so on.[22]

Wright's worldview was deeply informed by what Pierre Bourdieu calls "the popular ethos." As discussed in the Introduction, the popular ethos maintains a continuity between art and life, holds that art ought to fulfill a useful purpose, and eschews aesthetic distance for emotional engagement.[23] In one interview, Wright summarized his "popular" position: "As to the 'story for the story's sake,' nothing is farther from my mind."[24] Fans agreed that reading one of Wright's books deeply engaged one's emotions. Positive reviews (usually from small, regional papers or the religious press) repeatedly mentioned the tears the reader shed over the story rather than the formal aspects of Wright's novels. "It is a privilege to meet the people whom the author allows you to know," wrote the *Portland Spectator*. "They are worth while; and to cry and feel with them, get into their fresh, sweet atmosphere with which the writer surrounds them . . . these will repay you." Like Wright, these reviews made no distinction between art and life. They did not praise Wright for his fine characterization (which would have called attention to these characters as creations of a designing author), but instead talked about what wonderful people his characters were. As the *Boston Globe* maintained, "To the reader the characters will appear as real as friends they know—all of their aims, and likes, and hatreds being portrayed as true to life as snapshots caught by moving-picture cameras."[25]

Wright's "popular" or working-class ethos was no surprise; his schooling was highly irregular. It consisted largely of some haphazard reading and two years in the preparatory department at Hiram College. After his mother's death when he was ten, Wright worked on a farm and spent most of his adolescence and young manhood knocking around picking up odd jobs. He felt his lack of education profoundly: "While I have been for over a quarter of a century a professional writer of books, my lack of literary knowledge is appalling. When I am in the company of a bookish person, I am ashamed and ill at ease."[26] Despite this painful sense of intellectual inadequacy, Wright disdained what he described as useless knowledge. His novels frequently included overeducated, effeminate men who were rejected by the heroine for a manly man whose skill and intelligence were acquired on the job. In *When a Man's a Man*, beautiful, young Kitty Reid realizes she really wants to marry ranch foreman and real man Phil Acton, whom she has loved since childhood, rather than the overeducated Professor Everard Charles Parkhill, who has just proposed to her. Described by Acton as "the supreme representative of the highest highbrowed culture," Parkhill lacks masculine appeal.[27] Significantly, Kitty would never have been attracted to such an effeminate fop had her parents not sent her back east to a women's college, filling her head with all sorts of ridiculous ideas that made her unfit for ranch life.

Echoing the suspicions of self-contained intellectual life expressed by other Social Gospel novelists, Wright wondered if his burning desire to be of service to the human race could have survived a formal education: "Would I have held through colleges and universities my ideal of service? Or would I have lost my way in a wilderness of textbooks and lectures, and finally, out of touch with life, been content to live within the circle of my own individual intellectual interests?"[28] Wright clearly valued education and regretted his own lack of formal schooling, but he was deeply suspicious of a brand of useless intellectualism he associated with college men. "A sheepskin in itself," he wrote, "never entitled anyone to a degree of respect beyond that accorded the humble but useful animal who first carried it."[29]

Historian Richard Hofstadter traces the kind of anti-intellectualism Wright participated in back to evangelical religion, democratic politics, and a practical business culture that predominated in the nineteenth century. In an era when few business and professional men had much formal schooling, the purpose of education was assumed to be to further personal advancement, not train minds for a life of intellectual discipline. Practical life experience was held to be much better than book learning for setting a man up in business. Scholarly and cultural pursuits were widely held to be "unworldly, unmasculine, and impractical," suitable only for training a class of priests and aristocrats no longer relevant to modern American life.[30]

The Dickens of the Rural Route

Most evidence suggests that Wright's primary audience had only marginal access to higher education and the book culture it enabled. As a sparsely populated, geographically expansive country, the United States had a perennial problem with book distribution. A 1925 article in *Publishers Weekly* noted that there were only 1,500 book dealers in the entire country, most of them concentrated in large cities.[31] Most rural and small-town readers had great difficulty obtaining books and into the 1930s read much less than city dwellers as a consequence.[32] Publishers in the fifty years after the Civil War tried to solve these chronic problems with book distribution through two primary means—door-to-door subscription sales and mail-order distribution, strategies held in contempt by "legitimate" publishing houses in New York. The market was huge, however. Scholars estimate that before World War I, over 90 percent of all books were sold outside a bookshop, primarily through traveling agents.[33] These agents for the subscription book trade fanned out from their headquarters in midwestern cities like Cincinnati, St. Louis, Indianapolis, Kansas City, and Chicago into the surrounding countryside to offer certain kinds of steady-selling books door-to-door—Bibles, devotionals, reference books, and practical guides to housekeeping, gardening, livestock, and agriculture. Subscription companies targeted native-born, Protestant residents of rural areas and small towns—farmers, skilled workers, tradesmen, and small proprietors. Mail-order business focused on a similar demographic.[34] "Do you realize the great possibilities that await you out there in those farms, small cities and little towns," asked one bookseller, urging dealers to start mail-order departments in the pages of *Publishers Weekly* in 1923, "and does it ever occur to you, as a bookseller, that these people are book hungry?"[35]

From 1903 through 1920 (the years of his greatest popularity), Wright's work was published not by a regular trade publisher, but by book jobber Elsbery Reynolds of the Book Supply Company, who sold his books through the mail. Reynolds was a book distributor, engaging in no original publishing except for Wright's books. He was located in Chicago, far from the centers of trade publishing in New York, and the bulk of his business was Bibles, Sunday school literature, schoolbooks, children's books, encyclopedias, and other steady-selling reference works.[36]

Although the Book Supply Company's unpretentious 1918 catalog was largely composed of column after column of book titles and authors' names, Wright's work had twelve full pages of ads and a personal endorsement of Wright's latest novel over Reynolds's signature. Reynolds's statement shows that, for him, Wright's novels complemented the religious and educational books that were the company's bread and butter: "Over my signature I desire to give assurance, positive and absolute, to my friends of whatever nationality, political faith or religious belief that 'When a Man's a Man' is a story you should not only read yourself but one that must make you feel it your duty and your obligation to recommend and strongly indorse its reading to this boy or young man, or that girl or young woman. . . . It is a novel that you or I might read to the world for an audience and feel the kinship one with the other and with God and with Nature."[37] Geographic distribution of Wright's work kept its distinctive mail-order pattern long after his work became available in trade bookshops and through mainstream publishers.[38]

Wright sold better in rural areas and small towns than in cities, from the shelves of general stores, stationers, and drugstores rather than from those of trade bookstores.[39]

Almost everyone agreed that the majority of Wright's readers were nonreaders by book-trade standards.[40] Sales of his books dropped precipitously after he left the Book Supply Company for mainstream publisher D. Appleton & Company in 1920. The publishing industry was convinced that Wright's success had much to do with Reynolds's innovative distribution methods and the immense sums he spent on advertising appeals for individual titles. Wright was widely known in publishing circles after he left the Book Supply Company as, simply, "That Ingrate."[41]

Wright was also convinced his readers were disproportionately poor and rural. He wrote to his editor at Harper's (where he moved after leaving Appleton) in the 1930s about the declining sales of his work: "I venture to say . . . that among the twelve million unemployed and the hard hit farmers there are more of Harold Bell Wright readers than of any other author. It has always been significant to me that my following was built up so largely through the Book Supply Company mail order business. This means that by far the greater part of my readers have been farmers and the unemployed and those of small means who have been cut to the very quick."[42]

Even critics of the 1920s who could not come up with much nice to say about Wright's work did give him credit for his missionary work, converting the illiterate masses into born-again readers. Hildegard Hawthorne wrote in a 1923 article in *Bookman*, "It is to be remembered that many of those who read him are not readers at all, in the broad sense. If he did not write they would read nothing."[43] William Lyon Phelps thought of Wright's work as a kind of primer, training for the better books to which readers might someday graduate.[44] Even Appleton trumpeted Wright's gift for creating born-again readers in its promotional materials: "He has converted more non-book-readers into readers and book-buyers than any living American novelist," and "People to whom all other books but the Bible are idle and profane literature read Harold Bell Wright."[45]

The critical consensus in mass-market periodicals was that Wright's readers were a class apart from their own readers.[46] "Who reads Wright?" asked the *New York Times*. "Everyone you don't know," came the answer, "He is the Dickens of the free-delivery routes, the Dumas of the American countryside." Hildegarde Hawthorne told elite *Bookman* readers in 1923 that if they wished to understand "America in the bulk," reading one of Wright's novels was a good introduction to the psychology of the masses.[47]

One contemporary commentator, Grant Overton, described the ballyhoo accompanying the publication of a new Harold Bell Wright novel as follows:

> Six months before a new Wright story is to be published, thousands of tradespeople all over the United States know that the story is to be published, and when, and with what enormous advertising placed in forty specified periodicals and several dozen newspapers it will be "pushed"; and then begins the steady succession of personal letters and even telegrams, circulars and placards and posters, honest-minded persons in remote settlements discuss with enthusiasm and awe the prodigious sum of money to be expended on "just this one book, a *book*," librarians grow anxious and advertising men eager, preachers prepare sermons, in thousands upon thousands of homes the Christmas gift to Mother is pre-determined,—until at last, in a wide-rolling wave of excitement, a vast surge of the people of simple faith and worthy ideals, the day comes when the book is born.[48]

Overton clearly delineates the various networks through which Wright's books were promoted and sold. Not only did those in the book trade know about the new title, alerted by ads in *Publishers Weekly* and the *New York Times*, but the huge publicity campaigns got ordinary people talking about it. Ads were placed in the religious press, so that ministers could recommend this wholesome fiction to their congregants. Teachers paid attention (in part, because the book was advertised in education journals), so they could recommend the book to their pupils. Finally, parents bought the book for children, and grown children for their parents. For example, Ronald Reagan picked up *That Printer of Udell's* because he had seen his mother reading it.

As Overton's account indicates, the scope of these campaigns frequently became news itself. Traditionally, advertising books was believed to be too costly, since (unlike bars of soap or boxes of cornflakes) each individual title was unique. Reynolds and Wright understood that books could be marketed like other commodities and that Harold Bell Wright's name could operate as a trademark for wholesome, uplifting fiction. Reynolds mailed off promotional cards for each of Wright's books published by the Book Supply Company directly to his list of mail-order customers.[49] Reynolds also spent unprecedented sums on advertising in magazines and newspapers for

Wright's individual titles, never failing to mention "other books by Harold Bell Wright." The size of these promotional budgets was staggering, and their success revolutionized advertising in the book industry. Promoting *The Calling of Dan Matthews* (1909) cost $48,000; *The Winning of Barbara Worth* (1911), $75,000; *The Eyes of the World* (1914), over $100,000.[50] A 1915 *Bookman* article quoted one veteran bookseller, who explained Wright's success entirely in terms of advertising: "It is no mystery at all, just a matter of sheer advertising, like selling patent medicines or breakfast foods! Take any novel, I don't care how good or bad it is, and use the same methods . . . and I will guarantee that you will get similar results."[51]

After 1920, Appleton sank lots of money into advertising Wright's books, often promoting the size of the advertising campaigns themselves. One flyer captioned "Telling It to the World" promised "the greatest sales and publicity campaign ever conceived by any publishing house," featuring full-page ads in mass-market magazines, newspapers in large cities and small towns, religious newspapers and denominational magazines, and educational journals.[52] Seven months before its appearance, Appleton took out a full-page ad for *Helen of the Old House*, promising, "It will be brought forcibly to the attention of every English speaking person in America. Watch for the biggest sales campaign ever!"[53] Appleton got nationwide news coverage for one promotion—a phonograph record of Wright reading a dramatic scene from *Helen*. Advance mailings to booksellers proudly announced that this gimmick had won first prize from the National Convention of the Direct Advertising Association for "the most original and result-getting stunt." Book dealers were encouraged to loan out the record to women's study clubs and local radio stations.[54] Appleton promoted Wright's 1925 *A Son of His Father* with an essay contest. The hero of the book saves the family ranch from evil investors because he has inherited strength of character from his pioneer ancestors. Appleton prepared copy entitled "What Heredity Has Done for Successful Men and Women" and offered it to fifty major newspapers at no cost. It invited readers to submit essays called "What Heredity Has Done for Me" and promised a free copy of Wright's book to contest winners.[55]

Nobody pretended that Wright's books were anything but commodities. One Appleton flyer compared Wright's novels to Ford automobiles; both were "nationally known products," famous all over the world.[56] While contests and gimmicks were widely used in the 1920s to sell all kinds of consumer goods, books were largely exempt. Contests and giveaways, moreover, were not exactly good entry tickets into the ivory tower of the American literary canon.[57] Although his fellow Social Gospel novelists were squeamish, at best, about the intermingling of faith and commerce, Wright embraced the book-as-commodity as a potent weapon in the war for the souls of American readers.

Literary Scavengers

Both Wright's blatant commercialism and his evangelical fervor put him at odds with elite literary culture. So did his contempt for modernism. He wrote in his autobiography that "the taste of some of these modern, self-styled intellectuals, who soar so high over my lowly head, would gag a buzzard."[58] The great modernist writers of his time were publishing for tiny, highly educated audiences in "little magazines" featuring experimental writing. They believed in art for art's sake and concerned themselves self-consciously with aesthetics and literary form. Wright rejected the intellectual's vision of the literary life in a very public way. His *The Eyes of the World* (1914) was a fictional diatribe against artists and intellectuals for their dishonest, self-serving, prurient efforts to corrupt American society.

At the center of *The Eyes of the World* is a manly young artist, Aaron King, who promises his dying mother to use the three years of art-school training in Europe that she impoverished herself providing to redeem the discredited family name. The book is rife with artist figures—the manly hero/painter; the heroine, Sybil, musical prodigy and unspoiled child of nature; and Conrad La Grange, a modern novelist whose deformed body is a visual manifestation of the crookedness of his art. Like Sheldon's Judas figure, Jasper Chase, La Grange has shamelessly prostituted his art for wealth and good reviews. However, La Grange intends to protect Aaron King from the same fate. He introduces himself: "I am a literary scavenger. I haunt the intellectual slaughter pens, and live by the putrid offal that self-respecting writers reject. I glean the stinking materials for my stories from the sewers and cesspools of life. For the dollars they pay, I furnish my readers with those thrills that public decency forbids them to experience at first hand."[59] We never learn exactly what is in La Grange's novels, but King summarizes the one he has read: "The—ah—why—the one, you know—where the husband of one woman falls in love with the wife of another who is in love with the husband of someone else."[60] Innocent Sybil can only refuse to read La Grange's books, since she finds herself unable to play her hauntingly beautiful music afterward. In contrast, real art inspires her, making her feel "as I feel when I am at church."[61] Further, Wright makes clear that the artist has a great deal of help prostituting his art. In the novel, the corruption of the patrons and critics whose money, critical esteem, and networks of influential friends constitute an intellectual establishment is easily legible in the dissipation of their bodies and their immoral behavior.[62]

Our hero, seeing the light, destroys a very flattering portrait of a very immodest, immoral patroness and instead paints the ugly truth about the literary/intellectual crowd. The foremost literary critic in the United States, corrupted by all that "modern" fiction he has been reading, kidnaps the beautiful Sybil to force her to marry him, but she is rescued in the nick of time. The patrons and critics that constitute the literary and artistic establishment do not, however, use their influence to ruin King's reputation, because LaGrange knows some dirty secrets about them and he blackmails them into silence.

This novel was an easy target for ridicule. Owen Wister did a four-page send-up of it as a featured title in an article called "Quack-Novels and Democracy" in *Atlantic Monthly*. Some papers, however, thought Wright was right about modern novels. "His books are of a wholesomeness that is very comfortable in these days of thinly veiled literary pruriency," wrote one review of *Helen of the Old House*. "The book is clean and wholesome and has a freedom from suggestive scenes and conversation that is as refreshing as it is unusual in modern novels," promised another.[63]

Wright's Melodramas

Wright's books were repeatedly called to task for being melodramatic, a powerful clue to what these aesthetically bad novels might have been good *for*. Peter Brooks argues that melodrama is a "fictional system for making sense of experience" in a post-Enlightenment world. The Enlightenment dissolved what Brooks calls the "Traditional Sacred," a hegemonic belief in Christendom that structured the institutions, metaphysics, and hierarchically ordered society of western Europe. In its place were melodramas, which invested the events of daily life with larger meaning and significance.[64] Although he wrote about the desacralized liberal Protestant world of twentieth-century America rather than nineteenth-century France, Wright's melodramas are part of this paradigm.[65]

Wright, who briefly studied for the ministry after being saved by a revival preacher, engaged many critical issues in liberal Protestantism of the day, speaking out against denominationalism in *God and the Groceryman* (1927), exploring the benefits and possibilities of institutional churches in *That*

Printer of Udell's, and indicting the hypocrisy of the organized church in *The Calling of Dan Matthews.* His idea that belief in Christ ought to inspire the building of Christian institutions to feed the hungry, care for the sick, provide work for honest laborers, and support nuclear families at the center of Christian communities aligns him with Social Gospel thinkers such as Walter Rauschenbusch, Washington Gladden, and Richard Ely. However, the primary energies of Wright's work are melodramatic, investing a desacralized world with religious meanings that are usually profoundly personal rather than providing a revolutionary social vision.[66]

It is no coincidence that Wright chose melodrama as his vehicle. As discussed above, he did not spend a great deal of time reading Literature, and the texts most available to him for making sense of the world were popular plays.[67] He wrote many screenplays, adapted his novels into plays and participated in their production, and eagerly sold the rights to his novels to tent-show playwrights, whose adaptations turned millions of audience members on to his books.[68] Here is Wright describing a production of *Faust,* starring Lewis Morrison as Mephistopheles, that he saw as a young man and credits with being life-changing:

> I was as one in a trance. I was not in a theater, watching a play being acted upon the stage. I was looking upon life, my life. I was not conscious of Mr. Morrison acting a part; I was seeing the personification of evil. I was witnessing the eternal clash of spiritual forces which in every soul makes for ultimate salvation or final destruction. It was to me a tremendous spiritual experience that shook my very being.
>
> I left the theater to see the environment in which I was living and to view the influences to which I was being subjected in a new light. I had been accepting as a matter of course the only life I knew. I was becoming habituated to my surroundings. My vision was dimmed by familiarity. I saw life now in light of the eternal truth which Goethe's genius visioned and the art of Lewis Morrison made real. I do not in the least exaggerate, but state the simple fact as I know it after all the years have passed, when I say that this experience remained one of the most powerful influences in my life.[69]

Wright did not watch this play as one concerned in a distant, abstract way with its form. He was intensely, passionately involved with the story, completely unaware of the production *as a production* at all. Like his fellow Social Gospel writers and readers discussed in Chapter 1, there were no boundaries between art and life for Wright. This production commented immediately on his (degraded) life circumstances and inspired him to change. For him, this narrative gave structure and meaning to his life; it provided his "first vital conception of good and evil as definite life forces."[70] He began this story by describing the absence of Christian people and the utter lack of any spiritual influence since his boyhood. He asks rhetorically, "Is it strange, then, that I should look upon the theater with something of the feeling that one looks upon a temple?"[71]

Although all of Wright's books are melodramatic—peopled with spotless virgins, strong, manly men full of wholesome virtue, and leering, physically repulsive villains,[72] I will examine here his best-known novel, *The Shepherd of the Hills* (1907), which put the Ozark Mountains on the map as "God's country."[73] In *Shepherd*, a grief-stricken stranger from the city mysteriously appears in the Ozarks and decides to stay, working as a shepherd for the Matthews family, which is still grieving the seduction of their daughter by a sophisticated artist from the city and her subsequent death in childbirth. Pete, the illegitimate son of this coupling, is addle-brained and wanders the woods all day and night. Dad Howitt, as the stranger comes to be called, looks after Pete, helps out his neighbors, and (being in possession of a great deal of book learning) agrees to work as tutor to a beautiful young mountain girl named Sammy Lane, who wants to be a "real lady" by the time her fiancé returns from a trip to the big city. There is a contest over the hand of Sammy Lane between the Matthewses' son, a fine, virile specimen of mountain manhood, and Ollie Stewart, the effeminate, citified fiancé. The good mountain folks are persecuted by a villain named Wash Gibbs, who threatens Sammy's virtue, her father's safety, and the social fabric of the entire community.

When a doctor from the city arrives looking for Dad Howitt, he is outed as a well-known big-city minister and the father of the artist who seduced the Matthewses' daughter. Grief-stricken by the apparent suicide of his only son, Howitt had been sent by his doctor for a rest in the country. By an amazing coincidence (read: God's will), he took up residence in exactly the place where his son had seduced an innocent girl, abandoned her, and left her—insane with grief—to die giving birth to Pete. Howitt salves his grieving heart in the magisterial wilderness and does his best to make amends for his son's sin.

In the final pages, it is revealed that Howard, the artist-son, is still alive, hiding out in a nearby cave, caring for his addled son and doing good for the mountain folk. He is, however, mortally wounded, and lives only long enough to beg his father's forgiveness and obtain absolution from the wronged Matthews family before going to his eternal rest. Sammy Lane, having ditched her citified fiancé, marries the young Matthews boy, and the minister refuses to return to his big-city congregation, preferring to tend his flocks in God's country.

This is melodrama par excellence. Ben Singer identifies five characteristics that melodramas possess: pathos, overwrought emotion, moral polarization, nonclassical narrative structure, and sensationalism.[74] *Shepherd* has them all. There are innocent victims and dastardly villains, whose moral natures are clearly marked by their appearances.[75] As in traditional stage melodramas, the moral order is immediately legible. Moreover, *Shepherd* provides an excellent example of what Brooks calls the *"voix du sang"* of traditional melodrama, the uncanny ability of long-lost relatives to recognize their kinship on sight.[76] Howitt immediately feels an affinity for Pete, the grandson he did not know he had, and Pete is—of course—the spitting image of his handsome father.

These characters inhabit a remarkably Manichaean world. Wash Gibbs and Ollie Stewart do not have a redeeming bone in their bodies, but Sammy Lane and young Matt are pure, strong, and brave through and through. There are long-suffering, innocent victims: Maggie Matthews, the seduced and abandoned daughter; Mr. and Mrs. Matthews, the grieving parents; and poor addle-brained Pete, who is the living materialization of his parents' sin (and a stock figure from stage melodrama).[77] There is also persecuted innocence, for Howard Howitt, the artist-son who appears to be a seducing cad, really loved Maggie, had no idea she was pregnant when he left, and feared marrying her only because his proud, well-educated father would not have approved of his ignorant mate. He had, in fact, renounced his growing fame (won through a celebrated painting of his beloved) and his proud family in order to return and ask for Maggie's hand in marriage, only to arrive too late. So he made it appear he was dead and hid himself in the Ozarks to do penance.

As in much melodrama in America, the class conflicts of European melodrama are refigured as conflicts between the city and the country. The city is bad; the Ozarks are good. Ollie learns his superficial, effeminate ways in the city. The seducer is an urban interloper in the pristine wilderness. Dad Howitt tells a visitor from the city that he has much to learn in the Ozarks—"this page of His great book"—that will be of use to men in "the restless world over there."[78] Even religion is split along city/country lines. Howitt concedes that when he was a pastor in Chicago, "Christianity to him was but little more than culture, and his place in the church merely an opportunity to add to the honor of his name,"[79] but the mountains are full of good Christian men and women who never set foot in a church. Driven to the wilderness by grief—seeking peace, strength, and solace—the conventionally religious man Howitt had been died, and he was "born again in these mountains" as a humble shepherd.[80]

Shepherd is full of sensational scenes of excess. For example, manly young Matt saves the citified Ollie from a marauding cougar; he lifts an entire engine off the ground at the mill to win a bet for a friend; and he then lifts two grown men over his head—one in each hand—to demonstrate his strength. When the heavily foreshadowed fight with Wash Gibbs finally occurs, it is lovingly described for the better part of two pages—"a terrific struggle; not the skillful sparring of trained fighters, but the rough and tumble battling of primitive giants . . . the climax of long months of hatred; the meeting of two who were by every instinct mortal enemies." The summary comment belongs to Sammy Lane, who cries out after Matt has thrashed Gibbs and his knife-wielding thugs: "Oh, *what a man!*"[81] This is melodrama indeed, and—for the aesthetically inclined critic—often downright embarrassing to read. I think, however, we should take Wright at his word. He was not writing literature for intellectuals; he was sermonizing to the rural and the poorly educated, and his books were immensely successful for these specific readers in specific, nonliterary ways.

Ben Singer argues that melodrama spoke to the conditions of working-class modernity in two ways: (1) capturing the powerlessness of individuals within the harsh system of capitalism; and (2) reassuring audiences that a just, higher law still governed the chaotic world.[82] Maggie Matthews was seduced by a handsome stranger from the modern city; the Matthewses are in danger of losing their heavily mortgaged land to the bank; and Ollie Stewart seeks to seduce Sammy Lane with promises of wealth and urban sophistication. All of the Ozarks inhabitants seem vulnerable to forces beyond their control. In the end, however, Christian love brings forgiveness and healing to the wronged Matthews clan; "God's gold" (delivered by Howard Howitt) arrives on the doorstep in time to save the Matthews land; and Sammy Lane ends up staying at home with her God-given mate—all through a number of amazing coincidences that can only be read as the designing hand of God.

Moreover, Wright makes clear that he intends *Shepherd* to function like an allegory or a morality play, in which good and evil are clearly marked. *Shepherd* gives us explicit directions for reading in the introduction. The narrator writes:

This, my story, is a very old story.
    In the hills of life there are two trails. One lies along the higher sunlit fields where those who journey see afar, and the light lingers

even when the sun is down; and one leads to the lower ground, where those who travel, as they go, look always over their shoulders with eyes of dread, and gloomy shadows gather long before the day is done.

This, my story, is the story of a man who took the trail that leads to the lower ground, and of a woman, and how she found her way to the higher sunlit fields.

In the story, it all happened in the Ozark Mountains, many miles from what we of the city call civilization. In life, it has all happened many, many times before, in many, many places. The two trails lead afar. The story, so very old, is still in the telling.[83]

First, we are explicitly discouraged from reading *Shepherd* novelistically. Like widely circulated folktales, this narrative is a story a culture tells itself about itself, and the interest lies not in its originality but in the specific ways it is embellished or retold.

Second, we are explicitly told to read in typological or allegorical ways. The two paths are both actual trails through the woods in the Ozarks and material representations of life paths on a Christian journey. One path is good and true and (quite literally) leaves the pilgrim walking in the light; the other is dark and low and haunted by guilt and fear. The story happens both in the real time and place of the Ozark mountains and in the placeless, timeless realm of allegory.[84] Howard Howitt seduces an innocent girl and is haunted by darkness until his dying day. Sammy Lane turns down wealth and social status to marry her God-given mate and lives happily ever after. Sammy and Howard are both themselves (reportedly composites of real residents of the Ozarks) and types, figures for the countless men and women who have faced choices about the paths of sin and righteousness.

Gregory Jackson argues that the allegorical frames structuring homiletic fiction in the late nineteenth and early twentieth centuries created this kind of double vision for readers. They were both inside and outside time—"at the intersection of the temporal and the eternal"— simultaneously actors in their historical moment and part of God's eternal plan.[85] Moreover, as Michael Denning suggests, allegorical ways of reading were often "characteristic of subordinate groups." He argues that in allegorical readings, "the fictional world is less a representation of the real world than a microcosm. . . . Individual characters are less individuals than figures for social groups." Allegorical modes of reading also depend on culturally legible "master plots," of which Christian allegory is certainly one.[86] Indeed, Singer argues in his study of stage and film melodrama in America around the turn of the century that melodrama was "culturally segregated and stigmatized as a proletarian amusement." Numerous scholars link melodrama specifically to the economic and physical vulnerability and corporeality of working-class life in a market culture.[87]

Wright wrote several allegories—*Their Yesterdays* (1912) (whose everyman and everywoman protagonists did not even have names), *The Uncrowned King* (1910), and *The Eyes of the World* (discussed above). Some contemporary commentators maintained that Wright's work *was* allegory and specifically invoked *Pilgrim's Progress* as the most important intertext.[88] I am suggesting here that Wright's novels do not reward a traditionally literary reading but that they do reward an allegorical or typological reading more characteristic of popular or working-class audiences. It is also a way of reading with deep roots in the history of Protestant scripture-reading practices.

Meditations on ways of reading are scattered throughout *Shepherd*. While Sammy Lane is studying with Howitt, they spend as much time on nature walks as they do reading: "Always as she advanced, he encouraged her to look for the life that is more than meat, and always, while they read and talked together, there was opened before them the great book wherein God had written, in the language of mountain, and tree, and sky, and flower, and brook, the things that make truly wise those who pause to read."[89] Better than books written by men is the book of God—creation. As in the centuries-old practice called natural theology, science and religion are imagined here in perfect accord. Presumably, the better we understand the operation of the natural world, the more apparent will be the designing hand of God.[90]

The conclusion to *Shepherd* returns to explicit directions for reading the world. Pete dies, and Dad Howitt writes to his doctor/friend back in Chicago about the event's significance: "Here and there among men, there are those who pause in the hurried rush to listen to the call of a life that is more real. How often have we seen them, David, jostled and ridiculed by their fellows, pushed aside and forgotten, as incompetent or unworthy. He who sees and hears too much is cursed for a dreamer, a fanatic, or a fool, by the mad mob, who, having eyes, see not, ears and hear not, and refuse to understand."[91] Here, Howitt explicitly calls attention to several levels of meaning. The world available to us through our senses, the world the Enlightenment draws our attention to, is readily visible to everyone, but there is yet another level of meaning that Howitt is calling "more real," a transcendent meaning that invests the minutiae of everyday life with larger significance. To access this level of meaning requires looking with different eyes, looking in ways our culture identifies with children, fools, and other marginalized interpreters. Melodrama and the typological ways of reading that it invites or requires enact an inversion of customary power hierarchies, rendering the urban, middle-class reader marginal and granting a simple-minded backwoods boy epistemic privilege.

Shepherd concludes with the arrival of an artist coming to paint in the Ozarks. Dad Howitt, predicting the arrival of the railroad in these pristine mountains, warns the young man: "You must work hard, young sir, while the book of God is still open, and God's message is easily read. When the outside world comes, men will turn the page, and you may lose the place."[92] This passage is not only an elegy for the disappearing wilderness, but it is also a meditation on ways of reading. If the remnants of the sacred are legible in the pristine landscape, the moral order apparent in the simple appearance of things, this is because modern civilization has not corrupted the text. Just as the railroad replaces the woods, new ways of reading the world will replace the clear, unambiguous reading protocols of melodrama and allegory. The new worldview does not so clearly map the moral universe or so successfully place a reader in the social world.

The clear, moral order in *Shepherd of the Hills* is not, however, the return of what Brooks calls the Traditional Sacred—the single, unifying myth on which a coherent moral order and a set of social institutions could be built. As in all melodrama, the moral order *Shepherd* maps is highly personal and individualistic.[93] It closes not with a kingdom or a city or even a church community, but with a nuclear family. Sammy Lane introduces the visiting artist to her husband and children. They clearly embody what Brooks calls the "moral occult,"[94] the shattered fragments of the Traditional Sacred, in that they appear to the visitor "like young gods for beauty and strength."[95] They do not, however, provide an entire system of compelling, immediately evident meaning on which to build a society. *Shepherd* ends with the scene of narration. Sammy Lane unveils Mad Howard's long-lost masterpiece hanging on a back wall in her home, and she tells the visiting artist the story the reader has just come to know as *The Shepherd of the Hills*. In place of the myth of Christendom—a single story that made sense of the world—Wright offers the compulsive act of storytelling, the process of making meaning by shaping the events of everyday life into a coherent narrative.

Wright's novels offer new ways of reading the world to those whose class, regional, and educational backgrounds placed them outside mainstream culture. As the increasingly urban, increasingly literate, larger culture communicated to rural, poor, or poorly educated citizens that they mattered very little, Wright's melodramas invested their ordinary lives with transcendent meaning. *Shepherd* is not just the story of a pretty (but utterly irrelevant) mountain girl's selection of a mate; the very fate of the race hangs in the balance.

Mating, Breeding, and the Fate of the Race

Like the turn-of-the-century intellectuals described by historian Gail Bederman, Wright was deeply engaged in a conversation that located "civilization" at the intersection of gender, race, and a much-transformed, Darwin-influenced, Protestant millennialism.[96] His particular synthesis maintained that men and women of the "civilized" races (read: white) had a God-given responsibility to move humanity toward perfection. In this model, the other races had only subordinate places, if any. Women and men had distinct roles to play, since a high degree of sex differentiation was the mark of higher races. In addition, Wright's early novels were inflected by regional ideas about race. Aaron Ketchell argues that many writers throughout the twentieth century trafficked in a mythical image of the Ozarks as a kind of "ethnic refuge," an island of pure Anglo-Saxon stock in a sea of racial and ethnic diversity. The "Ozark hillbilly" figure functioned—for many—as a "racial redeemer in a country being overrun with unsavory shades of whiteness."[97]

The language of blood and breeding is ubiquitous in Wright's early novels. Preachin' Bill, the oracle in *Shepherd of the Hills*, says of Mr. Matthews and his son, "Men like them ought t' be as common as th' other kind, an' would be too if folks cared half as much 'bout breeding folks as they do 'bout raising hogs an' horses."[98] Matt and Sammy are "two splendid creatures . . . masterpieces of the Creator's handiwork; made by Him who created man, male and female, and bade them have dominion over every living thing that moveth upon the earth."[99] All of the voices of authority in the novel think Sammy and Young Matt ought to get married, since they "owed it to the race."[100]

The discourse about breeding in *Shepherd* is more complicated, however. Like Tarzan, who appeared on the scene in 1913, the heroes of Wright's novels combine unspoiled "natural man" and aristocratic blood. Sammy's father was the black sheep of an old southern family who was banished to the Ozarks, where he met and married a beautiful wild mountain girl, Sammy's mother. Mr. Lane has "something in his face and bearing that told of good breeding," but Sammy—hybrid of savagery and civilization—is even more impressive: "From her mother, and from her own free life in the hills, Sammy had a body beautiful with the grace and strength of perfect physical womanhood. With this, she had inherited from many generations of gentle-folk a mind and spirit susceptible of the highest culture."[101] The progeny of Matt and Sammy bear out the millennial predictions for the race. Matt and Sammy's first-born, Daniel, is the hero of *The Calling of Dan Matthews*, described as "the first born of the true mating of a man and woman who had never been touched by those forces in our civilization which so dwarf and cripple the race." He, too, reaps the benefits of being raised as a "natural man" in the Ozarks by parents who are blue bloods: "The boy was well born; he was natural. He was what a man-child ought to be . . . a revelation of that . . . best part of the race."[102] At the end of *The Calling of Dan Matthews*, when Dan has left the ministry to develop a mine on his family's property in the Ozarks, he, too, has found his true mate. She is a nurse he met while working as a minister, one who comes from a well-known family described as "thoroughbreds."[103]

The evolutionary stakes are even more obvious in *The Winning of Barbara Worth*. Here, Wright suggests that God—at work over centuries in the wind, rains, and rivers of the West—has created the almost impermeable California desert that has lain dormant while generations of human beings have evolved under His guiding hand into the supermen capable of conquering it.[104] Willard Holmes, hero of *The Winning of Barbara Worth*, is also "a thoroughbred and a good individual of the best type that the race has produced."[105] Although he enters the story as a tenderfooted easterner who has never ridden a horse, his baptism by fire in the desert activates his superior genetic inheritance: "It was as if in this man, born of the best blood of a nation-building people, trained by the best of the cultured East—trained as truly by his life and work in the desert—it was as though, in him, the best spirit of the age and race found expression."[106]

Wright gives us a tableau in the middle of *The Winning of Barbara Worth* that links gender, race, and millennialism. All of the peoples of the desert West are gathered in one place, and Wright makes clear that the individuals (as in all allegory) represent whole classes of people:

And not one of them thought of the significance of the group or how each, representing a distinct type, stood for a vital element in the combination of human forces that was working out for the race the reclamation of the land. The tall, lean desert-born surveyor, trained in no school but the school of his work itself, with the dreams of the Seer ruling him in his every professional service; the heavy-fisted quick-witted, aggressive Irishman, born and trained to handle that class of men that will recognize in their labor no governing force higher than the physical; the dark-faced frontiersman, whom the forces of nature, through the hard years, had fashioned for his peculiar place in this movement of the race as truly as wave and river and wind and sun had made the King's Basin Desert itself; the self-hidden financier who, behind his gray mask, wrought against one of the willow posts that upheld the arrow weed shelter; dark Pablo, softly touching his guitar, representing a people still far down on the ladder of the world's upward climb, but still sharing, as all peoples would share, the work of all; and, in the midst of the group, the center of her court—Barbara, true representative of a true womanhood that holds in itself the future of the race, even as the desert held in its earth womb life for the strong ones whom the slow years had fitted to realize it.[107]

Barbara is at the center of this enterprise in a number of ways.[108] Everyone thinks of it as "Barbara's desert," since she was found there as an infant, her parents having died in the crossing. Love of Barbara inspires the men from all classes to do their part in the reclamation of the desert. She is the beloved adopted daughter of financier Jefferson Worth and the lover of Willard Holmes, and she is looked after by her "uncles"—the Irishman, the frontiersman, and the Seer. She is widely considered to be an angel by the Hispanic families who work for her father, since she brings them food, clothing, and medical care when injury or illness keeps their men from gainful employment. It is in her name that the men seek to conquer the desert, and it is her love that inspires them and her womanly nurturance that mitigates the enterprise's harsh physical and emotional costs.[109] The glue holding all of this together is religion. God created the elemental forces that shaped both the hostile, rugged wilderness and the men strong enough to conquer it. He decreed that women should mate and bear children, not hold down jobs. In handing one's life over to God, one also restores these other God-given hierarchies—men over women, "civilized" white folks over people of color.

Wright's fusion of evolutionary theory with Protestant millennialism was common; many Protestant intellectuals responded to the scientific challenge to biblical truth with similar rapprochements. Their version of evolution—from

Herbert Spencer rather than Charles Darwin—suggested gradual, continuous, progressive development. Men were ascending toward perfection through the operation of God's will in the natural world. This worldview was particularly attractive to liberals, since it reconciled science, religion, and a progressive politics that served their needs and interests.[110]

Wright's books did, indeed, negotiate or finesse contradictions at the center of American life.[111] In addition to reconciling theories of evolution with belief in the designing hand of God, a rather painful contradiction for many Christians in the early twentieth century, *The Winning of Barbara Worth* also reconciles egalitarian ideology with inherited privilege. Although Wright suggests that men and women prove themselves in the West through talent rather than ancestry, all the transgressive class miscegenation is closed off at the end. Aristocratic Willard Holmes is about to take the foundling and adopted daughter of a new-money capitalist as his wife, when it is discovered that she is, in fact, the long-lost niece of his own blue-blooded guardian.[112] In Wright's world, one can be committed to both radical egalitarianism and the preservation of aristocratic bloodlines. One can be both an owner and a worker, a natural man and a born aristocrat, a foundling and a princess.[113]

Re-creating the Sacred

Unlike fundamentalists, who were convinced of the literal truth of scriptures, liberal Protestants were concerned with reconciling religion and science, with remaking themselves for the modern world. Less concerned with the second coming of Christ than with building His kingdom on earth through missions, institutional churches, and social activism on behalf of the poor and the disenfranchised, liberal Protestants were resolutely rooted in this world.[114] Their primary means of doing this was an individualization of faith, a remaking of American religion for the consumer capitalist world. In his work, Wright allowed readers to see the world as resolutely material and concrete (as mainstream modern life required) but also as ripe with transcendent meanings. Poor Pete was both an addle-brained boy and a divine seer, and the two worldviews were not contradictory in a typological or allegorical reading of the world.

In the closing pages of his autobiography, Wright addresses the distinction between his personal faith and the organized church, between the moral occult implicit in *Shepherd* and the Traditional Sacred, which no longer structured social institutions or seemed compelling to large numbers of (even Christian) Americans. He asserts, "I do not believe that the world today is as godless as we sometimes think."[115] It appears so only because people have confused the church as an institution with personal faith. Wright explains: "That I can no longer subscribe to the divinity of ecclesiastical councils, nor acknowledge as divine the authority of church courts, does not at all mean that for me, now, there is no God. It means simply that *I* am forced to restate for *myself my* understanding of Deity."[116]

In his personal understanding, science and religion, the secular and the sacred, were complementary. Wright was enthralled by biology and physics, believing wholeheartedly in the truth of these scientific disciplines, but he also found God in the mysterious forces holding atoms together and in the spark of life inhabiting kernels of grain. The implications of this theology are striking. Wright explained: "It exalts the commonplace and deifies the ordinary. . . . The sound of the harvester in a field of wheat is to me now a hymn of thanksgiving and praise. The smell of newly plowed ground is the incense of prayer; the acres of grain rippling in the breeze are the banners of Divine Glory; the sunshine is His strength; the rain His graciousness; the night His peace. All who in any capacity serve are God's ministers. The garb of the laborer is a priestly robe. The tools of the mechanic, the pen of the writer, the instruments of science, the needle of the seamstress, the utensils of the cook, the humble implements of the housewife, are the sacred furnishing of the temple of life which is the temple of the living God. To live is to worship; to worship is to live."[117] This worldview creates a vision of radical democracy in which all sorts of devalued occupations—farm labor, hand labor, housework—become valued equally with those of higher social status. Rather than robbing the ministry of the trappings of the supernatural (secularization), Wright argues that the supernatural inhabits us all. The personalization or individualization of the sacred supports the values of the modern marketplace in some ways, but it is also oppositional, locating the sacred in our work rather than in the consumer goods we increasingly buy and display.[118]

However, Wright's "moral occult," his populist re-visioning of the sacred for the individual, is nonetheless a millennial vision with disturbing gender and race politics and ambiguous class politics, at best. Women are, by divine decree and evolutionary necessity, wives and mothers. "True aristocrats" might look like ordinary mountain folk, but royal blood runs in their veins. Moreover, nonwhites do not enter the story at all except as comic relief or stereotypes.[119] For a particular set of rural and small-town, native-born, white

Americans, Wright's melodramas made inhabiting their particular place in early twentieth-century America much easier. These stories invested the lives of people like them with millennial importance and their ways of being in the world with a superior moral authority, just as the center of American life was becoming increasingly urban, increasingly complex, and increasingly filled with New Negroes, New Women, and large numbers of immigrants who looked less and less like them. Wright's allegories promised that they could be both citizens of a modern, disenchanted world and Christians inhabiting a sacred space, and that these identities would not be in conflict.

Wright's work and his literary reputation raise questions about how we study and teach American literature. Aside from dismissing ordinary readers as unintelligent and aesthetically challenged (as many of Wright's critics did), we have no way of explaining why so many Americans read such bad books with so much intensity and passion. I am suggesting here that American literary history ought to include all kinds of readers and writers, rather than just those engaged in self-consciously literary pursuits. Our literary marketplace includes writers who imagined themselves not only as artists, but also as wage earners, craftsmen, and missionaries, among other roles. People read not only for aesthetic pleasures, but also because certain kinds of stories offer ways of negotiating profoundly felt, painful contradictions at the center of American cultural life. Moreover, a literary history that takes popular books seriously will challenge some widely held critical commonplaces. For example, although many American cultural historians maintain that the process of "secularization" was largely complete by the end of the nineteenth century,[120] Wright's popularity suggests that the relationship between religion and American culture was (and is) far more complex and that it varies widely along the axes of class, race, region, and gender. Moreover, commerce sometimes mingles promiscuously with art and evangelism, rather than opposing them. Wright's literary career reminds us, then, that intellectuals are not the only readers and writers in America, and that ways with words are profoundly shaped by the communities and institutions—including religious and commercial ones—readers and writers inhabit.

PART II

The 1920s Religious Renaissance

THREE

Good Books Build Character
Promoting Religious Reading in the 1920s

The man in the street, who often seems concerned only with the stock market
and the World Series, is really immensely interested in religion.
—DR. S. PARKES CADMAN, Chair of the Religious
Book Club Editorial Board

If you do not commodify your religion yourself, someone will do it for you.
—R. LAURENCE MOORE

"Matters of the spirit are common subjects of conversation," asserted *Publishers Weekly* in 1924; "people may be heard discussing them in crowded elevators, in restaurants, in subway trains or between the acts."[1] The sentiment was widely held. Most cultural critics of the 1920s agreed that Americans were undergoing a "religious renaissance" that deeply influenced the print culture of the age.[2] A new translation of the New Testament was running in newspaper syndication. The front pages were filled with the Scopes "monkey trial" in Tennessee and the banning in Boston of Sinclair Lewis's novel about a thoroughly corrupt minister, *Elmer Gantry*. The year 1925 was the much ballyhooed 400th birthday of the Tyndale Bible, the first printed translation of the New Testament into English, and the Church of England spent much of the decade embroiled in well-publicized controversy over a new *Book of Common Prayer*. Mass-market magazines like *Pictorial Review*, *Woman's Home Companion*, and *Ladies' Home Journal* ran religious texts as their leading serials. The number of religious books published increased dramatically, and religious titles—Henrik Van Loon's *The Story of the Bible* (1923), Giovanni Papini's *Life of Christ* (translated by Dorothy Canfield Fisher, 1923), and Bruce Barton's *The Man Nobody Knows* (1925) and *The Book Nobody Knows* (1926)—held top spots on the nonfiction bestseller lists, even outselling most popular novels.[3] In the late 1920s, four trade publishing houses (Macmillan, Harper's, Henry Holt, and John C. Winston) added new religion departments. In 1927, amid this surge of activity in the world of religious print culture, the Religious Book Club was founded.[4]

This chapter examines the widely discussed "religious renaissance" in American book publishing in the 1920s. I pay particular attention to the 1921–27 industry-wide "Religious Book Week" promotional campaigns, the decade-long effort to better market religious books to a broader audience, and the 1927 founding of the Religious Book Club in light of the emergence of middlebrow institutions making high culture available to a mass audience. Drawing on a decade's worth of book advertising and editorial coverage related to religion in the industry journal *Publishers Weekly* and the monthly newsletters of the Religious Book Club from the 1920s and 1930s, I explore how faith, commerce, and consumerism interacted to shape what counted as a "religious" book and what kinds of faith were widely promoted. I argue that these efforts created a mass-marketable religion that reframed theological controversies as matters of consumer choice.

Religious Book Week

Although the number of religion titles published in the United States had long run second only to fiction, trade publishers had historically left religious publishing in the hands of denominational or religious publishing houses, whose distribution networks and marketing efforts were distinct from their own (and widely held to be better at reaching masses of widely dispersed readers).[5] The 1920s renaissance of public interest in religious books appeared to trade publishing houses and general booksellers as an immense and largely unexploited commercial opportunity. In 1921, representatives from trade and religious publishing houses met in New York to organize the Religious Book Week committee, charged with learning more about the market for and distribution of religious books and recommending ways to better exploit that market. The campaign was prominently featured in *Publishers Weekly*, which soon after dedicated an annual issue to religious books and designated an entire season during Lent for the promotion of religious books. One notable part of the campaign pushed giving books as Easter gifts. Twenty-one religious and trade houses participated in the initial Religious Book Week campaign—which subsequently grew to include not only trade and Christian publishers and denominational publishing houses, but also the Jewish Book Concern and the University of Chicago Press.[6]

Cultural commentators typically attributed the upsurge of interest in religious issues to the aftermath of World War I and the number of highly visible public controversies involving religion in the newspapers of the day. "The world, emerging from the war, is looking to its soul," announced *Publishers Weekly* in 1924.[7] The revival was, in fact, worldwide, with religious book sales on the upswing in Europe, Great Britain, China, and Japan. If the search for new hope and larger meanings for everyday life did not send readers to religious books, keeping up with current events might.[8] A representative of Fleming H. Revell, a prominent Christian publisher, maintained that "the prominence now given by the newspapers to doctrinal controversies has created a demand throughout the laity. Men and women in general are reading and are discussing in groups, serious books on both sides of the disputed questions."[9] The modernist/fundamentalist controversies that split Protestant denominations in the 1920s, most visibly around the Scopes trial in Tennessee, sent lots of people to bookshops and libraries to investigate these controversies more deeply. For the first time, the Revell representative suggested, the religious book market included large numbers of laymen and laywomen, rather than only the ministers and church workers who had long been its core constituency.

Religious Book Week was a blatantly commercial undertaking. After detailing the growth in church membership and the growing popularity of concern with religious issues, one article in *Publishers Weekly* cut to the chase—why any self-respecting bookseller should care: "This may all sound like the report of a church committee, but to the alert stationer and bookseller it means an opportunity to sell more books and win more customers, customers whom a store may hold for years, for an interest in religion is not an evanescent and fleeting thing as is an enthusiasm for Ping Pong or Mah Jongg, but it is an interest for life. Consequently the sale of religious books is a steady one for the store that meets the readers' needs sympathetically and intelligently."[10] The religious book market, then, had particular appeal for general booksellers. First, religious books that were general or nondenominational in character were steady sellers, offering a stable backlist to anchor more volatile sales in other areas. Second, buyers of religious books were steady, lifetime consumers of books. Moreover, many pleased religious book customers became "walking advertising agents for the bookstore." Readers who might casually mention a good book of general fiction or nonfiction to a friend became veritable missionaries for the religious books that changed their lives.[11] As the passage made clear, religion was seen as one of many possible niche markets for booksellers—a niche market that was more stable and consequently more worthy of cultivation.

In some ways, the pages of *Publishers Weekly*'s annual special religion issue were a powerful pep talk to trade booksellers, urging them to consider religious books *their* business and encouraging them with practical information and advice to learn enough about the field to be good merchants for this literature. For the novice at selling religious books, *Publishers Weekly* announced the publication of a semiannual catalog called "The Religious Bookshelf," which broke the religion category down into helpful subheadings (religious education, devotional books, Bibles, tools of the trade for clergymen, and so on) and offered a model for shelving books in the religion section. It mapped the field, so to speak, for the uninitiated. Edited by Harold B. Hunting, the manager of the Religious Bookshop in New York, it acquainted trade booksellers with new titles and functioned as a circular to mail to interested customers. It had notes on the best new books, supplementary lists of best books in selected fields, and space for advertising.[12]

Many booksellers and other participants in the Religious Book Week campaign, however, combined their pursuit of commerce with missionary zeal. Religious books were undoubtedly good for the bottom line, but they were also good for *us*, many believed. Publishers allied with ministers, churches, libraries, bookshops, women's reading groups, the YMCA, and the YWCA to get more religious books into the hands of readers. The Religious Book Week campaign, then, is best thought of as an alliance of missionaries for religious literacy with booksellers and publishers (some of whom shared their mission) hoping to reap financial rewards from their work. Selling more religious books would both save souls and improve the bottom line. American Studies scholar Matthew Hedstrom emphasizes the leadership role played by the liberal Protestant establishment in this campaign: "The transformation of the religious book business in the 1920s—exemplified by Religious Book Week—grew out of the hopes and fears of liberal religious leaders as they grappled with their declining social influence, the increasing sway of consumer culture, and a pervasive postwar spiritual malaise. The book men and church leaders tried to use religious publishing to reassert cultural influence and generate spiritual renewal, and in the process created a thriving religious middlebrow culture."[13]

What Is a Religious Book?

Before *Publishers Weekly* could urge booksellers to be better distributors of religious books, it had to define what—exactly—a religious book was. Throughout the decade, *Publishers Weekly* ran article after article entitled

"What Is a Religious Book?"[14] Although there was no universally agreed-upon definition, everyone was sure that a religious book was something quite different than it used to be—something better. Authors distinguished what were "formerly considered religious books" (one writer called them either "sectarian propaganda" or "tools for clergymen") from the "thousand and one practical applications of Christian principles to the social aims of our community."[15] One writer claimed that many book dealers experienced strong reader prejudice against books labeled "religious." "People have confused it with purely theological or pietistic literature," he explained. He was in good company with his proposed solution—a broad, inclusive definition of what constituted religious literature.[16] There were literally dozens of definitions put forth in the pages of *Publishers Weekly* in the 1920s, but a few will suffice. Gilbert Loveland of Henry Holt and Company called religion "a pretty big affair" and characterized as religious any book dealing "with some sort of adjustment to the universe." Harold Hunting maintained, "A religious book is one which helps us to get the really best out of any of the concrete interests of life." The Reverend J. F. Newton proposed in 1927 that "any book that tries to tell us what life means and what it is worth is a religious book."[17] Hedstrom argues that this broadened definition of religious books put forward in the 1920s served the interests of both liberal Protestant leaders and publishers, promising "increased sales, cultural redemption, and spiritual revitalization—while enhancing their own status as cultural arbiters."[18]

A religious book could be a novel, a theological treatise, or a discussion of science, politics, economics, psychology, or sociology. In many cases, it was not the subject that mattered, but the effect of the book on readers. For example, *Publishers Weekly* quoted directly from the liberal Protestant periodical *Christian Century*, which did a great deal of propagandizing for religious reading in the 1920s: "The subject-matter of a book may be religion, but if it arouses animosities, breeds bitterness, encourages selfish complacency, teaches small views of God and mean estimates of men, it is not a religious book. A book may deal with stars, or star-fish, with international or domestic relations, with organic evolution, political revolution, or the brain's convolutions, it may be poetry or science, philosophy or sociology, but if it quickens the imagination to lofty flights, warms the heart to generous deeds, and clarifies thinking about man as a citizen of God's world and about men as comrades in the great task of making that world a fitter dwelling place for God's children, it is a religious book."[19]

What was at stake in these definitions was what R. Laurence Moore calls the "commodification" of religion.[20] As religion engaged the marketplace of culture, it both transformed the literary field and underwent a transformation in its own character. Religion was no longer a professional field of study but a topic that touched on every aspect of daily life. If it helped us to be better people or discussed the larger meaning and significance of human lives, it was a religious book. In addition, the label had a moral valence. *Good* books (whatever they were about, whatever they advocated) were religious books. Any book whose consequences were moral and whose stakes were high was religious, independent of its theological position or content. Religious Book Week, then, rather than pushing a particular faith or creed, pushed *being religious*, whatever that might mean. Whatever one believed (and it really made no difference what), one should be buying books and seeking to know and live more deeply those beliefs. "These are stirring days in the religious world," wrote William C. Weber. "From one point of view they are days of a broadening of the horizon; from another a period of assault on the most sacred doctrines of religious belief." Weber felt no need to take a stand on this issue, since the common ground between these bitterly divided camps was that they both bought books: "Holders of both viewpoints are finding enlightenment and fortification in new books."[21]

Good Books Build Character

Since religious books were imagined as any texts that dealt with topics of significance and/or inspired us to be better people, advertising them required no reference whatsoever to specific faith traditions. The promotional materials for Religious Book Week included no crosses or menorahs or pictures of Jesus or Moses or Mary. "More Books in the Home," the 1921 poster urged. The 1923 campaign poster was a profile of Abraham Lincoln captioned with "Good Books Build Character." The 1922 poster pictured a family gathered around the fire reading. "Good Books Are Life Teachers," it asserted. A poster available for several years in the late 1920s was the interior of a Gothic cathedral with a caption stating, "Religious Books Build Character." Banners and flyers quoted not sacred scripture but Elizabeth Barrett Browning: "No man can be called friendless when he has God and the companionship of good books." Window cards defined a religious book ("A religious book is one which points the way to the highest goals of life") and explained what religious books would provide ("Moral Determination / Spiritual Strength / Mental Stimulus / Abiding Faith").[22]

"Good Books Are Life Teachers," Religious Book Week promotional poster, 1922. Miscellaneous Items in High Demand collection, Prints and Photographs Division, Library of Congress, LC-USZC2–181.

Invoking the sanctity of the home, the importance of good character, and the role of moral citizens in a democracy, the campaign created a specific kind of mass-marketable faith that urged one to be good but left what— exactly—that was up to the reader. The first Religious Book Week in 1921 had "More Books in the Home" as its theme, and a great deal of the publicity focused on the role of religious books in creating safe, moral spaces in which children could grow up. Dr. Henry Van Dyke was quoted in the pages of *Publishers Weekly*: "One reason . . . why some of the younger generation (and quite as many if not more of the older) seem to have frivolous, restless and

"Good Books Build Character," Religious Book Week promotional poster, 1923–26. Artist Posters collection, Prints and Photographs Division, Library of Congress, LC-USZC4–13135.

unsatisfied minds today, is because so many of our modern homes have no religious books in them."[23] The Methodist Church threw its support behind the 1921 week not because it saw opportunities for promoting Methodism, but because of the salutary effects it would have on the home. Religious reading would "stimulate the interest of the family in good books," "enrich the atmosphere and increase the attractiveness of the home," and "encourage the assembly of the family about the evening lamp," among others.[24]

President Warren G. Harding's 1922 letter of support for Religious Book Week—which was reproduced in *Publishers Weekly*—specifically connected the sanctity of the home to larger political issues—the fate of democracy, the presence of evil in the world: "I strongly feel that every good parent cares for his child's body, that the child may have a normal and healthy life and growth; cares for his child's mind, that the child may take his proper place in a world of thinking people; and such a parent must also train his child's character religiously, that the world may become morally fit. Unless this is done, trained bodies and trained minds may simply add to the destructive forces of the world."[25] President Harding was not alone in seeing political implications to religious reading. Dr. W. J. Smith, owner of a progressive bookstore, testified about his efforts in support of Religious Book Week in 1921: "I am sending out letters to all the pastors in my territory soliciting their co-operation in the Religious Book Week. It will not only mean the sale of books, but it will help to make our world safe for democracy."[26] The commercial and the moral/ethical were not in opposition for this bookseller, but happily complementary.

Religious Book Week was a two-pronged campaign. First, it sought to broaden the appeal of religious books from the core constituency of clergy and church workers to include laymen and laywomen more broadly interested in religious faith. Second, it sought to increase the number of books bought by clergy and church workers, making the case that their reading promoted the common good both by informing their work and by transforming them into reading role models for the laity.

The Laity: Great Armies of People Otherwise Educated, but Religiously Speaking, Morons

The religious leaders who wrote for *Publishers Weekly* in the 1920s were protesting what they saw as an epidemic of spiritual or religious illiteracy. Irving Kelly, for one, didn't care if anyone *wanted* more religious books in the home; they *needed* religious books. "In the average home library," he argued, "we can say of the religious book 'it is non-existent,' save possibly the Bible and a few devotional books as 'Pilgrim's Progress' and 'Imitation of Christ.'" Another crotchety clergyman claimed that "the typically modern Christian congregation is so illiterate spiritually that even Bible reading has declined almost to disuse." Preachers should take up the cause of religious reading from the pulpit, because, he claimed, religious reading might mitigate the negative intellectual consequences of the veritable "flood of modern novels" that was corrupting the minds of readers.[27]

W. H. Murray of Macmillan also took up the cause of "religious illiteracy" in his 1928 contribution to *Publishers Weekly*. He lamented the low percentage of "leading members" of churches who could honestly say, "Yes, I have bought and read one book upon our Christian religion carefully during the past year." Referring to American laypeople as "America's great armies of people otherwise educated but religiously speaking, morons," Murray proposed the founding of church libraries backed up by an educational program "whose object was to convert the whole parish into readers." A strategic alliance between booksellers and churches, he maintained, would be to the benefit of both.[28] The missionary zeal implicit in Kelly's call to arms was much more explicit in a 1929 article by William L. Stidger, who for ten years had been doing "dramatic book services" at his church and book broadcasts on the radio to build Christian readers' interest in religious reading. Seeing himself as "a sort of John the Baptist," he called the students he had trained "book missionaries."[29]

Although Stidger, a minister, was resolutely focused on selling books through the churches of America, other writers thought the unchurched might actually be a bigger audience for religious books.[30] Many such people were disgusted by what they saw as the corruption or hypocrisy of organized religion, its lack of tolerance for free thought, and its problematic contribution to world problems in the past. Nonetheless, they had spiritual longings or at least a curiosity about religion in the anthropological sense. Charles Potter suspected the non-churchgoers might buy more books because they got uplift and inspiration only from books, not from church services.

The Clergy: More Books for the Minister

The 1925 Religious Book Week campaign focused specifically on books for church workers, but this concern had long been part of the campaign. In 1922, Judson Press had sent copies of their Religious Book Week pamphlet to churches and Sunday school workers. By making a concentrated effort "to create a reading conscience" among religious workers, the publisher felt that these workers could serve as reading role models for their congregations. Specific suggestions were to offer a sermon on reading at least once a year, to use books in connection with all teaching in Sunday schools, to dedicate one Sunday school day entirely to books, and to provide a graded library for the use of students and teachers that would be widely advertised.[31] Ministers were clearly intended to be opinion leaders. At various points in the

1920s, *Publishers Weekly* urged getting ministers to write for church bulletins and local papers about important religious books that had changed their own thinking.[32] The best-publicized proposal of the campaign was a push to include fifty dollars in each church's annual budget expressly to buy books for the minister. This was an investment in the quality of his sermons and also (as one bookseller who did the math in pages of *Publishers Weekly* pointed out) a massive source of revenue for booksellers providing these books.[33]

Minister Dwight Bradley, proposing that the church take a leadership role in encouraging reading and guiding readers' book selections, agreed that the men and women in the pew had come there—in part—to get an education. The minister, he argued, was the best person to advise busy people on what to read. Bradley described his own practice of writing 300-word reviews of books that he placed in the church bulletin before his sermon on the book and then pasted into the flyleaf of the book before placing it in his church's lending library, an invitation for lay readers to engage with his ideas and interpretations.[34]

Throughout the 1920s, *Publishers Weekly* profiled specific churches or ministers or communities or bookshops whose success at selling religious books was extraordinary. These profiles were intended to be an inspiration to other booksellers, but they also offered practical pointers on how to replicate these noteworthy successes in other locations. For example, the Central Congregational Church in Newtonville, Massachusetts, was profiled in 1928 for the huge variety of book activities it undertook—book discussion at midweek meetings, selected reading lists for congregants, book reviews written by members in the bulletin, a book club in which each member bought a religious book and then circulated them among themselves, a book table where one could order or loan out books. Montclair, New Jersey, had a community-wide read-off pitting churches against each other to motivate them all to read more religious books.[35]

Booksellers were repeatedly urged to make themselves partners with churches in the selling and marketing of religious books. Booksellers should assemble a mailing list of pastors and Sunday school superintendents, YMCA/YWCA leaders, and other religious workers, who would receive announcements of new religion titles. Booksellers could advertise in church bulletins, have their religious book and Bible displays announced from the pulpit, install a book table in the church to sell books before and after the service, visit churches monthly with lists of new religion titles, display posters or banners in the social halls at churches, and provide assistance setting up book clubs or reading circles in congregations. They could help organize a self-service lending library at churches and cooperate with ministers who gave book sermons or literary vespers, so that interested congregants could easily purchase the featured book.

Religious Book Week did get a great deal of mainstream media attention, particularly in its initial years. Reflecting on the experience of the first annual campaign in 1921, *Publishers Weekly* maintained that although coverage was concentrated in the religious press, general interest periodicals had paid unusual attention to the promotional campaign. For example, there was coverage in *Literary Digest*, the *Independent*, the *New York Times Book Supplement*, and the Sunday book section of the *New York Herald*.[36] Religion coverage in *Publishers Weekly* was segregated, however. Aside from an occasional brief article, all of it occurred during the Lenten book season and most of it was concentrated in a single annual special religion issue in February or March. In this way, *Publishers Weekly* urged booksellers to better understand this market and exploit it, but also seemed to suggest that it was still a world set apart. The articles urging the removal of false boundaries between sacred and secular, religious publishing and trade, then, ran only during the Lenten religious book season. The lion's share of religious book advertising occurred in the special religion issue as well.

Religious Book Week was an example of one way to solve the problem of advertising books as commodities. Since each book (unlike toothpaste or cornflakes) was assumed to be different, booksellers engaged in comparatively little advertising until long after most other consumer goods had begun to be mass-marketed nationally. This experiment entailed advertising not specific books, but specific *kinds* of books by all members of an industry. Rather than trying to wrest market share from one another, they all engaged in redefining religious books as texts with broader interest and in advertising the good such books could do for general booksellers and their growing body of readers/consumers. The inspiration for Religious Book Week came from Children's Book Week, first held in 1919. Both were spearheaded by Frederic Melcher, described by Hedstrom as "perhaps the most influential book promoter of the twentieth century." Melcher professionalized the field by pioneering modern advertising and marketing techniques. He did so from a number of powerful positions: as editor of *Publishers Weekly* for forty years (from 1918), as executive secretary of the National Association of Book Publishers, and as secretary of the American Booksellers Association in the early 1920s.[37] As Hedstrom points out, it was—ironically—much easier to advertise children's books or religious books as a class, because these books carried moral weight and were thus less likely to be reduced to mere commodities in the eyes of readers.[38]

The Religious Book Club

The Religious Book Club (RBC), a mail-order book club modeled after the Book-of-the-Month Club, shared the dual focus of the Religious Book Week campaign on clergy and laity. It was created to both take advantage of the burgeoning interest of laymen and laywomen in religious topics and serve as a reading service for clergy and church workers.[39] Like those writing in the pages of *Publishers Weekly* in the 1920s, the RBC redefined "religious books" in broad terms—those "in which moral and spiritual ideals find effective expression."[40] Possible subjects included philosophy, history, contemporary domestic and international problems, psychology, fiction and poetry, some of which lacked an obvious connection to religion. For example, a number of manuals such as *Love and Marriage*, *Problems of the Family*, and *Sex and Youth* appeared as alternate selections. Occasionally, RBC editorial board members would point out the usefulness of such secular guides for ministers counseling young people or troubled congregants or offer reassurance: "An atmosphere of religious and social idealism surrounds the book."[41] The RBC further muddied the sacred/secular distinction by experimenting with general interest ("wholesome," "idealistic") alternate selections.[42]

Shortly after the founding of the RBC in November 1927, Dr. S. Parkes Cadman, the chair of the editorial board, explained its purpose in a *Publishers Weekly* article: "The Religious Book Club is one more indication of the extraordinary interest in religion today. The undertaking was born in the conviction that hosts of men and women all over the United States are hungrily seeking for light on the great problems of religious life and thought. Such people are eager to avail themselves of the opportunity to keep abreast of the best insight and scholarship in the realm of religion. And it is a great mistake to assume that they are found only among clergymen and professional religious workers. The man in the street, who often seems concerned only with the stock market and the World Series, is really immensely interested in religion."[43] The RBC was the brainchild of Samuel McCrea Cavert, editor of the *Federal Council Bulletin*, and his friend, Maxwell Geffen, president of Select Printing Company. Cavert and Geffen were inspired by a letter from a California pastor asking if the Federal Council of Churches (an umbrella organization of twenty-eight Protestant denominations) would start a reading service for ministers that would inform them of new developments in religious literature and make available the best such books. The council declined the proposition, but Cavert and Geffen formed their own company modeled on the Book-of-the-Month Club (founded in 1926), which would "create a wider interest in religious literature" by each month sending members "the best new book in the religious field as selected by an editorial committee of five outstanding religious leaders of the country."[44] The five original judges were distinguished leaders with significant ties to large, liberal Protestant churches and/or institutions of higher learning, and most were popular writers/speakers in their own right. They included Dr. S. Parkes Cadman (minister of Central Congregational Church, Brooklyn, and president of the Federal Council of Churches), Episcopal bishop Charles H. Brent (formerly chief of chaplains in the American Expeditionary Forces during World War I and chairman of the World Conference on Faith and Order at Lausanne), Dr. Harry Emerson Fosdick (pastor of Park Avenue Baptist Church, New York, professor of practical theology at Union Theological Seminary, and popular writer and radio personality), Bishop Francis J. McConnell of the Methodist Church (former president of DePauw University and president of the Religious Education Association), and Mary E. Woolley (president of Mount Holyoke College, president of the American Association of University Women, former head of the Biblical History and Literature Department at Wellesley, and a member of the National Board of the YWCA). Each brought prominence and experience in education and the popular media to bear on the endeavor of getting more religious books into the hands and minds of readers. The editorial panel was overwhelmingly liberal and Protestant, reflecting what Hedstrom calls "the Protestant establishment's sense of itself, of its values and the role it imagined for itself in society." He points out that the RBC and the Federal Council of Churches had overlapping personnel, and that the RBC functioned "as the de facto voice of the Federal Council in the world of books."[45]

What can we learn about religion and print culture in the 1920s from the book reviews and reader letters in the *Religious Book Club Bulletin* and a decades' worth of book advertising and editorial coverage related to religion in the industry journal, *Publishers Weekly*? What kinds of readers belonged to the RBC? What concerns and preoccupations shaped their reading? What kinds of communities—real and imagined—did it foster? What kind of religion did it sell to readers? With the exception of quotations from reader letters published in the *RBC Bulletin*, direct testimony about how religious texts functioned in the lives of readers is lacking. However, as Robert Darnton reminds us, information about the production, marketing, and distribution of texts can—in part—compensate for a lack of knowledge about readers and reception.[46]

What Kinds of Religious Books Did 1920s Americans Want to Read?

In 1928, Gilbert Loveland of Henry Holt and Company surveyed over one hundred laymen about what kinds of religious books they wanted to read. Loveland summarized their responses in six questions, with over 60 percent of respondents concentrating on the first two issues:

1. What kind of God can a man believe, in this scientific day?
2. How should a man think of Jesus?
3. What is left of the Bible, after criticism has done its worst?
4. Is prayer anything more than auto-suggestion?
5. Why is Christianity supposed to be superior to other religions? And what right has one religion to wage a campaign of religious imperialism?
6. What is the function of the church in modern society?[47]

Loveland noted that the bestsellers of 1928 were those that addressed these very questions. More important for my purposes, however, are the particular ways Loveland phrased these questions. Lay readers presumably felt defensive about and embattled in their religious beliefs. They asked not what prayer was good for, but whether it might be good for anything at all. They did not ask for help reading the Bible, but asked instead whether there was any point in reading the Bible, once modern criticism had done its worst. These are not so much questions about *kinds* of religious belief and practices as they are questions about whether it is possible to *have* religious belief in a modern, scientific society. Could one be religious without being a gullible, unintelligent fool?

That thousands of readers wanted the answer to be "yes" is evidenced by the offerings of the RBC, which presented book after book to readers that promised to reconcile religious faith with evolution and the other physical sciences, with modern psychology, and with people of other faiths at home and abroad. These books were popular because they addressed a deeply felt contradiction at the center of liberal Protestant life.[48] One could be modern, rational, and well-educated and also be a person of faith, and the RBC's offerings compulsively explained how—in accessible, lively prose.

The brief description of A. Maude Royden's *I Believe in God* in the *RBC Bulletin* made clear the sense of being embattled that was characteristic of

RBC readers: "The volume is not written for the theological or philosophical scholar but for the many men and women and young people who find themselves wondering whether religion is still intellectually respectable. In simple, nontechnical language, replete with concrete illustrations, a woman of rare insight reveals the dynamic quality that Christian faith brings into human life and sums up the practical reasons which have sustained belief in God across the centuries."[49] The review promises that the volume would give believers back their self-respect, and that it would do so not in theoretical or abstract terms, but in ways that resonate powerfully with readers' everyday lives.

Living at the Same Time in Two Separate Worlds: The RBC and Modern Life[50]

The majority of the RBC selections clustered around a few issues—religion and science, religion and psychology, the church in the world (including missions and relations with those of other faiths), and ecumenism. The most important of these, by number of offerings, was clearly religion and science.[51] The particular selection that received the most attention was the August 1928 selection, *Science in Search of God*, by Kirtley F. Mather. Chairman of the Geology Department at Harvard, Mather was a celebrity of sorts, having served as an expert witness for the defense at the Scopes trial in Tennessee.[52] Like many of the expert witnesses, he expanded his deposition in defense of evolution into a book of general interest. It had the lowest return rate of any of the RBC's offerings—around 3 percent. Return rates for other selections, particularly those that were written in scholarly language, approached 30 percent.[53] Loveland, whose company, Henry Holt, published the volume, explained the book's commercial success in terms both of its timeliness ("a subject of front-page interest") and its accessible style ("simple, vivid language without scholarly formulas"). It could be read in less than three hours.[54] In addition, the message of the book was reassuring to believers, reconciling science and religion—widely held to be in fundamental conflict—by asserting that the conflict existed only between *bad* science and *bad* religion, disappearing once one looked at both intelligently.[55]

Mather's was only the most successful of a sizable class of texts that sought to resolve the tension between science and religion in one of several (sometimes conflicting) ways: (1) that each was valid in its own distinct realm; (2) that science offered only partial truth; and (3) that *real* religion had nothing to do with outmoded scientific theories. The *RBC Bulletin* favorably reviewed two books which took diametrically opposed positions. Dwight Bradley's *The Recovery of Religion* argued that science needed to be "shoved back to its proper field," but Edwin A. Burtt's *Religion in an Age of Science* argued that science belonged everywhere in modern life, and that "religion must adopt the more radical procedure of regarding every conviction as tentative and as always open to fresh inquiry."[56] The sameness underneath the differing views becomes more apparent in the short blurbs the RBC used to remind readers that former selections could be purchased as an alternative to the current month's selection. Under the "On Religion and Science" heading were these representative titles:

THE NATURE OF THE PHYSICAL WORLD . . . A. S. Eddington $3.75
A world-famous astronomer discusses "the new physics" and suggests that religious values are in no sense ruled out.

OLD FAITH AND NEW KNOWLEDGE . . . James H. Snowden $2.50
A plea for the constant restudy and restatement of religious convictions, insisting that Christian faith and scientific knowledge are harmonious and supplementary.

SCIENCE AND HUMAN PROGRESS . . . Sir Oliver Lodge $2.00
The universe is found to be the scene of purpose and reason, with nothing to invalidate belief in God, Christ, prayer and immortality.

THE NEW REFORMATION . . . Michael Pupin $2.50
An American scientist reviews the advance of physical science and ends in an affirmation of spiritual realities.[57]

However these authors get there, they all conclude that the religion/science conflict is no conflict at all. Readers are given lessons in the tricky art of inhabiting two worlds at once—at being rational, scientific inhabitants of the modern world but also faithful believers in traditional doctrines that give meaning to their lives.[58] The work of these selections was to keep the contradictions in suspension, to structure and restructure people's imaginations so as to avoid painful cognitive dissonance.

The descriptions of these books sound remarkably old-fashioned, and there was a great deal of nostalgia in them for the nineteenth-century unity of science and religion taken for granted by the grandparents and great-grandparents of RBC readers. The field of natural theology was deeply respected until after the Civil War. In it, the laws of nature were elegant illustrations of religious truths, and naturalists describing and classifying the natural world were also explicating the mind of God. These RBC selections hark back to an era before the specialization of knowledge, when colleges trained gentlemen in the liberal arts and sciences and the opinion of an educated generalist still held sway over those with narrower, specialized expertise.[59] This nostalgia connects the RBC with middlebrow culture, which, Joan Shelley Rubin argues, was the remnant/reinvention of the nineteenth-century genteel tradition. The genteel tradition urged the cultivation of character through exposure to culture in the Arnoldian sense ("classic" texts held to contain the best ideas that had been thought and written in the world). Its survival in a "chastened and redirected form" as middlebrow culture in the 1920s and 1930s testified to the ascendancy in modern America of experts with specialized training.[60]

Similar kinds of arguments were made reconciling religion with psychology or psychoanalysis, areas also widely perceived to be in conflict.[61] RBC offerings insisted that modern psychology was not hostile to religion; that it was a useful tool for counseling troubled congregants; and that religion was—in fact—essential to mental health. For example, the July 1932 main selection, *Psychology for Religious Workers*, promised readers that psychology was no enemy; it could be made to do "yeoman service to the Christian cause."[62] Clifford E. Barbour's *Sin and the New Psychology*, an alternate selection, argued that psychoanalysis "confirms the fundamental truths of the Christian religion." Moreover, psychologists curing neuroses and ministers redeeming sinners were engaged in the same process. Psychoanalytic categories like repression, transference, and sublimation were merely new names for Christian categories like temptation, sin, forgiveness, and sanctification.[63]

Like the selections addressing religion and science, those concerned with psychology and religion promised to reconcile for readers the deeply felt contradictions between traditional faith and modern thought. As Cadman, the chairman of the editorial committee, told *Publishers Weekly*, the RBC was intended to facilitate the reimagining of faith necessitated by modern living: "The sweeping developments in science and world affairs today make it necessary for all thoughtful people to be rethinking constantly the meaning of religion for human life. Unless one does this he is in danger of finding himself swept loose from his old moorings and not knowing how to anchor himself to any spiritual realities."[64] The RBC offered readers an anchor in the stormy seas of contemporary life by demonstrating again and again that modernity and tradition were—all appearances to the contrary—not in conflict. Faith and modern thought were parallel sets of ideas in separate realms, complementary ideas that could render each other great service, or the same ideas expressed in different language. The rapprochement allowed readers to comfortably imagine themselves inhabiting two worlds at once.

Imagined Communities, Ecumenism, and the Nation: The RBC and the World

The RBC was also deeply concerned with religion in the world, particularly how to negotiate encounters with other faiths—in daily life, as part of missionary work, or in finding common cause to act for social justice. Most of the reviews in this category are characterized by a pattern of sympathetically exploring other faiths and then reaffirming the superiority of one's own. In this way, doubting Christians were reassured. Even people who spent many years studying other faiths and who deeply appreciated their nobility *chose* to be Christians. The short blurb for Oscar MacMillan Buck's *Our Asiatic Christ* concisely makes this logical maneuver: "An admirable illustration of the attempt to approach other religions in a spirit of warm appreciation of all which they have of value to the human spirit. Professor Buck studies the best in Hindu aspiration and points out how this is beginning to find fulfillment in Jesus Christ."[65] In this, as in almost every other case, looking at others leads us back to ourselves. In this review, Hindu aspirations are noble and valuable, but only because Hindus are reframed as people embarked (unknowingly) on an incomplete Christian journey.[66]

Most of the books about other religions were, in fact, alternate selections. However, in October 1928 the primary selection was *The Pilgrimage of Buddhism*, whose goal was "to discover the actual conditions of the religion as it is believed and lived today." Judges assumed that what readers desired was a kind of empathy: "Many books on the subject leave the reader wondering how any intelligent or spiritually minded person could adhere to such a religion. In contrast, Professor Pratt helps his readers to understand 'how it feels to be a Buddhist,' to catch the 'emotional undertone' of this alien faith, and to enter sympathetically into its symbols, its cult and its art."[67] The judges were clearly nervous about this volume, although they did choose it as the primary selection. "For those who may feel that Buddhism, however competently and fascinatingly treated, is a subject too remote from their daily experience," the judges recommended an alternate volume focused on Christian theism, John Wright Buckham's *The Humanity of God*. Although members were always free to select an alternate rather than the featured book, the RBC editorial board only rarely suggested a specific alternative on the front page.[68]

Like Hindus and Buddhists abroad, Jews and Catholics at home appeared in the RBC's offerings, but only as tokens. For example, the front page of the June 1932 *RBC Bulletin* trumpeted: "This is the first time in the history of the Religious Book Club when a primary selection has come from the pen of a Roman Catholic Author."[69] Similarly, the April 1929 primary selection, Ernest R. Trattner's *Unraveling the Book of Books*, a popularization of historical biblical scholarship, was marked as the first primary selection by a Jewish writer. In addition, these writers were assumed to speak for and to represent all Catholic or Jewish writers. Trattner's book, for example, was interesting "as indicative of liberal Hebrew scholarship today."[70] Further, like the Hindus abroad, the Catholics at home merely affirmed the universal validity of one's own faith: "The volume has a further significance as a disclosure of how much Protestants and Catholics have in common when they get down to the basic elements of the faith that both live by. Many Protestant readers will find themselves gaining a new sense of spiritual fellowship with Catholics as a result of this book."[71] Once again, the book has as its goal a sense of spiritual fellowship, of appreciation of other faith traditions, but again these others are mostly interesting as mirrors of our (Protestant and probably liberal) selves. Catholic faith is most engaging at the level of "basic elements"—which differ very little from those of Protestant Americans. They are important in that they affirm our own sense of universality or superiority (that is, they are really just like us, or given time and enlightenment, they will be just like us).

Selections aside, not many Catholics thought the RBC was for them. Less than a year after the RBC's founding, the Catholic Book Club (initially called the Catholic Literary Guild of America) was chartered. Funded by donations from laypeople, its purpose was twofold. First, it was designed to select for Catholics the books they should read and those they should not. Second, recognizing that not a single Catholic author appeared on the current bestseller list (although many books the Catholic Church opposed did), the Catholic Book Club wished to recognize and promote Catholic writers of merit.[72]

The RBC did, however, have an inclusive, ecumenical philosophy about most Protestants, offering many selections addressing interdenominational cooperation.[73] Again and again, readers were offered books that documented what was going on at the great ecumenical conferences of the day or that affirmed a central "core" Christianity and criticized the denominational squabbles that separated them from each other. H. R. L. Sheppard's *The Impatience of a Parson* is a case in point. Its brief summary called it:

" 'A plea for the recovery of vital Christianity'—and for a church that makes more of the things that were central in the experience of Jesus, and less of ecclesiastical and creedal forms, worldly prestige and the things that divide Christians into separate groups."[74]

In some ways, the RBC was engaged in creating an imagined community that intersected with and at times conflicted with other identities based on religion, race, gender, class, and nation. The "we" hailed by the *RBC Bulletin* needed to have Catholicism and Judaism made comprehensible in terms of liberal Protestantism. Conservative Christians who wished to avoid certain offensive liberal doctrines were given fair warning at the RBC and could custom-tailor their selections to meet their more traditional tastes. Hinduism and Buddhism, although interesting if considered in comparative perspective, were suspected of being so far off the beaten path as to lack interest. Perhaps the only foreigners who counted as "us" were the British—whose volumes filled the pages of the *RBC Bulletin* and seamlessly melded with the concerns of their New World brothers and (few) sisters.

Although there were a few offerings by women authors, most were by men, usually ministers or professors at divinity schools. Two alternate offerings were noteworthy as the exceptions that proved the rule; they made gender visible. Charles E. Raven's *Women and the Ministry* presented statistics about women in the church and argued for their ordination on the grounds that churches needed them. G. A. Studdert Kennedy's *The Warrior, the Woman, and the Christ* argued that Christ merged the best qualities of manhood and womanhood.[75] These selections were striking, however, precisely because most other texts just assumed an unmarked, universal human subject who was implicitly male. Similarly, the presence of a token woman, Mary Woolley, on the founding editorial committee, does not appear to have challenged the implicit equating of humanity with men. Although some of the offerings explicitly addressed the "race question," it too was usually absent from the discourse, assuming an unmarked, universal reading subject who was white. For example, Edwin Smith's *The Golden Stool* examined the relationships between white people and black people in Africa. The editors urged its relevance to religious life by linking these concerns to missionary work and asserting that it illuminated "the problem of race relationships as one of the most pressing issues confronting the Church today."[76]

In this way, the assumed RBC readership resembled what Michael Warner calls the "republic of letters," the imagined community of white, male, propertied citizens who constituted the public sphere and the new nation in eighteenth-century America. These citizens were held to be rational, disinterested, and capable of governing for the public good, unlike those whose humanity (and capacity for reason or self-governance) was compromised by their gender, race/ethnicity, or lack of literacy or property.[77] If the RBC was a free marketplace of religious ideas, it was nonetheless one to which not everyone had equal access.

The RBC and the Middlebrow

RBC readers clearly wanted books that reconciled faith and modern science, religious pluralism and Protestant superiority, but they only wanted books that achieved this reconciliation in particular—*middlebrow*—ways. Middlebrow institutions aimed to make high culture and all the benefits it promised accessible to a broader public. It typically involved joining the machinery of mass production and mass distribution to culturally esteemed texts— literature, art, classical music, and so on. Janice Radway has argued in her discussion of the Book-of-the-Month Club that the term "middlebrow" names not just a set of institutions or cultural texts, but also a distinct aesthetic and way of reading.[78] I will discuss here three specific ways in which the RBC engaged the middlebrow: (1) the promise to combine rigorous scholarship with lively accessibility; (2) the embrace of a pluralistic, conditional aesthetic; and (3) the opportunity for readers to engage affectively with characters, authors, and judges in ways that seemed intimate and personal.

First, much of the space in the *RBC Bulletin* was given over to reassuring readers that selected books were accessibly written and not overly abstract and theoretical—not what Cavert derisively described as "dog-eared tomes of out-of-date theology" and "goody-goody treatises on piety."[79] This lively, pleasurable presentation was not to be understood as a "dumbing down" of scholarship, however. The *RBC Bulletin* reviews always highlight *both* the writers' expertise and the accessibility of their prose. Clement F. Rogers's *The Case for Christianity* is a case in point: "The author, well known in British church circles as professor of pastoral theology in King's College, University of London, has for eight years spoken on Christian themes to heterogeneous audiences in Hyde Park on Sunday afternoons and undergone the blunt cross-examination for which the Park is notable. As a result, the author has the happy faculty of dealing with questions of Christian belief in a concrete and pungent manner."[80] As in many other reviews, oral and written language are seamlessly connected here. For example, the RBC prominently featured printed sermons and collections of addresses from religious symposia. Many reviews emphasized the distinctive "voice" of the author one "heard" in the (written) work. Presumably, one who regularly spoke to masses of ordinary people knew how to explain difficult theological concepts in accessible, lively language in print as well.

Besides learned language, the other bugbear the RBC editorial committee sought to avoid was overly abstract or theoretical works—works that readers could not make resonate with their everyday lives. In describing *Present-Day Dilemmas in Religion* by Charles W. Gilkey, for example, the editors insisted: "Dr. Gilkey possesses the rare faculty of presenting a profound subject in such a wealth of concrete illustrations and revealing incidents as to remove it far from the realm of the abstract or the academic. This it is which makes him listened to so eagerly both by student groups and by popular audiences."[81] As discussed in Chapter 1, Amy Johnson Frykholm describes a similar "life-application method" of reading characteristic of contemporary evangelicals. As when reading scripture, readers look for a take-home message in religious books to immediately apply to their own lives.[82] The boundary between books and readers' lives here is purposely porous, unlike the distanced, "pure" aesthetic ways of reading required by literary modernism in the same era.[83]

Second, the pluralistic and conditional aesthetic of the Book-of-the-Month Club was readily apparent in the RBC, its religious knock-off. Radway argues that Book-of-the-Month Club judges did not rank books along a continuum from good to bad but insisted instead that there were different *kinds* of books that were good for different kinds of readers.[84] Comparing a trashy mystery to the work of Henry James was like comparing apples and oranges. Henry James's work was good for certain kinds of pleasure; the mystery, for certain others. The Book-of-the-Month Club's goal was to pick the best book for each particular kind of reading experience.

Again and again, the editors of the *RBC Bulletin* made clear that certain kinds of books were good for certain kinds of readers, recognizing (for example) that a practical exposition of new Sunday school techniques that might be riveting to a Sunday school teacher might bore an amateur philosopher to death. A discussion of fund-raising for the church might be very useful to the chair of the stewardship committee but lack general appeal.[85] The effort to match particular readers with the right kinds of books sometimes required warning readers away from a primary selection. For example, Canon B. H. Streeter's *The Primitive Church* was the February 1928 main selection, but judges made clear that the book was perhaps a bad fit for nonspecialist readers: "The Editorial Committee desires to make it clear that this book is not written from the standpoint of general popularity and does not yield its treasure to casual skimming; it is rather a volume of most careful scholarship, the kind which will long be referred to as an authoritative work. Those (especially laymen) who prefer a volume for easy reading, or one dealing with less historical detail, should select as an alternative one of the important supplementary recommendations described on the following pages."[86]

The RBC recognized that people bought and read even the Bible for different (though equally valid) purposes. In the late 1920s and early 1930s, the RBC made two editions of the Bible available to club members. First was the quintessential middlebrow Bible, *The Living Bible*, christened "the whole Bible in the fewest words." It was shorter, not because important material had been removed, but because "repetitions, ceremonial details, land boundaries, genealogies of kings and other matters of less general interest" were omitted. To make the presentation more accessible, chapter numbers were moved to the margins and descriptive titles were put in their place. Second was *The Oxford Bible*, as important as a beautiful artifact as it was a text to be read. This King James Version, "printed in its entirety," was notable for the quality of its binding and printing rather than the qualities of its text: "Bound in blue buckram, with red leather label stamped in gold, with a gilt top and untrimmed edges, and beautifully printed in large type with wide margins, it is a volume the appearance of which at once suggests a literary treasure."[87] Some books are clearly understood to be valued for their other-worldly aura, whereas others are meant to communicate efficiently information we require for daily living. Neither kind of book is privileged as superior, but every effort is made to bring each book to the appropriate reader, to successfully match consumer desires with consumer goods without judging the social or cultural consequences of those desires.

Finally, the RBC promised readers what Janice Radway has called "middlebrow personalism"—the sense of communion with authors or characters as real, idiosyncratic individuals with distinctive personal voices.[88] The sense of intimate, meaningful dialogue was particularly appealing in the 1920s, since large numbers of readers were struggling with the transition from traditional rural and small-town communities characterized by face-to-face communication to large, bustling, anonymous cities. This personalism is most obvious in the *RBC Bulletin*'s discussion of biographies of saints and religious leaders from the past. Robert Norwood's *The Heresy of Antioch*, for example, presented the life of the Apostle Paul. The *Bulletin* promised, "Under Dr. Norwood's brush the outlines of the Apostle Paul stand out so clearly as to make him seem no longer a dim figure of the first century but a vital force in the modern world." The *Bulletin* explained to readers what Norwood's biography would do, in part, by telling them what it would not do. "The volume is not so much an attempt to set forth the historic facts of Paul's life," it explained, "as to interpret his meaning for today." Moreover, those interested in theology and dogma should look elsewhere: "The Great Apostle is portrayed, not as a theologian, but as a great human. His letters are described, not as the effort to formulate a doctrinal system, but rather as the outpouring of the heart of a great poet and mystic, throbbing with love for Jesus Christ, in whom he had seen God revealed as Love."[89] We are concerned less with Paul's thought, then, than we are with Paul, hearing him as if he were a personal friend confiding his feelings to us. The institution he spent his lifetime building pales in importance beside his individual experience of the divine; the Christian church he built impresses us less than his mysticism.

Tracy D. Mygatt and Frances Witherspoon's *Armor of Light* appeared on the RBC list of alternate selections. Although it was fiction, the RBC editorial committee claimed it possessed what they called "emotional realism," or an essential truth: "To be transported in imagination across the chasm of nearly nineteen centuries and to live vividly in the world of the first century Christians is the experience of the readers of this beautiful narrative."[90] It is noteworthy that the RBC did not initially distinguish fiction from nonfiction. They were run together in reviews and descriptions. Even the list of former selections, which were broken down into thematic categories (On Jesus Christ, On Religion and Science, On Psychology, Religious Education, for example), did not list "fiction" as a separate category until the late 1930s. Novels about Jesus, for example, appeared alongside nonfiction in "On Jesus Christ." A historical account of the Bible in English promised "the charm and glamour of fiction while recording historic fact."[91] The truth/fiction distinction was simply not useful when one's purpose for reading was a deep, emotional identification rather than a scholarly, contemplative distance.

Middlebrow personalism involved not only a way of identifying with vividly drawn characters, but also a kind of dialogue a reader experienced with the author through the act of reading. Comparing his popularizing work to what H. G. Wells did for secular history in his *Outline of History*, the RBC described Gaius Glenn Atkins's *Procession of the Gods*, the primary selection for October 1930, as follows: "Dr. Atkins takes the detailed data gathered by the researches of the specialists—the scholars in the fields of comparative religion, psychology, anthropology and archaeology—and lets this vast mass of material pass through his own reflection and imagination till it comes forth, no longer abstract and technical, but intensely human, rich in color and palpitating with life."[92] In short, Atkins is not only a scholar and a popularizer of the first order, but his book also gives us a sense of his own rich imagination. We as readers are educated, entertained, and feel as though we have made meaningful contact with a single, distinctive mind. The objective voice of science is not what makes Atkins's book so appealing; it is, instead, his personal voice. The "conversation" with him is part of the book's appeal.

Letters from RBC members published periodically in the *Bulletin* reveal further that some readers felt that reading the RBC's primary selections gave them communion not only with authors and characters but also with the judges. "I know the arrival of your choice will be an event looked for in each month," wrote one minister, "It is like being taken into the study of each of the members of your committee and given a share of an intimacy of which ministers in small towns are sorely in need." Others described the RBC as a strict tutor that kept them reading the best books on religion, whether they wanted to or not: "A man who is free to read what he will does not always read what he should." Another reinstated his subscription after canceling it, because he discovered that "buying and reading books without the monthly recommendation of the Religious Book Club is like trying to worship God in the great out of doors instead of going to church—you can, but you don't."[93]

The imagined community of the RBC was not only the communion of readers with the judges, authors, or characters. Readers were also asked to recommend the club to their friends in exchange for free books or a free six-month or year subscription, for example. Some readers did actually form real communities to read the offerings together. In Lorain, Ohio, a group of readers, many of whom were members of the RBC, met to discuss one of its offerings at their regular meeting after hearing a review from one of the members.[94] In this way, the *Bulletin* was a resource for readers who were forming their own reading and writing communities.

The RBC and the Marketplace

Reader letters make clear that the club made the literary marketplace knowable to readers overwhelmed by its size and complexity.[95] Many readers were intimidated by the number of books in print and appreciated help selecting which ones might be the best for them to read. "In this day of mass production of books such a service is a real one which will be taken advantage of by thousands of church people," editorialized one religious newspaper. "There are so many books coming from the press that your service makes our book dollars do double duty," wrote a minister from Cincinnati.[96]

Several letters made specific reference to book distribution difficulties that membership in the RBC alleviated. Like the readers who obtained Harold Bell Wright's novels through the mail-order Book Supply Company discussed in Chapter 2, some RBC readers lacked a convenient outlet for buying books. "I am very glad to have the opportunity of having my books selected by master minds, especially since I am much shut in during the winter," testified one letter. "I am greatly enjoying this service which you offer, especially since we live in the interior and are unable to secure selected new books when we desire them," wrote another from Huchow, China—undoubtedly a missionary.[97]

Whatever else could be said of the RBC's offerings, they hailed readers as individuals—usually as liberal, Protestant, white, male individuals. Although the offerings were uniformly critical of individualism and the therapeutic ethos that T. J. Jackson Lears claims came with it,[98] all were deeply complicit. The therapeutic ethos is a way of being in the world that focuses exclusively on improving and perfecting one's own physical and mental health to the exclusion of more traditional religious practices such as service to others or obedience to holy scriptures. Lears argues that around the turn of the century there was a shift of emphasis in psychological and religious discourses from salvation through self-denial to self-realization as manifested in this obsessive concern with individual psychological and physical health. This increasing focus on improving and perfecting the self minimized concern with larger social and moral questions and made it easier for individuals to see themselves primarily as consumers. The RBC participated in this reimagining of models of the self. Described as "a popular interpretation, for the general reader, of the views held by the principal groups of thinkers in the churches," Gerald Birney Smith's *Current Christian Thinking* appeared to be about social institutions and the beliefs shared by faith communities. The review explained: "The earlier chapters describe the viewpoint of the Roman Catholic, the Protestant, the 'Modernist' and the 'Fundamentalist,' and try to define, clearly and simply, the positions for which each of these groups is contending. The issues that are discussed are highly controversial, but the author handles them, in the main, in an objective manner. Other chapters are concerned with the present-day emphasis on Christian experience, the appeal to Christ, the controversy over evolution, and the various ways in which modern men are pursuing the quest for God."[99] The last chapter, however, reveals the author's own position—which presumably interested those seeking middlebrow personalism more. He is a proponent of the "Evangelical Movement"—not because of its superior doctrine ("which he shows to have been largely taken over from Catholicism") but because of its emphasis on "a genuine, first-hand, personal experience of salvation."[100] Institutions and ideas are of little importance (in spite of the careful, comparative discussion earlier in the text); what really matters is individual experience of the divine—which need not involve a community or a coherent set of beliefs at all. Rufus Jones's *New Studies in Mystical Religion* addressed religion specifically "as direct personal awareness of God," an alternate selection that—like many—focused more on mysticism than on institutions.[101] Some offerings even seemed to offer an anti-institutional bias. *Shoddy*, for example, a novel about how the spirituality and moral leadership of one minister are corrupted by the politics of the church, suggests that "pure" religion occurs outside the pew.[102]

The RBC also framed controversial theological questions as matters of consumer choice. The RBC took no stand on doctrinal issues and frequently offered books taking diametrically opposed positions. The RBC did not care what its members believed (within a Christian framework), as long as they believed something that required them to do some reading. For example, the April 1929 main selection was Ernest R. Trattner's *Unravelling the Book of Books*, a popularization of historical biblical scholarship. The editorial committee was enthusiastic about it, arguing that "the results of the foremost technical scholarship are presented to the lay reader in a brisk and captivating style, as readable as a novel and abounding in human interest and dramatic color." Nonetheless, the review was at pains to assuage any anxieties that investigating the *human* origins of the Bible might arouse. "The results of historical and textual criticism are held to be positive rather than negative," the review promises, quoting the author's belief that what the various versions of sacred texts have in common far outweigh their differences.[103]

All the praise and reassurances aside, however, the editorial committee named an alternate selection on the front page of the *Bulletin, The Authority of the Bible* by Charles H. Dodd, "for those who may prefer a volume interpreting the message of the Bible and the nature of its inspiration, rather than the historical processes by which it was produced."[104] Dodd's book seemed the perfect antithesis to the main selection and was offered in part to allay the anxiety that books like *Unravelling the Book of Books* created for some readers. The first paragraph of the review maintains: "The modern revolt against authority and the scientific study of the Bible have so combined to undermine the traditional views about it that a volume which builds up a tenable basis for belief in an authority still unshaken fills a sorely felt need. This is what Professor Dodd's book does. Not from any *a priori* assumption, but from an inductive study of the contents of the Bible and of their spiritual value, he arrives at a doctrine of authority which is certain to be reassuring to many."[105] If you need traditional faith, then the RBC is ready to provide it; if, on the other hand, you require a scientific investigation of the historical origins of those articles of faith, the RBC can provide that, as well. The club exists not to pursue *Truth* or *truths*, but to meet the spiritual needs of Christian/Protestant consumers, whatever they might be.

In the April 1930 *Bulletin*, the RBC recommended both *The Atonement and the Social Process* by Shailer Matthews (the liberal dean of the University of Chicago Divinity School) and *The Virgin Birth of Christ* by J. Gresham Machen (Princeton Seminary's foremost fundamentalist thinker). Reviews clearly marked these products with their (controversial) theological positions and made clear which readers would find them pleasing. Matthews's volume demonstrated that doctrines are not timeless truths but instead reflect the concerns of their specific, historical moment. Matthews did not care which theory of the atonement was "correct"; his purpose was to explain the social worlds from which each theory arose and the intellectual and spiritual needs it met. Two pages later, Machen's book is offered as "an exhaustive statement of the historical evidence supporting belief in the virgin birth of Jesus Christ," and Machen himself is identified as "presenting a thoroughly conservative interpretation of Christianity."[106] In some ways, what the RBC did was to reframe profound and painful differences in theology and worldview as consumer choices. If it did not resolve these contradictions, it at least offered ways of thinking about them that made the intellectual and cultural world of American Protestantism easier to inhabit. Although the presence of books like Machen's *The Virgin Birth of Christ* and Dodd's *The Authority of the Bible* might suggest a significant conservative Christian readership, the context in which these books were offered—as one of many possible sets of beliefs and values rather than as the Truth—participates in a liberal religious logic. As Hedstrom puts it, "Through the reading practices of the club—through this exercise in intellectual inquiry unfettered by doctrine—the club and its members performed, in their selecting, reviewing, and reading, the liberalism of liberal Protantism."[107] Moreover, whereas historical biblical criticism played an immense role in many Social Gospel novels, turning minister/heroes into effective, Christian crusaders for social justice rather than complacent church administrators, historical biblical criticism at the RBC is presented as one of many possible (and therefore distinctly nonrevolutionary) reading interests.

The highly ambivalent nature of the resolution between conflicting theologies was readily apparent in the review of the July 1928 main selection, Daniel Johnson Fleming's *Attitudes toward Other Faiths*. As in reviews of most books of this ilk, the RBC praised both Fleming's real reverence and respect for other faiths and his affirmation of "the unique place of Christ as the fulfillment of all the best aspirations of mankind." Fleming and the review sidestep the contradictions implicit in celebrating diverse religions and maintaining the ultimate superiority of one's own by invoking a common enemy—the materialistic, secular world: "The greatest rival of Christ today is not Confucius or Buddha or Mohammed, but the spirit of rampant materialism and sheer irreligion."[108] The logic of the marketplace deeply permeates this condemnation of the marketplace. It does not matter which God you choose to worship, which set of rituals and traditions you choose to embrace, as long as you choose one (and buy some books about it).

The RBC participated in the remaking of relationships among religious institutions, individual believers, and the literary marketplace. The RBC solved persistent problems with book distribution and provided expert guidance to readers in negotiating the overwhelming literary marketplace. The adamantly ecumenical RBC called into being an imagined faith community that was implicitly white, male, and Protestant, although it engaged with Catholics, Jews, Buddhists, and Hindus in a spirit of (albeit limited) empathy and tolerance. Its offerings reassured anxious readers that traditional faith and modern thought were easily reconciled, that one could be both a person of faith and a rational, scientific thinker. The club promised further that the best religious scholarship was available in lively, accessible prose that offered readers something that felt like authentic fellowship with characters, authors, and judges. It was selling a religious (and a literary) way of being in the world, but not necessarily a particular set of beliefs or doctrines. Readers were hailed as individual believers (even mystics) rather than as members of particular faith traditions or congregations. The RBC constructed a highly contradictory world in which faith is held up as the enemy of a materialistic, consumption-driven world, while participating in the remaking of faith to fit a liberal, consumerist logic. Here is Hedstrom describing the logic of selection at the RBC, a logic that implicitly relies on the invisible hand of the market in religious ideas to sort out the truth: "Rather than adhere to a single party line, then, the Religious Book Club simply operated on the presupposition that hearty disagreement and the give-and-take of honest intellectual inquiry constituted the best way to sort truth from error. As informed experts, committee members would steer readers toward the best books, and as autonomous consumers, readers would select those texts that best suited their intellectual and personal needs."[109]

Charles Sheldon would have been suspicious of Religious Book Week and of the RBC. Sheldon defined authentic faith in opposition to commerce and the extensive, promiscuous reading of contemporary books (recall that the Judas figure in *In His Steps* was a popular novelist). All that book reading by ministers resulted only in less Bible reading and in sermons that were little more than book reviews. Moreover, Sheldon juxtaposed the *right* way of reading—prayerful reading and rereading that motivated personal transformation and social change—with both self-contained intellectual/scholarly reading and the mindless and corrupting consumption of commercial fiction. For much of the 1920s, the RBC editorial board and trade and religious publishers attempting to increase sales of religious books argued the opposite—that selling more religious books not only made money, but also built better families and better citizens and spread democratic ideals around the world. Nobody engaged in the promotional campaigns to get more general readers to buy more religious books worried about *how* readers read or interpreted them, or if they acted on what they read at all. Buying religious books was enough. The rapprochement of a kind of mass-market faith and commerce was striking. As we'll see in Chapter 4, Bruce Barton went so far as to yoke Jesus and commerce together, making common cause against organized religion.

The Religious Book Week campaign and the RBC certainly commodified religion, but this is only the beginning of the story. As Colleen McDannell argues in her magisterial history of religious material culture, "If we immediately assume that whenever money is exchanged religion is debased, then we will miss the subtle ways that people create and maintain spiritual ideals *through* the exchange of goods and the construction of spaces."[110] As McDannell, Leigh Eric Schmidt, and David Morgan have argued, people make their lived religion from the materials their consumer capitalist cultures make available,[111] and to judge from the success of many popular religious books of the 1920s—Bruce Barton's *The Man Nobody Knows* (1925) and *The Book Nobody Knows* (1926), for example—these unabashed books-as-commodities had profound relevance for the lives of many ordinary readers/believers. Chapter 4 examines reader responses to these best-selling books by Barton, an advertising man whose books launched a major promotional campaign for a new-and-improved Jesus who was relevant to 1920s Americans.

FOUR

Jesus, My Pal

Reading Bruce Barton's Jesus

I had the privilege of reading your book by borrowing it from a church library,
but I want to own its contents, so I am copying it word for word on paper like this,
I am almost a quarter thro now, I write quickly and plain. I want to have it to
refer to as often as I do my New Testament.

Somehow the gap between His life and my own has been narrowed and whereas
before I felt that I never could hope to even approach His example, I now feel as
if I could apply His precepts to most of my own daily problems, whether they
be business problems or personal ones.

There is one question I would like to ask. Why did you stop at the death
of Jesus? As far as I am concerned the real divinity of Christ does not appear
until "the third day He arose." I have no desire to be a pest
but I would like that question answered.
—Letters from readers to Bruce Barton

In the Wisconsin Historical Society, there are hundreds of readers' letters like
those quoted above to Bruce Barton, author of the best-selling life of Jesus,
The Man Nobody Knows (1925), its sequel about the Bible, *The Book Nobody
Knows* (1926), and a practical guide to religion, *What Can a Man Believe?*
(1928).[1] Barton moonlighted as the author of popular religious books and
uplifting newspaper and magazine columns, but his real job was as president
of New York ad agency Batton, Barton, Durstine, and Osborn (BBD&O).
A longtime activist in the Republican Party, Barton represented the "silk
stocking" district of eastern Manhattan in Congress from 1937 to 1940,
making a name for himself as an isolationist. Barton's readers/correspond-
ents included businessmen; women's club members; servicemen; YMCA,
YWCA, and Bible class leaders; ministers; convicts; and such notables as
President Calvin Coolidge. They wrote to express their appreciation for his

work; to ask him questions about his own beliefs; to excoriate him for his irreverent discussion of Jesus; to ask for advice about their jobs, dealing with their families, coping with illness, unemployment, and depression; and for pointers on "getting ahead." These letters describe popular ways of reading in the early twentieth century, ways of reading intimately enmeshed with middlebrow culture and an ecumenical theology based in practice. Whatever the theological or intellectual limitations of Barton's books, they were—and are—nonetheless part of the lived religion of scores of ordinary Americans.

Like the readers of the Religious Book Club discussed in the last chapter, readers were less interested in Barton's theology or historical accuracy than they were in finding an emotional connection with the author and his characters and lessons for their own spiritual lives. Also like the readers of the Religious Book Club, many thanked Barton for his clear, accessible prose and his concrete illustrations. Barton's audience and the Religious Book Club subscribers were more interested in personal experience than they were in religious institutions. The reader in the first epigraph thought *The Man* was a sacred text. Like a medieval scribe, she was copying it out longhand so that she would never be without its counsel. The second epigraph, from the son of a minister, claimed *The Man* was the best representation of Jesus the reader had ever encountered, because it had immediate relevance to his personal struggles. The reader in the third epigraph was just irritated with this Jesus, who was sorely lacking in transcendent mystery.

Like the advertising of the 1920s, Barton's books were resolutely "modern," but they also offered compensation and comfort to those overwhelmed by the size, complexity, and speed of the modern world. Barton domesticated the unknowable complexity of modern life and the distance between an other-worldly God and men by having his Jesus approach readers as an old and well-meaning friend. Responding to a vacuum of advice created by the erosion of traditional communities, Barton—the consummate advertising man—reimagined Jesus as a personal adviser to modern, middle-class individuals. Moreover, he reframed deeply felt contradictions at the center of American Protestant life in ways that rendered them irrelevant to everyday religious practices. Like the Religious Book Club, Barton wanted to reconcile tradition and modernity and to reframe painful theological divisions as matters of taste or consumer choice.

A Prophet of Sanctified Commercialism[2]

Few historians or literary critics engage with Barton's work seriously.[3] Most often, he is dismissed as a third-rate writer of boosterish prose who embraced a theologically empty and intellectually bankrupt consumerism. In short, he used religion to rationalize the excesses of modern capitalist culture. For example, T. J. Jackson Lears argues: "Melding therapeutic religiosity with an ideology of consumption, Barton retailored Protestant Christianity to fit the sleek new corporate system. Rejecting the 'weightlessness' of liberal Protestant sentimentality, yearning for a more vigorous and manly religion, Barton produced a creed even more vacuous than its predecessor."[4]

Cultural historians of our own era have nothing on Barton's contemporaries, who indicted Barton for his self-serving sanctification of business and irreverent cheapening of religion from the day of *The Man*'s publication. The *New York Times Book Review* put it simply: "Possessed by this Rotarian vision of his, he swings the Gospels forcibly into line with the commandments of the business world." Gilbert Seldes of the *New Republic* called Barton ignorant of the history of Christianity, ignorant of events in the Roman Empire that shaped Jesus' life, and not so smart on human psychology either. Like many, Seldes suggested that Barton's representation of Jesus as "the father of modern business" was a sacrilege, claiming that Barton was so eager to represent Jesus as "a companionable and energetic Son of Man (read Brother Rotarian) that he must despoil him of all the attributes of the Godhead." In "The Rotarian Nobody Knows," Hubert C. Herring alleged that Barton's representation of Jesus as pleasant and popular was yet another metaphoric crucifixion.[5]

The religious press was—if possible—even less enthusiastic. The *Christian Century* put it plainly: "Here is an attempt to claim the authority of Jesus for the pseudo-morality which underlies modern business enterprise." Like many, it invoked both the Rotary Club and Sinclair Lewis's 1922 bestseller, *Babbitt*, to cast aspersions on *The Man*'s intellectual heft and moral authority. It suggested that Barton's readers were blandly materialistic white-collar workers lacking the brains and sophistication of artists and intellectuals or the traditional moral authority of working men.[6]

Negative publicity and subsequent scholarly condemnation aside, however, millions of people found the books compelling enough to purchase and recommend to friends, colleagues, and family. *The Man* was at the top of the nonfiction bestseller list in 1925 and 1926 and it was joined by *The Book* not long after.[7] I am less interested here in the intellectual rigor of Barton's books (which is sadly lacking) or in their theology (no doubt painfully inadequate) than I am in thinking about them as lived religion. How and why did so many readers appropriate Barton's books as "equipment for living?"[8] What did these texts provide that made it possible for many people to live less anxiously and experience the modern, rationalized world as less alienating and less unknowably complex? What were some of the personal and social consequences of a worldview shaped—in part—by Barton's texts? What the hundreds of carefully catalogued letters from readers to Barton demonstrate is that ordinary believers read differently than intellectuals and theologians, that they found in Barton's work a pragmatic, lived religion that helped them make sense of modernity and their place within it.

Religion, Consumption, and Masculinity: The Holy Trinity

Richard Fried summarizes the critical consensus on Barton as a "transitional figure" between rural and urban, between nineteenth-century entrepreneurial capitalism and twentieth-century consumer capitalism. Barton's real gift, he argued, was "building bridges of prose between tradition and modernity." In Warren Susman's terms, Barton "found a way of bridging the gap between the demands of a Calvinistic producer ethic with its emphasis on hard work, self-denial, savings and the new, increasing demands of a hedonistic consumer ethic: spend, enjoy, use up."[9] Barton did this by offering readers an ad campaign for a new and improved Jesus, who urged not the labor and self-sacrifice necessary for a producer economy of scarcity, but the pleasure and self-indulgence that a consumer economy of abundance required from its subjects. In the process, Barton had to reimagine both religion and shopping as acceptable manly pursuits. The transition from producerist to consumerist values that Susman and Fried describe, then, also required a thorough reimagining of the gendered order.

Barton's books labored mightily to reconcile consumer culture, American manhood, and Christianity, which had long been perceived as being at odds. Ray Long of the International Magazine Company wrote to Barton in 1924 offering advice on the best place for *The Man*'s initial magazine serialization. "If you publish 'The Man Nobody Knows' in a woman's magazine you're giving the readers a new version of an old story," he wrote. "For goodness sake, publish it where nobody ever heard of him—either in *Cosmopolitan*, *Saturday Evening Post* or *American*."[10] Long's assumptions about who would know the story of Jesus are noteworthy. Women (at least those with enough disposable income to subscribe to mass-market magazines) knew all about Jesus; they were the ones filling the pews in church on Sunday, teaching Bible school, and providing the volunteer labor that kept congregations functioning. Sophisticated young people, however—the readers of *Cosmopolitan*—concerned themselves with science, jazz, and fashionable novels rather than religion. The middle-class men who were the target audience for *Saturday Evening Post* and *American* were just too busy with the stock market, politics, and making a living to waste time on Jesus.

This particular gender and class framing of religion in America in the 1920s gets repeated often. Barton himself opened a much-ballyhooed radio interview in 1927 about *What Can a Man Believe?* by telling a story about a perfect stranger who had asked him a provocative question one day: "How did a fellow like you ever happen to write religious books?" Barton spent the next several minutes unpacking the question. What the man *really* meant, Barton explained, was something along the lines of: "You look normal. You're six feet tall and strong, and I see you around the golf links and the clubs and at prize fights, and having a good time generally. How did you happen to get tangled up with a subject that is supposed to be the exclusive province of women and the clergy?"[11] The question made clear how religion was framed in mainstream culture of the 1920s. People who took it seriously were a little *ab*normal. In 1924, H. L. Mencken helpfully explained that "Christendom . . . may be defined briefly as that part of the world in which, if any man stands up in public and solemnly swears he is a Christian, all his auditors will laugh."[12] Many of Barton's correspondents similarly testified to feeling embattled as Christians: "It is indeed refreshing to find here and there an author who throws the weight of his talents and influence on the side of righteousness and religion, in an age when it is popular to sneer at religion and to undermine the standing and influence of the Christian ministry."[13] In Barton's telling, men—real men (tall, strong, athletic)—were not much interested in religion. Religion ought to be contrasted with "having a good time generally." In this story, religion and consumer pleasures are opposed. One either spent money on golf, boxing matches, and going out on the town, *or* one went to church.[14] Manliness and religion are at odds in the framing of the question as well. Women and those effeminate, bookish men who lack the gumption for anything better spent their time policing other people's morals, but real men were too busy with athletics and all-male socializing to bother with it.

Barton's project was to prove the assumptions behind the stranger's question wrong. Historically, religious people raised in a Calvinist culture thought self-indulgent leisure was immoral. Since the colonial period, over two-thirds of the people in the pews had been women, but Barton was making the case for a new, modern religion—one perfectly compatible with men's interests and desires and in perfect accord with commercial leisure. Barton had a steep hill to climb, since the doctrine of separate spheres that had reigned since the mid-nineteenth century in middle-class America handed both consumption and religion to women. Barton thought he was equal to the task, however, if he could convince people that the man/God at the center of their religion—Jesus—was not, in fact, long-suffering, meek, and lowly, but a charming, muscular man's man who liked a good drink and the company of ruffians.

The Man begins with a preface describing how one man reclaimed Jesus from do-gooding women and the not-so-manly ministers in cahoots with them.[15] Entitled "How It Came to Be Written," the preface describes a little boy in Sunday school during his "weekly hour of revolt" against a kindly, absent-minded woman who was offering him "a pale young man with flabby forearms and a sad expression" as his Savior (3), a man with "a woman's face covered by a beard" (23). It's not that the little boy found religion inherently dull, only Jesus. He liked Daniel and David and Moses, all of whom were brave heroes of action-adventure tales in the Bible, but "sissified" Jesus—"the lamb of God"—was for girls (3–4). This Jesus was sorrowful and humble, and—like the Widow Douglas—spent time going around "telling people not to do things" (4). Could anyone blame the bored little tyke for wanting to light out for the territories?

Later, the narrative tells us, the grown-up boy decides to dispense with all the claptrap he has heard from ministers and Sunday school matrons about Jesus and just read what Jesus' friends said about him. He was astonished at what he found: "A physical weakling! Where did they get that idea? Jesus pushed a plane and swung an adze; he was a successful carpenter. He slept outdoors and spent his days walking around his favorite lake. His muscles were so strong that when he drove the money-changers out, nobody dared to oppose him!" (4). Barton's Jesus was no wet blanket either. To save a wedding party where the booze ran out, he once changed water into wine. Barton takes particular pleasure in debunking the notion that Jesus was a sad, ascetic man with similar expectations for his followers. He writes: "A kill-joy! He was the most popular dinner guest in Jerusalem! The criticism which proper people made was that he spent too much time with publicans and sinners (very good fellows, on the whole, the man thought) and enjoyed society too much. They called Him a 'wine bibber and a gluttonous man'" (4).

Barton's Jesus had a thoroughly consumerist streak. If he were alive today, he'd no doubt be at the prize fights, on the golf course, or just "having a good time generally." There is not much suffering and self-sacrifice in Barton's "discovery of Jesus" (the original subtitle) but a great deal of pleasure-seeking, many feats of manly prowess, and countless displays of the rhetorical power of the world's first and most successful advertising man, Jesus.[16]

Barton's book is full of other men, too, men Barton believes theologians have not given their due. First among these is "that quiet unassuming Joseph." "The same theology which has painted the son as soft and gentle to the point of weakness," Barton insists, "has exalted the feminine influence in its worship, and denied any large place to the masculine" (22). His paean to Joseph, the unsung hero, offers just the kind of reassurance professional-managerial class men who spent all of their time at the office while their wives raised the children needed to hear. It was not that the capitalist division of the world into private and public, feminine and masculine, made men irrelevant at home; it was just that their culture overlooked their significant influence. The questions about Joseph seem far more relevant to fatherhood in 1920s America: "Was he just an untutored peasant, married to a superior woman and baffled by the genius of a son whom he could never understand? Or was there, underneath his self-effacement, a vigor and faith that molded the boy's plastic years? Was he a happy companion to the youngsters? Did he carry the youngest, laughing and crowing on his shoulders, from the shop? Was he full of jokes at dinner time? Was he ever tired and short-tempered? Did he ever punish?" (22–23). Conceding that the Bible gives us no answer to these questions, Barton nonetheless concludes that Joseph must have been an amazing parent, for Jesus chose to explain the love of God for humanity by referring to him as "Father" (23).

Letters from readers confirm that the manliness of Jesus was one of *The Man*'s drawing points. One teacher described the effect of Barton's work on his Bible class of boys: "They were deeply interested and thinking about this new Jesus, who became a he-man and a real personality for the first time." Another correspondent wanted to found a group of businessmen, inspired by Barton's work, to promote teaching about a "virile Savior."[17] Repeated references to Rotarians testified similarly to the importance of Barton's work in constituting imagined communities of virile Christian men interested in commerce. Rotary and other fraternal organizations in the late nineteenth and early twentieth centuries were places where respectable middle-class men went to network; they provided all-male ritual and camaraderie and an occasion for social and public service. They were like churches for men, many of whom felt women and women's values had overrun Protestant churches in the early twentieth century, inspiring numerous related movements for "muscular Christianity."[18] Readers who had heard of Barton's book only in passing remembered this promise of manly fellowship, if nothing else. One letter asked (mistakenly) for a copy of *Jesus, the Rotarian*, making clear what part of a review or reference to *The Man* was most salient to this reader.[19] Hewitt H. Howland, Barton's editor, made the connections explicit: "If properly presented, I believe that even the world's best Babbitt can be induced to read your book, and when he has read it he will be as strong for Jesus as he now is for his local Rotary. For you have made Jesus a hero, a man's hero; so that no one can ever again think of him as the sacrificial lamb, the meek and lowly."[20]

The logic of consumer capitalism structures all of Barton's books. First, his Jesus is portrayed as a self-marketer par excellence. Barton makes clear that Jesus' absence from the contemporary marketplace is a travesty: "The present day market-place is the newspaper and the magazine. Printed columns are the modern thoroughfares; published advertisements are the cross-roads where the sellers and the buyers meet. Any issue of a national magazine is a world's fair, a bazaar filled with the products of the world's work. . . . That every other voice should be raised in such great market-places, and the voice of Jesus of Nazareth be still—this is a vital omission which he would find a way to correct. He would be a national advertiser today, I am sure, as he was the great advertiser of his own day" (66). Tellingly, the ten biblical heroes Barton chose to profile in *The Book Nobody Knows* were selected through market research. Ten thousand clergy were surveyed for the most important figures in the Bible, and Barton described the top ten. The version of Christianity Barton presented to the American public, then, was a carefully designed consumer product.

Moreover, like the Religious Book Club editors and Harold Bell Wright before them, Barton did not draw firm lines between sacred and secular. He maintained that all work was religious work, a claim for which his critics took him to task. "Though he tries manfully," Gilbert Seldes wrote in the *New Republic*, "he cannot convince us of the divinity of a Buick Service Station."[21] Further, Barton argues that much of the guidance the Bible provides is not religious guidance at all. For example, he explains that the Book of Proverbs does not offer religious ideas so much as provide "shrewd guideposts to worldly wisdom" that will further a man's material interests.[22]

In the fifth chapter of Barton's *What Can a Man Believe?*, he considers the church of the future ("The Church Nobody Knows"), which sounds remarkably like a spiritual convenience store. Because Barton does not distinguish life from spiritual life, the church is open all the time. Sunday mornings are often better left free for golfing, Barton argues. Moreover, Barton has organized the church along the lines of rationalized business. First, it specializes in spiritual life and training, so it does not waste time and energy with bazaars, motion pictures, entertainment and other services much better provided by people trained and paid to provide them. One hears sermons only at Christmas and Easter in the church of the future. Instead, the radio brings prayers, music, and devotional readings into people's lives every day. The minister is always a man over forty who has proven himself as an expert manager in some other arena of life. His job is to provide three short services in the morning and afternoon and then send congregants out into the world. There are no more denominations, and people come in when they desire for one-on-one counseling with the priest or minister, having their spiritual needs catered to on an individual basis.[23] This delivery of spiritual services is rational, efficient, and convenient for the consumer, who gets exactly what he or she desires, whenever he or she desires it. Moreover, as with consumer desires, people are hailed as individuals, interested not in traditions or communities, but in what can help them on their own spiritual journey. In the Bible, Barton insists, "we see *ourselves* . . . with all our passions and frailties, all our hopes and affections, our victories and defeats."[24] If we did not find practical help for our own situation, it would hardly be worth reading.

Advertising, the Ministry, and the Vacuum of Advice

As T. J. Jackson Lears points out in his history of American advertising, *Fables of Abundance*, a disproportionate number of pioneering advertising men were the sons of ministers.[25] Barton was no exception. His father, William Barton, was a Congregational minister who was ultimately settled in a congregation in Oak Park, a well-to-do Chicago suburb. The connection between childhoods in the parsonage and careers in advertising was no coincidence. Ad men were missionaries of a different kind, selling a gospel of consumption as the royal road to happiness, and they took many of their techniques from the ministry. Advertising in the 1920s was both a business and a calling. Ad men were hard-headed businessmen, using their talents to drum up sales of the product in question, but they also saw themselves in the business of education, public service, and cultural uplift. They were selling products, but they were also selling a way of life—modern, hygienic, stylish—in a word—better.[26] It was the advertiser's job to teach consumers how to engage with proliferating consumer choices in a world where traditional forms of authority were eroding. Advertising men stepped into a deeply felt vacuum of advice created by the increasing scale and complexity of rationalized institutions, the erosion of traditional communities, and the increasing anonymity of modern urban life.

A similar vacuum of advice existed for many with regard to their religious faith, and Barton saw no reason why he ought not fill both. Many of Barton's readers were raised in Protestant churches but found that their educations made the faith of their parents unworkable for them. College introduced some of them to historical biblical criticism and theories of evolution, some of which did not include a benevolent creator God. This left them without a moral compass. One reader spoke for many when she wrote to Barton in 1931: "Upon graduation from a large University I found myself entirely without any livable philosophy. The faith of my childhood had, of course, been rendered impossible by study and lectures, but my professors (myself as well) had neglected to supply anything to replace what had been taken away. Knowing that I could not live (I might exist, yes) without something to live for I browsed through the libraries hoping to find a book that might help me."[27] This reader discovered all three of Barton's books and read and reread them during a seven-month period in a hospital after her doctors had given her up for dead. However limited Barton's theology might appear to scholars and intellectuals, it was useful for people who felt they needed a faith to live by and could not find one that worked in a modern, industrial age.

Barton's books were clearly imagined as print substitutes for loving, personal mentorship formerly provided by parents, teachers, or ministers. Barton told the advertising staff at his publisher, Bobbs-Merrill, that one of the key points promotions should get across was that *The Man* was a good book for parents, teachers, mentors, and managers to pass along to their charges and employees.[28] They took his advice. One ad in particular asked: "Is there a young man in college whose education interests you? Is there a young man in business whose success concerns you? Is there a young man in any profession whose career is important to you? Send him a copy of The Man Nobody Knows."[29] Another claimed simply that "*every employer* in the United States ought to send a copy of this book for Christmas to the ten most valuable men in his organization."[30] James Angell, president of Yale University, imagined Barton's mentorship in larger terms: "I hope your book may be widely read, especially by young men."[31]

The Man was also a book that parents gave to children. One father wrote to Barton announcing: "I shall buy a copy to add to my six-year-old son's small library. He is too young now to understand it, but when he is fourteen I want to be sure that he has an opportunity to know a man whose human side is quite as, if not more[,] appealing than his so-called 'divinity.'"[32] Like a good parent, the books functioned for others as a force preserving them from youthful indiscretions that might have marred the course of their lives.

One reader wrote in 1955, "Many, many years ago my life was greatly blessed through the reading of your book, The Man Nobody Knows. I was eighteen and to me your book was a 'guiding hand.'" Now married with a son named after Barton, this reader enclosed a picture of his son on his twenty-first birthday. "Thank you, Mr. Barton," he concluded, "and God bless you."[33]

Young men, in particular, often wrote Barton seeking advice about getting ahead. For example, a twenty-two-year-old man wrote to Barton seeking help for dealing with what he believed to be a problem of motivation. He was working to support his widowed mother, attending night school three times a week, and studying books on advertising and journalism in his spare time. He desired a career in advertising. Although he devoted over 75 percent of his time outside of work to studies in the spring and summer, he found himself unable to buckle down and study as successfully in the fall and winter. Could Barton help? Barton wrote back with some advice about getting into the advertising business, but suggested that regular exercise, recreation, and the company of the "right sort of people" would be broadening and improving, perhaps more so than additional study. When the reader answered Barton's letter, he had joined the YMCA, planned to take up golf in the spring, and was much less anxious about life. "I thank you very, very much once again for your inspirational and helpful letter. Writing you is the best thing I have ever done for myself in my life."[34]

The Depression brought many letters from or about struggling young men to Barton's desk. "Just His Girl" wrote to Barton in 1934 describing a boyfriend—"ambitious, happy, and thankful that he was needed"—until he had lost his job six months before. She wanted Barton to write a newspaper column for all of the men out of work, telling them "something, anything, a new idea, a new thought" to help them stand the prolonged period of idleness and strain. She wrote: "Won't you help him, and the others, too? You can. Perhaps more so than you realize, because your writings each week—well, it's hard to explain, but somehow they make one see clearly and want to strive hard for that glorious something I call 'peace of mind.'"[35]

Young men with faltering careers were not the only ones seeking Barton's advice and comfort, however. An eighteen-year-old girl from Charleston, South Carolina, wrote to Barton from a tuberculosis sanatorium in 1929. She was surrounded by sick people, and many of her fellow inmates had already died. She had tried to read her Bible, but she understood very little of it. She was frightened and lonely and did not know what to believe, so she wrote to Barton. "Mr. Barton," she pleaded, "won't you tell me what *you* believe? Is their [sic] a God? Will there be an after-life?" Barton answered: "I am glad you wrote to me, and I wish we might sit down together and have a long talk." Since this was not possible, he sent her a copy of his book *What Can a Man Believe?*, which summarized his faith in ways he hoped might be useful to her. "Perhaps you will write to me again," he concluded. "I hope you will."[36]

All of these scenarios are examples of a vacuum of advice. The fatherless young man needed guidance in building a successful, balanced life. The unemployed young men lacked an identity outside of paid work and a community to ease them through the painful period of unemployment. The terrified girl in the sanatorium was isolated from family, friends, and religious community by her disease. Barton stepped in with concern, advice, and (sometimes) money. It says a great deal about our culture that they got this from a stranger whom they knew only through his prose rather than a supportive community of kin and neighbors or an adequate social welfare system. Desperate people wrote to Barton asking for money, career advice, comfort, and solace, and he sent them words of inspiration and praise—telling them to keep their day jobs, look after their kids, keep on keeping on, and so on. Like the advertising man that he was, he dispensed hope, advice, and soothing concern without raising any fundamental questions about the structure of the society they all inhabited. Barton's biographer, Richard Fried, calls Barton "a long-distance therapist, trying through his writings to help other Americans resolve some of the conflicts that came with modern living."[37] Fried is concerned with Barton's published writings—books and newspaper columns—but the same is true of his private correspondence with readers as well. Barton's "conversation" with the girl in the sanatorium included not only a personal letter but also a copy of his book, texts he presented as continuous with each other. *McClure's* magazine—which published many of Barton's newspaper and magazine columns—boasted that Barton had "the rare gift of making his readers feel that they are his personal friends."[38]

The letters readers sent to Barton can be usefully compared to Catholic women's appeals to St. Jude, discussed by Robert Orsi, who argues that the daughters and granddaughters of southern and eastern European immigrants in the 1930s to the 1960s were caught between a new world of work and family in the suburbs and the more traditional world of their parents, still living in urban ethnic enclaves. Appeals to St. Jude gave these women a way to narrate their own concerns within a Catholic tradition that silenced them and gave them a way to seek assistance and comfort from other women.[39] I am arguing analogously that Barton's particular imagining of Jesus responded to and was shaped by the needs of middle-class, white, mostly Protestant Americans who were struggling with the anonymity and the immense scale of modern urban life.

Jesus and Betty Crocker: On Middlebrow Personalism

Barton is widely (if not completely accurately) credited with being the brains behind the Betty Crocker ad campaign for General Mills.[40] Betty was a fictional character created in 1921 to sign company letters to housewives who had written to enter a contest. In 1924 and 1925, the cheerful and reassuring voice of Blanche Ingersoll as Betty entered the homes of countless American housewives through their radios. Eventually, Betty Crocker was signing over 4,000 letters per day.[41] Scores of women wrote to Betty not only about soufflés that would not rise and children who were fussy eaters, but also about feeling lonely and isolated in their homes, about husbands who drank and children who were a disappointment. The intimate confidences of thousands of strangers flooded General Mills, all addressed to an imaginary figure designed to sell products. As increased mobility separated daughters from mothers, removed neighbors from stable, traditional communities, and left young housewives to figure out how to run a household without much community support, Betty Crocker stepped into this vacuum of advice—a personal face on a fully rationalized, profit-seeking bureaucracy. She created the illusion that negotiating an immense marketplace as part of a mass public was not so different from encountering neighbors over the back fence.

Historian of advertising Roland Marchand argues that urban middle-class consumers in the 1920s ached for a sense of the personal in everyday life; they longed to feel that they were known and appreciated as individuals, rather than as part of mass audiences. Overwhelmed by the immense scale of modern life, the consumers Marchand describes were compelled to buy, not by objective information but by a friendly, personal voice pitching a product: "Through consumer response, through trial and error, and through close observation of the other media of popular culture, advertisers gradually observed and responded to a popular demand that modern products be introduced to them in ways that gave the appearance and feel of a personal relationship. People craved opportunities, through vicarious experience, to bring products within the compass of their own human scale."[42] By all reports, Barton was extraordinarily successful at this. Part of Barton's work reconciling the old world of entrepreneurial capitalism with the new world of mass consumption was to articulate corporate capitalist goals through the idiom of the small town and the small store. Richard Fried argues that Barton's institutional ads for immense corporations like General Electric and General Motors were designed "to humanize these vast bodies, to make them a 'family' or 'friend' who provided 'service.'"[43]

Barton's Jesus operated on the same principles. Letters that readers wrote to Barton or to his publisher confirm that this sense of personal connection with Jesus as someone like them had great appeal. A Baptist pastor in Houston wrote to Barton's publisher: "Mr. Barton gives us a fine portrait of the Friend, by whose side we would be happy to sit at a dinner, or with whom we would be glad to walk and talk on a sunny vacation day."[44] A hardware company president affirmed that the way he visualized Jesus had been changed profoundly by the book: "I think of him as a man like myself, with the same troubles and the same worries, and the same problems, which were not very much different with him than they are with us today. So this book of Barton's brings him close to me and makes him a more real personality than any that I have ever read." Another reader characterized Barton's Jesus simply as "Jesus, My Pal."[45]

Barton makes clear in his discussion of the Old Testament prophets that the intimate, chatty advice of someone like us was much preferred to advice from on high. He writes: "The Jewish prophets were stern-faced men; there are few if any gleams of humor in the Old Testament from beginning to end. It was the business of a prophet to denounce folks for their sins. Go to the Boston Public Library and look at their portraits. You are moved by their moral grandeur but rather glad to get away. They are not the kind of men whom you would choose as companions on a fishing trip" (33–34). Barton's Jesus, however, was. He was strong, tanned, and vigorous from work in the carpenter shop and a life lived outdoors. He was a leader of men, and he enjoyed the company of people of all kinds. He was charming and sociable—"the most popular dinner guest in Jerusalem" (4). He had a way with words that—coupled with his considerable personal magnetism—allowed him to build an organization that spread his teaching across the globe.

Barton's Jesus resonates with a shift in advertising techniques that occurred in the 1920s. Rather than imagining themselves as salesmen offering arguments in favor of buying a product (which might invite the reader to imagine counterarguments), copywriters increasingly saw themselves as confidants. This "side-by-side" approach cast the copywriter in the role of coach or adviser to a consumer faced with a difficult issue or problem— that is, they were allies.[46] What Barton's *The Man* did was to apply this same transition to the deity: "God ceased to be the stern, unforgiving judge, and became the loving, friendly Father. He, himself, was less and less the prophet, more and more the companion" (34). Barton catalogs all of God's roles from Genesis through Jesus in order to argue that they have all been supplanted by one—a sort of divine ad man who wants us to have all of our needs and desires met. Barton writes: "That was the message of Jesus—that God is supremely better than anybody had ever dared to believe. Not a petulant Creator, who had lost control of his creation and, in wrath, was determined to destroy it all. Not a stern Judge dispensing impersonal justice. Not a vain King who must be flattered and bribed into concessions of mercy. Not a rigid Accountant, checking up the sins against the penances and striking a cold hard balance. Not any of these ... nothing like these ... but a great Companion, a wonderful Friend, a kindly indulgent, joy-loving Father" (42). These letters and Barton's representation of Jesus and God invoke what Radway calls "middlebrow personalism," a way of being in the world that emphasized the particular and the local and offered compensation to subjects imagined as faceless parts of mass publics or giant, bureaucratic institutions. Identification, connection, a sense of communion with characters and authors/narrators, emotional engagement—all spoke to readers at sea in a thoroughly rationalized world.[47] Like the readers who subscribed to the Religious Book Club discussed in Chapter 3, Barton's readers sought a powerful, personal identification rather than theological or historical analysis. One reader commented particularly on his experience of a personal connection with Barton and his Jesus: "I have seen you in every word you have written and I have also seen Jesus. No greater compliment can be paid a man."[48]

I Pray You Be Saved Too[49]

The middlebrow personalism that Barton's Jesus enabled was like the image of Jesus as companion and friend that liberal Protestant ministers had been offering since at least the mid-nineteenth century as an alternative to the stern, judging God of Calvinism.[50] Cultural shifts are uneven, however, and for some conservative Christian readers, the radical leveling of the distance between an other-worldly God and human beings was still shocking in the 1920s. The minority position in letters to Barton comes from those who—however captivated by Barton's very human Jesus—were appalled by his neglect of Christ's divinity.[51] Although some readers assumed that Barton believed in the divinity of Jesus but merely chose to focus on his humanity in *The Man*, others were not so sure. Again and again, Barton was asked what he thought of the divinity of Christ.[52] Other correspondents peppered him with outraged questions about his dubious theology, accused him of having written a sacrilegious book, and/or promised to pray for his (clearly damned) soul. Many felt that Barton was truly well intentioned but had merely misunderstood the scriptures. Several suggested he pray for better understanding.[53] One reader, inspired by "love and knowledge of Jesus," wrote to Barton to criticize *The Man* as a book that would produce nothing but "infidels and agnostics." He produced a set of beliefs (Jesus' divinity, his virgin birth, the resurrection, the atonement for our sins) without which life was meaningless and the work of Christian ministers everywhere a fraud. "You must be born again by the Holy Spirit in order to understand and interpret the Bible," he admonished Barton. "You must be born again in order to understand the meaning of the life and death of Jesus Christ."[54]

Barton could not have been surprised by the outrage; the religious experts who had vetted the manuscript for publisher Bobbs-Merrill had made similar points, minus the promises to pray for his soul. William Jennings Bryan, for example, wrote to W. C. Bobbs at Bobbs-Merrill that Barton was a modernist who ignored the divinity of Christ: "He deals with Christ as he would with Lloyd George, Abraham Lincoln, or any other mere man." Campbell Morgan wrote to Bobbs-Merrill's D. L. Chambers that Barton's book only irritated him, since it was "purely Unitarian, and poor at that," compared to the much more sophisticated writings of theologians such as William Ellery Channing.[55]

Although Barton's sole emphasis on Jesus' humanity struck some readers as downright heretical, it is surprising how little difference this rather fundamental point of theology meant to most ordinary readers. One made clear that although his faith in Christ went beyond what Barton presented in *The Man*, he was nonetheless behind efforts to promote its study to businessmen and other lay readers: "Mr. Barton's book should refill the churches. It gives faith a common denominator. Many people will not find therein their whole conception of Christ. I, for one, do not. It is thus significant that I, as I believe, the majority, can go with the author, as far as he goes, with approval."[56]

Barton's Lived Religion

The effect of Barton's work (if not his intent) was to commodify religion, as scholars have rightly critiqued. However, he also gave people a workable religion. I am taking a functionalist approach to religion here, as the quintessentially middlebrow Barton did. As discussed in Chapter 3, Janice Radway argues that the middlebrow aesthetic or ethos was scandalous to cultural critics of the 1920s, because it imagined literature and culture as a means to the end of achieving social and professional status rather than as ends in themselves. "All books . . . achieved success and even greatness to the degree that they took up issues of everyday life," Radway explains. "Value was also a function of a book's capacity to be used in a pragmatic fashion to accomplish a particular end or purpose."[57] Similarly, Barton had little patience with religion as a transcendent realm of mystery or a system of consistent theological principles, but instead he insisted that it offer people practical guidance for daily living.

Again and again, readers wrote to thank Barton for making the life of Jesus and the material about the Bible accessible and relevant to ordinary men and women. Rather than relying on the minister or parish priest to tell them what Jesus' life meant, Barton told them that if they would just clear away all of the accumulated nonsense imposed on the life of Jesus, they could clearly see a man just like themselves, a role model in human trials. Theologians, he insisted, had made choosing the right way to live and the right things to believe unduly complicated. In short, pithy, eminently readable books with the "punch" of ad copy, a plain-speaking layman could give them what they needed to build a faith suitable for modern life. Barton's books in some ways liberated lay readers from the interpretations of clergy and scholars, but they did not encourage readers to find their own path as much as they substituted an advertising man for more traditional experts/authorities (parents, priests, ministers, professors). This was less a democratization of religious authority than it was a replacement of certain kinds of ecclesiastical authorities with others. It did, however, move emphasis from institutions and denominations to individual believers.

One reader wrote to Barton about what his accessible presentation of Jesus and the Bible meant to her: "I am eternally thankful that you had the mental stamina to wade through the begats and road blocks in the old testament and give me the real story. I don't think I could have ever cleared that to my satisfaction."[58] Not only did Barton render opaque or confusing passages clear, he honored readers' sense of difficulty in ways that preserved their self-esteem. The Bible, Barton insisted, is an amazing library—a masterfully condensed history of civilization, a collection of aesthetically magnificent literature, a textbook in human nature, and a biography of Jesus (a role model)—but he does not mince words about its limitations: "There are long chapters of genealogy which are no more edifying than pages of the telephone directory. There are First and Second Chronicles, which recite the tedious mistakes and sins of kings who were no better than the kings of

England and not half so important in their influence on our lives."[59] Consequently, Barton's *The Book* promises readers "the high points" and tells them the reasons the Bible still matters, in engaging, often humorous prose, complete with quizzes before each chapter to guide readers' attention and give them a sense of mastery.

Blurbs from ministers in advertising for Barton's books and positive reviews almost always made mention of Barton's accessible style. The *Wichita Eagle*, for example, claimed that what set *The Man* apart was that, "different from all the hundreds of other books about Christ, it talks a language most easily understood by millions."[60] In the mid-1930s, research on "readability" conducted at Columbia Teacher's College confirmed that accessibly written nonfiction books were a scarce commodity. One news source covering this dilemma offered readers a list of suitable titles, on which Barton's books appeared.[61]

Many readers specifically juxtaposed Barton's accessible presentation with the incomprehensibility of their minister's: "I've sought and questioned and listened to sermons of all faiths and crawled around in the hair of half the preachers in town trying to get the story that you gave so simply and beautifully and so clearly that even muddle headed me feels that I do not have to ask a question. You answered them all for me."[62] This gap between ministers/scholars and ordinary people comes up repeatedly. The gap highlights the difference between theology and lived religion, between the world of church leaders and intellectuals and the practices of ordinary laypeople in their homes and communities. Although the tenets of institutional religion and the everyday practices of laypeople can be related in any number of ways—complementary, supplementary, contradictory, and so on—in this case, there was a significant gap between scholarly condemnation and popular approval of Barton's work. Barton produced what I call middlebrow religion—which spoke to and continues to speak to millions of readers—although it earned him, and continues to earn him, the scorn of intellectuals and theologians. Like middlebrow culture more generally, middlebrow religion was scandalous because it failed to respect the separation between sacred and profane, culture and commerce, and because of its resolutely practical ethos that insisted texts be useful in readers' everyday lives.[63]

The clergy who wrote Barton or reviewed his work for Bobbs-Merrill found one error after another in his work. He could not call a particular chapter "Heresies" if it was just a criticism of the church, since no doctrines were challenged in his catalog of bad deeds done in the name of religion in the past.[64] His descriptions were full of errors and misunderstandings of

Syrian/Jewish customs. He described Palestine as if it were in Ohio or New England. One correspondent gave him the name of a knowledgeable scholar who might proofread his next book before it went into print.[65] Barton kidded his editor after the return of a particularly vitriolic reader report from a minister that *The Book Nobody Knows* ought to have been called *The Book with Which Nobody Will Agree.*[66]

Nevertheless, most readers could not have cared less. One wrote a letter to the *Boston Herald* praising its courage in printing a favorable review of Barton's *The Man* after many others had criticized it for being materialistic, irreverent, and downright unscholarly. He wrote: "The Herald has stood out in courageous fashion for the new book of Bruce Barton, 'The Man Nobody Knows.' It is proof of the intellectual integrity of the Herald that it praises a book scathingly reviewed by the intellectuals and ridiculed by the professors of Biblical criticism."[67] It is not that this reader is questioning the judgments of intellectuals and professors. He all but concedes they are right, but he asks why any of this is relevant. "What if the work is not precisely historical?" he inquires. "What if it is 'low-brow'? What if its hero is a back-slapper and a Rotarian?"[68] The intellectuals and professors are not wrong; they are just engaged in the *wrong conversation*, spending a great deal of time and energy discussing irrelevant issues and questions while ordinary Christians yearn for useful information and sensible spiritual guidance. Another correspondent suggested as much when he wrote to Bobbs-Merrill to praise *The Man*: "It's a great book. It will do much to rob organized Christianity of its sterility. True it may not follow classical exegesis. What of that? Its 'explanation' appeals not to the scholar but to the man on the street. Possibly it is not logical according to rote and rule. The common people will read it gladly. It is a splendid contribution to practical popular religion. . . . Possibly 'fantastical' in some paragraphs, but it is a fantasy that will catch the attention and create a fresh helpful saving acceptance of the religion of Jesus."[69]

This gap between clerical authorities and laypeople is readily apparent in another letter to Barton from 1926. This reader and his pastor were at odds over *The Man*, and the reader could not get his pastor to see through his layman's eyes, despite his best efforts. He wrote: "It may interest you to hear of my experience with my own pastor just the other day. He was visiting at my house and we came to talk about your book. . . . The pastor claimed you were making a mere man of Jesus, no place pointing out His Divinity[,] and for that reason the pastor had come to the conclusion that you were doing more harm than good with those publications. I tried to tell him my viewpoint as a layman and how a business man would take the contents of those abstracts published day by day."[70] Although the divinity of Jesus looms large as a theological question, getting people excommunicated and causing schisms in denominations, this letter suggests that at the level of lived religion it made little difference, to some at least. Even if the emphasis on the humanity of Jesus is a theological flaw, the book does good work for businessmen trying to lead moral lives, much better work than a theologically correct and utterly uninteresting account might. Rather than asking, "Is this book orthodox?" the reader suggests that his pastor ought to be asking, "Does this book make Christians feel better, stronger, and more prepared to face the challenges and disappointments in modern life with courage and kindness?" Like middlebrow culture more generally, middlebrow religion was judged on its practical function in individuals' daily lives. Most often, readers reported that Barton's books granted them peace of mind and sanctified their workday labors in service of others rather than leading them to critique mainstream culture (as fundamentalist writing did) or inspiring them to work to transform social institutions (as liberal Social Gospel writing did).

Barton's work appealed not because its theology was liberal or conservative, but because it provided a way for readers to negotiate or sidestep the deeply felt contradictions at the center of American Protestant life.[71] Was one a believer or not? Were the miracles real or not? If scholars could not agree on it, what were we to think? Barton reframed the issues and questions in such a way that the answers no longer mattered—one practiced this kind of faith whether one embraced a particular doctrine or not. On some level, Barton made it seem that these painful contradictions and controversies were really quite meaningless.

Again and again, the narrator of Barton's *The Man* explained the irrelevance of formal theology and the importance of narrative and human emotion: "Theology has spoiled the thrill of his life by assuming that he knew everything from the beginning—that his three years of public work were a kind of dress rehearsal, with no real problems or crises. What interest would there be in such a life? What inspiration? You who read these pages have your own creed concerning him; I have mine. Let us forget all creed for the time being, and take the story just as the simple narratives give it. . . . Stripped of all dogma this is the grandest achievement story of all! In the pages of this little book let us treat it as such" (9). Scholars of American culture have long lamented the decline of American letters from the vigorous, masculine Calvinism of the founding fathers to the sentimental, intellectually empty pap dished out by domestic fiction writers and popular authors of the later century. Ann Douglas calls this decline the "feminization of American culture" and puts it in a direct line to what she sees as the vapid, politically retrograde popular narratives of our own day. T. J. Jackson Lears similarly laments the transition from "salvation" to "self-realization," as a therapeutic worldview thoroughly complicit with consumer culture replaced the Calvinism of earlier generations.[72] I am not suggesting that Barton trafficked in defective or dumbed-down theology—that the Platonic ideal is represented by Jonathan Edwards and this is a degraded form. On the contrary, this was self-consciously different theology. Barton provided what I am calling "middlebrow religion"—a religion based in practice rather than creeds. David Hall distinguishes the writings of Puritan divines from the lived religion of people he called "horse shed Christians"—those who left the service to congregate around the stables outside, smoking, shooting the breeze, and exchanging information about crops and the weather. Ordinary Christians were enthusiastic consumers of some of what the churches had to offer (baptism was quite common, for example), but were clearly at odds with preachers on other key points (only a small percentage of congregants took communion).[73] The distinction between laypeople's religious practices and the ideas of clergy and theologians about what those practices and beliefs ought to be is a real one.

Similarly, Nancy Ammerman's study of contemporary congregations uncovers a large body of churchgoers she calls "golden rule" Christians. Ammerman argues that such people have long been measured by scholars against evangelical Christians, who have a theologically consistent belief system—the literal truth of the Bible, the divinity of Christ, our redemption by his death and resurrection, the virgin birth, Jesus' imminent return to earth, as examples. Golden rule Christians seem like much less devout people. They do not have the same rigorous set of beliefs and are not particularly articulate about their beliefs at all. Ammerman claims this is because their theology is based in practice—one is not a good Christian because of what one believes, one is a good Christian because of the life one lives. If you do unto others as you would have others do unto you, then you are a good Christian. Ammerman thinks golden rule Christianity is the most common type of faith for white suburban Americans, calling them "a pervasive religious type that deserves to be understood on its own terms."[74] As in Barton's work, the individual actor is paramount, not the religious institutions to which she or he might or might not belong. Injustices built into social institutions are rendered invisible in golden rule definitions of Christianity.

Barton was writing what might be described as "golden rule" books with wide popular appeal in the 1920s and beyond, but scholars and religious leaders have measured him with a theologian's yardstick. Barton's theology of practice (if you live a life of service to humanity, you are a good Christian) renders most traditional theological questions utterly irrelevant, *and this is precisely why I think it had/has such wide appeal.* For example, in his discussion of Jesus' temptation after his baptism, Barton writes: "The narrative describes them as a threefold temptation and introduces Satan to add to the dramatic quality of the event. In our simple story we need not spend much time with the description of Satan. We do not know whether he is to be regarded as a personality or as an impersonalization of an inner experience. The temptation is more real without him, more akin to our own trials and doubts. With him or without him, however, the meaning of the experience is clear" (11–12). Barton's discussion of Jesus' miracles proceeds similarly. First, Barton reminds readers that Jesus "was very reticent about his 'miracles.'" He "did not interpret them in the same way that his followers did, nor attach the same importance to them. He was often reluctant to perform them, and frequently insisted that the individual who had been healed should 'go and tell no man'" (25). Although Barton has expressed his doubts about the orthodox interpretation of Jesus' miracles, he is careful not to place this theological position at the center of his discussion. Later he writes, "The whole problem of his 'miracles' is beyond our arguments, at this distance. We either accept them or reject them according to the makeup of our minds" (33). Whatever we decide (and Barton leaves it up to us), he thinks there is considerable power to shape all of our lives for the better in the stories of the Bible, however interpreted. Like the offerings of the Religious Book Club, Barton came from a liberal Christian perspective, but (also like the Religious Book Club) he framed theological perspectives as matters of consumer choice or personal taste and minimized their consequences for everyday life.

Barton's anti-intellectualism and dismissal of theology gets more pointed in his later books. In discussing the heated debates about which books of the Bible are canonical, which apocryphal, and which just do not make the cut, Barton has little patience: "The mountain range of the bible shades off into foot-hills, and we do not know just where the range begins or ends. But the range is there, towering magnificently above all other literature. Scholars may discuss its measurements and limits; the theologically minded may battle over its 'inspiration.' Let them argue. What the world needs is fewer folk to argue and a whole lot more to read."[75] At base, Barton's aesthetic/theology (they are the same thing) is utilitarian. At the end of *The Book*, Barton argues that the Bible endures because it meets men's and women's spiritual needs, not because of divine origins or the efforts of theologians.

Indeed, he suggests, it survives in spite of the best efforts of its scholarly interpreters.[76]

Barton's 1928 *What Can a Man Believe?* is written entirely as a substitute for the useless theorizing of ministers and theologians. It begins with a letter Barton claims arrived in the mail from a husband, father, and president of a major company asking Barton to write a book for people like him. The fictional letter reads:

> I should like to see a book written which would answer the following questions:
>
> 1. Would the world be better or worse off if it should abolish religion?
> 2. Has the church done more harm than good?
> 3. Of the various religions now extant, which is the best?
> 4. What few simple things, if any, can a business man believe?
> 5. If there is to be a 'faith of the future,' what kind of a faith will it be?
>
> . . .
>
> Consider this letter an order for the first copy. The theologians may shoot you at sunrise, but these questions that I have asked are what we ordinary fellows want to know.[77]

The pulpits, denominational newspapers, and mainstream press are so full of religious controversy, Barton suggests, that ordinary thinking men and women are fed up. They want a clear explanation of a kind of faith that will work for them, not pages of print and hours of arguing over fine points of theology that separate creed from creed, denomination from denomination, which matter little in the practice of everyday life.

The favorable reviews Barton's books did receive hailed him for his pragmatic approach to faith and his eschewing of divisive issues of theology. For example, Harford Powel Jr., in Sunday's *Herald Tribune*, offered *What Can a Man Believe?* his highest praise: "It sweeps away denominations. It throws the modernist and fundamentalist on the same scrap heap." Promotional materials affirmed that *The Man* was being read by both modernist and fundamentalist clergymen and also "by every man and woman who finds practical Christianity inspiring and new ideas invigorating." Such materials quoted supportive reviews from places like the *Des Moines Capital*: "A strikingly beautiful picture of the man Christ. It must enrich the reader's life, whatever his theology."[78]

However, not all distinctions among Christians got tossed out. As was the case for the Religious Book Club, Catholics were poorly served. Because Barton gave short shrift to Jesus' virgin birth, carefully included Jesus' siblings (left out of the Vatican's account of his life), and alleged that Catholics worshipped Mary and utterly neglected Joseph, he got a lot of angry letters from Catholic readers.[79] Many threatened to cancel their subscriptions to the *Woman's Home Companion*, which ran *The Man* in serialization in 1924. Finding newspapers to run *The Book* as a serial was difficult because of fears about alienating Catholic subscribers.[80] Barton's middlebrow America, then, was largely (although not exclusively) white, privileged, and Protestant. In addition, having reminded readers that Jesus and the writers of the Gospels were certainly much less concerned with Jesus' virgin birth (or lack thereof) and with his miracles than many contemporary Christians were, Barton was surprised at how little flak he caught from fundamentalists.[81] The most compelling theory is that fundamentalists had their own probusiness position that made them less likely to condemn this work, even if its liberal theology was readily apparent.[82]

Selling *The Man Nobody Knows*: Individuals and Mass Publics

The presentation of Barton's books as examples of a middlebrow religion based in practice or as texts through which many individuals created a lived religion for a modern, consumer capitalist society should not be seen as in any way opposed to their status as commodities. As an advertising man, Barton took particular interest in the promotion of his own books. Bobbs-Merrill asked Barton's advertising firm to advise them in promoting *The Man* and *The Book*, and Barton pestered them mercilessly about every step of the campaign.[83] He did not like the visual advertising—a Gothic window with the title of the book—since it smacked of the rarefied ecclesiastical atmosphere the book was written against. He noted that *The Man* and *The Book* were number one and number three on the nonfiction bestseller list—a rare occurrence for any author—and suggested this fact be used in future advertising.[84] Letter after letter from business acquaintances are filed by date, thanking Barton for the endless stream of complimentary copies he had Bobbs-Merrill send.[85] Barton also made sure that the editors of twenty-five trade papers—*Iron Age*, *National Petroleum News*, *Hotel Management*, *American Builder*, among others—got copies, since he saw the book as good for business.[86] Could Bobbs-Merrill get a blurb from Charles M. Schwab? Could Dr. Cadman answer a question about the book over the radio? Could they get fundamentalist preacher John Roach Straton to "roast" it?[87] What about a special promotion with the Rotary Club? Could they send copies to Sunday school classes, which might use the book and write a blurb promoting it to other classes, groups, and Bible studies?[88] Barton's inexhaustible self-promotion is, in fact, the main impression a reader of his business correspondence gets.[89]

Sales of *The Man* also illustrate the ways modern mass markets could best be conquered through more traditional, personal relationships often imagined as being in conflict with them. Like Harold Bell Wright's novels, *The Man* sold better in smaller cities—Indianapolis, South Bend, Detroit, Buffalo, Kansas City, Cincinnati, Cleveland, Dayton, and Columbus, in particular. D. L. Chambers of Bobbs-Merrill attributed this to the "determined personal interest" of a single dealer in each city.[90] One mailing that Bobbs-Merrill sent out detailed the special promotional efforts for *The Man* by six particular dealers, arguing that each might serve as a model for the bookseller receiving the flyer. One bookseller sent a copy to twenty local ministers, asking them to return their impressions of the book, "blurbs" from local opinion leaders that were subsequently used in flyers, banners, mailings, and other promotional efforts. The complimentary copies to ministers resulted in several mentions from the pulpit that stimulated sales. Other booksellers detailed their counter and window displays and efforts by clerks who had a personal interest suggesting the book to those seeking a religious title. One bookseller sent copies to all of the Rotary Club members on his mailing list on approval. Fully 60 percent paid to keep their copy.[91]

The efforts of one bookseller in particular, Otto Ulbrich Company of Buffalo, were written up in *Advertising and Selling Fortnightly* and *Publishers Weekly*. Alex Osborn, Barton's business partner at BBD&O, was friends with the owner of the Otto Ulbrich Company, Christopher Grauer, and urged him to make a special effort with his partner's book. Grauer sent advance mailings about *The Man* to all of Ulbrich's credit customers; there were two window displays and a table display inside the store; all of the salespeople "pushed" the book; every customer got a package insert about *The Man*; and there were signs on the delivery wagon. The company took out advertising space in the local newspaper and sent circulars to all of the *Woman's Home Companion* readers in the area, who had been introduced to *The Man* in serialization in 1924. The other component of the plan was a letter campaign aimed at opinion leaders: high school English teachers, bosses and managers who supervised a number of workers who might benefit from the book, clergy, Boy Scout leaders, and Bible class teachers.[92] Osborn wrote about the experience in *Advertising and Selling Fortnightly*, arguing that it worked much better for retailers to come up with a way to market the book and then share it with their colleagues than for decrees about the best way to market coming down from either publishers or advertising executives, who lacked the credibility of those engaged in the day-to-day business of selling books.[93] In this way, the logic of modern advertising deeply affected this campaign. Instead of offering instructions on marketing the book from Bobbs-Merrill or BBD&O (distant authorities), this campaign offered "side-by-side" advertising tips on Otto Ulbrich letterhead. The national mass public introduced to *The Man* encountered this commodity through the efforts of traditional local opinion leaders—teachers, ministers, managers, coaches, and others—easing their transition into mass markets by taking advantage of local friendship and community networks.

Barton's Place in American Culture

Barton offered readers a Jesus who was a personal friend in a world in which people were increasingly imagined as undifferentiated masses or place-holders in bureaucratic structures. His books were accessibly written and intended to have immediate consequences for people's lives. Finally, they offered readers a way to negotiate profound splits in American culture between modernism and fundamentalism, between religion and science, not by answering or settling these controversies, but by reframing religion as a matter of practice rather than belief.

This kind of reading confounds our categories. Paradoxically, these books-as-commodities were both sacred and commercial, and buying them was one way to participate in a transdenominational Christian community. Whatever his political or intellectual limitations, Barton's work was taken up to an unusual degree as lived religion, his theology of practice woven deeply into the fabric of everyday life. One correspondent described her use of Barton's books: "I have given them as presents and loaned them as 'best books' and one of them is usually in the place of honor on my beside reading table.... Those I have are well-worn with constant handling and many re-readings, but I don't think you will be insulted by that fact! I'm afraid the replacement market is nil, however, for those old copies have been with me through storm and stress and are like war-comrades, not to be thrown away in times of peace."[94] Although this letter explicitly invokes the exchange value of books in the marketplace (usually associated with mass publishing and the extensive, cursory reading of many books), it is clear that the correspondent's ways of reading were more akin to the intensive Bible readings of her nine-teenth-century ancestors. Barton's books were commodities, but they were sacred books for many nonetheless. Another reader wrote Barton in 1925 that *The Man* had the place of honor on his bookshelf, "between my Bible and Roy Durstine's book on advertising." Another put it more simply: "You have written the Fifth Gospel."[95]

Barton's blatant commercialism and boosterism for business cheapens the value of his work in our world, where we are accustomed to separat-ing the sacred from the profane, culture from commerce. However, as I argued in Chapter 3, people make their lived religion from the materials their consumer capitalist cultures make available, and Barton's work was both commodity and resource for self-expression, community creation, and the remaking of religious ideologies. The study of lived religion, which emerged in the early 1990s in the United States, resituates the study of Chris-tianity not in creeds or doctrines but in the practices of ordinary people. David Hall argues that one of the many goals of the study of lived religion is to establish the importance of formerly trivialized texts and practices that traditional religion scholarship has ignored or ridiculed.[96] Barton's books—with their immense sales, lack of intellectual heft, and flawed theology—are the perfect site for investigating lived religion. They were (and continue to be) immensely useful to modern Christians in a consumer capitalist world, and they are equally useful to those seeking to write a more representative history of both reading and religion in the United States. Barton's example suggests that much of America enthusiastically read (and continues to read) books that are intellectually suspect and theologically incorrect, because these books provide solutions to the historically specific economic, social, and psychological circumstances in which they find themselves. The next section turns to the best-selling religious self-help books of the 1940s and 1950s, which more explicitly addressed themselves to the problems of ordi-nary Americans.

PART III

America's God and Cold War Religious Reading

FIVE

Pealeism and Its Discontents
Cold War Religion, Intellectuals, and the Middlebrow

The plain fact is that one cannot lose two religions—the traditional one, and the
flamboyant utopianism of the progressive intellectual—without having a bad
conscience about it. It is this bad conscience which, I think, is at the base of
today's "turn towards religion."
—PAUL KECSKEMETI

My problem is not only that I find that there are real things in the world
about which we legitimately can be apprehensive, negative, unhopeful, and even
gloomy from time to time, but that one of the surest causes of such negative
thinking, in me, is Dr. Peale's own kind of "Religion."
—WILLIAM LEE MILLER

Historian William McLoughlin calls the first two decades after World
War II the "Fourth Great Awakening," a religious revival discussed endlessly in the popular press of the day.[1] In 1949, the best-selling fiction
book was Lloyd Douglas's biblical epic, *Big Fisherman*, and three-fifths
of the top nonfiction titles were religious books. In January 1950, nearly
half of the books on the *New York Times* and *New York Herald Tribune*
bestseller lists were religious books.[2] Newspapers battled each other for
ministers who could write advice columns in language accessible to ordinary laypeople. Periodicals of every stripe were increasing their coverage
of religion and selling more copies as a consequence.[3] *Publishers Weekly*
asserted in 1950 that "the phenomenal interest in religious books" was at
one of its all-time highs. Although all kinds of religious texts were selling
well, the most noteworthy were self-help books that promised readers
escape from spiritual emptiness through the fusion of religion and psychology.[4] These titles included Harry Emerson Fosdick's *On Being a Real
Person* (1943), Rabbi Joshua Loth Liebman's *Peace of Mind* (1946), Bishop

Fulton Sheen's *Peace of Soul* (1949), Norman Vincent Peale's *The Power of Positive Thinking* (1952), and Billy Graham's *Peace with God* (1953). This chapter traces a gap between intellectuals and ordinary readers in their ideas about religion and religious reading. I contrast the largely negative critical reception of these religious self-help books with the largely positive, deeply appreciative letters written to their authors by ordinary readers. I argue that these books' significant intellectual failings in no way compromised their usefulness to Americans struggling to navigate an increasingly bureaucratic society and an increasingly anxious international scene. I also survey coverage of the religious revival in the periodical press, paying particular attention to a 1950 "Religion and the Intellectuals" symposium in the highbrow *Partisan Review* and responses to it in mass-market magazines. This, too, illuminates different understandings of reading and religion in the Cold War that were shaped by education and cultural capital. Although intellectual journals and mass-market magazines were at odds about the role of religion in American life, each positioned itself on the side of American individualism. Chapter 6 examines how these texts operated as propaganda for "the American way" at home and abroad, participating in what Alan Nadel calls "containment culture."

The Cult of Reassurance: Religion and Cultural Capital

In a 1955 article for *Life* magazine entitled "Have We a 'New' Religion," Paul Hutchinson, editor of the liberal Protestant periodical *Christian Century*, began by considering class-specific religious practices. "Russell Lynes divides America into high-brows, low-brows and middle-brows," Hutchinson explained. "This renewed attention to religion characterizes all three."[5] Highbrows read (and pretended to understand) the works of Reinhold Niebuhr, Paul Tillich, and Jacques Maritain, among other cultural achievements. Lowbrow "ecstatic sects" that appealed disproportionately to "Negroes, West Indians, and Puerto Ricans" were growing faster than any other group, their storefront congregations encouraging snake handling and speaking in tongues. However, Hutchinson's primary concern was with what he called the "cult of reassurance," which was uniquely middle class and, for that reason, uniquely influential. He explained: "It is a flocking to religion, especially in middle-class circles, for a renewal of confidence and optimism at a time when these are in short supply. It is a turning to the priest for encouragement to believe that, despite everything that has happened in this dismaying century, the world is good, life is good, the human story makes sense and comes out where we want it to come out. Most of us find these things hard to believe these days."[6] Citing the Holocaust and other wartime atrocities, the atomic bomb, and the Cold War balance of terror, Hutchinson argued that fear, insecurity, and despair were running rampant. The "cult of reassurance" was a rejection of this ubiquitous hopelessness. As preached from pulpits and expounded on the pages of best-selling religious self-help titles, it insisted on "positive thinking" and the achievement of peace of mind through relaxation, meditation, and the repetition of scripture and other inspirational texts. Calling the psychologist "our Western tribal medicine man," Hutchinson described the "cult of reassurance" as a rapprochement of sorts between religion and science. It repackaged American faith in the individual and his boundless capacity for achievement in psychological and theological language.[7]

Hutchinson traced the cult's origins back to the 1946 publication of Rabbi Joshua Loth Liebman's best-selling *Peace of Mind* and claimed that every publishing house had been angling for a copycat success ever since. Much of the article profiled Norman Vincent Peale, author of the 1952 *The Power of Positive Thinking*, whom Hutchinson called the "high priest of this cult of reassurance."[8] Although Hutchinson did not name them, some of the other ghosts haunting his article were Fulton Sheen, Billy Graham, and Harry Emerson Fosdick. Other articles made the connection explicit. In a 1955 profile, The *New York Sunday News* put Peale in the company of Sheen and Graham, authors of *Peace of Soul* and *Peace with God*, respectively, whose books similarly promised the alleviation of psychic distress through enlightened religious living.[9]

Hutchinson's *Life* article sought to offer a balanced consideration of this new "cult of reassurance." The rapprochement between psychology and religion was often uneasy. Many psychologists were appalled at the oversimplifications and misleading appropriations of their science by ministers; many ministers were horrified that important religious doctrines were tossed aside by the emphasis on feeling good and accomplishing one's goals with the help of God. Moreover, Hutchinson felt that the effects of the "cult of reassurance" on individuals and the larger society were not yet clear. In its favor, it did bring people back to church and synagogue in record numbers, and it forced religious leaders to attend deliberately to the distressed souls of their members. Undoubtedly, many people were helped out of anxiety, depression, and hopelessness by its promises and techniques. Moreover, the cult helped to keep American optimism alive, which was important, Hutchinson argued, since most of the hope these days seemed to be emanating from Soviet Russia.

However, Hutchinson also invoked Reinhold Niebuhr's idea that all human efforts are necessarily tinctured with failure to raise doubts about the glib, neatly packaged solutions offered by the "cult of reassurance." When the inevitable sorrows and disappointments arose, would people decide that God wasn't doing the trick and flee the churches? What kind of a bastardized religion promised happiness and prosperity but had nothing to say about evil, darkness, and despair?

The Rage of the Intellectuals: Pealeism and Its Discontents

Paul Hutchinson's article in *Life* was among the more measured considerations of these religious self-help books; most were uniformly critical. In 1955, William Lee Miller wrote, in "Some Negative Thinking about Norman Vincent Peale":

> As a result of reading Dr. Peale's one point in every simple, easy book, chapter, and paragraph, I am so full of "confidence-concepts," "faith-attitudes," and "energy-producing thoughts," of "thought-conditioners" and "spirit lifters," of "10 simple workable rules," "8 practical formulas," "7 simple steps," "2 fifteen-minutes formulas," and a "3 point program," of "proven secrets," "true stories," and "actual examples," of "healing words" ("tranquility," "serenity") and "magic words" ("Faith Power Works Wonders"), so adept at "Imagineering" and "mind drainage" (also "grievance-drainage") that I have the Confidence, Faith, Vigor, Belief, Energy, Efficiency, and Power to write an article criticizing Dr. Peale. Believe me, Dr. Peale, without you I never could have done it.[10]

Although his had more wit and style than most, Miller's critique of Peale was typical. Peale's most recent biographer describes reception of his work as characterized by both enthusiastic popular reception and "savage critical attack."[11] Although *Reader's Digest* and small, regional periodicals tended to be quite positive, most of the educated religious elite—university professors, seminarians, theologians—condemned the book. Peale's first biographer referred to the learned backlash against *The Power of Positive Thinking* (which nearly drove Peale to resign his ministry at Marble Collegiate Church) as "the rage of the intellectuals."[12] Although reviewers often took issue with "this new religion of reassurance" or "the peace of mind cult"—offering a few scornful words for Liebman or Sheen—their favorite whipping boy was clearly Peale.[13] In part, this was because Peale was richer and more successful than the others, and because he often stood in for the whole class of writers.

Religious intellectuals had a laundry list of grievances against the "cult of reassurance." The first was that it offered a partial, incomplete, or bastardized version of Christianity. Pealeism was "very nearly blasphemous" and "a parody of religion" and offered "a completely false concept of Christianity."[14] Dr. Liston Pope, dean of Yale Divinity School, argued: "This criticism of the new religion of peace of mind is no theological quibble; it is not to be taken in the spirit of a mild difference of opinion between preachers. The peace of mind cult represents a redefinition of the Christian faith and its central themes."[15] Not only was Peale theologically incorrect; he and his followers were beyond the religious pale, dismissed as a "cult." Others failed to see any connection at all between Pealeism and Christianity. One commentator plaintively asked: "Where, in all the morass of false witness, whether in quests for successful living or in saccharine sentimentality—where are the great, historical central themes, subjects, words of Christianity through the ages? Where are considerations of the Trinity, Incarnation, covenant, atonement, redemption, salvation, sin, offering, judgment, worship, sacrament, sacrifice, communion, and the idea of the Holy?"[16]

The particular offense committed by Peale and his ilk was that they distorted Christian doctrine into an apology for pursuing self-interest. Reinhold Niebuhr put it best: "The basic sin of this new cult is its egocentricity. It puts 'self' instead of the cross at the center of the picture."[17] The result was the "instrumentalization" of religion, its reduction to a means to the end of worldly success. Dr. Franklin Clark Fry, president of the United Lutheran Church in America, admonished, "The true Christian asks 'What does God want to do *through* me?' not 'What can He do *for* me?' "[18]

To a man, these critics were suspicious of how easy Peale's religion was, how free of trials and suffering. One argued that the "Peale products" promised "easy comforts, easy solutions to problems and mysteries that sometimes . . . have no comforts or no solutions at all, in glib, worldly terms." In place of the heart full of gladness Christ offered even in the midst of suffering, believers got a cheap "happiness," and some risked mistaking the latter for the former.[19] Dr. A. Powell Davies of All Souls' Unitarian Church, in Washington, D.C., insisted: "The good life is just not that easy. . . . The kingdom of God was never intended to be a fool's paradise."[20] Others feared not that the religion was too easy, but that Peale's psychology was—that readers who needed serious professional counseling under medical supervision to heal would mistakenly turn to positive thinking instead.[21]

Some finished the indictment about "easy" religion that centered on the self by characterizing Pealeism as guilty of the ultimate in shallow consumerism. In the pages of *Atlantic Monthly*, Curtis Cate described the new figure of the evangelist/author as "a zealous promoter of psychic comfort, a super-salesman of salvation who has revolutionized the traditional methods of propagating piety by learning to peddle faith with all the *élan* of a Madison Avenue advertiser plugging a new barbiturate."[22] Peale's brand of faith was a mass-produced product designed to please consumers. Although Sheen was constrained by Catholic dogma and Graham by his "fundamentalist gospel," Peale freely remade the gospel—unencumbered by theology or religious tradition—to meet his congregants' needs and desires.[23]

In addition to being theologically bankrupt, Peale's books suffered from a profound lack of intellectual heft. One critic explained, "Dr. Peale's rejection of 'negative thinking' may be a rejection of any real thinking at all."[24] Miller, whose sarcastic review serves as an epigraph to this chapter, demonstrated that a Peale text was not so much the development of an intellectual argument as it was an endless repetition of a single assertion. "If you have read one," he explained, "you have read them all." Moreover, since there was no development, the chapters and paragraphs were utterly interchangeable. One could move a chapter from the beginning to the middle or the end with no loss of coherence. Similarly, one could shift a chapter from one book to another. The paragraphs could be shuffled around at will.[25] This was because Peale's book repeated versions of the same scene again and again: "Peale meets Great Man; Peale humbly asks Great Man for his secret (his formula, technique); Great Man tells Peale strikingly Peale-like secret (formula, technique) upon which Peale then expatiates." Moreover, Miller explained, the Great Man was always a businessman or a military leader or a sports hero. There were no thinkers in Peale's books—no authors, artists, professors, or intellectuals.[26]

Critics argued that the effect of the "peace of mind" cult was uncritical support for the status quo. In part, Peale's popularity was due to the utterly unchallenging (and therefore deeply reassuring) nature of his message. Miller explained that Peale "need say nothing that might cut across his hearer's expectations, challenge the adequacy of their goals, or make demands of them."[27] Miller was deeply suspicious of the number of employers who bought *The Power of Positive Thinking* in bulk to give away to

their employees as motivational gifts.[28] The book was said to give salesmen "renewed faith in what they sell and in their organization," without
regard to whether the company or the product warranted this faith. If the
book worked—inspiring the sales force and replacing labor grievances with
inspirational thoughts—profits increased.[29] Peale's books did not ask readers to question whether personal "success" was what the world needed, or
if access to it was equitably and justly available to all. As evidence of the
support Pealeism offered for the status quo, Miller sarcastically noted that
God kept steering Peale to endorse Republican candidates.[30]

Although Peale earned the most invective, critics had similar things to
say about Fosdick, Liebman, Sheen, and Graham. The critique of Fosdick
was that his therapeutic gospel simply acclimated people to prosperous,
comfortable lives. The most famous such critique was made by Reinhold
Niebuhr about an early collection of Fosdick's magazine articles called
Adventurous Religion (1926). Niebuhr argued that Fosdick's religion was
not actually adventurous at all: "It develops within the limits of the age and
does not challenge the age itself."[31] Indeed, critics since have pointed out that
Fosdick's examples were overwhelmingly white, middle- and upper-class,
urban, and northern. His illustrative anecdotes were about servants and
golf and stocks, a worldview that excluded much of the American public.[32]
Donald Meyer called his chapter on Fosdick in his study of mind-cure in
America "The Empty Adventure," since he maintained, with Niebuhr, that
Fosdick's religion was really about making comfortable people comfortable with the world they found themselves in rather than challenging social,
racial, and economic injustices in the world.[33]

Similarly, Andrew Heinze argued that the most vitriolic responses to
Liebman's *Peace of Mind* came from Jewish intellectuals. Some were merely
disdainful of the book's mass cultural status. Irving Kristol, for example,
suggested that Liebman possessed "literary ties to the fraternity of vulgar
journalism."[34] His most important critic, however, was Will Herberg, author
of the 1955 *Protestant-Catholic-Jew*, discussed in the next chapter. Herberg
was a devotee of Niebuhr, and he was deeply influenced by the neo-orthodox
critique of liberalism. Just as Niebuhr had earlier challenged Fosdick on
how complacent his "adventurous religion" really was in the face of social
injustice, Herberg called writers like Liebman a "swarm of cult priests and
panacea-mongers," whose rosy worldview failed to engage the evil in our
fallen world.[35]

Similarly, although it was immensely popular, Graham's *Peace with God*
was not a book that appealed to the religious intelligentsia. Graham claimed

he wrote it "not for the theologians and philosophers but for the man in the streets."[36] Repeated dismissals by scholars and intellectuals, who characterized Graham as an "undereducated zealot," never seemed to cool the ardor ordinary people felt for him, however.[37] Like Niebuhr's dismissal of Fosdick, some critiques of Graham also focused on the complicity of Graham's message with consumer culture. Descriptions of his crusades—carefully orchestrated media and publicity events—also inspired invective like that hurled at Peale. For example, the German press described Graham as "a Hollywood version of John the Baptist" and "a salesman in God's Company." He reportedly "advertise[d] the Bible as if it were toothpaste or chewing gum" and was preoccupied with the size of his commission.[38]

Intellectuals—even those sympathetic to religion—were deeply suspicious of the "cult of reassurance" because it was complicit with consumer capitalism, because it enabled a kind of smug, prosperous complacency, and because it reduced a revolutionary religion that challenged us to build a better world to an easy acceptance of the status quo. Its intellectual limitations were readily apparent in its failure to engage meaningfully with theology and religious tradition and its facile dismissal of the problem of evil. Although much of this critique is probably warranted, to accept it at face value would be to assume that ordinary readers—who bought and read these books in record numbers—were cultural dopes, victims of this vacuous, consumerist message.[39] Readers' letters to these authors suggest otherwise.

The Promises of Middlebrow Religion

These books were unambiguously "middlebrow." This is to say that they sought to make complicated theological and psychological material accessible and engaging to ordinary readers. Indeed, in all the reviews and letters to Fosdick, Liebman, Sheen, Peale, and Graham, the accessibility of their language was repeatedly noted. For example, in letters to Fosdick, readers consistently acknowledged his clarity. "What I like about your books is the simple style in which they wrap up great ideas, so that the average person can, with one reading, tell what you are driving at," explained one. He contrasted Fosdick's clear, accessible presentation with that of Reinhold Niebuhr, whom he and other "ordinary pastors" no longer even tried to read, because Niebuhr's writing was so obscure.[40] Gordon Allport, one of the psychologists Fosdick cited in *On Being a Real Person*, told Fosdick, "We psychologists must learn from you how to make our thought accessible to John and Jane Citizen."[41]

Readers by the thousands also wrote to thank Peale for his simple, accessible directions to finding health, happiness, and success, which had given them a new attitude and transformed their lives.[42] One explained why Peale's sermons did her so much good: "They are not over my head, but down to the ground to help in everyday living."[43] Wrote one reader of *The Power of Positive Thinking*: "I have not read over 10 books in my entire life time and I thank God that this was one of them." He needed this book desperately, he insisted, because there was no other way he could have found God. He pledged to reread the book in order to grasp its "full meaning."[44]

As these letters suggest, many readers (like Bruce Barton's readers in the 1920s) found accessible religious books hard to come by. Indeed, readability was an enduring problem in the field. In a 1950 article in *Publishers Weekly*, one author lamented the dry, dull difficulty of most religious books. The writing, he explained, was "generalities and abstractions." He insisted that C. S. Lewis continued to be immensely popular, because—unlike most theologians or biblical scholars—"he can be read without tears and an anguished struggle to compel voluntary attention."[45] The gratitude of many readers for the accessible, engaging prose of Peale and Fosdick made sense, given how rare it was in religious books.

The "voice" of these writers also enabled what Radway calls "middlebrow personalism." As discussed in Chapters 3 and 4, middlebrow personalism created an emotional connection between the writer and the reader that felt like authentic friendship.[46] In this way, readers of mid-century self-help books were not so different from the readers at the Religious Book Club in the 1920s and 1930s. One of Peale's devoted readers put it simply: "I feel you are my friend. Your broadcasts, books and pamphlets have been a great help to me."[47] Many readers also experienced reading Fosdick's books as a kind of conversation with the famous pastor himself. "I have never met you and have only heard you preach once and yet it seems as though you have been a lifelong friend," explained one minister/reader. "For all that you have shared with me through your many books, I am most grateful."[48] Fosdick cultivated this kind of connection by referring to his personal experience in letters. For example, he repeatedly described his own crisis of faith in college and a nervous breakdown he suffered early in his years at seminary to reassure readers that he understood their difficulties and had felt their pain. "It is entirely a natural and familiar experience that young people, reaching the age of intellectual independence and stimulated by the various courses at a university, should find difficulty with their religion," he reassured one nineteen-year-old college girl who had lost her orthodox faith. "I went through that experience myself and so I understand very well what you are facing."[49]

Liebman's readers, too, repeatedly returned to the idea that they experienced a sense of communion with Liebman, a distinct and caring self, through the reading of his books. Many thanked him for the account of his own changing religious faith, their favorite part of *Peace of Mind*.[50] One magazine profile of Liebman explained: "Thousands reading the book get the feeling that it must have been written expressly for them."[51] Letters testified that this was indeed the case. One reader, struck by the timely appearance of this book in her life at a moment of great emotional need, explained: "Divine inspiration must have guided it into my hands."[52] Describing *Peace of Mind* as a "blessing," another explained, "I feel god has given me a real friend in you."[53] Many became convinced that Liebman was the only one who could assist them with their anxieties and distress and wrote requesting a personal meeting.[54] Again and again, Liebman and his secretaries referred these readers to psychiatrists near their homes or offered an appointment with Liebman's assistant instead.

Not only did *Peace of Mind* engage in a kind of middlebrow personalism that gave readers the sense of real, personal communion between Liebman and themselves, but the book was also greeted with the highest form of middlebrow praise—for its "usefulness."[55] "Beyond all else, it is a useful book," trumpeted one advertisement, "useful to the average man struggling to make something of his inner life, and equally useful to the clergyman and physician for its pioneering into that realm where religion and psychiatry meet." Although several blurbs mentioned Liebman's vast learning and wisdom, most were at pains to point out how accessible and lively the prose was.[56] Advance publicity emphasized that the book offered practical help rather than theory. The *Chicago Tribune* summed it up best: "If you have ever been beset with fears or doubts . . . this book will be tremendously helpful to you."[57]

In a radio interview, Liebman explained that he was shocked by the hundreds of letters from readers insisting that reading his book had changed their lives. Readers read the book in the hospital, after nervous breakdowns, following the death of a child or spouse, in AA meetings, in the aftermath of a divorce, or in the midst of struggles with an abusive spouse. Some received the book as a gift from loved ones during times of trouble.[58] The most compelling parts of *Peace of Mind* were those addressing grief. Readers wrote Liebman about sons they had lost in the war or children who had died in infancy. Some sent marked-up copies of the book or sections of it to friends in mourning.[59] The chapter "Grief's Slow Wisdom" was the most often abridged or digested section of the book. For example, it appeared in a 1947 issue of *Reader's Digest*, and a 1948 feature article in *Look* magazine profiling Liebman was followed by excerpts from it. These chapters may have had particular appeal to women, many of whom had lost sons, husbands, brothers, and fathers in the war.[60]

Scores of postwar Americans were filled with grief over their killed and wounded loved ones, terrified by the continuing hostilities of the Cold War and the nuclear standoff, and overwhelmed by the scale of large corporations and government bureaucracies that robbed them of a sense of agency and control over their own lives. The "cult of reassurance" placed readers *as individuals* at the center of American life and made the case that their happiness and success were the highest good. These writers made this case in accessible, engaging prose that addressed readers' practical daily needs. The claims of religious intellectuals—that these books were blasphemous and/or theologically incorrect, intellectually bankrupt, complicit with consumer capitalism and the status quo—seemed to many beside the point. Whatever their theological, political, and intellectual failings, these books *worked*, making it easier for grief-stricken, overwhelmed, and anxious individuals to navigate daily life with some semblance of equilibrium and grace. This gap between critics and ordinary readers is emblematic of a larger cultural disagreement between intellectuals and the middle class over the appropriate role of religion and reading in American culture, a disagreement carried out in the pages of elite literary journals and mass-market magazines in the 1950s.

Religion and the Intellectuals: *Partisan Review* Weighs In

Inspired by a number of high-profile conversions to Christianity, *Partisan Review* organized a four-month-long symposium called "Religion and the Intellectuals" in 1950. Described as the "house organ of the American intellectual community" in the period after World War II by historian Richard Hofstadter, *Partisan Review* was one of the most influential "little magazines" in history and perhaps the most influential in the post–World War II period.[61] It began as a literary house organ of the New York City John Reed Writers Club with Communist Party funding in 1934. It soon folded but was reborn in 1936 as an independent radical (anti-Stalinist Marxist) journal, with William Phillips and Philip Rahv as editors. Although widely known as the "*Partisan Review* crowd," or simply as "Partisans," regular contributors were called "the New York intellectuals" by the 1960s. Core members of the group, although often bitterly divided over key issues, shared a commitment to anti-Stalinist socialism in the 1930s and anticommunist liberalism by the 1950s.[62] Key figures included Sidney Hook, Meyer Schapiro, Lionel Trilling, Dwight Macdonald, Philip Rahv, Clement Greenberg, Alfred Kazin, Daniel Bell, Irving Howe, Irving Kristol, and Nathan Glazer, most of whom weighed in on the "Religion and the Intellectuals" symposium in 1950.

The New York intellectuals were as close to a self-conscious intelligentsia as the United States ever had.[63] They were apostles of high culture, of modernism, of the European intellectual and cultural tradition, and—above all—of cosmopolitanism. The appeal of Marxism for many was that it transcended race, religion, and nation, applying equally to all.[64] They were mostly rationalist Jews, overwhelmingly second-generation immigrants, and overwhelmingly graduates of City College in New York. They pursued what Alan Wald calls "universalist internationalism," seeking to avoid what they saw as religious and cultural parochialism.[65] They were public intellectuals seeking to transform public life, and they specialized in cultural critique.[66]

The "Religion and the Intellectuals" symposium certainly fulfilled this mission. It ran in four successive numbers in *Partisan Review* in early 1950.[67] The editorial statement introducing the symposium explained that growing numbers of intellectuals were embracing religion, although—as a group— they had been suspicious of it in the recent past. In addition, the idea that religion would wither away in the face of human progress was increasingly challenged by the idea that the survival of Western civilization depended on widespread religious belief. This pressing cultural issue demanded serious consideration, more serious than that offered by the popular press, "with its noisy publicity for the latest conversion of one or another prominent personality" (105). The disdain was mutual. For example, *Saturday Review* subsequently dismissed the *Partisan Review* symposium as intellectual posturing irrelevant to the rising religious fervor of ordinary people.[68]

As the editor, William Barrett, pointed out halfway through the four-month symposium, the positions taken by intellectuals were all over the map—from traditional creedal statements to cranky Marxist assertions that religion was just false consciousness—and they differed from each other in approach, tone, presuppositions, personal beliefs, and experiences (456–57). Five key themes that emerged from the symposium were (1) a debate over whether a religious revival was in progress or whether it was a superficial form of social conformity or false consciousness; (2) a widespread, although not unchallenged, assumption that religion be good *for* something (that is, have social and psychological benefits) rather than being true; (3) that religion was a substitute for faith in reason and science and secular notions of "progress" that had been challenged by recent world events; (4) that, for intellectuals, religion was a kind of authoritarian ideology that undermined their status as free thinkers; and (5) that the revival among intellectuals was intimately enmeshed with ideas about art and literature and that its "literariness" undermined its authenticity.

Unlike most popular magazines of the day, *Partisan Review* debated the existence of a "religious revival." Some contributors were convinced of its authenticity. For example, Paul Tillich (one of the writers *Life* magazine insisted only highbrows read) argued: "That there is a turn toward religion among intellectuals cannot be questioned," citing as evidence recent work by poets, philosophers, playwrights, novelists, and social scientists (254). Paul Kecskemeti summarized the (qualified) sea change in intellectual circles over the last fifty years: "Unmitigated loathing and derision are no longer *de rigueur* when it comes to discussing religious phenomena" (472).

Others argued against attaching such historical significance to the "revival" in progress. William Phillips insisted that it was "restricted to certain literary circles in America" and had little or no effect on the larger culture (480). Newton Arvin called it a "temporary phenomenon" (118). Hannah Arendt thought the current religious fervor was part of a perfectly predictable swing in the history of ideas between supernatural religion and materialism that occurred every twenty years or so (114). Sidney Hook called it "part of the more inclusive movement of irrationalism in modern thought" (226), a movement fueled by folks unable to face harsh Cold War realities without the consolation provided by mystical faith (228).

Others conceded that the revival was real but insisted that it had little to do with religion per se. Robert Graves argued that the revival was social rather than religious, an increase in "mere church-going," proof only of "a national urge to parochial respectability." Genuine religious revival—"old-fashioned prophetic Salvationism"—was restricted to "poor whites and the Negroes" (133), a claim that made a *Saturday Review* columnist livid. Philip Rahv called the revival "perverted historicism" and insisted that the *real* return was to "Tradition," not belief in God (237). Kecskemeti concurred: "It seems to me that nostalgic longing for religion is more characteristic of today's typical intellectual than the possession of religion" (475). Robert Gorham Davis identified this longed-for idealized past specifically—as preindustrial folk culture—and argued that Catholicism was merely its most important carrier (315).

Most striking about the *Partisan Review* symposium were the assumptions underlying it. The editors thought religious belief required rational explanation and justification by its personal and social utility. For example, the editorial statement launching the symposium asked contributors to respond to a number of specific questions about the causes and effects of the religious revival, including, "What has happened to make religion more credible than it formerly was to the modern mind?" and "Is a return to religion necessary in order to counter the new means of social discipline that we all fear: totalitarianism?" (104–5). Although the editors offered a number of explanatory possibilities for rising religious fervor—failure of radical politics, loss of faith in human progress, social breakdown—that religious beliefs might be *true* was not one of them. As with the "cult of reassurance," the reduction of religion to a means to an end was controversial.

Many of the intellectuals contributing to the symposium noticed this materialist bias and called *Partisan Review* to task for it. For example, Alfred Kazin described the questions/prompts for contributors as "loaded with a disdainfully 'sensible' positivism" (232). James Agee discussed the assumptions behind *Partisan Review*'s prompts at length, arguing that conversions were not fueled by rational ideas about religion's historical necessity or utility, but by nonrational faith. "Those whose primary concern with religion is to make it useful are as wide of the mark as those who try to use art for purposes other than its own," he concluded (112–13).

Several contributors urged shifting the burden of proof. W. H. Auden explained that if "naturalism" is assumed to be true, then one must look for nonreligious reasons for embracing Christianity (what the *Partisan Review* editors did), but that if one is a Christian, what requires explaining is the failure of others (and one's earlier, unconverted self) to see the obvious inadequacies of atheistic/agnostic worldviews (120). Jacques Maritain—yet another one of *Life*'s highbrows—summed it up this way: "What needs to be explained is why human beings are *not* always and everywhere intent on the word of God" (323). Others noted that the functionalist mode of speaking about religion characterized not only *Partisan Review* but the newly converted intellectuals themselves. Irving Howe pointed out: "Most of the recent religionists do not ask us to accept God because they are ready to assert that the statement *God exists* is true, but because they feel it might be useful or good to behave as if it were" (470).[69]

Many argued that the revival of religious faith was related to the loss of secular faiths—in science and technology, in radical politics, in human progress. Kecskemeti argued that we were not moving from a lack of religion to an embrace of religion, but from one religion (faith in science and human progress) to another (traditional religious faith). In these terms, progressive intellectuals of the 1930s were much more "religious" than contemporary religious intellectuals, clinging to their utopian faith in the salvific effects of science in spite of a stunning lack of evidence (474). Agee, one of the most passionate defenders of religion in the symposium, argued: "The religious man is aware of his faith; the nonreligious man, as a rule, is unaware. There seems hardly a question which kind of faith is the more childlike" (110).

There was plenty to say about the limits of reason, science, technology, and human progress from intellectuals of every stripe in the symposium. Agee argued that intellectuals who undergo religious conversions were "ripened" by the loss of their (misguided) faith in science. They "have outgrown the still popular delusion that 'science' is potentially omnipotent and omniscient—i.e., is God," and that science will soon provide answers to all our contemporary problems. Agee and Kazin believed that a rationalistic, scientific worldview was directly responsible for the revival of religion by starving individuals of the sustenance their souls required. As Kazin put it: "When man is deprived both of security and emotional wholeness, but is still regarded as a machine, in a world of machines, he will revolt—sometimes to amazing extremes, and even if he is a scientist—to reclaim his marvelous and indestructible belief in himself as a spiritual being" (233).

Alongside science and technology was the other failed alternative to traditional religion: Marxism. Citing the inadequacy of the socialist and liberal philosophies that once functioned as what he called "undogmatic substitutes for religion," Meyer Schapiro insisted that "religion now has its fellow-travelers" (333). Many contributors thought orthodox Christianity was the new Stalinism. Davis bemoaned the reductive thinking that set up only two false intellectual alternatives—"Moscow or Rome, materialistic totalitarianism or medievalism, truth or Truth" (316). Rahv was most critical of the slide from revolutionary politics to traditional religion: "The pity of it is that not a few gifted writers are plunging from one debauch of ideology into another without giving themselves time to sober up. Actually what they need is not more of the same medicine but a dose of skepticism" (241). Disillusioning though Stalinism might be, the solution was not to mindlessly embrace yet another totalizing system but to become a free and independent thinker. Graves concurred: "When a self-styled intellectual . . . deliberately embraces a mediaeval faith in the supernatural, I cannot see that he places himself on any higher intellectual level than his despised and pitied Stalinist counterpart" (137).[70]

Many maintained that being a man of faith and being a clear thinker were mutually exclusive. Arvin insisted that embracing Christian "myths" involved violating one's critical intelligence (118). Davis fumed that the recent converts "have leaped over two centuries of critical thought as if they had never occurred" (316). Graves insisted: "Intellectuals who turn Catholic and submit to Church discipline . . . surrender their critical rights, and cease to be intellectuals" (136).[71] Religion, then, was imagined as something for the weak-minded masses, not for intellectual elites. Schapiro proposed that the religious revival was evidence only of an incomplete socialist revolution. As long as we live under conditions of "authority and fear," he argued, religion will have mass appeal and will be appropriated by unscrupulous authorities to control the populace (331). Religion, then, was just false consciousness. The better road to individual liberty, social justice, and thriving communities was socialism (339).[72]

These condemnations of religion were no surprise. *Partisan Review* regulars had been articulating such sentiments since before World War II. In 1940, Rahv wrote that "socialism and theology turn out to be mortal enemies," and James T. Farrell argued that a "class struggle of the mind between religion and science" was going on. "Catholicism is the oldest and greatest totalitarian movement in history," declared Hook at the opening of one essay. These were all noncontroversial utterances in the *Partisan Review* circle. The church was widely held to play a "reactionary" role in the world.[73]

As many contributors made clear, the de facto religion of *Partisan Review* intellectuals was the unencumbered pursuit of knowledge. After they became convinced that Marxism (even anti-Stalinist Marxism) was a kind of intellectual authoritarianism and not a theory that would ensure universal freedom, their guiding ideology was a commitment to free and independent thought. By the postwar period, most held that intellectual freedom was "a bulwark against absolutism in all of its guises."[74] To subject one's thinking to church discipline, then, was to abdicate one's status as both intellectual and advocate for freedom and democracy.

Structurally, these positions make sense. Between 1870 and 1930, U.S. intellectuals were in the forefront of the struggle for secularism, successfully challenging the Protestant establishment to free universities, the press, science, mental health, and other endeavors from the cultural control of churches.[75] Intellectuals saw their interests as a knowledge class as opposed to religious orthodoxy and the power of religious institutions. First, intellectuals' influence came from cultural capital—education and expertise—rather than religious tradition. Promoting their professional interests and autonomy thus necessarily involved the waning of church influence over ideas.[76] Second, intellectuals conceived of themselves as an alienated avant-garde and cast themselves in the role of prophet, leading efforts toward reform or revolution. At least in nineteenth-century America, the status quo to be challenged was the Protestant establishment.[77] Third, religion stood in the way of establishing ideal speech communities at the center of intellectual life. If intellectuals believed in the free play of ideas and open debate unconstrained by tradition or orthodoxy, religion was clearly the enemy.[78] In addition, the church often involved itself in censorship (a cardinal sin for intellectuals) and in anti-intellectual revivals.[79] Thus, the act of self-definition, of giving birth to oneself as an intellectual, involved opposing religion. As a consequence, religion became associated with "the uncultivated mass of ordinary people" against whom intellectuals defined themselves.[80] This dynamic played out clearly in the war of words between *Partisan Review* and the mass-market magazines that commented on its "Religion and the Intellectuals" symposium in 1950.

Some contributors to the symposium did express hope for the emergence of a different kind of faith, one that did not require abdication of one's reason and intelligence. Two of *Life*'s highbrows, Paul Tillich and Jacques Maritain, offered their own visions. Tillich thought that what was required was a new theology that did not require the rejection of rational thought or scientific truths (256). Maritain sought to create a rapprochement among radical politics, social justice, and traditional religious faith. He argued that atheistic Marxism inevitably ended in totalitarianism and that religion was central to struggles for nationhood and freedom. Moreover, one could not have social justice without faith, since the animating power to fight for the former came from the latter (323–25).

Noting that most of the high-profile recent conversions were American literary figures, *Partisan Review* prompted its contributors to meditate on the relationships among religion, literature, and the arts. Clement Greenberg affirmed that the newly religious were overwhelmingly poets (466). Rahv went so far as to dismiss the whole "so-called religious revival" as "high talk of literary men and journalists about the necessity of returning to traditional Christianity" (240). Many contributors thought it made sense that literary types were the most preoccupied with religion, since poets and artists inhabited the realms of mystery, subjectivity, and imagination.[81]

For the most part, however, the *Partisan Review* intellectuals had nothing but scorn for the literary converts, with the possible exception of T. S. Eliot, to whom many gave a pass.[82] The myth-and-symbol critics came in for particular ridicule. Agee argued that the literary critical turn to "myth" was the way science-minded agnostics sought to reap the aesthetic and literary benefits of religion without troubling themselves to actually believe in anything (112). Similarly, Farrell called the myth-and-symbol literary types "crypto-religious," "the hollowest of the hollow men," and "shoddy apostles of an emptiness which they conceal with cultivated obscurantism" (322). Howe pointed out that God was suspiciously absent from the narratives of the new converts. He explained: "Intellectuals attracted to religion invoke theology, myth, metaphysics and psychoanalysis, but seldom publicly ask or answer the central question facing anyone who professes to faith in the twentieth century: do I, how can I, believe in the existence of God?" (469). Again pointing to the centrality of myth and tradition to the converts, Phillips called the results of religious belief "mainly literary" and charged that this "smacks more of art fetishism than of true belief" (481). Several contributors pointed out that the lives of these new converts were virtually indistinguishable from those of nonbelievers, including their earlier selves.[83]

The confusion of literature/art and religion came in for a great deal of criticism. Davis protested that "art cannot be a substitute for religion," arguing that religion possessed both an institutional character and a claim to truth that art did not (313). Similarly, Phillips insisted that the new religious revival produced "a religious attitude to literature," not a religious literature. This produced neither good religion nor great art (481). Mass-market magazines also took up the question of the proper relationship between art and religion. There was little agreement.

The Novel Goes to Church: The Middlebrow Response

Saturday Review ran a piece of its own at the conclusion of the *Partisan Review* symposium called "The Novel Goes to Church." The author, H.S., was full of disdain for the intellectuals who dismissed the rising church rolls and the popular success of religious books and movies as merely social. How many pages had they filled debating the reality and sincerity of the religious revival, when any idiot could see that faith was clearly on the rise? "The explanation of the growth of a new religious ardor in the United States does not require the investigations of philosophers or intellectuals," he argued. "There can be no doubt that a true religious revival is in progress."[84]

H.S. was furious about the functionalist bias of *Partisan Review*'s editors and many of its contributors. He wrote: "In most of these confusing declarations there appears to be a central lack of belief in any kind of Christian religion which has the power to move the mind, the heart, and the soul of man."[85] H.S.'s irritation aside, it wasn't only the highbrows who thought about religion in functionalist ways. Paul Hutchinson's *Life* magazine article on the middle-class "cult of reassurance" a few years later also assumed that one should embrace religion because of the benefits it provided a believer in this life. Popular religious self-help books—of which Norman Vincent Peale's *The Power of Positive Thinking* was the best example—all talked about guilt, anger, fear and anxiety, grief and depression, and other negative emotions, promising that religious belief would bring peace, contentment, meaning, and energy for daily struggle to this life.

Although he came to different conclusions than most of the *Partisan Review* intellectuals, the *Saturday Review*'s H.S. did agree with them about many of the precipitating factors of the religious revival. The philosophers were wrong, H.S. asserted, when they maintained that humanity possessed the ability to end human suffering through science, education, and technology, and that religion would "wither away" in the face of human progress. He insisted: "When the people became convinced that there was no certain hope in politics or science or academic learning it was inevitable that the moment must come for a return to the Church."[86]

Whereas many *Partisan Review* authors thought it was a tragedy that so many intellectuals were being seduced into unthinking obedience by Catholicism as they had once been seduced by Stalinism, mass-market magazines saw tragedy elsewhere. For example, the *Saturday Evening Post* editorialized in 1950 that "If People Ever Required Religious Faith, It's Now." The editorial characterized as a "major tragedy" the "drift . . . in intellectual and scientific circles . . . away from the basic religious concepts which bind men of all ages and races together." It called for an interfaith resistance movement of ordinary people working to place religion at the center of community life to oppose the increasingly prominent "procedures by which masses of men are 'processed' and 'conditioned' for life in the socialist anthill."[87] If many intellectuals thought the unquestioning embrace of religious orthodoxy put human freedom and dignity at risk, many mass-market magazines thought that it was socialistic, irreligious (they were the same thing in the Cold War context) intellectuals who endangered human freedom and dignity.

H.S., the author of the *Saturday Review* postmortem on the symposium, paid particular attention to the phenomenal growth in sales of religious novels and autobiographies in the late 1940s and early 1950s, imagining the relationship of religion and literature quite differently than *Partisan Review* intellectuals did. The "literariness" of the revival made many *Partisan Review* authors suspicious—that converts were really engaged in "art fetishism," or trying to reap the benefits of engagement with myth and mystery without actually having to believe in anything or substantially transform their lives. Conversely, H.S. described it as a "minor miracle" that hundreds of thousands of readers read these religious books in which writers expressed "their belief in God and hope for salvation." He wrote: "We need more novelists who can believe in Man and God, in the romance and grandeur of the smallest village, in which every individual is a new experiment of the Creator, and in a world in which there is some sense to living."[88] If most intellectuals scorned the new literary converts for having mistaken literature for religion, *Saturday Review* thought that the purpose of literature was to bring hearts and minds closer to God. That is, popular fiction was—quite rightly—propaganda for religion. If the literary converts' religion seemed to be adamantly not about God, but instead about myths and symbols, middlebrow religious fiction was presumed to create meaning and order by representing individuals and the world as products of God's designing hand.

If Cold War periodicals are to be trusted, the rules for thinking/reading about religion differed by class. In intellectual circles, faith in science, human perfectibility, and radical politics had eroded, and religious belief was no longer characterized as part of the problem. Nonetheless, religious belief made one suspect in intellectual circles and compromised one's status as a deep and rational thinker.[89] Mass-market periodicals thought that what America needed was more traditional religion and that it was a tragedy that so many intellectual and scientific leaders were so irreligious. Although many mass-market magazines wrote that the purpose of good books was to instill old-fashioned religious values and morals into readers, intellectuals were suspicious of the "literariness" of the religious revival among intellectuals and faulted those who would confuse religion with literature or art.

That said, there was some common ground between the *Partisan Review* intellectuals, many of whom manifested a great deal of disdain for ordinary people, and the positions taken in the pages of *Life, Saturday Review*, and *Saturday Evening Post*. Both sides increasingly engaged the idea that religion was good, not because it was *true* but because it was *useful* to individuals or societies. Both saw the return to religion as being a result of the failure of widespread secular faiths—in science and technology, in human perfectibility and progress, in radical politics and the "American way." Whatever their different positions, however, they agreed, above all, that the fates of reading and religion were joined. As a 1950 *Publishers Weekly* article put it: "There is among many persons an increasing recognition of the fact that religion has a tremendous stake in keeping the habit of reading alive. For religion depends on the printed word as one of its chief instruments."[90]

Religion and reading were intimately enmeshed in the culture of the Cold War. Not only did religion function as a retreat from Cold War anxieties, but religious thinking and reading effectively became another front in the Cold War. In mass-market magazines, religion was the glue that held American society together. It was what distinguished Americans from their atheistic Soviet opponents and a bulwark that stood between Americans and a society that looked and felt like a "socialist anthill." It insisted on the importance of *individuals*, on the significance "of the smallest village, in which every individual is a new experiment of the Creator."[91] It insisted that individual souls mattered, even amid what President Eisenhower would come to call the "military-industrial complex." In mass-market magazines, religion insisted on the persistence of individual agency and autonomy as the quintessential American virtues.

Although intellectuals were making quite different arguments about religion—that it compromised one's status as a free and independent thinker, that it was a form of intellectual totalitarianism, that it was merely a form of social conformity or false consciousness—they made these arguments in similar terms. Intellectuals claimed the moral high ground in the same way writers for mass-market magazines did—by emphasizing the importance of individual agency and autonomy. Intellectuals rejected religion on the grounds that it robbed citizens of their right to free and independent thought. To reject religion, then, was akin to rejecting totalitarianism and embracing liberty—and what could be more American than that? While these commentators articulate different definitions of what religion is and what it means, they all do so in ways that align themselves with "the American way." If mass-market magazines aligned themselves with God and against the godless communists, intellectuals aligned themselves against totalitarianism by rejecting God. Both saw their position as a way of affirming the sanctity of the individual soul or the individual mind.

This was precisely the rhetorical move at the center of best-selling religious self-help books of the period. God wanted you to have more energy, be less anxious and depressed, and experience love and self-esteem. For postwar Americans—plagued by grief, anxiety, and little sense of control over their daily lives—this privileging of *individual* health and happiness was compelling reading. The "cult of reassurance" placed individual readers at the center of American life and offered them practical, accessible guidance. Intellectuals worried that the religious revival was evidence of a weak-minded retreat from the cold realities of the postwar world and a surrender to the newest form of intellectual totalitarianism, but they, too, were concerned with the freedom and autonomy of *individual* thinkers. Religious intellectuals, committed as they were to faith as a psychological and social necessity, worried that the "cult of reassurance" offered not real religion, but a theologically and psychologically vacuous apology for the status quo that unwitting readers might mistake for the real thing. The danger, then, was that "success"—defined in the most shallow and consumerist of ways— might replace salvation.

"And so what does the Peale phenomenon mean?" asked William Lee Miller at the conclusion of his scathing review of *The Power of Positive Thinking*: "It means that an old, wrong answer to our new American problems is very popular, and that we have a hard choice to make. We are a people accustomed to simplicity and success and unprepared for tragedy, suddenly thrust into mammoth responsibilities in a complex world and a tragic time. In the face of hard and unexpected facts we can rise to a new maturity, or we can turn instead to those who pat us on the head and say it isn't so at all, like the Reverend Doctor Norman Vincent Peale."[92] Having laid out the options in stark contrast—immaturity or a kind of enlightened, Niebuhrian faith tinged with fatalism; meaningful engagement with the tragic world or delusional denial of its evils; hard work to build a better world or easy affirmations to placate us into inertia—Miller left it in his readers' hands. That so many seemed to embrace the "cult of reassurance" with their pocket books and their inadequate minds was cause for deep concern among intellectuals. Moreover, Miller's explicit invocation of "American problems" offers critical clues to how these books functioned at home and abroad. The individual good testified to by readers in their letters to Peale, Fosdick, and Liebman had national and international implications. If Americans were locked into a Cold War with the Soviets over political and economic ideology, happy, well-adjusted Americans were both better prepared for battle and better advertisements for America. I turn to the role of these books as propaganda for "the American way" at home and abroad in the next chapter.

SIX

The Cult of Reassurance

Religion, Therapy, and Containment Culture

Fused together by terrible necessity, religion and psychology now bend
forward, as one, to succor stumbling humanity, to lift it up, anoint its
wounds, and fill its cup to overflowing with the oil of peace.

—RABBI JOSHUA LOTH LIEBMAN

There are many souls stretched out on psychoanalytic couches today
who would be far better off if they brought their consciences to a confessional
box. There are thousands of patients on their backs who would be made
better today if they were on their knees instead.

—BISHOP FULTON SHEEN

In June 1947, a fan wrote to Rabbi Joshua Loth Liebman to express her appreciation for his best-selling religious self-help book, *Peace of Mind*. She wrote:
"It is a masterful accomplishment and I am grateful with all my heart for the
wealth of information you revealed. Through its pages I reached the mountain
top and the realization of His presence. It is the most inspiring book I have
ever read." This fan was an avid and eclectic religious reader. Although raised
a Lutheran, she also read Unity publications and the works of New Thought
leader Emmet Fox. Her hunger for religious knowledge was "insatiable," she
wrote, and she hoped Liebman would send her a list of recommended reading (he did—Harry Emerson Fosdick, philosopher Edgar Brightman, and
Quaker mystic Rufus Jones). She read voraciously, in part because she was
not getting what she needed from church leaders: "Many times I've wondered
about the forces of good and evil and often discussed it with many pastors,
but never received a satisfactory answer." Liebman's book presented new ideas
and provided spiritual insights. She was most grateful, however, for his hon-
esty ("there are some things we don't know and probably won't ever know")
and for his practical advice ("not just verbosity but real aids in living").[1]

She added a lengthy postscript (as long as the letter itself), because she feared she had given Liebman the wrong impression—that she might be "unhappy in my faith" (Missouri Synod Lutheran). She wasn't, but she did offer a list of things she had been taught that she no longer believed—that it was wrong to be a Freemason; that Buddhists, Muslims, and Jews (like Liebman) would go to hell, since only Christians could be saved; that the Bible was inerrant and required no interpretation. Like Liebman's account of his own evolving faith in *Peace of Mind*, her views of God had changed as well.

This letter is representative. There were many "insatiable" religious readers in the aftermath of World War II and the early Cold War years, as discussed in the last chapter. Among the most popular texts were self-help books—like Liebman's *Peace of Mind*—that promised readers escape from spiritual emptiness through the fusion of religion and psychology.[2] The most popular titles included Harry Emerson Fosdick's *On Being a Real Person* (1943), Liebman's *Peace of Mind* (1946), Fulton Sheen's *Peace of Soul* (1949), Norman Vincent Peale's *The Power of Positive Thinking* (1952), and Billy Graham's *Peace with God* (1953). Although Graham and Peale were especially concerned with reaching men, evidence suggests that most readers of these religious self-help books were women, like Liebman's admiring fan.

Like her, their reading (and viewing and listening) habits were ecumenical. More than 30 percent of the mail from listeners to Sheen's radio show, *The Catholic Hour*, was from non-Catholics.[3] Liebman's sermons from Temple Israel in Boston were broadcast to a radio audience of more than a million, approximately 70 or 80 percent of them Christians.[4] The Peale archives include letters from readers testifying to how helpful they found the work of Peale and Fosdick, Peale and Sheen, Peale and Mary Baker Eddy.[5] Even the publishing histories of these books suggest overlapping reading and writing communities. Peale's publisher wrote to Liebman in 1948 to ask if he might be willing to blurb Peale's new book, *Guide to Confident Living*. *Reader's Digest* issued a hardbound volume in 1948 that placed condensed versions of Fosdick's *On Being a Real Person* and Liebman's *Peace of Mind* side-by-side. Peale prevailed on *Reader's Digest* to reissue its original abridgement of Liebman's book in 1962.[6]

The same readers who read Peale's *The Power of Positive Thinking* were also quite likely to watch Catholic Fulton Sheen's prime-time television program, *Life Is Worth Living*, write fan letters to the Jewish Liebman, listen to liberal Protestant Fosdick's sermons on the radio, and/or follow Graham's enormous evangelical Christian revivals through the media. Historian of

American religion Martin Marty described the period after World War II: "A congenial public found it could enjoy the soothing ministries of both Catholic Sheen and Protestant Billy Graham as if there had never been a war between the faiths."[7]

The eclectic religious reading testified to by Liebman's fan was made possible by profound changes in the social institutions of reading during and after World War II.[8] Although members of the Religious Book Club in the 1920s and 1930s were exposed to non-Protestant faiths in a limited way, it was massive wartime media campaigns launched by a private interfaith organization, the National Conference of Christians and Jews, and enabled by U.S. military mobilization that introduced large numbers of ordinary Americans to cross-faith reading. The National Conference of Christians and Jews made the case that victory over fascism required religious tolerance, interfaith dialogue, and an appreciation of Americans' shared spiritual heritage. The civil religion of American democracy was "Judeo-Christian," it argued, a concept revived in the 1930s to describe the common history and scriptures of Christians and Jews and to highlight their shared values that were critical to founding and maintaining American democracy. The National Council of Christians and Jews exposed millions of Americans to books, pamphlets, films, radio programs, and workshops led by a "tolerance trio" of a minister, a priest, and a rabbi that made the case for this civil religion. Millions of Americans—primed by exposure to people of other faiths by wartime dislocations, horror at Nazi anti-Semitic atrocities, and a belief that national unity was necessary for victory—embraced the notion of the United States as a Judeo-Christian country. One key campaign was the 1943–48 Religious Book Week initiative, which created and widely publicized four recommended reading lists—Protestant, Catholic, Jewish, and "Goodwill" (interfaith). It was an immense success. By the 1950s, "Judeo-Christian" was everywhere in public discourse, and ordinary Lutheran laywomen like Liebman's fan were reading—and being transformed by—a book written by a rabbi. American Studies scholar Matthew Hedstrom describes the effect of these wartime interfaith campaigns: "The vast majority of Americans did not cease being Protestants, Catholics, or Jews, of course, nor did a new hybridized religion emerge. But for the first time, in the 1940s middle-class Americans began turning in significant numbers to other faith traditions for inspiration, wisdom, solace, and insight."[9]

This ecumenical consumption of religious media did not compete with church or synagogue attendance; it was an adjunct to institutional religious activity.[10] Liebman's fan reported herself perfectly satisfied with her Missouri Synod Lutheranism, but she read widely in search of enlightenment from any available source. She both faithfully attended Lutheran services and found a book by a rabbi the most inspirational she had ever read. Moreover, she was at pains to demonstrate her respect for Liebman's faith. When she felt her Lutheran beliefs and her extracurricular religious reading were in conflict, she adjusted her beliefs to accommodate the books that were important to her. In this way, she participated in booming postwar religious life as both a member of a historic denomination and an autonomous individual who exercised agency through her religious reading. In claiming her religious tradition and at the same time expressing support and respect for religious freedom and tolerance, she was articulating her identity as an American. Her Lutheranism connected her to her ancestors and differentiated her from the atheistic communists in the Soviet Union. In an era still reeling from the Holocaust, her religious tolerance and ecumenism marked her participation in American freedoms. Moreover, as Americans became more anxiously preoccupied with conformity created by corporate capitalism, mass culture, and burgeoning new suburbs, she could assert her identity as *an individual,* an independent thinker who followed her own conscience, through her eclectic religious reading.

In this chapter, I consider best-selling religious self-help books by Fosdick, Liebman, Sheen, Peale, and Graham in light of what Alan Nadel calls "containment culture." I summarize their common concerns; analyze each major text in turn; examine how they conflated democracy, religion, and capitalism into the "American way of life"; and discuss foreign readers' encounters with these books, which functioned as Cold War propaganda in the developing world.

The Cult of Reassurance and the Triple Melting Pot

These religious self-help books from the 1940s and 1950s came from a variety of different religious perspectives and were at odds with each other on many critical points. Some were explicitly intended as challenges to their wrong-headed predecessors. Nevertheless, they shared a family resemblance. First, all targeted an audience of laypeople rather than ministers, theologians, or psychiatrists.[11] Their intention was to make sometimes dense and complicated psychological and religious ideas accessible and relevant to ordinary people, and they harnessed the machinery of mass production and mass distribution to do so.

Second, all were certain that modern selves suffered from psychological fragmentation. Fosdick argued that mental and emotional health meant being an integrated person, one who "achieves a high degree of unity within himself." Liebman explained that "man is like an omnibus with many little egos jostling each other as the vehicle of life hurtles down the highway." Sheen described modern man as "so dissociated . . . that he sees himself less as a personality than as a battlefield where a civil war rages between a thousand and one conflicting loyalties."[12] The goal of these books was to integrate a person, to organize/hierarchize the many competing selves and agendas under the guidance of a strong ego with the help of God. Fosdick explained, "The primary command of our being is, Get yourself together, and the fundamental sin is to be chaotic and unfocused." Sheen completely conflated the integration of selves and the salvation of souls: "Human beings need to be put together more than they need to be taken apart. Sin divides us against ourselves; absolution restores our unity."[13]

Third, although these books were focused on the anxieties and sorrows of individuals, they were profoundly shaped by World War II and the Cold War. For these writers, the achievement of individuals' psychic wholeness had profound social consequences. For example, consider the prefatory passages below from Liebman's *Peace of Mind* and Sheen's *Peace of Soul*, respectively:

> I have written this book in the conviction that social peace can never be permanently achieved so long as individuals engage in civil war with themselves. I maintain that a co-operative world can never be fashioned by men and women who are corroded by the acids of inner hate, and I believe that our much-heralded "society of security" will remain a Utopian vision so long as the individuals composing that society are desperately insecure, not only economically but emotionally and spiritually.

> Unless souls are saved, nothing is saved; there can be no world peace unless there is soul peace. World wars are only projections of the conflicts waged inside the souls of modern men and women, for nothing happens in the external world that has not first happened within a soul.[14]

The society these books imagined, then, was merely the sum total of the psychologies of its citizens. Although most paid lip service in their prefaces to the impact of social and cultural forces shaping readers' life satisfaction, attention to the structure of social institutions—government, businesses, families, churches, schools, and so on—was almost completely absent.[15]

Finally, all of these books were concerned with the relationship between modern psychology and religion, between health and faith. Whatever position they ultimately took, all promised that religious faith of some variety would bring peace, meaning, and energy for daily struggle to *this* life. Like the editors of *Partisan Review*, these writers maintained that religious faith—whatever else might be said of it—was *useful*.

The presence of so many clergy from every major faith tradition promising 1940s and 1950s Americans relief from psychological distress through religion was noteworthy. It testified to the emergence of what Will Herberg called the "triple melting pot" of Protestant-Catholic-Jew in his 1955 bestseller of the same title. The problem concerning Herberg was the coexistence of mounting religiosity in postwar America with profoundly secular ways of being in the world. The *real* religion of Americans, Herberg insisted, was the "American way of life"—which included belief in things like democracy, free enterprise, self-reliance, progress, and optimism.[16] As a nation of literal and metaphoric third-generation immigrants, America embraced religion as the idiom through which individuals preserved their connection to the past, since most had left behind their nationalities, their languages, their customs, and even their ethnic enclaves in the process of assimilation.[17] Being a Protestant, a Catholic, or a Jew, then, was a way to claim one's heritage, while simultaneously exercising the American right to freedom of religion and differentiating oneself from the atheistic communists who threatened the "American way of life."[18]

However different their denominational backgrounds and theological positions, Fosdick, Liebman, Sheen, Peale, and Graham were often understood by readers and critics to be engaged in the same endeavor, as fellow travelers in what *Life* magazine called the "cult of reassurance." Historian William McLoughlin claimed that the "ecumenical revivalism" of the 1950s placed Sheen, Peale, and Graham together as religious leaders opposing the increasing influence of secular liberalism. Donald Meyer called Fosdick, Liebman, Sheen, and Peale "positive thinkers," trafficking to a greater or lesser degree in a dumbed-down version of religion/psychology that was utterly complicit with consumer capitalism.[19] Reviews in contemporary periodicals, discussed in the last chapter, repeatedly discussed these texts together.

The popularity of all these books—often across faith lines—demonstrated that the "cult of reassurance" imagined specific faiths as different roads to the same destination (that is, American individualism and optimism). In addition to promising Americans of Judeo-Christian faiths the prosperity, happiness, and optimism that were their birthright, these books presented the "American way of life" to foreigners, who received them from missionaries, soldiers, and development programs funded in part by the U.S. government.

These books were part of containment culture at home and abroad. They resolutely focused the attention of American readers on their *individual* health and happiness, rather than on structural inequalities and social injustice. None, for example, suggested that anxiety, depression, and despair might be perfectly rational, healthy responses to poverty, racism, and the threat of nuclear war. Further, they were exported to the developing world as a way of instructing foreigners in American individualism, democratic freedoms, and the happiness citizens reaped from embracing "the American way." In both contexts, these books made *functional* arguments: (1) religion would bring Americans psychological health and wholeness; (2) "the American way"—a mélange of political, economic, and religious principles exported by the United States—would make citizens of developing countries happier than communism ever could.

Fosdick's *On Being a Real Person*: Religion as the Road to Mental Health

Before Billy Graham, Harry Emerson Fosdick (1878–1969) was "America's preacher." Famous for his weekly Sunday evening radio addresses broadcast by NBC on *National Vespers* from 1927 to 1946 and almost fifty popular devotional/self-help books and articles in countless mass-market magazines, Fosdick was the founding minister of the interdenominational Riverside Church in New York, a professor at Union Theological Seminary, and a founding member of the editorial board of the Religious Book Club. Opponents christened him "Modernism's Moses" after he preached a controversial sermon in 1922 called "Shall the Fundamentalists Win," in which he argued for a liberal interpretation of the Bible and acceptance of varying theological viewpoints. His best-selling book was *On Being a Real Person*, which distilled his insights from many years of pastoral counseling into a popular guide to living a healthy, well-adjusted life.[20]

Fosdick defined the central struggle of his life as "the endeavor to be both an intelligent modern and a serious Christian,"[21] and he worked tirelessly to make such a faith accessible to ordinary people. "My vocation was to be an interpreter in modern, popular, understandable terms, of the best that I could find in the Christian tradition," he explained in his autobiography.[22] Consequently, he published in places such as *Harper's*, *Ladies' Home Journal*, *Atlantic Monthly*, *Reader's Digest*, and *Physical Culture*. "I must try to reach people where they are," he insisted.[23]

Fosdick's interest in pastoral counseling dated back to the 1920s, when he announced to his church that he would be available for one-on-one consultations several afternoons a week. He found himself overwhelmed with distressed congregants and utterly unequipped to address their psychological problems. He consulted with a noted psychiatrist, Dr. Thomas W. Salmon, medical director of the National Committee for Mental Hygiene and the former chief psychiatric consultant to the armed forces overseas. Salmon's untimely death quashed their plans to collaborate on a clinic to be affiliated with Fosdick's church. Nonetheless, Fosdick staffed his Riverside Church with a team of psychiatrists, psychologists, and social workers to meet the needs of his distressed congregants. Often called the father of pastoral counseling, Fosdick supported several national disciplinary organizations and advocated for training in the field at seminaries. In his autobiography, he insisted: "I should not put preaching central in my ministry. Personal counseling has been central. My preaching at its best has itself been personal counseling on a group scale."[24]

Advance sales of *On Being a Real Person* were brisk, and it spent weeks competing for the top spot on the nonfiction bestseller list. It ranked fourth in sales for nonfiction books in 1943. Over 300,000 copies sold in hardcover alone. In addition, it was selected as an alternate for the Book-of-the-Month Club, and *Reader's Digest* issued a condensed version, even before Harper & Brothers issued the book itself.[25] The War Department issued a special edition of 50,000 copies for free distribution to the troops.[26]

Unlike his fellow travelers in the "cult of reassurance," Fosdick did not cast himself as an apologist for religion in *On Being a Real Person*. He insisted, "My main purpose in writing this book has not been to present an argument for religious faith."[27] Nonetheless, this was exactly what he did. Fosdick began by defining a healthy personality (a "real person") and exploring how to achieve a mature, integrated identity. He insisted that what makes us uniquely human is that we consciously participate in the unfolding of our potential, that we are in some way "self-creators" (2). Healthy selves are characterized by wholeness rather than fragmentation and inner conflict, and they possess the strength and energy to integrate various social faces, competing desires, social stressors, and personal limitations into a coherent, unified identity. Fosdick was willing to translate from psychological terms ("integration") into religious ones ("salvation") (34), but his emphasis was clearly on mental health.

Most of Fosdick's book was full of secular good sense about maintaining psychological equilibrium. A good life includes self-acceptance, creative and fulfilling work, commitment to important causes or beliefs beyond oneself, the love and companionship of friends and family, commitment to building a better world, healthy exercise, time in nature, good books, and time for play. Nonetheless, he warned against integrating oneself around any or all of these: "When one has granted the worth of such proffered substitutes for religion as faith in friends, in personal possibilities, in creative work, in man's power to build a better world, it still remains true that the hour comes to a man and perhaps to most people when friends die or betray trust, personal possibilities peter out, creative work confronts failure and building a better world seems dubious, and when, lacking religion's basic belief in God and so in life's spiritual source, intrinsic meaning, available resources and worth-while destiny, all values seem in the present precarious and in the future doomed" (131). If Fosdick did not intend to be an apologist for religion, he nonetheless suggested that happy, well-integrated atheists were rare birds, indeed.

Faith not only provided hope, but also the energy necessary to get oneself out of bed in the morning to do that creative and fulfilling work, commit oneself to great causes, and nurture those relationships with family and friends. In chapter 9, "The Principle of Released Power," Fosdick (who sounds remarkably like Norman Vincent Peale here) explained that people need not generate the energy to build fulfilling lives out of their own spiritual resources, but instead need only take it in through an attitude of "hospitable receptivity" to a power greater than their own (216).[28]

At the close of many otherwise quite secular chapters and again in the final chapter, "The Practical Uses of Faith," Fosdick suggested that a mature religious faith was the best or the only foundation for avoiding depression, accepting oneself, quieting one's conscience, finding the energy for daily life, and so on. He believed the "faith faculty" was inborn, and that those without a constructive philosophy of life were more prone to neuroses than believers were. However, this faith was thoroughly commodified. One should have religious faith not because its claims were true, or out of concern for the fate of one's immortal soul, but because it would make one's life less anxious, empty, and sad. Further, Fosdick showed no preference for *which* religious faith one embraced in this text (although he certainly did elsewhere). They were all equally useful for the practical purpose of filling human lives with meaning; one should choose a faith as one made other consumer choices—on the basis of personal preference.

Although he embraced religion (*any* religion) as the road to happiness, part of Fosdick's project in *On Being a Real Person* was to critique orthodox Christianity. He insisted that the old religious model of judgment and condemnation for sin was both bad for mental health and ineffective in changing behavior. Instead, he embraced a medical model—"diagnosis" rather than "denunciation." Fosdick often preached against the limitations of "conscience" for guiding people through life, equating it at some points with the superego.[29] In *On Being a Real Person*, Fosdick described the consciences of many modern individuals as being like stuck car horns, distracting and alarming us way out of proportion to the scale of our offenses, long after confession and restitution had been made (148). This was the source of the "guilt complex," and Fosdick blamed orthodox religion for facilitating this kind of needless suffering.

His early reputation as "Modernism's Moses" aside, Fosdick minimized the importance of theology.[30] Again and again, Fosdick explained in letters, books, and articles that he believed in "abiding stars and changing astronomies," that our ideas about God were conditioned by our social and historical milieu, even if God himself was unchanged.[31] It was to be desired that our theologies would change as our knowledge and circumstances did. There was a huge market for Fosdick's therapeutic message and eschewing of theological debate. When he retired in 1946, *Time* magazine estimated that his books and radio addresses had brought him 125,000 letters a year from grateful readers/listeners.[32] Moreover, Fosdick was soon writing to congratulate a young rabbi, Joshua Loth Liebman, on his own best-selling religious self-help book, *Peace of Mind*, which had been deeply influenced by Fosdick's example.[33]

Mature Religion: Joshua Loth Liebman Reconciles Science and Religion

Of his friend Joshua Loth Liebman, Rabbi William Braude argued: "Had he remained alive, he would have become a kind of Jewish and more intellectual Billy Graham."[34] Liebman was the rabbi of Temple Israel in Boston, where his sermons were broadcast to over 1 million radio listeners across the Northeast. He was also visiting professor of philosophy at Boston University and visiting professor of Jewish philosophy and literature at Andover Newton Theological School, the first Jew to hold a faculty position at a Protestant seminary. He held a Ph.D. from Hebrew Union College in Cincinnati, earned while pursuing studies to be a rabbi, and he spent a year pursuing graduate work at Hebrew University in Jerusalem. He was a Zionist and an outspoken advocate for civil rights. Liebman was also a wildly popular lecturer at colleges, universities, and seminaries.[35] His enduring fame was established through his best-selling self-help book, *Peace of Mind*.

Peace of Mind was published by Simon and Schuster in the spring of 1946, and within three weeks it was a *New York Times* bestseller. According to a

Look profile of Liebman, sales were more than 400 times that of the average book published in the United States, and Liebman's publisher estimated that fully one in five readers wrote to the author. *Peace of Mind* was translated into ten languages. It was a selection of the Religious Book Club and a dividend for the Book-of-the-Month Club.[36] In 1948, when Liebman died at the age of forty-one, *Peace of Mind* was still among the top ten on the nonfiction bestseller list.

In a meet-the-author radio interview, Liebman explained what the success of *Peace of Mind* and the thousands of letters from grateful readers had taught him: "I've had confirmed for me what I earnestly believed when I wrote the book. That major problems are not denominational in nature—there is no sectarian label to a phobia, an anxiety, a grief, a loneliness. . . . Rich and poor, Catholic, Protestant, and Jew are all equally susceptible and equally curable."[37] This sentiment confirmed Liebman's human universalism and his longtime commitment to interfaith ecumenism, a tradition begun at Temple Israel by his predecessor.

Although a follower of Freud, Liebman did not share Freud's antipathy to religion. Like Fosdick, Liebman thought that religion was critical to mental health. Although he conceded that there might be some nonbelievers who were merely wary of unproven knowledge claims, he generally characterized atheism and agnosticism as mental disorders. Nonbelievers were not loved well enough by their parents in early childhood; they suffered from "endocrine disturbances" in adolescence; and they had an "overtly hysterical fear of emotion in adulthood."[38]

More than any other popular religious self-help writer, Liebman set out to reconcile psychoanalysis and religion (any religion), although his examples largely came from Judaism. Liebman's definition of religion was remarkably nonsectarian, although clearly Jewish in its origins. He described it as "the accumulated spiritual wisdom and ethical precepts dating from the time of the earliest Prophets and gradually formulated into a body of tested truth for man's moral guidance and spiritual at-homeness in the universe" (12). Implicit in this definition was the necessity of religion's development over time to meet changing needs. This was the central argument of Liebman's book, and part of his project was imagining what an appropriate religion for the modern world might look like.

Like the Religious Book Club authors in preceding decades, Liebman argued for the reconciliation of science and religion: "Am I being unorthodox when I suggest that it is in the mighty confluence of dynamic psychology and prophetic religion that modern man is most likely to find peace of mind?" (20). Liebman explained that religion as traditionally practiced had left us with "morbid consciences" and "infinite confusions" (20). He was especially critical of the doctrine of original sin. Nor was abandoning religion to embrace a modern, scientific worldview the answer. Like Fosdick, Liebman insisted that religion could offer benefits science could never provide—a sense of purpose, a feeling of connection to God and to others, and the harnessing of individuals' lives to transcendent moral and spiritual projects (13). Skillfully steering a course between the Scylla of unthinking obedience to orthodoxy and the Charybdis of atheistic science, Liebman concluded that secular salvation lay in combining the best insights from religion and psychoanalysis.

The right kind of religion was "mature," a word Liebman used throughout the book. Part of his critique of religion was that much of it was childlike. It assumed that what was expected of us was blind obedience to a Father God, to whom we appealed to have all our needs met. He described the "immature" faith of the majority: "To them the Lord is a master chef at a gigantic fish fry—a cosmic bellhop who should respond to their every summons" (156). He asked if it was not a gain rather than a loss to give up such ridiculous and intellectually untenable ideas.[39] In his concluding chapter, Liebman offered up a reconstructed ten commandments that reiterated the importance of adult faith: "Thou shalt search thy heart for the traces of immaturity and the temptations of childishness. Thou shalt reject all flight from freedom, all escape from maturity, as unworthy of thy person. Thou shalt turn away from all supine reliance upon authority, all solacing slavery to an omnipotent social father. Thou shalt seek together with thy brothers a kingdom of mature equality" (203). Just as individuals outgrew childish ideas about God as their minds developed and grew, societies must also embrace new ideas about God as they matured and progressed. Echoing Fosdick's ideas about enduring stars and changing astronomies, Liebman explained, "Our new idea of God does not mean that God Himself has changed, but that we have changed as we have grown in insight and experience" (168–69). This project of achieving a new, more mature idea of God was an interfaith endeavor, involving Christians and Jews, scholars, professors, and ministers like Fosdick, whom he invoked by name.

Unlike most other religious self-help writers, Liebman made explicit metaphoric connections between subjectivity and social life. For example, he argued that people have an ethical duty to become warm, free, loving, and mature, since their identities shape the larger world. In a section entitled, "Tolerance Is Love," Liebman argued that tolerating others' uniqueness was a way of loving them. Opposing "private imperialism," the desire to make over spouses, children, siblings, and friends into one's own image, he insisted that secure people allow others to be themselves (74). Loving people, he argued, were not "totalitarians within the family circle" (74). He developed the metaphor further, arguing that "*Democracy is the principle of tolerance extended into the sphere of politics*" (78). Because it preserved minority ideas and positions, tolerance was critical to democratic societies.

In urging readers to accept their negative emotions—rage, aggression, and hostility—he made further use of the political analogy: "As mature men and women we should regard our minds as a true democracy where all kinds of emotions and ideas should be given freedom of speech. If in political life we are willing to grant civil liberties to all sorts of parties and programs, should we not be equally willing to grant civil liberty to our innermost thoughts and drives, confident that the more dangerous of them will be outvoted by the decent and creative majority within our minds?" (93). Liebman repeatedly used metaphors likening mental health to a democratic (and American) form of government. In his 1947 radio address, "Peace of Mind," he maintained that "the human mind should be a little democracy with checks and balances between the three branches of our inner government"—the id, ego, and superego.[40] Similarly, in his final article, "The Art of Happiness" published posthumously in *Cosmopolitan* in 1948, Liebman argued that "the goal of familial relationships should be to make the home a little democracy."[41]

Liebman was harnessing widely shared ideas about the superiority of American forms of governance to convince readers that psychoanalysis was all-American, and—therefore—right and effective. In part, he was engaged in redrawing in-group/out-group lines. If the most important cleavage in American religious life was once between Christians and non-Christians, Liebman offered new boundaries between "mature" believers (liberal Christians and Jews whose reason and tolerance make them authentically "American") and immature ones (the conservative or orthodox). The effect of Liebman's *Peace of Mind*, then, was to mainstream liberal Judaism and to suggest that the distinctions between his Jewish and Christian readers were much less important than their shared commitment to American values and their shared anxieties about living in a postwar atomic world. Simon and Schuster furthered this end by trying to avoid marketing *Peace of Mind* as a Jewish book. Although one or two Jews might appear in a list of excerpts from reviews, most of those puffing the book were liberal Protestant clergymen or mental health professionals. Posters and advance publicity called

Liebman "a great and erudite preacher with many years of experience helping people help themselves"—*not* a rabbi.[42]

Historian Andrew Heinze makes the case for Liebman as a *Jewish* thinker, challenging the still-influential misreading of Liebman by Will Herberg (author of the 1955 *Protestant-Catholic-Jew*). In Heinze's telling of it, Herberg's miscasting of Liebman as part of the "cult of reassurance" created a "caricature" that has distorted fifty years of criticism on *Peace of Mind*. The triumph of religious pluralism was apparent in Peale, Sheen, and Liebman preaching to the same highly literate, ecumenical audience. However, this religious pluralism was also a reduction of the great faiths to a shallow common denominator. Heinze insists that Liebman was neither shallow nor committed in any simple way to religious pluralism; he was—first and foremost—a Jew.[43]

Heinze compellingly places Liebman in the intellectual history of Jewish thinking on the self, arguing that he self-consciously participated in *musar*, the Jewish discipline of ethical and moral striving. Moreover, *Peace of Mind* offered a radical critique of orthodox Christianity's notion of original sin, much as Fosdick's *On Being a Real Person* had. Liebman and Fosdick agreed that this kind of guilt caused great psychic damage to humankind, but whereas Fosdick urged the embrace of a medical model, Liebman urged instead the kind of self-acceptance preached by Judaism, which emphasized that men were created in the image of God. In place of anti-Semitic ideas about Judaism as a religion of laws and Christianity as the religion of love, Liebman cast orthodox Christianity as the religion of judgment and shame and preached what Heinze calls "a new Jewish gospel of love" and self-acceptance for everyone. Appropriating William James's notion of "healthy-minded" religion—a religion that gave people hope, energy, and resilience—as his own, Liebman argued that the healthy-minded religion was, in fact, Judaism. Jews, who had survived persecution and genocide, were the models for the resilient psyche necessary to thrive in the modern world.[44]

Heinze is absolutely right to characterize *Peace of Mind* as a Jewish book and place it in Jewish intellectual history. Liebman's colleagues were engaged in the same project in eulogizing him and defending his reputation after his death.[45] Nevertheless, there is significant evidence to suggest that Liebman was widely *misunderstood* or appropriated by rogue readers who *did* read him as part of the "mind-cure" cult. Regardless of Liebman's own goals and intentions, to write a reader-based history of religious reading in America, one must wrestle with popular readings of these books, however misguided they might seem to scholars. Herberg was not the only one to group Liebman with Sheen and Peale; it was a popular move. Many articles in the popular press discussed in the last chapter grouped together Sheen, Liebman, Peale, and sometimes Graham, and indictments of Peale frequently also condemned Sheen and Liebman as lesser offenders. Readers clearly considered these authors to be engaged in the same project, even if they themselves had quite distinct missions, goals, and approaches. Moreover, Liebman's argument for the superiority of Judaism is a functional (middlebrow) argument: Judaism was better, not because it was true, but because it *worked better* (created healthier people). Jews had more resilient psyches because they assumed they were modeled after God rather than marked by original sin. In addition, as Liebman argued in the chapter "Grief's Slow Wisdom," Jewish grieving rituals should be respected, not because they were traditional, but because they *worked*. They were uniquely effective in facilitating the expression and overcoming of grief on a healthy timetable.

Peace of Soul: Bishop Fulton Sheen and the Critique of Psychoanalysis

Unlike Liebman, Fulton Sheen was no friend of psychoanalysis. A *Time* magazine profile in 1952 quoted him insisting that modern-day Pharisees might pray as follows: "I thank Thee, O Lord, that my Freudian adviser has told me that there is no such thing as guilt, that sin is a myth, and that Thou, O Father, art only a projection of my father complex."[46] Sheen (1895–1979) was an erudite scholar and a popular media celebrity. He earned his doctorate in philosophy from the University of Louvain in Belgium, where he was the first American to be awarded the Mercier Prize for the best philosophical work. He taught for twenty-five years at Catholic University. He was the national director of the American wing of the Society for the Propagation of the Faith (Catholicism's international missionary society) from 1958 to 1966, sending millions of dollars to Rome for international missions. He did radio broadcasts for *The Catholic Hour* Sunday evenings from 1930 to 1950. His Emmy-award–winning popular television show, *Life Is Worth Living*, aired for five years, first on the Dumont network (1952–55) and later on ABC (1955–57).[47] Billy Graham called Sheen "one of the greatest preachers of our century."[48]

Sheen was also the author of sixty-six books and sixty-two booklets and pamphlets, in addition to two regular syndicated newspaper columns and numerous articles in secular magazines and newspapers.[49] His most famous book was *Peace of Soul*, which had a long run on the bestseller list and joined its interfaith cousins in promising distressed Americans mental health and wholeness through religion. It spent the first two months of 1950 as number six on the *New York Times* bestseller list, far ahead of Paul Blanshard's anti-Catholic screed, *American Freedom and Catholic Power* (number sixteen). It was the selection of four Catholic book clubs, and it was translated into several foreign languages.[50]

All of this proselytizing on the radio, on television, in the classroom, and in the pages of books and magazines honed Sheen's formidable rhetorical skills. He became famous for winning over challenging, high-profile converts to Catholicism. One *Time* magazine profile included a list: Colonel Horace Mann, who led the character assassination campaign against Al Smith, the 1928 Catholic presidential candidate; Louis Budenz, who—until the day his conversion was made public—was the managing editor of the communist periodical the *Daily Worker*; Heywood Brown, described by *Time* magazine as an "arch-liberal freethinker"; ambassador, writer, and wife of *Time* magazine publisher Henry Luce, Clare Boothe Luce; Henry Ford II; and violinist Fritz Kreisler.[51] The three chapters of *Peace of Soul* on the psychology, theology, and effects of conversion were widely held up as evidence of Sheen's formidable persuasive powers.

Sheen's major message in *Peace of Soul* was that there was a significant difference between Liebman's peace of mind, won through psychoanalysis, and peace of soul, which could only come from God. Starting with the anxious, guilt-ridden souls of modern men, Sheen's tour de force ended up as an amazingly complete justification for Catholic faith. In its opening pages, Sheen described apologetic literature as "about fifty years behind the times," not because it was any less true, but because the men and women who read it were too muddled by the noise and confusion of modern life to take it in.[52] Once upon a time, men elucidated the mind of God through study of the natural world. Modern individuals were no longer interested in natural theology, however; they were utterly and completely taken up with themselves. Sheen explained: "Not the order in the cosmos, but the disorder in themselves; not the visible things of the world, but the invisible frustration, complexes, and anxieties of their own personality—these are modern humanity's starting point when people turn questioningly toward religion" (2). So Sheen, ever the pragmatist, abandoned metaphysics and started with people's anxious, miserable souls instead. No matter, Sheen suggested, because God had created an orderly universe, and rational engagement with any part of that universe would ultimately point to universal principles of faith (7).

Sheen described modern individuals as "jailed by self." Psychoanalysis imagined individuals as captives of their own minds and victims of forces beyond their control (4). Sheen pointed out that the determinism of Freud ("psychological materialism") bore a striking resemblance to the determinism of Marx ("historical materialism"), and that "both deny spiritual freedom" (5–6). Neither Freud nor Marx offered suffering souls what they needed— release from the prisons of their own minds and their own material circumstances. Sheen insisted: "One thing is certain: The modern soul is not going to find peace so long as he remains locked up inside himself, mulling around in the scum and sediment of his unconscious mind, a prey of the unconscious forces whose nature and existence he glorifies. . . . Peace of soul cannot come from the person, any more than the person can lift himself by his own ears. Help must come from without; and it must be not merely human help, but Divine help" (13).

Although Sheen's book was structured like Fosdick's and Liebman's—with chapters on frustration, anxiety, conflicts, guilt and remorse, fear of death, and so on—ultimately he moved through these topics to an accessible, rational exposition of Catholic theology (including the seven deadly sins, the sacraments, why birth control is a sin, and the necessity of confession). Moreover, he was certain that liberals like Fosdick and Liebman had it all wrong. They claimed that orthodox religion's emphasis on sin had left men and women with crippled souls, haunted by "guilt complexes" that called not for condemnation but for acceptance and cure. Conversely, Sheen maintained that guilt was the rightful consequence of sin. People felt guilty because they had done bad things (106). Further, as members of the human family, which had fallen from grace with Adam, everyone participated in original sin. In chapter 5, "Morbidity and the Denial of Guilt," Sheen argued, "There has been no single influence that has done more to prevent man from finding God and rebuilding his character, has done more to lower the moral tone of society than the denial of personal guilt" (67).

While psychoanalysis might quiet our internal turmoil, it could offer no lasting solutions. In chapter 7, "Psychoanalysis and Confession," Sheen argued that psychoanalysis was a secular reinvention of confession and that its popularity was evidence that people required this sacrament much as they required food or water. Confession gave us peace, Sheen insisted, because we entrusted our wrongs to priests, God's designated representatives, who were authorized to instruct us to do penance and assure us of God's forgiveness. Psychoanalysis offered no such lasting relief, since the analyst represented nobody but himself.

Sheen's book also differed from Fosdick's and Liebman's in its emphasis on conversion. Three of the fourteen chapters focused on the psychology, theology, and effect of conversion. If psychoanalysis integrated us into a backward, unjust world, conversion oriented us to the next world, which shrank our petty anxieties and fears about this one down to size (245–46, 275). The only real reason to be anxious was about the fate of our immortal souls, and conversion lifted us above the worries of this world and into that higher realm. But Sheen was careful to list the positive benefits that come from conversion *in this world*. First, conversion oriented us, imposing a natural hierarchy on the confusion of modern life: "The senses are subject to the reason, the reason to faith, and the whole personality to the Will of God" (275). Suddenly, the overwhelming weight of all that fragmented modern knowledge became part of a unified hierarchy of truth. The exhaustion that resulted from living a scattered, meaningless life or from doing battle with our baser instincts lifted, and the convert's energy could "be released to serve a single purpose" (276). As Sheen explained, conversion solved a great many problems of this world: "It makes somebodies out of nobodies by giving them a service of Divine Sonship; it roots out anger, resentments, and hate by overcoming sin; it gives the convert faith in other people, whom he now sees as potential children of God; it improves his health by curing the ills that sprang from a disordered, unhappy, and restless mind; for trials and difficulties, it gives him the aid of Divine power; it brings him at all times a sense of harmony with the universe; it sublimates his passions; it makes him fret less about the spiritual shortcomings of the world because he is engrossed in seeking his own spiritualization; it enables the soul to live in a constant consciousness of God's presence, as the earth, in its flight about the sun carries its own atmosphere with it" (276–77). Although he did concede that conversion made one the target of hate from nonbelievers, the emphasis was clearly on better living through Catholicism. Saint Thomas Aquinas aside, Sheen made clear that conversion simply did a better job at equipping people for modern life than psychoanalysis ever could.

Moreover, all those converted souls would build a better world, Sheen insisted. "The tormented minds of today are not the products of our tormented world. Rather, it is our upset minds that have upset the world," he argued (259). Atomic weapons were not a problem, Sheen continued, people were: "A bomb in the hands of a Francis of Assisi would be less harmful than a pistol in the hand of a thug" (14). Religion trumped politics every time: "In the Divine reckoning, it is Carmelite nuns and Trappist monks who are doing more to save the world than the politicians and the generals.

The alien spirit that preempts civilization can be driven out only by prayers and fasting" (238).

Whereas Fosdick and Liebman thought there was something wrong with religion—that it was "immature" or unsuitable for our time or made us miserable—Sheen was certain that the problem was in ourselves. Whereas Fosdick and Liebman wanted to remake religion for the modern world, Sheen wanted to remake confused modern men and women, so that they could once again see the timeless truth in religion (be "reborn"). Sheen wanted to set the record straight in *Peace of Soul*, to offer to Americans buying religious self-help books by the truckload one that promised them *real* peace, not through newfangled psychological notions and "modernized" religion, but through presenting the eternal truths of Christianity in a new, reader-friendly format.[53]

Although the period from 1947 to 1954 was the high-water mark in Protestant-Catholic hostilities, historians believe that Sheen's popularity marked a turning point in American Catholic history. David O'Brien calls the decade after World War II the "climax of American Catholic history," because it marked the arrival of Catholics into the American cultural mainstream.[54] Herberg maintained that the late 1940s and early 1950s marked the years when the Catholic Church emerged as an unambiguously American institution, leaving behind its immigrant roots and its status as a foreign church.[55] For many critics, then, Sheen was an icon of Catholicism's emergence into mainstream American life, a figure whose emphasis on spiritual freedom in *Peace of Soul* and elsewhere was really an endorsement of the "American way of life."[56]

Based on an analysis of five years of Sheen's television program, *Life Is Worth Living*, Mark Massa challenges this characterization of Sheen as a "positive thinker" and makes the case for Sheen's worldview as Catholic (that is, neo-scholastic or Thomistic) to the core.[57] Sheen's biographer concurs, maintaining that Sheen answered all the modern challenges to Catholic faith with "a brilliant adaptation of St. Thomas' truths."[58] Although Massa is absolutely correct to characterize Sheen as "relentlessly Catholic, Thomistic, and neo-scholastic,"[59] Sheen was repeatedly read or misread (like Liebman) as being part of the "cult of reassurance." Sheen might not have been so simple-minded as Peale, but popular press sources indicate he was not read as a Catholic apologist of the traditional type, but as one of the new interfaith religious media celebrities promising to bring us peace and serenity through the strategic application of religion. A history of religious reading that starts with religious readers must—like those popular readers—understand these books as engaged in the same cultural project. Herberg was right that in some ways Peale, Liebman, and Sheen represent the "triple melting pot" and that they all—at base—endorsed the "American way of life." However, what they provided was not necessarily a dumbed-down or emptied-out brand of religion.[60] That Liebman's was a resolutely Jewish book and Sheen's an orthodox Catholic one in no way changes the fact that they shared a set of assumptions about how religions worked and their necessity for mental health. To embrace a middlebrow way of being in the world religiously (what was religion good *for*?) in no way ruled out also embracing a Catholic or Jewish or evangelical or liberal Protestant way of being in the world. Theological differences aside, popular religious books from whatever faith tradition shared a common set of assumptions about the place of reading and religion in modern life.

God's Salesman: Norman Vincent Peale and the Gender of Positive Thinking

Fosdick felt great personal affection for Norman Vincent Peale (1898–1993), but he maintained that "his harp has only one string."[61] Peale plucked that string with great zeal, turning his ideas about the power of positive thinking into a major media empire. Historian of American religion Sydney Ahlstrom claimed that Peale was as important to the 1950s religious renaissance as George Whitefield had been for the Great Awakening in the 1730s and 1740s.[62] Peale was the minister at Marble Collegiate Church on Fifth Avenue in New York; the founder of the inspirational periodical *Guideposts*; author of a weekly syndicated newspaper column with 10 million readers and an advice column in *Look* magazine; preacher for a weekly radio program with 3 million listeners; co-host of a television show with his wife; a regular writer for *Reader's Digest* and other popular periodicals; and the founder of the nonprofit Foundation for Christian Living. At one point, he even had a line of Hallmark greeting cards.[63] Media profiles characterized him as the "jet propulsion man" for his awe-inspiring schedule of travel, lectures, preaching, and writing. Denominational distinctions were largely meaningless for Peale, who was born and raised a Methodist but spent most of his career preaching for a Reformed church. Although his theology was liberal, his politics were definitely not, and he felt much more at home with the conservative National Association of Evangelicals than he ever did at the liberal National Council of Churches, which sponsored his television and radio shows.[64]

Like Fosdick, Peale was a pioneer in the field of pastoral counseling. Finding that he, too, was in over his head trying to address the psychological ills of his constituents in the 1930s, he turned to psychiatrist Smiley Blanton, a student of Freud, for consultation on his more difficult cases. Blanton and Peale started the Religio-Psychiatric Clinic at Marble Church, where more than twenty mental health professionals were available to address the needs of the city's troubled souls. Peale and Blanton also collaborated on several books early in Peale's career, and Peale raised a great deal of money for one of the earliest professional associations for pastoral counseling, the American Foundation of Religion and Psychiatry.[65]

Peale was a self-declared "missionary to American business."[66] He started a ministry for businessmen at Marble Church and after 1955 spent much less time preaching in churches (including his own) and much more time addressing gatherings of salesmen, Rotary Clubs, and conventions of managers and other business professionals, hoping to spread his message to those who might never darken the door of a church. In 1954, Peale was named one of the "Twelve Best U.S. Salesmen," and he appropriated the epithet of "God's Salesman" as a way of celebrating his zeal for and skill in winning converts.[67] Although his ministry was largely focused on businessmen, and—to a large extent—bankrolled by them, the majority of his audience were lower-middle-class Protestant women.[68]

At the center of Peale's media empire was *The Power of Positive Thinking*, the book that cemented Peale's reputation as the high priest of the "cult of reassurance" and made him rich. "I am not, never was, nor never will be a writer," stated Peale, who ultimately became the author of forty-three books.[69] Explaining that he lacked both scholarly credentials and literary talents, Peale described *The Power of Positive Thinking* as a "practical, direct-action, personal-improvement manual."[70] Aesthetic and intellectual failings aside, it promised to teach the reader simple, specific, scientific techniques for building a happy life with the help of God. Unlike Liebman and Fosdick, Peale did not waste any time arguing for the reconciliation of science and religion. For Peale, Christianity was a science (178). Peale's goal in *The Power of Positive Thinking* was to teach readers that science.

The Power of Positive Thinking spent two and a half years on the *New York Times* bestseller list, a record at the time. A full-page ad that ran in 1955, three years after its initial printing, announced that over 2 million copies had been sold; that there had been twenty-five printings to date; that it had spent a new, all-time record 179 weeks on the *New York Times* bestseller list; and that it had been translated into fourteen languages and serialized in eighty-five newspapers and thirteen national magazines.[71] The various versions of *The Power of Positive Thinking* had sold 15 million copies by the late 1980s, still one of the top-ten self-improvement books of all time.

Peale's *The Power of Positive Thinking* participated in what Elaine Tyler May calls "domestic containment," discouraging subversion inside the United States by privileging the "traditional" nuclear family ideal and the suburban home ownership that came with it.[72] Home ownership gave workers a vested interest in the success of American capitalism, and it required them to buy appliances and cars, which fueled the economy. The ideal of domesticity imagined men as wage slaves and contained women in the home to make consumer purchases and raise the children, who represented the future for this anxious age. The home was a warm, safe, protected haven from the Cold War balance of terror, and (ideally) it preoccupied Americans, shutting out questions about poverty, racism, the nuclear arms race, and social inequality that might undermine faith in "the American way of life."

Alan Nadel argues in *Containment Culture* that the Cold War was "a particularly useful example of the power of large cultural narratives to unify, codify and contain—perhaps intimidate is the best word—the personal narratives of its population."[73] Peale's *The Power of Positive Thinking*, with its resolutely psychological, individualistic worldview, participated in the disciplining of personal narratives.[74] Peale wrote: "Many of us manufacture our own unhappiness. Of course not all unhappiness is self-created, for social conditions are responsible for not a few of our woes. Yet it is a fact that to a large extent by our thoughts and attitudes we distill out of the ingredients of life either happiness or unhappiness for ourselves" (59). Peale did not have much to say about those social conditions, but he had much to say about disciplining our thoughts and attitudes. In seventeen chapters, he offered "scientific" formulas and techniques to feel confident, stop worrying, have constant energy, and get along well with people. Although he offered some helpful instruction on progressive relaxation and meditation techniques, most often he urged the reader to repeat passages of scripture or other affirmations out loud several times a day. One critic described this as "old-fashioned Couéism with organ music."[75]

The book was largely composed of illustrative anecdotes—primarily about down-and-out businessmen who achieve spectacular professional and social success once they embrace Peale's techniques of positive thinking.[76] In Peale's world, individuals succeed not because of education, class privilege, and white skin, but because they fill their minds with positive thoughts—period. They are anxious and fearful not because of the nuclear stand-off and social unrest but because they allow their minds to be filled with negative thoughts. Peale resolutely focused the attention of these organization men on "success"—narrowly defined by social status and income. "The system" in Peale's world was always fair, and so taken for granted that it seemed an unremarkable, unquestioned fact of life.[77] Within the pages of a Peale self-help book, it was impossible to imagine an alternative world. One's goal was to utilize "prayer power" to achieve conventional success in this one.

In one representative anecdote, a salesman, testifying to his colleagues over breakfast at their hotel, pitches the power of positive thinking with the same zeal as he pushes his products. One of the salesmen had just taken some foul-tasting medicine for his nerves, and our hero offers a more effective alternative—the Bible: "This book will do the job, and I really mean it. I suppose you think it strange that I carry a Bible around in my bag, but I don't care who knows it. I am not a bit ashamed of it. I have been carrying this Bible in my bag for the past two years, and I have marked places in it that help keep my mind at peace. It works for me, and I think it can do something for you too. Why not give it a trial?" (20). Salesman that he was, Peale also urged his readers to experiment with new techniques in order to pray more "efficiently" and "profitably" (43).

Historian James Gilbert describes these anecdotes as "stories of regenerated masculinity," since turning to prayer power brought not only this-worldly success, but also new manhood described in heavily gendered language—"growing firmness," "stiffening of resolve," for example.[78] Peale's autobiographical illustration of his own "inferiority complex" was also deeply gendered, detailing his "namby-pamby" boyhood as a skinny minister's son and his longing to be a "hard-boiled fellow" (4). As Gilbert argues, Peale and Billy Graham had particular interest in reaching men—who converted in much smaller numbers than their wives, daughters, and sisters, since the highly emotional process of accepting Jesus as personal savior and submitting to his will in all things cast converts in a "feminine" role.[79]

Just as Peale's anecdotes inspired salesmen to be more content wage slaves, his anecdotes about women inspired them to be better wives/mothers/consumers. In Cold War terms, a beautiful, submissive housewife was a living object lesson about the superiority of capitalism and democracy. During his "kitchen debate" with Soviet premier Nikita Khrushchev in 1959, Vice President Richard Nixon contrasted the beauty and leisure of American housewives with the haggard working women of the Soviet Union, arguing that this was proof positive of the superiority of the "American way." Peale did his best to inspire American women for their role as propagandists in the Cold War.[80]

The few women in *The Power of Positive Thinking* were worried either about finding a husband or about keeping one who had strayed. In both cases, they were sent to "God's beauty parlor," and they emerged having gained a pretty smile and lost their domineering, nagging ways. In the chapter "Try Prayer Power," one woman—whose husband had fallen in love with another woman and asked for a divorce—used Peale's full-proof formula: "(1) PRAYERIZE; (2) PICTURIZE; (3) ACTUALIZE" to reclaim her husband's love and save her marriage. This woman confessed that she was a "careless homemaker" and that she had become "self-centered, sharp-tongued, and nagging," character flaws that no doubt inspired her wayward husband's extramarital adventuring (46). Nonetheless, the couple agreed to put off divorce for ninety days, time the wife put to good use by imagining her wayward husband (who was out with his mistress) at home in his chair reading the newspaper, puttering around the house, and going golfing with her. She was so resolute in her unfailing cultivation of this image that one night he did stay home and read the paper, which was followed by more nights at home and a golf game. At the end of ninety days, he could not imagine living without her. While the contemporary reader might think her time would be better spent picturizing his cheating ass out the door, the lesson was clear. Peale summarized the triumph: "The formula proved a powerful mechanism. She prayerized, she picturized, and the sought-for result was actualized. Prayer power solved her problem and his as well" (48).

Under the heading, "Expect the Best and Get It," Peale gave us another woman—bright, determined, ambitious, but getting on in years—who opened their private consultation by announcing, "I want to get married." Noting that she had reprimanded him for being several minutes late for their appointment, he characterized her severity as a "pretty serious fault." Although he offered a little amateur beauty advice—to make her dress hang better, to wear a whiff of sweet perfume, to do something about her "floaty" hair—he was primarily concerned with the "domineering attitude" manifested in the firm lines on her face. "The average male, I might as well tell you, does not like to be dominated, at least so that he knows it," Peale explained (92).

I spent a week one summer in the Peale archives at Syracuse University reading a small sampling of the more than 2,000 letters per week that readers wrote to Peale.[81] What I learned is that—Peale's overwhelming emphasis on the troubles and salvation of businessmen aside—his readers were over-whelmingly women. His biographer estimates that 90 percent of those writing letters to *Guideposts*, his inspirational periodical, were women, and these large female majorities seem accurate for his general correspondence as well.[82] There were scores of miserable, depressed, anxious, and desperate women in America in the late 1940s and early 1950s, and—on my bad days—it seemed to me that every one of them had written to Peale. They were young and grieving widows; their children had died or were in the hospital; they themselves were bedridden or had suffered nervous breakdowns; they needed housing; their husbands drank and beat them; racism excluded them from the only nearby church; they desperately needed a job to support themselves and their families; they suffered from "inferiority complexes."

One correspondent began her letter: "This morning I was in the depths of despair, contemplating leaving my three children and completely disappearing. This afternoon I turned to your book, and found faith and tools to face life again." This woman's husband had fallen in love with another woman and wanted a divorce. By turns hysterical and despondent, the letter writer finally turned to Peale's *The Power of Positive Thinking*. She read the anecdote about the woman who used prayer power to save her marriage (discussed above) and decided to do the same: "It has been a beautiful day for me. Her husband came back, so will mine."[83]

Not all of Peale's readers were so satisfied, however. A good many—sometimes in the course of asking for prayers or advice—took him to task because they had been praying and thinking resolutely positive thoughts for years but their difficulties had persisted. One correspondent was inspired to write by an article of Peale's in the *Akron Beacon Journal*, which concluded, "Having done all, stand." She wanted to know how this inspirational, pull-yourself-up-by-your-bootstraps-and-persevere advice pertained to her family. Her husband, a dentist, suffered terribly from asthma. Consequently, they had been forced to move to a better climate; he had lost his practice; and they had borrowed money from relatives to survive. A day after his latest discharge from the hospital, he was back at work—still struggling for breath—because her two sons were unemployed and they needed to eat. "Does that mean *for my husband*," she asked "stand—at the dental chair until you drop?" Lest he tell her that they had not been trying hard enough (his standard response to why positive thinking did not work for all), she added, "I want you to know that not once have we lost faith or stopped praying. We do it morning and night and many times through the day."[84]

The scope of these women's problems becomes apparent in the part of the finding aid that lists topics in the "problem files" (Peale's office filed letters by subject under the problem readers wrote to him about). I reproduce the list of subheadings under the category of "spouses" below:

IID Box 35

SPOUSES

Unpleasant Personal Characteristics of Husbands
Jealous Husbands
Cruel, Abusive, Domineering Husbands
Indifferent, Inattentive Husbands
Irresponsible, Shiftless Husbands
Disagreeable, Bad-Tempered, Moody Husbands
Jealous, Discontented, Errant Wives
Misc. Husbands
Flirtatious, Philandering Husbands[85]

Even the letters about jealous, discontented wives are disproportionately from women, writing about their own (often justified) jealousy or about the bad behavior of some other woman.

At the conclusions of many of these letters, I thought to myself that these women did not need Norman Vincent Peale, they needed Betty Friedan. Peace of mind was the least of their problems—what they needed was access to political, economic, and social power. Paradoxically, their powerlessness was precisely why Pealeism had such appeal. In his classic study, Donald Meyer insists that mind-cure—the idea that one could overcome difficulties and achieve health and prosperity through the power of mind alone—had particular appeal to women, especially women of the privileged class.[86] The doctrine of separate spheres had left them without useful work to do and without access to public power. Positive thinking, in this formulation, was a source of (at least symbolic) power for those who lacked it. If you do not have an independent income or social/political influence, the idea that sitting in your home thinking could arrange events to your liking might be a powerful fantasy indeed.

Although *The Power of Positive Thinking* resolutely shaped its readers into organization men and attractive domestic wives, compulsively focusing their attention on their own families, homes, and white-collar success rather than on international affairs, politics, peace, or social justice, there were seams and ruptures in the message that reader letters in the archives make visible. If *The Power of Positive Thinking* invited readers to understand the world in starkly individualistic terms, the fervency with which they had to say their affirmations and the frequency with which they had to repeat them testifies to the power of the social unhappiness, anxiety, and terror they were attempting to conquer.[87]

Billy Graham's *Peace with God*: The Exception That Proves the Rule

In the middle of a sixteen-city tour through New England in 1950, evangelist Billy Graham (1918–) fell ill in Hartford, Connecticut. While he was in bed recovering, a colleague spent several days at his bedside reading to him from Sheen's *Peace of Soul* and Liebman's *Peace of Mind*. Graham became convinced that he should write a book of this type, and in 1953 *Peace with God* appeared.[88] Graham saw to it that President Eisenhower received one of the first copies. As of 1991, it had sold more than 2 million copies and had been translated into thirty-eight languages.[89]

Graham lacked the formal education of Fosdick, Liebman, and Sheen, having attended college at the unaccredited Florida Bible Institute and later graduating from Wheaton College. He began his career as a traveling evangelist for Youth for Christ International but soon struck out on his own to win souls. He came to national attention in 1949 during a Los Angeles revival that received blanket coverage from William Randolph Hearst's publicity machine. He subsequently built the Billy Graham Evangelical Association, which became an international media empire incorporating television and radio programs, films, magazines for clergy and laypeople, a syndicated newspaper column, and countless books written with collaborators or ghost writers. Graham was known not only for the immense crusades he held in cities throughout the world and the conferences and workshops to train missionaries and evangelists for service worldwide, but also for his immense political influence, especially during the Johnson and Nixon years.

Although initially dubious about Graham as the rising star in evangelical circles, Peale ultimately christened him "the greatest living preacher of the Gospel of Jesus Christ."[90] Peale was one of the local New York clergy who supported Graham's New York revival in 1957, and Peale's Marble Church received the largest number of converts.[91] The New York revival allowed Peale and Graham to build some common ground. Peale introduced Graham to the members of the inner circle at the National Association of Evangelicals, and—theological differences aside—they found common cause in their conservative political positions on labor, anticommunism, and containment.[92]

In many ways, Graham—the great conservative revivalist—seems an odd bedfellow for Peale, Fosdick, Liebman, and Sheen, but his name appeared frequently with theirs in contemporary coverage of the "religious revival" in the 1950s. Moreover, Graham's own religious self-help books, *Peace with God* (1953) and *The Secret of Happiness: Jesus' Teaching on Happiness as Expressed in the Beatitudes* (1955), targeted a similar audience. In the latter, Graham described the beatitudes as Jesus' self-help book—"a formula for personal happiness that applied to anyone, no matter what his race, geography, age or circumstance!"[93]

Graham was at pains to distinguish his project from those other volumes in the "cult of reassurance." In a chapter entitled "Search for Happiness," Graham distinguished the peace Jesus offered from the worldly variety: "Not merely a nondescript, so-called peace of mind—but a peace which frees him from all of life's distracting conflicts and frustrations, a peace of soul which permeates his entire being, a peace that operates through the trials and burdens of life."[94] Jesus maintained his equanimity even in the face of death, Graham argued, and that was the kind of peace he promised us as well. Having distinguished his project from Liebman's, Graham went on to distinguish his project from Peale's: "There are others who say that our mental attitude toward life needs to be changed. 'If we *think* right, we *are* right.' To them the problem of evil is a psychological one. 'Think positively,' they say."[95] Pointing out that positive thinking of this sort was all the rage, Graham maintained that it was a doctrine easily appropriated by the greedy and self-seeking. God did not say, "Blessed are they who think happiness thoughts," Graham concluded; instead, He promised, "Blessed are the pure in heart: for they shall see God."[96]

Graham also challenged key points of Fosdick's *On Being a Real Person.* Fosdick was sure the moralizing judgment of religion was not what sinners needed; they needed compassion, psychological diagnosis, and cure. Graham was convinced this was precisely the problem with modern life—people like Fosdick putting sin in a dress. Graham wrote: "We've tried calling sin 'error' or 'mistakes' or 'poor judgment,' but sin itself has stayed the same, no matter how we try to salve our conscience."[97] Moreover, the only solution to sin, sorrow, and death was Jesus Christ, Graham argued. In case anyone had missed the point, he dismissed the Koran, the Vedas, and the holy books of other religions to argue that the Bible "is the only Book that offers man a redemption and points the way out of his dilemmas" (24).

Moreover, all that faith in science that Fosdick, Liebman, and Peale manifested in their works seemed misguided to Graham. For Graham, science was both a blessing and a curse, and it had brought us to the brink of Armageddon with the atomic bomb (16). Although he offered Jesus as the answer, Graham first dwelled at length on sin and suffering: "No matter how we try to salve our conscience, we've known all along that men are still sinners; and the results of sin are still disease, disappointment, disillusionment, despair and death" (21). Peale would have prescribed some "spirit lifters" and castigated Graham for all that negative thinking.

Although Graham claimed not to have written a sectarian book, theology loomed much larger in *Peace with God* than it did in books by Fosdick, Liebman, or Peale. Graham explained, "My object is not to get you to a particular denomination or church—but to get you to a saving knowledge of the Lord Jesus Christ" (7). He tried to avoid controversies that divide Christians from each other, he insisted, but he also refused to compromise the Truth. For example, he explained that the Bible was true in its entirety; it always had been; and it required no amendments, interpretation, or selective reading from us to fit it for the modern world (27–28). Moreover, he dismissed the inevitable progress of humankind as a myth and scoffed at the idea that men could bring about the Kingdom of God here on earth (postmillennialism) (208). In suggesting that Jesus offered us peace, hope, energy, and happiness, Graham was not willing to open the fold to all, even all Christians.

In addition, *Peace with God* was not structured like its fellows. In place of chapters on anxiety, fear, depression, and so on, it was divided into three parts: (1) "The Problem"; (2) "The Solution"; and (3) "The Results." Spiritual malaise was the subject in "The Problem," which called this an "age of anxiety" and maintained that everyone was suffering from the same emptiness and confusion (14). Unlike his fellow travelers in the "cult of reassurance," Graham knew the precise source of our soul-sickness—Satan (19). Graham spent part 2 narrating how Jesus' sacrificial death and resurrection have freed us from all that (much as Sheen spent his final three chapters talking about conversion and its aftermath). Part 3 provided the nuts and bolts of Christian living and the logistics of finding and attending a supportive church. Although he differed on emphasis, Graham's convert sounded remarkably like those businessmen revivified by positive thinking: "There is a new sparkle in your eye. There is a spring in your step. There is a smile on your face. Even your friends notice the change that has taken place in your life. You have now been born again" (140). Although he conceded that psychiatry had helped many people, he insisted that real peace came only from God: "The Bible says: 'He is our peace.'"[98]

Nonetheless, this book, although in many ways the rejection of all that came before, oddly resembles its fellows. It ends with chapter 18, "Peace—At Last," and a listing of all the *this*-worldly benefits converts would reap. Many of these were physical benefits: "Sin and a sense of inner unworthiness impair physical and mental well-being. The sense of physical impurity and physical immorality, the sense of hatred directed toward our fellow man, the awareness of our own inadequacy and frustration and our inability to achieve the goals to which we aspire—these are the real reasons for physical and mental illness. The sense of guilt and sin that natural man carries with himself renders him unfit for the performance of his duties, renders him sick in both mind and body. It was no accident that Jesus combined healing with his preaching and teaching when He was on earth. There is a very real relationship between the life of the spirit and the health of the body and mind" (220–21). However uncompromising he was in his embrace of orthodox Christian theology, Graham had accepted the "cult of reassurance" set of assumptions. In the course of justifying an embrace of evangelicalism, Graham ended by singing the praises of its *this*-worldly benefits. Ultimately, religion was justified because it made us better, healthier, happier, and more energetic. Graham might disagree vehemently with his cohorts on which religion best brought that about, but he accepted the premise that this was what religion was *for*, or at least that if one were to justify religion, one must argue in these terms. Here's what the all-important afterlife did for Christians, for example: "Our sorrows and problems here seem so much less when we have keen anticipation of the future. In a certain sense the Christian has heaven here on earth. He has peace of soul, peace of conscience, and peace with God. In the midst of troubles and difficulties he can smile" (79). The concluding sentence was—of course—about Christ, but it was not about eternal life or eternal damnation. Instead, it was about peace: "In Christ we are relaxed and at peace in the midst of the confusions, bewilderments, and perplexities of this life. The storm rages, but our hearts are at rest. We have found peace—at last!" (222).

In spite of their significant theological and political differences, these writers were engaged in a common project. All embraced the same goal—peace, happiness, energy, and focus for *this* life. Although they differed about which product was the best one, they were united in presenting religion (or particular religions) as a product that could deliver energy, contentment, and success. This orientation was profoundly middlebrow. It imagined religion as a means to an end—as something *useful* to the reader engaged with his/her daily struggles rather than as a transcendent realm that existed outside our daily lives.

A New God Idea for America: Religion and Containment Culture

In the spring of 1958, fifteen public figures were recruited by the Boston Public Library to participate in a new reading campaign called "Celebrities' Choices." Librarians asked which six books readers would choose to save, if all the others were to be destroyed. Such luminaries as first lady Mamie Eisenhower, boxer Gene Tunney, scientist Wernher von Braun, author Thornton Wilder, and FBI chief J. Edgar Hoover answered. Hoover's list included both Peale's *The Power of Positive Thinking* and Liebman's *Peace of Mind*.[99] His selections were no coincidence. The "cult of reassurance," which promised Americans peace of mind, and containment culture, which focused on fighting communism at home and abroad, were intimately enmeshed. In *Containment Culture*, Alan Nadel argues that containment was a privileged cultural narrative that divided the world into two competing camps: (1) those propagating an inextricable combination of capitalism, democracy, and religion; and (2) those dedicated to destroying the "American way of life" (read: atheistic, totalitarian communists).[100] Many of these religious self-help writers were dedicated anticommunists, and their books propagandized for capitalism/ democracy/God.

For example, Billy Graham was christened "Communism's Public Enemy Number One" by the *Chicago Daily News* in 1955.[101] The first printed sermon he mailed out to listeners of his radio program, *Hour of Decision*, in 1951 was called "Christianity versus Communism." In another sermon about communism, "Satan's Religion," from 1953, he characterized the struggle between Christianity and communism as a "battle to the death" and described Marx and Lenin as "disciples of Lucifer."[102] In the concluding chapter of *Peace with God*, Graham called communism "the greatest, most well-organized and outspoken foe of Christianity that the church has confronted since the days of pagan Rome!" and suggested that it might be the Antichrist foretold in ancient prophecies (215). Moreover, religiosity, anticommunism, and "Americanism" were almost always conflated for Graham in the 1950s and 1960s.[103] Although he hated the label, Graham was known as the "High Priest of the American Civil Religion" during the Johnson and Nixon years for a reason.[104] For example, throughout *Peace with God*, Graham metaphorically linked God and America. The Bible is like the Constitution, applying equally to all: "Just as America has grown and prospered within the framework of our Constitution, so Christianity has flourished and spread according to laws set forth in the Bible" (26–27). The difference here was that the Bible never required amendment, for its authors were inspired by the Holy Spirit. Graham even explained the doctrine of original sin by analogy to the U.S. presidency: "We forget that Adam was the head of the human race, even as in this country our President is the head of our government. When the President acts, it is really the American people acting through him. When the President makes a decision, that decision stands as a decision of the entire people. Adam stands as the federal head of the human race. When he failed, when he succumbed to temptation and fell, the generations yet unborn fell with him" (46). This rhetorical strategy both made Christian doctrine comprehensible to American readers and sanctified American ways of life. In Graham's telling of it, to lack patriotism was unchristian; to reject Christianity was un-American. Moreover, political subversion at home came from a lack of religiosity. Graham insisted, "Fascism and Communism can find no place in the heart and soul of a person who is filled with the Spirit of God, but it floods with the greatest ease into the minds and hearts of those who are empty and waiting" (18). In this way, saving souls for Jesus and defeating the communist menace were the same battle. Every soul converted to Jesus was also converted to Americanism and free-market capitalism. Moreover, the battle between the United States and the Soviet Union for the hearts and minds of the developing world had everything to do with Christianity. Graham explained in *Secret of Happiness* that "the reason Communism is making such inroads in the world today is that somewhere along the line the people who were supposed to live Christian lives failed."[105]

Peale, too, spilled a lot of ink on the evils of communism. For example, although *The Power of Positive Thinking* made very few references to 1950s society and politics, Peale did make one overt reference to communism.

> It is important to eliminate from conversations all negative ideas, for they tend to produce tension and annoyance inwardly. For example, when you are with a group of people at luncheon, do not comment that the "Communists will soon take over the country." In the first place, Communists are not going to take over the country, and by so asserting you create a depression reaction in the minds of others. It undoubtedly affects digestion adversely. The depressing remark colors the attitude of all present, and everyone goes away with a perhaps slight but definite feeling of annoyance. They also carry away with then [sic] a mild but definite feeling that something is wrong

with everything. There are times when we must face these harsh questions and deal with them objectively and vigorously, and no one has more contempt for Communism than I have, but as a general thing to have peace of mind, fill your personal and group conversations with positive, happy, optimistic, satisfying expressions. (22–23)

Although he did not like to dwell on it, Peale was, in fact, a dedicated anticommunist. For example, he authored a *Reader's Digest* article called "Let the Church Speak Up for Capitalism" in the 1950s.[106] Peale was involved in a great many right-leaning political groups, advocating for patriotism, anticommunism, laissez-faire economics, and family values. Although he imagined his inspirational magazine *Guideposts* as apolitical, he described it as "an inoculation" against communism or socialism and insisted that it would "refertilize the soil of American life by widely spreading religious ideas, [so] we can counteract the communistic virus . . . and defeat left-wing influences such as Communism."[107]

In addition to his role as celebrity apologist for the Catholic Church, Fulton Sheen was what historian Donald Crosby called the "prophet and philosopher of American Catholic anticommunism," a struggle in which he had engaged since the 1930s. In addition to many newspaper columns and radio and television addresses on the topic, Sheen was the author of *Freedom under God* (1940) and *Communism and the Conscience of the West* (1948) and one of three religious leaders who consulted on a House Un-American Activities Committee report called *Ideological Fallacies of Communism*.[108] Historically, communist governments had suppressed the Catholic Church, often engaging in the persecution of priests and nuns. Moreover, the battle against communism was useful to the American Catholic Church, because it united Catholics across ethnic divisions and it cast them as "real Americans." Anti-Catholicism of the day maintained that the Catholic Church was a "foreign" influence made up largely of immigrants and governed by a totalitarian ecclesiastical government in Rome. Sheen was so sensitive to the charge that Catholics were un-American that he spent several pages in *Peace of Soul* explaining how obedience to the Catholic Church was fundamentally different from obedience to a totalitarian state and that the church was not teaching its adherents fascist or undemocratic ways of being in the world (271–74).

Sheen's particular gift was his exhaustive knowledge of communism. He had read all of Marx, Lenin, and Stalin and could cite the Soviet constitution better than many of the communists he converted.[109] Although he made dozens of high-profile conversions, Sheen seemed most pleased to narrate how he returned Louis Budenz, managing editor of the communist *Daily Worker*, to the Catholic fold. Sheen was a "Special Service Contact" for the FBI in the 1950s and 1960s, where he frequently gave lectures. He exchanged warm, personal letters on several occasions with J. Edgar Hoover, and the FBI investigated the loyalty of potential converts for him.[110] Sheen was widely celebrated for his patriotism. The American Legion of New York awarded him its gold medal for "exemplary work on behalf of Americanism," and the University of Notre Dame awarded him its second annual Patriot Award, which recognized "an outstanding patriot who exemplified the American ideals of justice, personal integrity, and service to country," the year after J. Edgar Hoover was awarded the inaugural prize.[111]

A 1955 profile of Sheen in *Time* magazine described him as the "product of two unique historic forces"—the Catholic Church and America. The article spun out the surprising juxtapositions: "Into the making of Fulton Sheen went Saint Paul and Thomas Jefferson, Savonarola and George F. Babbitt."[112] For Sheen, however, the two were almost indistinguishable. His biographer explained, "American democracy and Catholic Christianity were virtually one to Sheen."[113] In his 1940 *Freedom under God*, Sheen argued that "Americanism is the political expression of the Catholic doctrine concerning man," citing in particular the idea that rights came from God and that both the gospel and the Declaration of Independence affirmed the dignity of man.[114]

Liebman similarly conflated religiosity and Americanism, going so far as to propose a "New God Idea for America."[115] His distinction between mature and immature religion, discussed above, mapped onto the distinction between democratic and totalitarian regimes. A democratic state required citizens who were prepared by liberal faith for rational participation in civic life. "Immature" religion—religion that asked blind obedience to God—formed subjects prepared instead to obey a dictator. Liebman's goal was to replace the immature "feudal" God with one more suitable to modern American life, a God who wanted "mature partners" in building a brave new world. He insisted: "There is a chance here in America for the creation of a new idea of God. . . . The church and the synagogue alike can, if they will, help men everywhere to resist the economic and political slavery threatening to engulf human dignity and freedom, by teaching belief in a God who wants co-operation, not submission; partnership, not surrender."[116] Only the experience of participatory democracy would fit us for our joint venture with God, and this experience of democracy was uniquely American. Liebman's hope, however, was that these American democratic ideals would remake the world. In a 1948 *Ladies' Home Journal* essay called "Hope for Human Brotherhood," Liebman argued that American "national psychology" was uniquely equipped for peace and brotherhood, and thus Americans could lead the entire world away from violence and ancient hatreds.[117] Hedstrom characterizes this aspect of Liebman's work as "a kind of psychic and spiritual Marshall Plan for a war-torn world."[118]

Only Fosdick was a less-than-enthusiastic Cold Warrior. In chapter 10 of his autobiography, "Ideas That Have Used Me," Fosdick wrote at length about the challenges presented by communism. He warned that the reactionary nature of some hard-line anticommunists obscured the idea that the world needed progressive social change and that Americans had represented the promise of democracy, equality, and freedom long before the communists arrived on the scene. He explained: "I certainly am anticommunist—anti its totalitarianism, its atheism, its Marxism—but I am also sure that the only way to beat the communists is to match and surpass them in proclaiming a new day for the world's common people."[119] Nonetheless, reviews repeatedly ran together patriotism and the psychological wholeness for which Fosdick proselytized. One urged: "High on your reading list, if you would become a real person, a real American, [should be] Fosdick's 'On Being a Real Person.'"[120] Further, letters from soldiers and sailors serving at home and abroad testify to the role of Fosdick's books in preparing and sustaining them for battle against fascism and (later) communism.[121] Finally, *On Being a Real Person* was selected for an Armed Forces Edition by the Council on Books in Wartime, a consortium of large publishing houses that produced roughly 100 million cheap paperbacks for the troops. Their motto was "Books Are Weapons in the War of Ideas," and Fosdick's *On Being a Real Person* was deemed worthy for battle.[122]

It is no coincidence that so many religious self-help book writers were also Cold Warriors. These books were not just tracts promising happiness to anxious Americans; they were also propaganda for "the American way," both inside and outside the country. Therapeutic culture and containment were intimately enmeshed, and those books promising peace of mind to distressed Americans were also selling America to readers abroad.

Exporting the American Way: The Cult of Reassurance and the Developing World

In addition to promising Americans of Judeo-Christian faiths the prosperity, happiness, and optimism that were their birthright, these books were weapons in the contest with the Soviets for the hearts and minds of readers in the developing world. Peale's *The Power of Positive Thinking* was translated into fourteen languages, including Afrikaans, Indonesian, Arabic, and Japanese. Liebman's *Peace of Mind* was available in ten foreign languages; Graham's *Peace with God* was translated into thirty-eight languages. Fosdick's *The Meaning of Prayer* and *The Manhood of the Master* were translated into fifteen and eighteen languages, respectively. *On Being a Real Person* was translated into Arabic, Persian, Urdu, Bengali, and Indonesian with U.S. government funding.[123]

Letters from readers testified to the international prominence of these books. For example, one reader wrote to Peale's publisher about her experience in two bookshops in South Africa, neither of which could keep *The Power of Positive Thinking* in stock.[124] Alexander Haraszti, a Hungarian Baptist who later became the point man for Graham's crusades in eastern Europe, encountered Graham's work in the mid-1950s from typewritten pages passed from person to person underground. In 1955, he got his hands on an English copy of *Peace with God* and a German translation and began translating Graham's work into Hungarian. Sure that he would be denied government permission to publish the book, he instead distributed mimeographed copies of the translation to his students at the Baptist seminary in Budapest, offering the chapters as examples of sermons to emulate. His bootlegged translation circulated in Lutheran, Reformed, and Roman Catholic seminaries in Hungary in this way.[125] At his crusade in Moscow in 1982, Graham discovered that almost half of his audience had read *Peace with God*, although most had access only to hand-copied or mimeographed versions, which circulated outside official publishing and bookselling networks.[126]

In Graham's authorized biography, there are stories from all over the world about people who came to Christ through reading *Peace with God*. For example, many Christians in the Indian state of Nagaland (whose intertribal lingua franca was English) read *Peace with God* and listened to Graham's *Hour of Decision* over short-wave radios from Manila. At his Irish crusade in 1972, one of the Catholic priests who chaired the local crusade committee told an overflow audience that he found Christ after reading *Peace with God*. The president of the Supreme Court of Cambodia converted from Buddhism to Christianity after reading *Peace with God*.[127]

Fosdick—who in his boyhood dreamed of becoming a foreign missionary—became a virtual missionary through the circulation of his books abroad, and he was especially appreciative of letters written from the mission field thanking him for his work.[128] In Fosdick's archived correspondence, his texts were inevitably portrayed as useful to people of many faith traditions, because they avoided theological controversy in favor of practical attention to the needs of ordinary people and because they presented contemporary examples in accessible language.

For example, a missionary in Cairo, Egypt, wrote to Fosdick about a young Muslim man who came to him desiring guidance in leading a Christian life. The missionary described most of the books available in Arabic as "hopelessly theological and antiquated," but he gave the boy a copy of Fosdick's *The Meaning of Prayer* to begin his faith journey. The boy returned several times to tell the missionary how helpful the book was and to acquire two more copies to give to his Muslim friends. The missionary had given away copies to Jews and Christians as well. "They are unanimous in their testimony to its usefulness," he concluded.[129]

Although sometimes, as in the case above, these texts were tools for converting people of other faiths, more often they were sites for interfaith dialogue. Another correspondent passed along a story from a missionary woman in India, who had been talking about Christianity with an Indian man she described as "a high caste Hindu, well educated and as keen as a razor." She had loaned him many books, but he usually returned them—unfinished—because the English was too difficult or he was bored. Fosdick's *The Meaning of Prayer* changed all that. He came back to her, clutching the book to his chest, to implore her to let him keep it: "You have given me a great many good books but this is the only one you have given me that I want to keep forever. I want just this copy. I have read and read it, and find so much for me and my family in it, that you must let me keep it for good."[130] In this account, an educated Hindu pleaded with a Christian missionary to let him keep a cheap, borrowed paperback of one of Fosdick's most popular and accessible works. The book did not convince him to become a Christian, but it did inspire him to work toward a better life for himself and his family. Although a great reader, he had never before even finished a book, because they were all frightfully dull or full of difficult language or both. Fosdick's book, then, promised him spiritual guidance in accessible, nonexclusive terms.

Letters detailed other similar scenes. In 1946, one teacher's letter cast Fosdick's work as a compelling site for interfaith dialogue:

Both in India and in Egypt I found your books amazingly helpful
in my work with non-Christian as well as Christian students. I shall

never forget using "The Meaning of Prayer" with a group which included three Mohammedans, three Hindus, two Budhists [*sic*], a Parsee and one Christian (myself). For two college years this group met in a student's room and studied together. Twenty years later, the organizer, a Mohammedan—now a professor in Bombay University, visited me in Cairo and recalled the group meetings and testified to the contribution to his conception of God which that book had made. He is still a Moslem, but the story of his development, the development of the thirteen year old illiterate girl he married and their joint effort to be of service to their students on the campus in Poona made me realize how deeply he had been influenced.[131]

In this account, the process of reading, studying, and discussing Fosdick's work converted no one but did enrich and deepen the experience of all faiths. If the students did not hold the same creeds, they could nonetheless agree on admirable ways of acting on their beliefs. This letter engaged what Christina Klein calls "Cold War Orientalism." She explains that middlebrow intellectuals sought to distinguish themselves from imperialists. They repudiated military conquest, colonization, and religious conversion, instead imagining American global influence in terms of reciprocal, voluntary exchange.[132] The letter writer suggested that these exchanges involved face-to-face conversations across racial and religious lines, but they could also be facilitated by strategic use of the right kind of printed materials.

Of course, such letters present a maddeningly vague and incomplete picture of cultural and religious exchange. These representations came from American missionaries and teachers, not from the Buddhists, Muslims, and Hindus they encountered. Maybe the Muslim boy was reselling Fosdick's books on the black market. Maybe the Indian gentleman bragged to his friends about having scammed a personal copy of Fosdick's work from a naive missionary woman. Maybe the college students came to the study group not for the reading and discussion, but for the snacks. Nevertheless, the frequency and the similarity of these accounts (such letters appear from the 1920s through the 1950s) suggest that "positive thinking" was not just about the commodification of religion at home, but was also a necessary part of remaking American identities for the global, decolonizing world.

The fantasy at the center of these accounts was similar. The Muslims, Buddhists, or Hindus never appeared as poor benighted savages in need of redemption by missionaries bearing the word of God. The woman missionary in India encountered a "high caste Hindu, well educated, and sharp as a razor." The gentleman engaged in interfaith reading was part of a college study group learning together in a dorm room at night. Nor were the natives passive recipients of Western/American/Christian knowledge. These narratives cast them as shoppers—and choosy ones at that. The Muslim boy was so satisfied by the Fosdick product (so useful!) that he returned to "buy" two more copies for his friends. The high-caste Hindu returned one lousy product after another for being dull or difficult—but he wanted to keep the Fosdick book, which finally satisfied his consumer desires (so helpful to him and his family!). Each narrative prominently featured Muslims, Hindus, or people of other faiths engaging in a voluntary, mutually beneficial exchange with American/Christian missionaries. They were willing customers, so to speak, for the American/Western/Christian merchants.

This relationship of exchange has historically been gendered. Men produced and advertised products, and women consumed these products for their families. Successful commerce depended on advertising men "wooing" women shoppers by attractively presenting the wares.[133] In these narratives, Fosdick's book was the right kind of merchandise—useful, accessibly written, not overly theological—to entice choosy, independent-minded natives (maybe not so smart as we, maybe much less rational and more impulsive) to buy these products. Melani McAlister suggests that the biblical epic films of the 1950s imagined the relationship between the United States and developing nations of the world like a marriage. Rather than succumbing to coercion, Third World nations—like good wives—would voluntarily subordinate themselves to the United States in exchange for foreign aid and military protection.[134] Similarly, these narratives from missionaries cast America and Americans as masculine and the natives as feminine, willingly subordinating themselves to American wares/ways with words in order to reap benefits for themselves. They were not coerced into becoming American, however (these were not narratives of imperialism). In most of these narratives, the natives kept their indigenous religious identities but were "made over" into acceptable partners through their embrace of these quintessentially American books and their participation in a quintessentially American voluntary exchange. These American books were products the natives wanted, not the propaganda of colonial overlords engaged in acts of real and symbolic violence.

These narratives of cross-cultural understanding relied on sentiment, on the personal emotional connection between individuals, to build cross-cultural peace and understanding. As an example, I reproduce below Fosdick's English introduction to the Japanese edition of *On Being a Real Person*:

It is gratifying to know that this book of mine is being translated into Japanese. I am sure that Mr. Motoo Takei [the translator] has not found the task an easy one, for the book came from intimate dealing with the inward problems of Americans and is full of allusions, illustrations and questions which may well be difficult to render into Japanese.

Deeper than the local differences which distinguish us from each other, however, are the common problems associated with this difficult, tumultuous era in which we all live. Fear, anxiety, disillusionment, depression—such inward enemies of the spirit are common to us all.

I have been in Japan and I love your beautiful country and its people. If through this book I can be of help especially to your young men and women facing, as we in America also do, this disordered and often frightening world, I shall be grateful. We must win an inward victory over ourselves before we can win a victory over the world's bitterness and war madness.

In this book, I hope that I may speak personally to some who will be helped by its message.[135]

Fosdick assumed that—cultural differences aside—we were united by a shared set of universal human values.[136] Much as Liebman declared that anxiety and despair knew no racial or religious bounds, Fosdick assumed our most fundamental worries were shared. Further, he engaged here with what Radway calls "middlebrow personalism," the idea that social institutions and international politics were best understood through personal identification with a single individual.[137] Fosdick ended his introduction not by imagining the United States and Japan at peace, but by imagining Harry Emerson Fosdick making a single Japanese individual feel better about his or her life—an exchange facilitated by the international circulation of print.

On Being a Real Person was a Franklin book. The Franklin Book Program was a quasi-governmental, nonprofit organization founded in 1952 to facilitate the translation and distribution of American books abroad. Its mission soon broadened to include education and literacy programs, libraries, publishing, and bookselling. The Franklin Program was, at base, a development agency, and its administrators imagined that books and reading would modernize the commercial and knowledge economies of emerging nations, from which would inevitably follow the embrace of American-style freedoms, democracy, and free market capitalism.[138] In addition to economic development, the Franklin Program was intended to develop new global markets for American book publishers and to win over the hearts and minds of people in the developing world from communists.[139]

There were tensions among the Franklin Program's competing goals: development, commerce, and propaganda. The program's primary source of funding in the 1950s was the newly founded United States Information Agency (USIA), although additional support came from local governments in developing countries and philanthropic organizations like the Ford Foundation. Whereas Franklin Program leaders embraced a "modernization" mission, the State Department and the USIA viewed books as overt forms of propaganda for the American way. In 1953, a State Department press release made clear that books should (1) educate foreigners about the United States, the American people, and American policy goals; (2) provide the scientific/technical knowledge necessary to grow economies and cement alliances in the developing world; and (3) convince people of other nations that the United States possessed a distinct, valuable cultural tradition.[140] Although the Franklin Program did distribute thousands of USIA-approved books in the 1950s, it did not wish to be cast as a "purely propagandistic agency."[141] The program employed local intellectuals as writers and translators and to run regional offices in the developing world; it encouraged the growth of indigenous publishing, bookselling, and libraries; and it sponsored dictionary and encyclopedia projects intended to facilitate nation building.[142]

Certainly, *On Being a Real Person* offered the opportunity to make Americans, American individualism, and the American way of life comprehensible to foreign readers, and in that it was perfectly in line with the USIA mission. However, readers and intellectuals in the developing world frequently appropriated books and libraries for their own purposes (most users of USIA libraries read the technical/scientific books, not the books about America, for example).[143] For this reason, some speculation about the appeal of books like this in the developing world might be in order. What if foreign readers were not put off by the quintessential "Americanness" of *On Being a Real Person*, as Fosdick feared, but instead were reading it for that very reason? Rather than a tool for figuring out how to live "the good life," this book might have been a tool for figuring out the people on whose influence and resources the fate of one's own country depended—the Americans. The translation of these religious self-help books facilitated the export of "the American way," but readers' transactions with print were inevitably more variable and more self-interested than models of modernization or cultural imperialism might suggest. The 1940s and 1950s were the heyday of "national character studies," which shaped the early years of American Studies as a discipline both in the United States and abroad.[144] The quintessential "Americanness" of these books—their optimism, individualism, and emphasis on prosperity and happiness—made them not only self-help books, but also accessibly written studies of national character for foreigners.

My intention here has been to think about Cold War religious reading and consumer culture in a transnational frame. If Fosdick, Liebman, Sheen, Peale, and Graham all believed that religion—or a certain kind of religion—could bring Americans the happiness that was their birthright, they also shared a belief that a certain kind of religiosity was indistinguishable from "the American way" that promised them this happiness. It should come as no surprise that their work was recruited into the battle with the communists for the hearts and minds of the developing world, or that readers in the developing world might appropriate these texts for their own ends.

The fan whose account of reading Liebman's *Peace of Mind* began this chapter expressed her "Americanness" through her freedom to worship as her ancestors did and her cosmopolitan, eclectic religious reading across faiths. This free access to the marketplace of religious ideas allowed her to both "fit in" and express herself as an autonomous, thinking individual rather than as the other-directed, conforming suburban housewife intellectuals feared Americans of her class were becoming. Similarly, readers in the developing world had access to a religious marketplace of ideas, determined in part by the interests of American book publishers, American policymakers, and development agencies. Like her, they were "shoppers" for the right kinds of religious books, and—like her—they appropriated these books in ways that served their own needs and desires. At home and abroad, these religious self-help books were taken up as ways to engage with America and Americans, as practical guides to navigating postwar life.

PART IV

Reading the Apocalypse

Christian Bookselling in the 1970s and 1980s

SEVEN

The Late Great Planet Earth
and Evangelical Cultures of Letters
in the 1970s and 1980s

> When the world shakes . . . those in it grab onto something of substance and
> durability. The Bible, and books that build on it, are such stabilizers.
> —GARY WHARTON OF ZONDERVAN

> The volume of Christian publishers has doubled and in some cases
> tripled over the past 10 years. If your store is not carrying Christian
> books, you are missing out on a very important market.
> —RICHARD BALTZELL OF FLEMING H. REVELL

In the 9 March 1970 special issue of *Publishers Weekly* devoted to religious
books, Zondervan, a nondenominational evangelical publishing house in
Grand Rapids, Michigan, announced the publication of Hal Lindsey and
C. C. Carlson's *The Late Great Planet Earth* and the kickoff of a marketing
campaign placing ads in evangelical and campus periodicals nationwide.[1]
The Late Great Planet Earth, an accessible guide to end-times prophecy,
proved to be a major hit. In the next year's special religious books issue,
Zondervan trumpeted that *The Late Great Planet Earth* had been through
eight printings in less than six months and had over 130,000 copies in print.
A nearby ad announced the ninth printing of *The Late Great Planet Earth*
and touted its enormous sales.[2] It went through twenty-one printings in
its first twenty-six months.[3] Nevertheless, Lindsey's book—the best-selling nonfiction book of the 1970s—seldom appeared on any bestseller list,
because those lists were drawn from a select few urban trade bookshops, and
The Late Great Planet Earth sold primarily through Christian bookstores.
Publishers Weekly acknowledged this injustice the following year in an article describing how religious books that had sold more copies than trade

titles on the bestseller list nevertheless got ignored. *The Late Great Planet Earth*, which sold something like 60,000 copies per month, was exhibit A.[4]

The Late Great Planet Earth was only the tip of the iceberg, however. The whole field of evangelical publishing was burgeoning during the 1970s and early 1980s, and *The Late Great Planet Earth* had encountered the perfect storm—disenchanted youth, economic recession, unrest in the Middle East, distrust of social institutions, and an evangelical revival. All combined to create an immense, engaged audience for books for laypeople about the apocalypse. This chapter examines the field of religious publishing in the 1970s and early 1980s and situates *The Late Great Planet Earth* in its culture of letters.[5] The next chapter looks specifically at how readers engaged with *The Late Great Planet Earth* and the debates surrounding it.

Crisis in Religious Publishing

"Religious book publishing is in trouble," declared Martin Marty in the pages of the liberal periodical *Christian Century* in 1971. Marty, an associate editor and a professor of modern church history at the University of Chicago, surveyed forty-four members of the "fraternity" of religious book publishers whose titles had been featured in the pages of *Christian Century* in the previous two years. They were almost unanimous in declaring the field in crisis.[6] Since the late 1960s, church membership and church attendance had been in decline; youth had grown suspicious of all institutions, including churches; and sales of religious books had fallen. *Publishers Weekly* noted that title output was down; many firms had failed; and only one-quarter of publishers with religion lists in 1960 still had them in 1970.[7]

Transformations in religious institutions and the changing social scene loomed large in explanations for flagging sales of religious books. First, Vatican II had disrupted the stable audience for Catholic books—nuns, priests, Catholic schoolchildren—and many Catholic publishing houses had failed as a consequence. National and international movements for Protestant unity had put denominational publishing houses under stress both by reducing subsidies from parent denominations and by shrinking the loyal audience of denominational leaders. In addition, economic recession and inflation had cut into the disposable income of book buyers, especially ministers, who had historically been the best customers.[8] One publisher told Marty: "The old clientele of 'automatic' buyers is disappearing and new buyers are hard to locate."[9] Youth, for example, were believed to be so preoccupied with exploring alternative spiritual paths—astrology, Eastern mysticism, drugs, environmentalism—that traditional religious books held little appeal.[10]

The Religious Publishers Group of the American Booksellers Association emerged from an all-day conference in New York in March 1970 resolved to meet the challenges of this crisis. Its leaders launched a major effort to study the new contours of this market and develop industry-wide marketing methods to adapt to it.[11] Why were sales in decline? Who would replace the ministers and church workers who used to be their stable customer base? How could they reach the unchurched? Why did people seek out religious books, and where did they buy them (religious bookstores, trade bookshops, campus bookstores, mail-order book clubs, for example)? Finally, because the secular media were widely held to be a lost cause—either ignorant about or openly hostile to religion—how could they best advertise their wares?[12]

Religious publishers and religion departments of trade houses began reimagining themselves for this brave new world. First, they sought to diversify their offerings in order to appeal to a broader audience. Many religious publishers included more general interest books on their lists, and denominational houses became more ecumenical in their offerings. Rather than focusing on denominational or doctrinal issues, they rededicated themselves to books that addressed social issues (the war in Vietnam, divorce, race discrimination, poverty) with "an underlying religious orientation."[13] Second—like 1920s religious booksellers—they sought to redefine "religious books" more broadly. One Catholic publisher, for example, redefined a religious book as one that dealt with "human concerns and humane needs." Westminster Press stopped classifying many of their new titles under the "religion" rubric, arguing that it was a "red flag" for college students and laypeople who were alienated from organized religion. Instead, new titles got marketed as sociology, philosophy, or ethics.[14] The high-water mark for reimagining religious books in broader, more inclusive terms was a promotional poster distributed at the 1973 American Booksellers Association convention by the Religious Publishing Group declaring: "Religious books are also about love, sex, politics, war, peace, ecology, theology, philosophy, drugs, race, dissent, ethics, technology, hippies, morality, revolution, rock, god, beauty, psychology, dogma, the underground, the establishment, death and . . . life."[15]

Everyone knew what didn't sell—books about the institutional church and theology. Marty concluded his 1971 *Christian Century* piece by declaring that "cozy treatises on religious institutions" and "far-out radical theology" were out and that "works that speak helpfully . . . to the actual problems people face" (that is, self-help and practical religion/psychology titles) were in.[16] Trying to sell theology was a particular nightmare. What Marty called "serious, scholarly, academic-style theology" had experienced some commercial success in the 1960s, but those days were over. His informants in religious publishing complained that "theologians no longer talk about anything except what concerns theologians; they write to impress their academic peers and have no regard for the less learned faithful."[17]

As it did in the 1920s and the 1950s, the language of religious books received particular attention. In 1972, *Publishers Weekly* declared that religious books not only needed to address "today's spiritual and social needs," but that they needed to do it in "today's language."[18] Publishers—particularly in the field of theology—were looking for a more readable style, one Marty described as "lying midway between incomprehensible Teutonic jargon and flashy faddist fashion."[19] "What we need in the field of religious writing is a renewal of good language," declared Dr. John Havlik of the Home Mission Board of the Southern Baptist Convention in 1978, pointing out that jargon was not useful for winning hearts and minds for Jesus.[20]

Although Marty would no doubt have classed Lindsey with those writing in a "flashy faddist fashion," Lindsey was the darling of many readers for just this reason. *Publishers Weekly* called *The Late Great Planet Earth* "old-fashioned Doomsday preaching in a contemporary idiom" and praised Lindsey's "folksy style" and sincerity.[21] Even historians looking back include references to Lindsey's language in their brief descriptions of the text. They call it "an apocalyptic reading of Ezekiel in funky '70s slanguage," "a tale of biblical prophecy told in countercultural vernacular," and "a slangy update of Darby's teachings," invoking the nineteenth-century British theologian John Darby, whose theories about the end times (premillennial dispensationalism) Lindsey popularized.[22]

Things looked quite different by the end of 1973. In September, *Publishers Weekly* declared that the "well-publicized crisis" was over and religious publishing had returned to normal, with new versions of the Bible, daily devotionals, and books for religious professionals all coming back into print. The stabilized market could support those firms that had survived the depression and a few new houses, which were increasing the number of new titles offered and reporting increased sales. It had been a rough road—"the upheaval of the 1960s"—with cutbacks, layoffs, shrinking lists, and failing firms, but those that survived were stronger and better for it.[23] By 1976, *Publishers Weekly* characterized religious book sales as strong across the board—from denominational and nondenominational publishers and from those offering Protestant, Jewish, Catholic, and Eastern books.[24]

Church attendance did not improve, however, and the paradox— declining attendance at church and rising sales of religious books— preoccupied those interested in the market for religious literature in the mid-1970s. A 1974 Yankelovich study showed that fewer people believed religion was important and that fully 70 percent declared that religion's influence was on the wane, yet all kinds of religious books from cheap devotionals to expensive theological texts were selling like crazy. How to explain this?[25] One editor maintained that Americans were increasingly suspicious of all institutions—including churches—but that their needs for moral and spiritual guidance remained. In the absence of compelling institutional sources of help, people were reading to get advice on dealing with overwhelming and complex social and moral problems: Watergate, Vietnam, racism, poverty.[26]

Two material changes in the book industry influenced the sales and mar-keting of religious books, as it did publishing more generally. First, the 1970s saw the rise of chain bookstores in suburban shopping malls, an attempt to solve the perennial problem of book distribution. Since fully 60 percent of prepublication orders for religious books took place in general stores, these chain bookstores made religious books available to a much larger audi-ence.[27] During this period, the Religious Publishing Group of the American Booksellers Association and the Christian Booksellers Association (CBA) repeatedly held workshops, conferences, and panel discussions trying to convince general booksellers that religious books were good business. The CBA underwent astronomical growth in number of members and sales receipts, and this captured the attention of the chains. B. Dalton and Walden were both sending buyers to the CBA annual convention by the late 1970s. By the early 1980s, B. Dalton was doing a major expansion of its religious book section.[28]

The second major change was the rise of the mass-market paperback, a format that came slowly to the religious book marketplace, because religious books were often much cheaper than trade books, so the price advantage was less.[29] Nonetheless, like the rest of the industry, mass-market paperbacks revolutionized the distribution of religious books. However, because paper-backs had a reputation for being lurid and sleazy, many publishers were con-cerned that religious book buyers might never think to look for titles that interested them among the popular paperbacks. Publishers maintained that if these books were to be successful, they had to be packaged and promoted in ways that identified them as religious or family-oriented books.[30] Lindsey was among the first to ride this wave. "I've never gone for the hardback market," he explained. "In fact, I've always insisted on publishing the hardback and the quality paperback at the same time. I'm writing for the youth culture—and the average young person doesn't even look at hardbacks of any kind."[31]

The mass-market paperback was also important for "crossover" books appealing to a general audience that might not venture into a specialized religious bookshop. "We are getting our books out there where the unbeliever action is," trumpeted one religious publisher about mass-market reprints for the trade market.[32] Initially, such crossovers were managed by splitting the religious and the secular rights. For example, Marabel Morgan's *The Total Woman*, an evangelical guide to marital sex, was sold to the religious trade by evangelical house Fleming H. Revell and to the secular trade at the same price by Pocket Books.[33] *The Late Great Planet Earth* was sold in the religious market by Zondervan and in the trade market by Bantam. Evangelical houses were happy about the larger audience for biblical truth; paperback publishers were happy to have the profits.[34]

In fact, many give credit for bridging the gap between general and religious publishing to Lindsey's *The Late Great Planet Earth*, which was Zondervan's all-time bestseller and a book that reached millions through its Bantam mass-market reprint. Although he maintained that Zondervan's core constituency was evangelical Christians, the managing editor insisted that "nominal Christians" and those who did not attend church at all were increasingly encountering Zondervan books through mass-market paperback reprints.[35] Bantam seemed as pleased as Zondervan with the partnership on *The Late Great Planet Earth* and other titles. "There is a big religious revival going on," asserted Grace Bechtold, Bantam executive editor and vice president, and Bantam created a special order form directed specifically at readers of religious/inspirational titles. By 1978, Bantam was no longer interested in splitting secular and religious rights, however, because the market was so lucrative.[36]

Identifying good crossover titles was not always easy, however. Alongside the immense success of *The Late Great Planet Earth* and Billy Graham's books were the duds—books by Watergate figure Charles Colson and Ruth Carter Stapleton, for example.[37] Zondervan was careful about which titles to sell in general stores, since many evangelical titles were simply not appropriate for a trade audience.[38] Further, even if it were the same text, it *meant* a different thing to buy a mass-market paperback at a newsstand or trade bookshop than to purchase it through a religious bookstore or a mail-order religious book club. Michael Leach argued in the pages of *Christian Century* in 1974 that this increasing public accessibility made it "easy to 'pick up religion with your groceries,' as it were."[39]

The Boom in Evangelical Publishing

The real news in religious publishing in the 1970s and early 1980s, however, was the huge growth in evangelical publishing. "Sometimes I am much more optimistic about religious publishing than I am about the world tomorrow," asserted Gary Wharton of Zondervan in 1974. "The greater the world pressures . . . the greater the need for an answer, and the greater the future of religious books that provide answers."[40] These twin sentiments—worry about the state of the world and optimism about the booming sales of evangelical books—filled the pages of *Publishers Weekly* in the 1970s and early 1980s. Indeed, the growth in sales of evangelical books was nothing short of breathtaking. The annual convention of the CBA experienced double-digit annual rates of growth in sales and a long series of broken attendance records. *Publishers Weekly* coverage of the CBA annual meeting in Dallas in 1973 declared it an "understatement" to call religious book publishing a "booming business."[41] Sales at Zondervan rose 48 percent from 1970 to 1971, primarily because of Lindsey's *The Late Great Planet Earth*.[42] Between 1972 and 1977, overall religious book sales grew 112 percent, compared with an overall industry growth rate of 70 percent during the same period. In 1981, the *New York Times* estimated that religious publishing was a yearly $1 billion business, having nearly doubled in size since the early 1970s. Moreover, it continued to grow at something like 15 percent a year, with evangelical books being the fastest-growing part of that market.[43]

Why the amazing growth? "Difficult times mean better Christian sales," asserted one commentator, citing the moribund economy and the lack of faith in government and other institutions as driving factors.[44] "One reason why Christian publishers are so successful is that the world they publish in is geopolitically unstable," explained an early 1980s *Publishers Weekly* report on the booming business at the CBA annual convention.[45] The sense of moral and economic helplessness went deeper, however. "There is a widespread sense of insecurity," argued one religious publisher, citing student unrest, dissolving families, inflation, and unemployment as examples.[46] The Bible and Bible-based books provided a stable life raft in this storm of uncertainty. "The Bible has a lot of answers," offered William Barbour, president of evangelical publisher Fleming H. Revell, by way of explanation.[47]

Looking back on the era from the turn of the twenty-first century, Charles Krauthammer argued that Americans had their millennial panic early—in the late 1970s and early 1980s. Why? Because millennial panic requires bad times, and the late 1990s were pretty good. The 1970s and early 1980s were not. *The Late Great Planet Earth* and its ilk sold so well, Krauthammer insisted, because of "oil shocks, stagflation, and post-Vietnam demoralization."[48] Similarly, speculating on why so many readers' imaginations were captured in the 1970s and early 1980s by Lindsey's vision of saved Christians being raptured to heaven before the apocalypse, religion journalist Mark Silk asks, "Perhaps it was simply the prospect of getting off the planet as quickly as possible—away from Cambodia and Saigon, Watergate and OPEC, from the Rev. Jim Jones and the Ayatollah Ruhollah Khomeini?"[49]

Similarly, a so-called post-Watergate morality explained some of the appeal of evangelical books, since conservative Christianity touted its own high moral standards as an alternative to the corruption and deceit running rampant in the larger culture.[50] The turn to evangelicalism was only one among many possible paths available to troubled Americans, however. As Lindsey himself pointed out, books on the occult, Eastern mysticism, and astrology all offered answers, but evangelicals were simply more aggressive and better organized than these other movements.[51]

Bad times and uncertainty aside, the other reason often given for the skyrocketing sales of evangelical books was the heightened profile of evangelicals themselves. William Barbour Jr., the president of Fleming H. Revell, explained: "Never before these mid-70s has so much secular media attention been focused on evangelical Christians—politicians, athletes, entertainers, businessmen, 'Watergaters,' preachers."[52] For example, the cover story of one 1976 edition of *Newsweek* was entitled "Born Again!" and it used the rapidly approaching presidential election as a lens for exploring "the most significant—and overlooked—religious phenomenon of the '70s: the emergence of evangelical Christianity into a position of respect and power." Gallup concluded that 1976 was "the year of the evangelical."[53] The consensus on the exhibit floor at the 1978 CBA convention was that the once-insular world of Christian publishing was opening up to secular publishers and secular audiences, because evangelicalism had been big news in recent years; because the movement itself was increasingly nondenominational; and because so many "star authors" known to the secular world were bringing media attention to their books.[54]

Finally, sales were increasing because Christian publishers and booksellers were producing better books and getting better at marketing and promoting them. That is to say that the field—once dominated by mom-and-pop stores imagined by their proprietors as a form of evangelism—was becoming increasingly professional. The CBA held all kinds of workshops at annual and regional meetings on budgeting, accounting, inventory control, money management, and promotion.[55] In addition, the Religious Publishing Group of the American Booksellers Association held panels on selling religious books in a general bookstore in which they proselytized for the profitability and steady sales of religious books and offered practical advice and guidance on starting, expanding, and maintaining a religious books section. "Religious books cost less, last longer, and give higher profitability," declared Zondervan's Gary Wharton at one such event.[56] The trend continued into the 1990s, as evangelical publishers moved beyond their traditional CBA outlets and into Walmart and Costco and focused more attention on packaging and marketing their books to niche audiences.[57]

What were these popular evangelical books like? At an American Booksellers Association panel in 1976 focused on selling religious books in the general bookstore, Zondervan's Wharton described them as "experience-oriented, life-centered and Bible-based."[58] The emphasis on the Bible was critical for evangelical houses. Dan Malachuk, president of Logos International, told the evangelical periodical *Christianity Today* that "the secret of our success is that Jesus is the chairman of the board." Zondervan maintained that "editorial policy . . . begins with its commitment to the Bible" and that all books had to pass a conservative theological litmus test.[59] The impressive sales of evangelical titles drew interest from trade publishers with nonsectarian religious lines. Alex Liepa of Doubleday announced the intention to expand its evangelical publishing in 1977 and trumpeted the launch of an evangelical imprint soon after.[60] The "Galilee" imprint was designed to guide evangelical readers to the religious books that met their needs. Liepa described it as "a guarantee to the reader that the book is Evangelical in content and outlook." The imprint was strictly about the orthodoxy of content, since the line would feature new books and reprints, hardcovers and paperbacks.[61]

For the most part, these books made a personal appeal to individual believers, bypassing theology and institutional issues (as had popular religious books in the 1920s). "Personal testimony" books were popular throughout the 1970s, and "issue-oriented" books detailing Christian approaches to dealing with issues like divorce, pornography, and troubled youth also sold well.[62] Liepa at Doubleday maintained that best-selling titles offered readers practical, personal guidance and hope through inspiring stories or autobiographies.[63] Books were intended to inspire dispirited Christians through first-person narratives of believers overcoming obstacles. Self-help titles were also among the most popular.[64]

Others agreed that the Jesus movement was big and that books about controversial contemporary issues—"current event titles"—sold well.[65] Although Lindsey's *The Late Great Planet Earth* appeared in 1970 (arguably both a Jesus movement and a current events book), the interest in prophecy was enduring. Books on prophecy and the situation in the Middle East were still numerous and selling extraordinarily well (including new ones by Lindsey) in 1980.[66] What these books had in common was that they spoke to readers' personal situations in immediate, concrete ways. Current events and prophecy books took the overwhelming complexity of the nightly news and placed it in a religious context that gave it meaning and placed readers both "in the know" and on the right side of history. They were "self-help" books in that they addressed needs in an immediate, accessible way and inspired readers for daily life, much as other people's accounts of overcoming obstacles and practical guides to better living did. These books were so ubiquitous that when Lindsey took the manuscript of *The Late Great Planet Earth* to Zondervan in 1969, his old seminary colleague and soon-to-be publisher tempered his hopes by drawing attention to an already crowded marketplace: "You've got to be realistic. . . . After all, there are already lots of books on Bible prophecy in the Christian book stores."[67]

Agreeing on the definition of an "evangelical book" was no easy task, however. For example, at one of many seminars/workshops on marketing religious books in the general bookshop in 1975, one audience member asked the religious publishers and booksellers on the panel for a definition of an "evangelical book." The Zondervan representative offered that evangelical books "cater to the Billy Graham–type people," a definition his fellow panelists would not unanimously endorse. Others offered that evangelical books dealt with "orthodox Biblical Christianity" and defined evangelicals as "people who look to the Bible for what it is they ought to believe about the nature of man and God." It got even more complicated when a representative from Word, Inc., a Waco, Texas, evangelical publisher, tried to offer some historical perspective. Evangelical publishing had been transformed in the last decade or so, he insisted. Whereas evangelical books had once been "critical of other faiths," this was no longer the case. Those texts (the ones critical of other faiths) were now called "fundamentalist books," he explained, but books published by evangelical houses like Revell,

Zondervan, and Word now covered a broad range of topics and interested many kinds of readers.[68]

The Jesus People and the Youth Market

Much of the growth and excitement in the evangelical book market focused on youth. Although widely held to be checked out or preoccupied with drugs, sex, rock music, or forms of Eastern mysticism, in fact youth were one of the two critical markets for evangelical publishers. The primary buyers of evangelical books in the 1970s and early 1980s were married women aged twenty-six to forty-nine and youth between sixteen and twenty-two.[69] Hardcover books targeted married women; paperbacks aimed for the youth/student market.[70] Between 1969 and 1974, the average age of a Christian book buyer dropped dramatically, with half of consumers under the age of thirty-five (in line with the average age of the general population).[71] As early as 1970, evangelical publishers proclaimed a new emphasis on the "burgeoning youth market," an emphasis one publisher glossed as "Try Jesus, Not Junk."[72] Publishers were convinced that youth were particularly turned off by jargon and irrelevant or abstract theoretical arguments. To reach this market, one publisher maintained, required "a free-wheeling way of talking about religion."[73]

The Late Great Planet Earth tapped into this youth market. For seven years in the 1960s, Lindsey was an evangelist for Campus Crusade for Christ, preaching to crowds of college students at the University of California at Berkeley and San Francisco State University. This experience profoundly shaped his presentation style. In a *Publishers Weekly* interview, Lindsey explained, "That's how I learned to communicate with the youth culture. . . . I was constantly challenged to not just spout theological jargon but to tell people something they could understand."[74] In 1969, Lindsey retired from Campus Crusade and began a teaching ministry near UCLA, as co-director of a forty-person residential house called the Jesus Christ Light and Power Company. Here he honed his material in lectures and Bible studies. He explained his process: "As I wrote, I'd imagine that I was sitting across the table from a young person—a cynical, irreligious person—and I'd try to convince him that the Bible prophecies were true. . . . A young person isn't hesitant to call you on something, and it forces you to come to grips with people who aren't in the religious 'club.'"[75]

Publishers Weekly was especially interested in the youth market, because cultivating it promised long-term sales growth for publishers and booksellers. One explained, "The Jesus People were not a fad; they are attending conservative schools and churches, and buying conservative books." Moreover, many campus organizations like Campus Life, Campus Crusade for Christ, Navigators, and Inter-Varsity had record memberships in the mid-1970s, and all of them were engaged in publishing of their own.[76]

"Jesus People" were featured in cover stories in *Time, Life, Look, U.S. News and World Report*, and other mainstream media in the early 1970s. The Jesus movement was a vast, amorphous revival/renewal movement among youth that had many faces (churches, communes, coffeehouses, free newspapers, street ministries) and that shared an anti-institutional approach to religion and a fundamentalist theology. *Time* magazine's 1971 cover story characterized the movement as "a May-December marriage of conservative religion and the rebellious counterculture."[77] The generational conflict between rebellious teens devoting their lives to Christ and personal evangelism and more conventional, churchgoing parents was at the center of a 1971 *Life* article about the Jesus movement in Rye, New York.[78] Jesus People were like the counterculture—placing subjective experience at the center of spiritual life, emphasizing alienation from and protest against organized institutions and social elites, seeking a "high" experience understood as a form of spiritual transcendence. They were unlike the counterculture, however, in that they pursued these ends not through drugs, but through Bible study and prayer.[79]

Lindsey's relationship to the Jesus movement was somewhat tenuous.[80] The movement was centered on the West Coast in street ministries, communes, and coffeehouses that ministered to drug addicts and runaways. Lindsey's ministry at the Jesus Christ Light and Power Company near UCLA was comparatively straight and conventional—appealing to athletes and college students. It involved Bible study and group discussion but bore little resemblance to the communes whose residents turned their back on this world to study the Bible and evangelize on the streets.[81] Evangelical sociologist Ronald Enroth described Lindsey's ministry as "on the fence between Jesus Freaks and the Establishment" and argued that because his followers were university students or recent graduates, he gave some intellectual depth to the movement.[82]

However marginal to the Jesus movement Lindsey himself was, *The Late Great Planet Earth* was arguably its textbook. Contemporary commentators agreed that although the Jesus People were not great readers of any book except the Bible, *The Late Great Planet Earth* was a critical text for many. Religion scholar Robert S. Ellwood noted that *The Late Great Planet Earth* is "one of the few volumes besides the Bible found in virtually every movement commune, home, and church parlor."[83] Although these young activist Christians were an important core audience, the crossover sales to the general audience made *The Late Great Planet Earth*'s reputation. The mainstream media, however, did not extend much respect to *The Late Great Planet Earth*'s audience.

Mencken Redux: Conservative Christians in the Mainstream Media

Evangelical publishers frequently felt like second-class literary citizens. "The large chains ignored them. The media didn't understand them. The National Book Awards didn't even recognize religious books," one retrospective account explained. As a consequence, the Evangelical Christian Publishers Association, an international nonprofit organization, was founded in 1973 to organize its members and advocate for their interests. The organization sought to create a united voice for the industry, to share data, to increase professionalism and efficiency, to expand its members' market, and to promote Christian fellowship among members.[84]

Along these lines, Leslie H. Stobbe, editor in chief of Moody Press, wrote to *Publishers Weekly* protesting the lack of coverage given to religious books in 1974. In the letter, he asked why the "year-in-review" feature in the previous issue had neglected to mention CBA bookstores. He offered a few suggestions about critical trends in religious publishing that *Publishers Weekly* ought to be paying attention to but was not: growth in religious paperbacks, record-setting sales of religious bestsellers, and the initiation of rack jobbing in department stores, discount drugstores, and discount chains by religious publishers.[85] He had a point. Although *Publishers Weekly* had a special religious books issue in the spring (and another in the fall later in the decade), trends in religious publishing seldom made it into regular publishing/bookselling news at other times of the year.

Further, *Publishers Weekly* accounts of the CBA annual meeting every summer (usually in some conservative southern or midwestern city) dripped with condescension in the early 1970s. It presented the CBA conventioneers as quaint, exotic creatures who (whatever else they might be) were certainly not *us*. For example, the opening paragraphs of CBA convention coverage usually featured not the record attendance and the book sales, but the gimmicks (costumed characters, free giveaways).[86] One such account quoted a regular American Booksellers Association convention-goer who found the CBA meeting unnervingly unlike most booksellers' conventions he'd attended. The hotel bars were deserted, he noted in astonishment, and they might as well have just turned off the cigarette machines for the weekend.[87] Over the course of the decade, however, *Publishers Weekly* reports on the CBA convention grew more serious and respectful as the size and profitability of this sector of the literary marketplace skyrocketed.[88]

The liberal *Christian Century* dedicated a lot of print to the world of religious books, featuring weekly book reviews and periodic special book issues. It had nothing good to say about evangelical bestsellers, which it characterized as narrow, parochial, and anti-intellectual. A 1974 article quoted one book salesman who was critical of evangelical bestsellers. "They show a steady growth," he conceded, "but I fear it is immature." In the long term, this growth was simply untenable, since these books left the needs of "the rational thinker" unmet and their "overemotional status" was not sustainable. "The brainwashed" would be reading these kinds of books forever, but other readers—"thoughtful," "substantial," "rational"—would surely move on.[89] The problem with "bad" religious books (the evangelical ones) was the same as the problem with their readers—they were irrational and overly emotional—and the newfound prominence of both these books and these readers was cause for grave concern.

Christian Century just assumed its readers would have no idea what these evangelical books were like. In his 1971 review of the field, "Religious Publishing: A Decline but Not a Demise," Martin Marty maintained that "to most of our readers few titles on this market [the evangelical market] would be recognizable," but he characterized them as books that sell a lot of copies, have little larger social impact, and seem to many outsiders to be "maudlin, repetitive and lacking literary qualities." They sell, Marty maintained, because evangelicalism was an immense, intact subculture in which people read each other's books, whereas mainline readers and writers "tend to phase out of religious culture into the 'world at large.'"[90] Liberals had a whole vibrant literary world to explore, but evangelicals were trapped in their own maudlin, repetitive, not-so-literary ghetto. Marty reported respect for those successful evangelical publishers who had identified a niche market and filled it, but he (incorrectly) thought they were headed for a fall. The older readers were dying off, and Marty saw no new market developing. Moreover, this fad did not seem likely to stick around, and major houses would get burned if they attempted to take advantage of this market.

Christian Century grew less confident of this assessment over the course of the decade as evangelical bestsellers continued to make history and evangelicals rose to social and political power. In the preface to the 1975 book issue, the editors distinguished between all the "junk" out there promising little more than "self-serving spiritual kicks" to millions of consumers and the less popular religious titles of substance. "They may not have the wealth of the exploiters and sensationalists [Lindsey's publisher is specifically mentioned], but they are offering spiritual wisdom to serious readers."[91] A 1977 article distinguished between the serious books of substance put out by denominational publishing houses and the "popular" books that made bigger profits—"celebrity salvation books, the Christian bed-partner manuals, the TV evangelists' potboilers, the Second-Coming guides."[92] Another 1977 article bemoaned the "literary cholesterol" being sold by the truckload from "Ma and Pa Christian bookstores." The author called for a healthier literary diet of intellectually sturdy religious books and offered the following pages of *Christian Century*'s book issue as a first step along that path.[93]

Christian Century tied the popularity, over-emotionalism, and anti-intellectual nature of these evangelical bestsellers to corporate mergers that shifted the terrain out of which religious literature had emerged. In a 1977 editorial entitled "Publishing in an Age of Mergers," the writer declared, "Church culture has been overwhelmed by television culture," and explained that popular religious books were aimed at the "Dinah-Merv-Johnny crowd," who were interested in Elvis, Lawrence Welk, and country-western music. It was simply not profitable to target more elite audiences, who "prefer symphony or jazz, social criticism or upper-middle-brow magazines." As a consequence, most readers thought "Christian book" meant some vacuous volume by Pat Boone or Marabel Morgan (*The Total Woman*) or Miss America. While such celebrity claptrap had its place, it had preempted the books that considered other aspects of faith—"the cross . . . or the mind."[94] As the references to jazz, the symphony, and "upper-middle-brow magazines" indicate, this was an argument about social class. The problem with evangelicals (and their books) here is not presented as a theological issue (the metaphoric versus the literal truth of the Bible, for example), but as a class issue. Evangelicals have no breeding. They have *bad taste*—and that bad taste is for books that lack appropriate attention to reason and are overly emotional in their tone.[95] As the editor put it in the preface to the May 1978 spring books issue, "Catering to popular taste is not by itself necessarily a vice; failing to try to improve it is."[96]

In some cases, the popularity of these books was—ipso facto—evidence of how bad they were. To not make money on your books, to have your books remaindered, meant that you were a serious author, one making credible religious/theological claims rather than selling out to the Dinah-Merv-Johnny crowd. For example, Martin Marty wrote an editorial, "You'll Never Get

Rich," in which he used the royalties on his own books as a case in point. He estimated that mowing lawns paid about five times more per hour than writing serious books about theology or religious history. He concluded that you weren't going to make any money as a religious author "unless you write gothic novels, are a born-again sinner-turned-saint for televising, or believe that the world will end soon and that Jesus wants you to get yours quickly."[97]

There were additional potshots at Lindsey, whose sales and profits surpassed all the others. In May 1979, *Christian Century* ended the series "The Books That Shape Lives," which had featured lists of influential books from important religious leaders. *Christian Century* asked its staff to submit their own lists as a farewell to the series. Marty had done one in 1962 for another occasion, so his column revisited that list and asked what—if anything—he ought to change, given the intervening seventeen years of publishing. At his crotchety best, Marty didn't change a damn thing. Sarcastically, he asked, "In place of 'my elementary school atlas,' which had taught me love of the earth, should I substitute Hal Lindsey's best-selling *The Late Great Planet Earth*? It teaches that because Jesus is coming soon, I should hate the earth and love not the things of the world. The author hates the earth enough to plow his royalties into long-term real estate investments and loves not the world enough to spend the rest on Mercedes Benzes. A good book."[98] Similarly, in a 1983 *Publishers Weekly* article entitled "Welcome to a New Breed of Religious Writers (and About Time, Too)," Floyd Thatcher declared triumphantly, "The time is past . . . when the traditional religious marketplace can be duped by an author who attempts to cash in on the fears and fantasies of an apocalyptic head-trip."[99]

Lindsey did have a public relations problem. Similar to Marty's article, much of the popular coverage of *The Late Great Planet Earth* cited the presumed disconnect between Lindsey's end-times prophecies and his expensive tastes. A *Publishers Weekly* profile described him: "Hal Lindsey . . . is an Advent-and-Apocalypse evangelist who sports a Porsche racing jacket and tools around Los Angles in a Mercedes 450 SI. And even though his best-selling books of Bible prophecy warn that the end is near, Lindsey maintains a suite of offices in a posh Santa Monica high rise for the personal management firm that sinks his royalties into long-term real estate investments."[100] Not only did such riches seem unseemly for an evangelist purportedly concerned with higher things, but the ostentatious way Lindsey displayed his wealth testified to the lack of breeding that critics suggested characterized evangelicals.

As Robert Orsi notes, much scholarship on religion was concerned with dividing the "good" religion (the middle-class, liberal kind) from the "bad" religions (the overly emotional, primitive, rural and/or working-class kind). Mainline liberal Protestantism was "good"; Catholics, Fundamentalists, Pentecostals, and Charismatics were bad. Although Orsi is concerned with religious studies scholarship, this pattern certainly characterized popular coverage of religious publishing at *Publishers Weekly* and the liberal *Christian Century* as well.[101] What much of the coverage of evangelical publishing in general and Lindsey in particular did was to dismiss this brand of religion as "bad"—hysterical, sensational, anti-intellectual, narrowly parochial. In the meantime, a controversy was raging over how to accurately measure the relative influence of mainstream bestsellers and popular evangelical books like Lindsey's.

The Controversy over the Bestseller List

The Late Great Planet Earth was the best-selling book of the 1970s. It sold 10 million copies during the 1970s, yet it never appeared on any bestseller list because it sold primarily through Christian bookstores—a mode of distribution not counted in assembling the major bestseller lists (*New York Times, Publishers Weekly*).[102] This was cause for controversy, even at the time. Zondervan, Lindsey's publisher, took out an ad in *Publishers Weekly* next to the bestseller list at the end of the periodical. "A Bestseller You Will Not Find Listed on the Opposite Page," it was headlined, and it advertised Lindsey's blockbuster bestseller.[103] A 1972 article in the evangelical periodical *Christianity Today* entitled "Unlisted Bestsellers" summarized the catch-22 in which religious publishers found themselves. Although their books sold scores of copies (over a million copies in the first two years for *The Late Great Planet Earth*), they never got the recognition, publicity, and boost in sales from appearing on *New York Times* or *Washington Post* or *Publishers Weekly* bestseller lists. This arose from several idiosyncratic practices. First, in the early 1970s, most bestseller lists considered only hardcovers. Lindsey's book was out in hardcover and trade paperback, and the paperback outsold the hardcover by thirty to one. Second, lists were compiled by calling up a small number of selected bookstores. Cheryl Forbes, the author of the *Christianity Today* article, had one informant who insisted that the *New York Times* bestseller list was based on numbers from only ten stores in Manhattan.[104] Excluded from the list were book club sales, mail-order sales, sales at general stores (Kmart or racks at the grocery store, for example), and books sold in religious bookshops or genre bookstores. Moreover, there was some suspicion that the (unrepresentative) booksellers surveyed were not always entirely honest about sales figures. Some reportedly claimed that moribund titles were selling like hotcakes in an attempt to create sales by getting them labeled "bestsellers." Third, because the raw sales numbers or rankings from booksellers in the survey needed to be averaged out, those numbers could be manipulated in the process of being turned into a list.[105] One *Washington Post* book critic characterized these newspaper bestseller lists as "rife with charges of bias and skullduggery." A book wholesaler called them "completely inaccurate, grossly misleading, a farce."[106]

Such practices meant that bestseller lists were not accurate reflections of the world of books and reading. *Washington Post* reporter Clive Thompson argues that they were, instead, "a reflection of cultural consensus, antiseptically cleansed of the reading that's done outside the traditional range of the nation's cultural capitals."[107] Rural and small-town religious readers in the South and Midwest did not count for much. Compilers of the lists conceded as much. The *Washington Post* book pages were "adamantly regional," based on only a few select bookshops inside the Beltway. Bestseller lists were not impartially reporting numbers but instead providing "a snapshot of the culturati" to their disproportionately wealthy, well-educated, urban readers. As Eliza Truitt of slate.com noted in 2003, the *New York Times* and other publications frequently "prune out the lowbrow riffraff" to maintain a literary tone.[108] "I don't think we're missing the boat on popular books. We're missing the boat, calculatedly so, on things like religious books," insisted the *New York Times Book Review* editor. "I don't think we have to apologize for that." Daisy Maryles at *Publishers Weekly* agreed: *Publishers Weekly* lists are "a form of reporting—they're not based on absolute numbers."[109]

The bestseller list controversy got major press. In 1976, *Time* magazine noted that almost fifty current religious titles had sold over 1 million copies, and numerous others had passed the 100,000 mark, many more than the average fiction title on the trade bestseller list.[110] *Newsweek* ran a 1977 article entitled "Holy Writ" on the controversy. Although religious books outsold all but the "showiest" entries on trade bestseller lists, books like Lindsey's (8.5 million copies) and Billy Graham's latest (*Angels*, at 2.5 million copies) never appeared, because religious bookstore sales were excluded.[111] Even *Christian Century*—exasperated as it was with all those vapid, saccharine evangelical bestsellers—conceded this was not fair play.[112] Lindsey—registering his annoyance in a *Publishers Weekly* interview—argued: "We'd already seen that 'The Late Great Planet Earth' could outsell everything else without

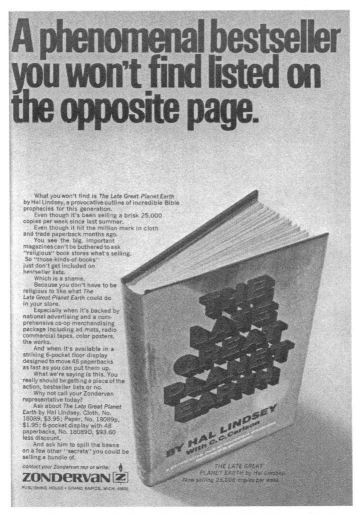

Advertisement for *The Late Great Planet Earth*, *Publishers Weekly*,
27 March 1972, 107.

getting on the list because of the prejudice against religious books. . . . But when we managed to put two books on the list at the same time, we proved that people really want to read what the Bible says about the future."[113]

In part because of this exclusion, the CBA *Bookstore Journal*, a periodical for Christian booksellers, began compiling its own bestseller list in 1972 by calling twenty-four religious bookstores from major markets across the country.[114] In this way, it hoped to offer guidance on the most popular books for member stores, for independent religious bookshops, and for general bookstores that might want to start or expand a religion section and be at a loss about which current books to stock. By 1975, the religious bestseller list was being compiled by the Christian News Service based on a monthly poll of fifty to seventy-five religious bookstores from a variety of denominational backgrounds in the United States and Canada. Catholic books were compiled as a separate annual list.[115]

As *Publishers Weekly* noted in 1974, the numbers on the "National Religious Bestsellers" list were breathtaking. To be number ten on the list, a book typically had to sell 75,000 copies, a higher hurdle than that required to appear on the general bestseller list. *Publishers Weekly* mused about the cultural meaning of the phenomena—that religious bestsellers outsold general bestsellers. "Using these sales as a starting point, one could easily argue that Anita Bryant has more followers than Germaine Greer, that Pat Boone speaks to more important needs than David Reuben, and that Marjorie Holmes will be savored long after Jacqueline Susann is remaindered," the author speculated.[116] You can hear the awe and anxiety over the deemphasizing of trade books, trade audiences, and secular life in America. What kind of a world is it when evangelicals like Bryant, Boone, and Holmes have a bigger audience and a bigger influence than the liberated, secular, sexy celebrities who fill the society pages and the book sections of major newspapers? Werner Linz of Seabury Press, an Episcopalian publishing house, speculated on the exclusion of religious books from bestseller lists: "It's embarrassing to them. . . . No one wants to admit that some crummy religious book—and a lot of them are crummy—sells more copies than John Cheever."[117]

Soon after, *Publishers Weekly* began running articles on "The Phenomenon of the Religious Best Seller" in its special religious books issue.[118] Most of this coverage was imported—that is, the Christian News Service writer submitted the article and the interviews with evangelical publishers, so that they could speak for themselves (and so that *Publishers Weekly* need not dedicate staff and resources to covering the evangelical market). The special Religious Books issue had a guest editor every year to cover the field for the magazine.

Religious bestsellers were different than trade bestsellers in several ways. First, the market was gendered. Of hardcover religious bestsellers, 90 percent were authored by women (only 15 to 20 percent of the trade bestseller list was).[119] Second, religious bestsellers tended to be shorter than trade bestsellers, averaging only 190 pages. Third, they were cheaper, with the average retail price of a hardcover religious bestseller only half the price of a trade bestseller.[120] Fourth, returns for religious books were much lower (averaging less than 11 percent), because of "built-in" sales to churches and religious institutions.[121]

Finally, religious bestsellers stayed on the list much longer than trade bestsellers. For example, of the thirty books on the July 1975 list of religious bestsellers, five had appeared on the first (1972) list. In addition, 80 percent of religious bestsellers had remained on the list for at least a year.[122] Even if they were not bestsellers, religious books were steady sellers over the long run.[123] As a consequence, an active backlist was crucial. Peter Kladder of Zondervan told the New York Times in 1980 that fully 70 percent of Zondervan's sales volume was from backlist titles.[124] Because religious books sold steadily for years and each new title from an author brought new sales of his or her older titles—even in hardcover—a bookseller had to think about them differently than secular bestsellers.[125]

Low cost. Low returns. Long life. What wasn't to like? Evangelical books took the risk out of bookselling. The Late Great Planet Earth was the quintessential religious book of the 1970s and early 1980s; it set the pattern and pointed the way for sales of evangelical titles across the decade and beyond. As traditional denominational publishing floundered in the late 1960s, losing readers as religious institutions remade themselves and lost "built-in" readerships, The Late Great Planet Earth became a blockbuster bestseller, because it appealed to a new, nondenominational youth audience in an exciting new format, the religious paperback. It was accessibly written, eschewing both esoteric theology and difficult religious jargon, and it was marketed in innovative ways. Zondervan sold it alongside other books on Bible prophecy and the apocalypse in Christian bookstores; Bantam issued an edition to capture the "unbeliever action" in trade bookshops. Although evangelicals and evangelical publishing were growing increasingly prominent in public life—like Lindsey—they did not always get a great deal of respect from mainstream media, which dismissed these books as hysterical, hypocritical, and shallow, if quite profitable. Increasingly, however, Lindsey and other best-selling evangelical writers protested their systematic exclusion from mainstream media and the minimizing of their substantial cultural influence. Readers, too, had a great deal to say about The Late Great Planet Earth and the debates surrounding it. These readers are the subject of Chapter 8.

EIGHT

End-Times Prophecy for Dummies:
Reading *The Late Great Planet Earth*

> This book [*The Late Great Planet Earth*] contains incontrovertible proof that
> Christianity is the one true way. Everybody should read this.
>
> Every 3 years Hal Lindsay [*sic*] writes a new book denoting how the world will
> end in 5 years. Each subsequent book explains how he WASN'T wrong in the previous
> book and the world will really end in 5 years. . . . He has followed this pattern for 3
> decades and is now acknowledged as "the fore-most authority on Biblical prophecy
> in the world today." . . . I'm an electrician. If I had been doing my job POORLY
> and WRONG for 30 years I doubt I would be "the foremost authority." In fact,
> I dare say I would have ceased to make a living in my
> chosen profession in the first 10 years.
>
> —Readers of *The Late Great Planet Earth* on Amazon.com

American Studies scholars have been preoccupied with the politics of texts about end-times prophecies. For example, Paul Boyer, in his magisterial *When Time Shall Be No More: Prophecy Belief in Modern American Culture* (1992) argues that a belief that the end of the world is inevitable—held by a large number of Americans and American policymakers, including Ronald Reagan—profoundly shaped American foreign policy at the end of the Cold War. If the end of the world was inevitable (that is, it was God's will), what was the point of trying to reduce nuclear weapons stocks or sign new non-proliferation treaties?[1] Similarly, Melani McAlister argues in *Epic Encounters: Culture, Media, and U.S. Interests in the Middle East since 1945* (2001, 2005) that what Lindsey's book accomplished was the politicization of white evangelicals. Although they had largely eschewed involvement in worldly politics in favor of attention to personal sin and salvation in the wake of the Scopes trial in the 1920s, evangelicals were admonished by Lindsey that understanding the Bible required their engagement with Middle East politics and foreign policy.[2] Lindsey's *The Late Great Planet Earth* freely mingled quotations from defense intellectuals and diplomats with prophecies from the Bible, illustrating how one confirmed the other. Moreover, although most books about Bible prophecy assumed that readers were deeply interested in and knowledgeable about scripture but less engaged by contemporary politics, Lindsey's book tried to engage those interested primarily in contemporary international affairs but less knowledgeable about scripture.[3] In this way, current events became the bridge over which readers could come to Bible prophecy and—ultimately—to Christ.

Although books like Lindsey's no doubt did shape how Americans thought about nuclear weapons, the Middle East, the environment, and militarism, the "politics" of these texts is much more complicated.[4] Readers encounter texts in complex ways, as part of communities of readers that shape what they read and how they read it; and they encounter these texts as *books*, whose packaging and marketing shape the genre tradition in which they are placed and the particular kinds of reading they invite or enable. *The Late Great Planet Earth* was explicitly marketed to two distinct audiences—evangelical and trade—in two distinct packages. Moreover, the people who read it were not passive recipients of its political message—"cultural dopes" in Stuart Hall's terms.[5] Some were clearly resisting readers, and—as the epigraphs to this chapter suggest—they spent a great deal of time on Amazon.com engaging with one another in sometimes vitriolic terms. I look here specifically at narratives from readers for whom *The Late Great Planet Earth* was important. I have collected these narratives from two sources—eighty-one reader reviews posted on Amazon.com and nine I solicited from either H-Amrel (an online discussion group on the history of religion in America) or Theolog (a blog associated with the liberal periodical *Christian Century*).[6]

A Tale of Two Books

The Late Great Planet Earth was the best-selling nonfiction book of the 1970s, with 10 million copies in circulation by the end of the decade. It had sold more than 28 million copies by 1990 and an estimated 35 million by 1999. It was translated into over fifty languages; a 1977 movie version narrated by Orson Welles ran in theaters nationwide; and the film was later broadcast on HBO.[7] One critic called Lindsey "the most widely read interpreter of prophecy in history." Another claimed that only the Bible itself had outsold *The Late Great Planet Earth*.[8]

Although it may appear to those of us looking back as a single, immensely influential book, it was really two books with distinct but overlapping audiences—religious and trade. These two audiences each had their own reasons for reading the book and their own ways of reading it. Zondervan, an evangelical publisher based in Grand Rapids, Michigan, first published an edition in 1970 for evangelical readers, which was sold primarily in Christian bookshops and through the mail. Only after it had sold something like half a million copies did Bantam pick up the secular rights and release a mass-market edition available in trade bookshops and grocery and convenience stores.[9] Although the text itself is identical, the editions are clearly marked as belonging to different genre traditions that invite distinct reading protocols. The Zondervan edition was marketed as Bible prophecy. That is, it was an interpretation of the Bible (or at least the difficult, prophetic parts of it in Daniel, Ezekiel, and Revelation) for committed believers. Although it was written in far more engaging, accessible language than most, it was part of a long tradition of books on prophecy in an already-crowded evangelical marketplace.[10] The Bantam edition had a different cover—one explicitly modeled on Erich von Däniken's *Chariots of the Gods*, an immensely popular speculative history of how aliens from outer space had visited earth in ancient times.[11] It was shelved with New Age or occult or science fiction books and marketed to a secular audience as what McAlister calls "doomsday exotica."[12]

Although the words on the page differed not at all, the reading protocols invited by these two modes of packaging and marketing the book differed markedly. Evangelical Christian readers were convinced of the truth claims made in *The Late Great Planet Earth* and read it in order to connect the disturbing events in the world with predictions made in the prophetic books of the Bible. *The Late Great Planet Earth* made the scary, uncertain contemporary world look as though it were completely under God's control and that events were unfolding exactly as He intended. The reader had a special role to play in this historic moment in convincing others of the truth in time for them to accept Jesus as their personal savior and be rescued from the impending apocalypse. To these readers, the book was true and called them to take action based on their reading. The "New Age" or "science fiction" readers saw *The Late Great Planet Earth* as engaging, speculative fiction. They were not bound by its truth claims; they found its fantastic elements appealing precisely because they had few ties to contemporary life (that is, it was "escape" fiction); and they were not necessarily moved to take action because of reading it.

This duality appears repeatedly in readers' recollections of the book. Some were clearly evangelical readers; some were clearly speculative fiction readers;

and others were aware of its dual function and audience and commented specifically on this. One reader remembered talking about the book with his girlfriend, whose brand of countercultural evangelicalism was connected to her attraction to "proto-New Age things," including von Däniken's *Chariots of the Gods.*[13] An Amazon.com reviewer situated the book in this genre tradition for other potential readers in a review headlined "Interesting Fiction," describing *The Late Great Planet Earth* as like Nostradamus and Edgar Cayce. Another reviewer identified its genre as "the sensationalist exposé," listing similar books—*The Bermuda Triangle, Chariots of the Gods, Philadelphia Experiment, The Population Bomb.*[14] A 1977 *Publishers Weekly* interview noted that "general bookstores shelve Lindsey's titles next to books about the I Ching and Transcendental Meditation."[15]

Others recognized that it was both religion and speculative fiction. One reader wrote to me that he had discussed the book with his colleagues when he was in seminary (it was religion), but that it was in the science fiction section of his local bookstore.[16] For some, its sci-fi/fantasy elements were what made the book so bad. To call it fiction was to dismiss it as useless and wrong. One Amazon.com reviewer scoffed, "Suffice it to say that Lindsey's take on the book of Prophecy might as well be a fantasy concocted as a science fiction novel." Another review titled "What a Load of Baloney" explained, "This book depends upon (count 'em) five works from the nineteenth century all of which have been debunked by scholars. It is a wonderful fantasy. If you like reading fantasy, and can accept it as such, it will be a great book for one to read."[17]

Others submitted more ambivalent reviews, explicitly invoking the two genre traditions in their critique. "Horrible Scholarship but Entertaining," insisted one Amazon.com reviewer, awarding the book two stars, a loose averaging of the 0–1 stars for logic and quality of scholarship and the 3–4 stars for "entertainment value."[18] One reader, remembering the engagement of his younger self with the text, recalled conscious engagement with the theology and unconscious engagement with its speculative tone. Although he narrated his embrace of and subsequent disenchantment with *The Late Great Planet Earth* as a story of his evolving understanding of eschatology, there was something else going on as well: "Some years later, I also realized that one of the reasons I had been so fascinated with LGPE and its clones was that I was a science fiction fan & LGPE had the tone of a sci-fi novel."[19]

The science fiction connection is commonly made. Lindsey himself, contemporary cultural commentators, and subsequent scholars have linked the popularity of prophecy books with other obsessions of the time: UFO

Front cover, *The Late Great Planet Earth*, original Zondervan edition.

narratives, the occult, New Age texts, conspiracy films. What they shared was a belief in supernatural intervention in human affairs and a profound suspicion of official (rational, liberal humanist) narratives about public life.[20]

Religious Institutions, Divided Publics, and the Individual

At least initially, readers of the Zondervan edition of *The Late Great Planet Earth* were conservative Christians who read the book as part of religious reading communities in the 1970s and 1980s. Evangelical publishers like Zondervan made most of their sales through Christian Booksellers Association (CBA) bookstores. The book was "invisible" in the secular mainstream until Bantam's mass-market paperback edition, and most of the mainstream

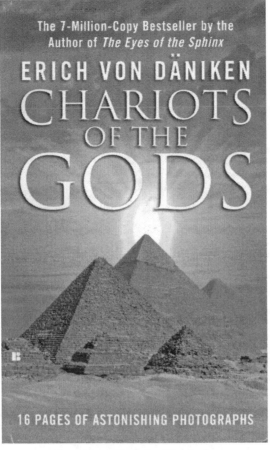

Front cover, *Chariots of the Gods*.

press coverage assumed that "we" did not read such books, and that the immense numbers of people who did were cause for grave concern.[21] As such, buying and reading *The Late Great Planet Earth* was a way of participating in a transdenominational Christian community that defined itself against a hostile or dismissive secular mainstream.

Church historian Martin Marty called *The Late Great Planet Earth* a "flag book"—a book whose purpose was—at least in part—the "rallying of the troops." As he surveyed the religious books landscape in 1976, Marty discerned ecumenical movements crystallizing out of reading communities around popular books by Corrie ten Boom, David Wilkerson (*The Cross and the Switchblade*), and Lindsey. Readers made themselves partisans of their flag book but did not associate with those outside their reading clique. Lindsey's premillennial dispensationalist readers, for example, were profoundly

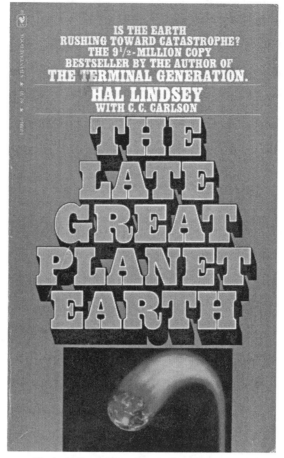

Front cover, *The Late Great Planet Earth*. The Bantam cover image was designed to suggest that of *Chariots of the Gods*.

suspicious of the Pentecostal/charismatic readers of Wilkerson. Readers did not read these books for information as much as they did for "belonging-ness," Marty argued.[22] To read and talk about these books was a way of publicly claiming a particular religious identity and membership in a privileged community of believers.

Indeed, the most striking fact about the eighty-one Amazon.com reviews is the vitriolic debate between insiders and outsiders. Although there are a few in the middle, most of the reviews give the book either five stars (the maximum) or one star (the minimum), with many expressing the fervent desire to award zero stars or even negative numbers.[23] The total includes twenty-four five-star reviews, ten four-star reviews, seven three-star reviews, two two-star reviews, and thirty-eight one-star reviews (most of which are

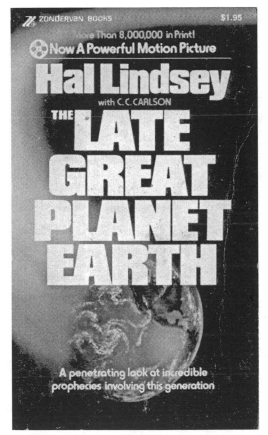

Front cover, *The Late Great Planet Earth*. Later covers
repeated the earth-as-comet image.

really zero or negative-star reviews). Readers are either full of contempt for
Lindsey and his work, are true believers, or are those whose lives were transformed by the book but who have since reevaluated their commitment to
Lindsey and his theology. It is clearly a book for "insiders," and those from
liberal religious backgrounds who wrote to me overwhelmingly explained
their "immunity" to its appeal by invoking their enlightened, liberal Christian upbringing.[24]

Clearly, *The Late Great Planet Earth* changed many readers' lives. "This is
the classic Bible prophecy book of all time," wrote one reviewer. "I first read it
in the early 70s and it moved me to seek out God." Another explained: "*The
Late Great Planet Earth* provides everything a Christian needs to know to drive
him or her to want to spread the message of Christ's salvation to a needy world."
For some, Lindsey had a divine mission to bring the truth about the end times

Front cover, *The Late Great Planet Earth*, current Zondervan edition.

to ordinary Christians: "Hal Lindsey has definitely been called by Our Lord and Savior to help us understand what was written thousands of years ago."[25]

Not surprisingly, many readers—whose own lives had been transformed by reading *The Late Great Planet Earth*—were eager to share the book with others. "I first read this book over 30 years ago and it changed my life. . . . I shared it with everyone I knew," wrote one grateful and representative reviewer.[26] Many recalled having bought multiple copies they gave away to friends, family, and strangers whose own faith they perceived to be lacking.[27] Testimony about transformed lives abounds. "One of my college roommates is a Christian largely because of reading 'The Late Great Planet Earth' in the 70s, and he has spent his adult years in Mexico as a missionary," wrote one.[28]

Those who disliked the book were—if possible—even more impassioned. A one-star review described *The Late Great Planet Earth* as "idiotic, gullible, credulous, superstitious, fanatical, irrational, etc." "Pure bunk," proclaimed another. "I read this book in 1971. It was pure bunk back then and it's even purer bunk 35 years after its publication. All of its 'predictions' didn't happen. Yet the author continues to be admired in fundamentalist circles. What does that tell you?"[29] As this case illustrates, criticism of Lindsey and *The Late Great Planet Earth* often slipped into criticism of those who read his books. Under the heading of "Fundamentalist Nonsense for the Ignorant and the Stupid," one argued: "What's amazing is that no matter how wrong he [Lindsey] is, no matter how shoddy his scholarship, and no matter how ludicrous his predictions, his books keep getting published and the dumb sheep out there just keep on buying this stuff."[30] Many reviewers suggested that Lindsey and his ilk kept cranking out books on the end times, in which they kept pushing doomsday out further into the future, in order to make money.[31] Lindsey was characterized as a snake-oil salesman and a scam artist.[32] Those who kept buying his books were just suckers. Several critical reviews invoked P. T. Barnum's adage that "there's one born every minute."[33] Even those critics who seemed more sympathetic characterized Lindsey's faithful readers as childish or immature. They, too, had been profoundly moved by *The Late Great Planet Earth* back in the 1970s, their reviews maintained, but they were unsophisticated and easily duped teenagers then, and now they have moved on, implying that those who have not exhibited a childish lack of sophistication and knowledge.[34]

Many readers continued to be angry about the misspent lives and misdirected energies that belief in Lindsey's claims had caused. For example, one explained, "I put off planning college and a career for a number of years because I couldn't see the point—after all, who wastes their time rearranging the deck chairs on the Titanic? When I think of the years I wasted because of this book, I get really, really angry!"[35] Others urged readers to place their energies in more productive directions—to worry about clothing the naked and feeding the hungry rather than end-times prophecy. It's a book, some maintained, that missed the point—loving your neighbor, living as Jesus did.[36] Many readers offered suggestions to potential buyers about better books to read on the end times or on Bible prophecy.[37]

Lindsey had his defenders, who explicitly took on the critics in their reviews. "Boy have some reviewers got it wrong!" insisted one. "This is a fantastic book and a good starting place for more study!" "I read most of the reviews of this superb book, and wonder why there is such vitriol—and then kick myself for the momentary lapse," began another. "When you shine a light in the dark, the bugs scurry for cover and it's much the same with people who don't want to know the truth, and spend enormous amounts of energy debunking truth that they don't want to hear."[38] There is a lot of quoting of scripture about scoffers who will burn in hell and smug "I-told-you-so's" directed at those who will be left behind.[39]

In some ways, the divided opinions are to be expected. *The Late Great Planet Earth*—like most evangelical books—defined itself against the sinful, secular mainstream and the liberal Protestant institutions allied with it. For example, Lindsey explicitly invoked the National Council of Churches and the World Council of Churches in a discussion of "The Ecumenical Mania." The amalgamation of all these churches, he insisted, watered down the true doctrines of the church and substituted worldly politics and "ecclesiastical shenanigans" in their place.[40] He dismissed such ideas as institutional racism and "Marxist-Christian dialogue" as silliness and insisted that the goals of the Communist Party USA and the liberal churches were identical. He was further critical of liberal theologians who late-date the Book of Daniel in order to challenge its supernatural record of prophecy. Lindsey insisted, "All through the Scriptures we find that Christ dealt strongly with the religious leaders and false prophets who put on their many-colored coats of righteousness and led people astray. Jesus called them hypocrites, fools, and vipers."[41] Jesus would not want you to be tolerant, ecumenical, and "broad-minded," Lindsey urged. He would want you to stubbornly and closed-mindedly stand up for the truth.

The Late Great Planet Earth clearly distinguished itself from liberal institutions and the secular world, but it also aimed its invective at evangelical institutions—especially those that denied or minimized end-times prophecy. The typical reader of *The Late Great Planet Earth* encountered the book in the 1970s or early 1980s as a teenager. Sometimes the book had the endorsement of church leaders. For example, one reader remembered, "This book practically replaced the Bible in the fundamentalist church I attended in the 70's."[42] But in many other cases, the book circulated underground among the young people of the church, even as it was roundly condemned by the minister in the pulpit.[43] One reader explained that the circulation of this book among the youth of his church helped create oppositional identities between hidebound parents and elders and truly Christian youth.[44] That is, it redrew the lines between "them" (religious leaders/elders) and "us" (youth), such that the institution was undermined.

The Late Great Planet Earth moved the center of Christian life from the institutional church to the individual believer. "We need to be alert," Lindsey insisted. "When we hear church leaders, teachers, or preachers questioning the visible return of Christ, this is a doctrine of apostasy."[45] Lindsey distinguished between those who say that Jesus returns every time people accept Him spiritually and those who say that Jesus may return at some point in the future but that it is irrelevant to our lives, although he gave both classes the label of "False Prophet." As evidence of widespread apostasy, he cited a 1961 *Redbook* study of seminarians: 56 percent rejected the virgin birth of Jesus; 71 percent rejected life after death; 54 percent rejected the bodily resurrection of Jesus; and 98 percent rejected that there would be a personal return of Christ to earth.[46] Citing end-times prophecies about false prophets, Lindsey insisted, "If you pass this book around to many ministers you'll find how true this prediction has become."[47]

Lindsey distinguished between the apostate church ("visible, physical gathering of people who may call themselves Christians") and the true church. He argued that apostate churches ("religious country clubs") could be of any denomination, and he urged readers to embrace true belief, however "anti-church" or "narrow-minded" or "dogmatic" that true belief might be labeled.[48] He placed particular emphasis on the distaste many young people felt for organized religious life: "In talking with many young people from various backgrounds I have found that the institutional churches are viewed by them as a reflection of all they despise in what they consider materialistic, hypocritical, and prejudiced elements within our American culture."[49] Lindsey insisted that the failing here was all the church's. Young people eagerly received Jesus, when they realized that the alternatives—"welfarism, socialism, or drugs"—would not provide lasting meaning for their lives. Churches, Lindsey maintained, either could not communicate the truth about Jesus in ways that young people found compelling or were not seeking the truth at all. As a consequence, they could not "compete" with radical political organizations that (falsely) promised the salvation young people were seeking.[50]

One astute reader, reflecting back on his experience attending Lindsey's Bible studies in Los Angeles in the 1970s, recalled how resolutely individualistic his thinking about salvation and the church were at the time. He wrote, "I ended up assuming that God's primary concern was with me and my personal salvation. The idea that my salvation was part of a larger, grander story, the formation of Christ's body the church . . . went largely unrecognized and unexpressed."[51] Although many commentators blame dispensationalist theology for this anti-institutional bias, this reader claims larger social forces mattered as well. As children of the 1960s, new converts to the Jesus movement were "deeply suspicious of institutional authorities"—religious or secular—coming in.[52]

Fear and Excitement: On the Appeal of *The Late Great Planet Earth*

Readers also encountered *The Late Great Planet Earth* in a larger historical context of slightly premature millennial panic. The nuclear arms race, environmental degradation, Cold War hostilities, unrest in Asia, Africa, and the Middle East, and a global economic downturn prepared readers to be anxious about humanity's future.[53] Mainstream press coverage focused on the comfort a belief in the designing hand of God could bring in such anxious times. The book offered to place the unsettling contemporary events of the 1970s and early 1980s within a larger framework of divine meaning and promised Christians personal salvation and hope. "For the Christian, these books are the comfort we seek while the world seems to spiral out of control," explained one Amazon.com reviewer.[54]

Fear was, in fact, the most common topic in discussion about the book on Amazon.com.[55] For example, one reader insisted that the book and film of *The Late Great Planet Earth* "literally traumatized me for many years." Another explained that the book was "a sure-fire prescription for scaring the daylights out of young kids (I know, I was one of them)."[56] Some of the adult Amazon.com reviewers reflected back on the reading of their teenage selves: "This book's strength lies in its ability to terrify a nonbeliever into becoming a Christian, and probably millions of non-Christians (or lukewarm Christians) out of stark fear became believers, some even pastors and missionairies [*sic*]."[57] This was one reason many readers criticized the book: "Faith should be more based on love and God's goodness, not fear of destruction."[58] Some of Lindsey's supporters defended him against charges of being a fearmonger. For example, one insisted, "There is nothing in this book to provoke fear, other than fear if you reject Christ, and you are left behind!"[59] Others maintained that there was nothing at all wrong with fearmongering: "Yes, Christians use scare tactics just like Jesus BECAUSE THERE IS SOMETHING YOU SHOULD BE AFRAID OF, IT'S CALLED HELL."[60]

For many, the fear was fear for their own salvation.[61] For others, the fear was for the nation and the world. One reader remembered the teen Sunday school class where she read *The Late Great Planet Earth*: "We got lots of end times paranoia, the cold war still going on, fear of nuclear war. Lindsey and writers like him . . . play on these fears."[62] Recalling members of a carpool who talked about the book incessantly, another wrote, "It seemed to fill them with anticipatory fear about our nation." Another remembered, "I can remember reading Lindsay [*sic*] type stuff and it was totally conflated with fear-mongering about the Russians invading and taking over the U.S. I can remember waking up from a nightmare about this."[63]

Several readers claimed that their worldview was—at least temporarily— transformed by reading *The Late Great Planet Earth* and consuming similar narratives (*Thief in the Night* films, Jack Chick comics). One remembered, "For a few years I tended to look at world events as being part of an elaborate 'end times' scenario that had been predicted in detail in the Bible." Another wrote, "I recall thinking that the Pope's near assassination, followed by Reagan's near assassination were surely some sort of harbinger of the end."[64] Several readers returned to *The Late Great Planet Earth* in the immediate aftermath of September 11 and found renewed meaning in it.[65]

Some remember not fear but thrill. One of Lindsey's previously quoted Bible study students from the 1960s remembers: "What I most vividly recall... is the deeply felt urgency of the times . . . the sense of excitement, intensity, and urgency we felt as Hal linked the Scripture to our world, our dilemmas, our questions. . . . Tremendous hope and fervor enveloped me and other students."[66] Reading *The Late Great Planet Earth* and talking about it with others could create the same sense of anticipation and excitement. One reader wrote to me: "I talked about this book a great deal, as you can imagine, with other friends as we went through high school, and as I recall I found the idea that we were soon to be taken out of this world absolutely thrilling. I have no idea how this interplayed with my own development as an adolescent, but I know that when times got tough, I was really looking forward to this great new thing that was about to happen (I wasn't going to have to finish high school. I wasn't going to have to put up with the intense pressures of my peers, etc.). I was a skinny kid with big glasses and I wasn't really happy with myself or very confident with peers. Man, did I look forward to an end to all that."[67]

Commentators struggled to explain how the suffering and devastation that were to occur during the end times were not frightening or horrible to believers. Robert Elwood, a scholar of the Jesus movement in the 1970s, called this sense of anticipation and excitement "apocalyptic happiness" and argued that it involved visualizing and hoping for a new, better world and experiencing a kind of "high" as a consequence. Rather than being afraid, then, believers would find the end times "thrilling, like a Technicolor movie."[68] In part, what Lindsey did was to speak to a desperately insecure generation of students about achieving a kind of absolute certainty and security. Erling Jorstad, another scholar of the Jesus movement in the 1970s, explained: "Speaking to a generation reared on a diet of science fiction, atomic bombs, and global pollution, Lindsey shows how the 'signs of the times' prove Jesus is coming. The teenagers find this fact not frightening, but immensely reassuring. To them it is the final proof, beyond human wisdom or logic, that the Bible must be literally true."[69]

Lindsey himself sounded oddly enthusiastic about the agonies and devastation that would come to an unbelieving world—"bloody battles" and "frightful carnage" that were beyond human imagination. "Imagine, cities like London, Paris, Tokyo, New York, Los Angeles, Chicago—obliterated! John says that the Eastern force alone will wipe out a third of the earth's population (Revelation 9:15–18)," he enthused.[70] Lindsey's apparent relish for the death and destruction that would occur at the battle of Armageddon earned him criticism—especially from liberal Christians.[71] Readers on Amazon.com echoed concerns about Lindsey's apparent satisfaction: "If I didn't know any better, I'd swear this was a book written by a Satanist. The author seems to be rejoicing in the prospect of Armageddon, including mountains being blown up and the destruction of all the world's cities."[72]

Does Theology Matter?

Lindsey's worldview was premillennial dispensationalism, made familiar to many contemporary Americans by the popular *Left Behind* series of novels (1995–2007). Lindsey was a follower of nineteenth-century Englishman John Nelson Darby's ideas about the division of history into seven great eras or "dispensations" and the imminent return of Christ before the final dispensation, a thousand-year reign of peace on earth ("premillennial"). Premillennial dispensationalism as an approach to interpreting prophetic books of the Bible (Daniel, Ezekiel, Revelation) was codified in 1909 by Cyrus Scofield in the influential Scofield Reference Bible. Scofield's notes—the "keys" to cryptic passages of scripture—appeared on the same page as the text itself and in identical type. This made Scofield's notes (the interpretation of God's word) almost indistinguishable from God's word itself.[73] The new Scofield Reference Bible was released in 1967; it was a powerful intertext for Lindsey's *Late Great Planet Earth*.

Although there was and is considerable debate over specifics, premillennial dispensationalists believe that ambiguous passages of scripture reference events that will occur as the second coming of Christ approaches. In Lindsey's version, the harbingers of the end times include the return of

Jews to the Holy Land (founding of Israel in 1948); Jews regaining control of Jerusalem's sacred sites (1967 war); and the rebuilding of the Temple (not yet). As the end times approach, the Antichrist, disguised as a global peacemaker, comes to power. True Christians will be transported to heaven (the rapture). This will be followed by seven years of tribulation—floods, famine, disease, plagues, war—at the end of which Jesus will return to lead Israel's army against the combined armies of the world. Christ's victory will usher in His thousand-year reign (the final dispensation).[74]

Not surprisingly, theology looms large in readers' discussion of *The Late Great Planet Earth*. First, many reviewers felt compelled to identify their theological positions before passing judgment on the book—stating that they were no longer Christians, or that they were premillennialists or simply that they believed that Jesus will return to earth and that they were very much looking forward to it.[75] Much of the most vitriolic criticism comes from those who believed Lindsey was misinterpreting scripture, that is—his theology was wrong.

There were a number of books that came out in the late 1970s from theologians who made this argument at length.[76] For example, T. Boersma's *Is the Bible a Jigsaw Puzzle . . . An Evaluation of Hal Lindsey's Writings* (1978) took on the task of debunking Lindsey's interpretive method. Boersma concluded that "on the basis of Scripture," one must reject Lindsey's approach, and he offered his own (presumably correct) way of reading the passages of Daniel, Revelation, Ezekiel, and Zechariah that were important to Lindsey's worldview.[77] Cornelius Vanderwaal, author of *Hal Lindsey and Biblical Prophecy* (1978), argued, "Pity those who look to Lindsey's books to lead them through the Bible. Lindsey's views represent yet another link in a long chain of mistaken interpretations of God's Word."[78] Ministers who wrote to me had similar convictions: "Bottom line the book is—pardon my language—crap from a theological perspective although as an historical text, really valuable."[79] Even the lay readers on Amazon.com could be rather sophisticated theologically. One explained to fellow customers that the rapture cult started in Britain in the early nineteenth century and that it was not biblical. The rapture—the idea that Jesus will take Christians alive from earth before the sufferings of the end times—was not widely accepted by biblical scholars.[80]

Oddly, however, Lindsey's theological errors seemed to bother most readers very little. The man who remembered finding Lindsey's vision of the end times "thrilling" to his skinny, adolescent self also narrated how he ceased to believe Lindsey trafficked in the truth: "I don't recall when I quit thinking that the world was going to end soon (or ever). I think what happened was that 1981 passed [when Lindsey initially predicted the end], and then things got better for me. I gained some weight, made some more friends, got contact lenses and started looking forward to college. When I got to college and studied religion I was, of course, very interested to learn about Darby and the whole dispensational thing. But I wasn't shocked to discover that the system was not very sound biblical theology. I think I was sort of tired and bored with the whole thing by then. I think somewhere along the way I had determined it was stupid."[81] Remembering a Sunday school teacher who kept a dispensational chart on the classroom wall and located each passage they read together on the timeline, this reader mused: "I do remember, by the time I was a senior, that I was terribly frustrated and bored by all this. He probably bored me out of my dispensationalism way before I rejected it theologically or biblically."[82]

In this narrative, a theological education alerted the reader to the limits of Lindsey's arguments, but the reader had lost interest long before. The knowledge of Lindsey's theological errors might have been the nail in the coffin, but Lindsey's narrative had ceased to have a meaningful place in his life much earlier. To be "boring" and "stupid" indicates that this story no longer made sense of his daily life and his social and psychological needs the way it formerly had. This story was simply not *useful* anymore.[83] In her 2012 ethnography of two Vineyard Fellowship churches (founded in 1982 by John Wimber, one of the central figures among leaders of the Jesus People on the West Coast during the 1970s), T. M. Luhrmann similarly found a pragmatic focus on what faith could accomplish. These descendants of the Jesus People have a faith that she describes as "practical, not philosophical." "People stay with this God not because the theology makes sense," she argues, "but because the practice delivers emotionally."[84]

Even those who thought Lindsey wrote a great book acknowledged his theological failings but didn't seem to care. One Amazon.com reviewer explained: "Many, many people were led to a saving faith in Christ after either reading this book or seeing the movie. . . . I beleive [sic] that even the most learned among us will get a 5 out of 8 for theology. Jesus said you will know them by thier [sic] fruits, I have only seen good fruits come from this book."[85]

Although theologians and ministers were critical of his errors of biblical interpretation, for many ordinary readers the theology was beside the point. Even Lindsey's fans conceded that he might be misreading scripture, but they asserted that it mattered little. The book did good work, brought them closer to God, and helped them to convert their friends. Its theological incorrectness was easily overlooked. Even those who dismissed the book said that the theological critique was not what really changed their minds.[86]

The Scandal of Middlebrow Religion

"I first heard the gospel in a context, manner, and form I could understand from a former tugboat captain named Hal Lindsey," declared Chris Hall, writing in the evangelical periodical *Christianity Today* in the late 1990s.[87] Hall was recalling the Wednesday night Bible studies he had attended in the late 1960s at the Jesus Christ Light and Power Company, a former fraternity house near UCLA, where Lindsey did his teaching and evangelism. There was nothing new in Lindsey's message (his colleagues complained that he merely repackaged his lecture notes from seminary),[88] but his mode of presentation was both innovative and compelling. "He knew how to package the dispensational eschatology he had learned at Dallas Theological Seminary in a fashion that Americans, many of them young, countercultural types emerging from the turbulent sixties, could understand and embrace," Hall recalled.[89]

Fundamentalists had long been interested in the apocalyptic books of the Bible—Daniel, Ezekiel, Revelation—and there is a long tradition of interpreting them in light of contemporary events believed to be harbingers of the end times.[90] Most of these other books were for "insiders," however. McAlister describes them as "academic, inbred books aimed at audiences of the already-converted."[91] Most readers were enrolled in evangelical seminaries and Bible colleges, and the emphasis leaned much more heavily on scripture than on the current events believed to confirm the prophetic power of those scriptures. Conversely, Lindsey presumed that his readers were fascinated and terrified by the wars and unrest in the Middle East, although they might have lacked familiarity with the prophetic scriptures that identified these events as harbingers of the end. His book was much more easily appropriated by "outsiders" than its competitors. Lindsey's job was to weave together contemporary political, scientific, and foreign policy accounts of nuclear proliferation and scenarios for World War III with the prophetic scriptures that predicted them, convincing lay readers that the Bible offered a framework to give meaning to the terrifying events of the day.

Initially, neither Lindsey nor Zondervan imagined that his repackaging of the premillennial dispensationalism he learned in seminary would have a big market among the unchurched. Lindsey explained, "If I had been writing 15 years ago, I wouldn't have had an audience. . . . But a tremendous number of people were beginning to worry about the future, and they were looking everywhere for answers. The turn to the occult, astrology, Eastern religion, and other movements reflected the fear of what was going to happen in the future. And I'm just part of that phenomenon."[92] If Zondervan sold *The Late Great Planet Earth* at Christian bookstores as a short, accessible book of prophecy for conservative Christians, the Bantam edition engaged members of this larger audience who were looking to all kinds of alternatives to make sense of the world and allow them to feel more secure about the uncertain future. *The Late Great Planet Earth* was eschatology, but it was also pop psychology, futurism, or pseudo-science in some bookstores.[93] It was an extraordinarily successful commodity, because it was niche marketed to audiences of "insiders" and "outsiders."

Lindsey's rhetorical strategies enabled this kind of crossover. His goal was to make Bible prophecy, an often esoteric intellectual discipline, accessible and compelling to lay readers. He framed it not as an exercise in scriptural exegesis, but as one among many ways of divining the future. "This is a book about prophecy," he wrote, "—Bible prophecy. If you have no interest in the future, this isn't for you. If you have no curiosity about a subject that some consider controversial, you might as well stop now."[94] His chapter explaining biblical prophecy began by talking about astrology and other popular forms of divining the future, before finally turning to Bible prophecy at the close of the chapter as a more accurate, proven method.[95] That is, you should be interested in end-times prophecies not because they are the authoritative word of God, but because the Bible has a better track record than other forms of fortune-telling. Quite simply, it is better at placing the scary, confusing mess of contemporary events into a narrative that provides meaning and hope than the alternatives. The rhetorical argument is not that end-times prophecies are *True*, but that they are useful. This quintessentially middlebrow claim—however compelling it might have been to lay readers—infuriated theologians.

For example, Cornelius Vanderwaal, a Reformed theologian who authored one of many book-length debunkings of Lindsey's bestseller in the late 1970s, was appalled by Lindsey's chapter casting Bible prophecy as fortune-telling. Vanderwaal explained that by reducing Bible prophecy to a means to an end—satisfying our curiosity about future events—Lindsey "drags the Lord's prophets down to the level of the heathen seers."[96] Vanderwaal's explicit goal was to uphold the Reformed confession, and he was furious that Lindsey's amateurish Bible interpretation was winning more converts than orthodoxy. He is angered by the way Lindsey presents the Bible as one among many choices a consumer of fortune-telling commodities might make. How dare Lindsey judge the scriptures according to their effectiveness or usefulness for our own lives? How dare he think about God's word as a means to an end? At base, Vanderwaal and critics like him fault Lindsey for taking a functionalist approach to religion, a quintessentially middlebrow (and consumerist) approach. Just as the middlebrow aesthetic was scandalous to cultural critics of the 1920s because it imagined literature and culture as a means to the end of achieving social and professional status,[97] Lindsey's religion was scandalous because it imagined Bible prophecy as a means to the end of divining the future and providing practical guidance for everyday life.

The Late Great Planet Earth was clear and engaging to general readers, as good middlebrow texts are. Lindsey made prophecy accessible in two ways. First, he explained the strange and unfamiliar in familiar terms. For example, he explained the rapture—the physical taking up to heaven of true Christians before the beginning of the tribulation—as being like another kind of fantastic journey most people had found unimaginable—the trip to the moon witnessed the year before by Americans watching television.[98] Second, he warned readers when he engaged in detailed exegesis, so that they could skip it if they found it unpalatable: "It is necessary on the next few pages to establish some documentation from ancient history. Some people find this subject 'a little dull,' to say the least. If this is your case, you may wish to skim over the high points. For others, it will prove to be rewarding to check carefully the grounds upon which the historical case is built."[99]

Lindsey's accessible presentation divided lay readers and theologians. Enthusiastic lay readers repeatedly invoked the engaging, accessible prose in which Lindsey presented premillennial dispensationalism. "Mr. Lindsey knows his material well and the presentation is both clear and simple," one asserted. Another reassured potential readers: "Written in a clear and understanding way, this book will move you to not only seek out Biblical prophecy for yourself, but examine your own heart in this last hour that we are living."[100] Lindsey's critics heaped scorn on *The Late Great Planet Earth* for precisely these reasons. For example, Vanderwaal maintained that the public was easily duped by Lindsey and others like him, because they were so ignorant and poorly read: "A public that reads nothing heavier than the *Reader's Digest* is ready to consume and digest great quantities of the terror treatment."[101] He dismissed Lindsey and his ilk as sensationalists and bad scholars: "Thus the history of exegesis doesn't concern them in the slightest. All they're interested in is 'the latest'—especially if it's startling or sensational. The problems with which theologians have wrestled for centuries are quickly forgotten. . . . [They] make no attempt to refute earlier interpretations of the Bible passages on which everything is made to depend. The views of past scholars are simply shaken off as dead weight. . . . The democratization of our society has now gone so far that *anyone* can be an authority on biblical interpretation. Do it, brother! Don't let anyone stand in your way!"[102] If Lindsey judged eschatology by its usefulness—that is, its accuracy in predicting future events—Vanderwaal maintained that good eschatology was self-consciously situated in a centuries-long tradition of scriptural exegesis. Lindsey's work was engaged with today's world; Vanderwaal's was concerned with the self-contained historical/textual world of theologians.

Lindsey's opponents were, in fact, almost uniformly critical of his lack of historical grounding.[103] Chris Hall characterized the Jesus movement as a whole as suffering from a "drastically shortened exegetical perspective" and "theological and historical amnesia." He recalled: "As a young believer birthed during the Jesus movement, I knew nothing of Justin or Irenaeus [church fathers]. The model of exegesis I received, and in turn practiced myself, was a highly individualistic affair. . . . I was shockingly unaware of the Christians who had read, pondered, and interpreted these texts before me."[104]

This eliding of historical and cultural context should sound familiar. Like Frykholm's "life-application method" readers of scripture, Lindsey's readers wanted a take-home lesson with immediate relevance to their daily lives rather than competing interpretations or historical context about a book or passage.[105] Similarly, the secular "middlebrow" reading that—I argue in the Introduction—descends from Calvinist modes of reading scripture, immediately connects historically distant texts with readers' daily lives. In some ways, Lindsey was asking his readers to read the prophetic books of the Bible as if they were parts of the Great Books curriculum—as if they had something immediate and direct to say to readers' own life situations rather than as texts that emerged from and participated in particular historical and cultural debates of their own time. Lindsey took the prophetic works of the Old Testament—written during periods in ancient history when the survival of the Jews as a people was in question—and recontextualized them as writing about the 1970s that engaged events in the daily newspaper.

Like the Great Books curriculum, which promised folks who could not afford an expensive education in the classics at Harvard the benefits of these

texts without all the tuition money, training in ancient languages, and leisure such an education required, the debate over *The Late Great Planet Earth*
was profoundly inflected by cultural capital. Vanderwaal was part of an elite
class of religious intellectuals desiring to protect their status as privileged
interpreters of the Bible. Lindsey's anti-intellectualism was a huge problem. How could you not care what centuries of expert exegesis say about
these passages? How powerful could the interpretations be, if millions of the
uneducated could understand them?

Vanderwaal explained that readers were taken in by Lindsey because
they were completely unaware of what rigorous scriptural analysis looked
like: "Since we live in a democratic age, an age in which all knowledge has
to be packaged in some simple 'Reader's Digest' style, they fail to recognize what superficial methods of Scriptural interpretation the dispensationalists are using."[106] This was, in part, because their leaders were pretty
ignorant as well. Vanderwaal lamented: "The time when every preacher
had a classical education is long gone. Not many of today's preachers
are experts in theological scholarship and the languages of the Bible."[107]
Many ministers these days were less scholars than social revolutionar-
ies, he argued, and they preferred mining the Bible for political slogans
rather than entering the centuries-long conversations about the meaning
of scriptures.

This gap highlights the difference between the study of religion from the
top down (starting with clergy, theologians, and church leaders) and the
study of religion from the bottom up (starting with laypeople). Lindsey produced a kind of popular religion which spoke to and continues to speak to
millions of readers, although it earned him and continues to earn him the
scorn of intellectuals and theologians. Like middlebrow culture more generally, Lindsey's brand of religion was scandalous because it failed to respect
the separation between sacred and profane, culture and commerce, and
because of its resolutely practical ethos.[108] If Lindsey made a lot of money
from *The Late Great Planet Earth*, it must not be a holy book. If end-times
prophecy interpretation was undertaken by professors and theologians with
years of training and in a language of almost unreadable complexity, then
Lindsey's brevity and clarity were evidence of his intellectual bankruptcy. If
the Lord's affairs transcended human understanding, then an insistence that
religion improve the lives of believers on their terms was utterly corrupt.
If Lindsey engaged in theologically incorrect fearmongering that appalled
intellectual elites, his way of interpreting scripture nonetheless engaged a
worldview that resonated with many ordinary readers. Historian George

Marsden calls prophecy belief a kind of "folk piety." Boyer calls it a "theology of the people."[109]

Conclusion: Two Books, Many Readings

In this chapter, I investigated how *The Late Great Planet Earth* might look different if we studied it from the bottom up, rather than from the top down. Theologians are critical of its intellectual failings; scholars despair over its historical inaccuracies and, indeed, its failure to engage with history at all. If we start with texts and authors, with scholars and intellectuals, the story of *The Late Great Planet Earth* is about theology (bad) and politics (ditto—which is to say, hawkish and right-wing). If we start with laypeople reading, a different and much more nuanced story emerges.

American Studies scholars have historically focused attention on the ways end-times prophecy media shape readers/consumers into political actors. Such texts are an antimodernist critique of contemporary America and express anxiety about global systems and the secularism that comes with them.[110] They are also, as Boyer argues, texts that shaped American discussions about the Middle East, the Soviet Union, nuclear weapons, and the environment. One of their effects was no doubt the politicizing of white evangelicals, as McAlister rightly insists. Undoubtedly, some readers of *The Late Great Planet Earth* were politicized to support right-wing causes and to be complacent about the inevitable nuclear holocaust the Bible presumably foretold. However, as narratives of lay readers make clear, this is only part of the story. Readers encounter texts embedded in what Clifford Geertz calls "webs of significance"—both material and human—that shape what kind of meaning readers make. As scholars like Robert Darnton and Roger Chartier have long made clear, one cannot "read" the politics of a text from the words on the page. Readers take up these texts as books—material artifacts that shape how and by whom they are read—and as part of interpretive communities that shape their interpretations.[111]

The Late Great Planet Earth was two books—Truth and speculation, prophecy and sci-fi, scriptural exegesis and paranoid conspiracy fantasy— and these two ways of packaging the text privileged certain kinds of readers and certain kinds of reading over others. If these accounts offer evidence that readers of a single text encountered at least two books, they further suggest an even larger number of readings. Readers of *The Late Great Planet Earth* were grateful, terrified, thrilled, obedient, transformed, bored, amused, resistant, paranoid, angry, disgusted, and everything in-between.

The reports of these readers as they argue over meaning with each other, with authors and publishers, with religious leaders, and with their younger selves suggests that reading is a good deal more unruly and unpredictable than scholarly accounts indicate.

The vast majority of scholarship on end-times prophecy comes from historians and literary scholars, who are engaged in textual analysis.[112] That is, they produce close, attentive "readings" of these texts, readings I often find quite compelling and smart. Ordinary readers of these texts are not nearly so consistent in their interpretations, however. Whatever designs writers and publishers might have on their audiences, what emerges is often much more complicated and contradictory. Ideologies have holes in them; readers bring their personal histories and social situations to bear on their reading. If most commentary on *The Late Great Planet Earth* has focused on its social and political implications, the narratives from readers are frequently more personal. Texts like *The Late Great Planet Earth* have implications for nuclear nonproliferation and foreign policy in the Middle East, but they also have implications for miserable kids who desperately want out of their suffocating high school worlds, young men engaging their countercultural girlfriends who are into both Jesus and New-Age stuff, and people who want to fit into church youth groups where *The Late Great Planet Earth* has replaced the Bible. Moreover, the social and political implications emerge only in and through the individuals who decide if such stories are useful, given their current concerns and circumstances. Truth and theological correctness seem less important to these readers than the usefulness of these stories for making sense of their lives and larger world events. Luhrmann describes what contemporary evangelical Christians seek: "What they want from faith is to feel better than they did without faith. They want a sense of purpose; they want to know that what they do is not meaningless; they want trust and love and resilience when things go badly."[113] This seems true of Lindsey's 1970s and 1980s readers as well. The politics of this kind of faith is really up for grabs. Perhaps the most disturbing political implication of *The Late Great Planet Earth* is that it encourages readers to imagine their lives, their interpretive world-making, and their salvation in strictly individual terms.

The Late Great Planet Earth was accessibly written and widely available in affordable editions, carefully packaged to appeal to both insiders and outsiders to Bible prophecy. For some, it was engaging fiction. For others, it invited them to connect other-worldly religion with contemporary life and made them over into (they thought) better people. Although intellectual elites were greatly troubled by errors in Lindsey's theology and his aesthetically bad prose, ordinary readers seemed largely untroubled by these, preferring to privilege what texts do in readers' lives over style, form, aesthetics, or scholarly standards. The story of *The Late Great Planet Earth* suggests that scholarly modes of reading exist alongside popular ways of reading that emerge from religious contexts. As an extraordinarily successful commodity niche marketed to different consumers, it also suggests the entanglement of lived religion and consumer culture. I look more closely at the contemporary religious marketplace and the books that succeed in it in the following chapters.

PART V

The Decade of the Soul

The 1990s and Beyond

NINE

Books for the Seeker

Liberal Religion and the
Literary Marketplace in the 1990s

The marketing of "church" books, those with a denominational or creedal
slant, is an uphill battle, whereas books that espouse a disaffiliated or
institutionally disengaged religious posture ride a crest of public interest.
—*Toronto Star*, 17 April 1999

God has become a modern celebrity.
—*Washington Times*, 29 April 1995

The mail-order book club One Spirit offered readers "Resources for the
Spirit, Mind and Body." In October 2001, its website explained: "Today,
more people than ever are realizing the value of a balanced, healthy lifestyle.
But with so many choices, and so many different directions, how can you be
sure you're selecting the path that's right for you? You can trust One Spirit to
offer you only the best books, CDs, videos, audiotapes, and more. Whatever
your needs are–and wherever your heart leads you—you'll find the guidance you seek at One Spirit."[1] One Spirit categorized titles under rubrics
like world religions, feng shui, herbal medicine, animals, getting your desk
organized, vegetarian cooking, codependency, New Age, and great sex—
all represented as parallel or complementary paths toward enlightenment,
liberation, or empowerment. In these paragraphs, readers/consumers were
cast as pilgrims on a spiritual journey (which path is the right one?) rather
than as members of traditional religious institutions. Further, they were
seeking not salvation but a "balanced, healthy lifestyle," which could be
achieved in any number of equally acceptable ways. One Spirit remained
agnostic on the question of right belief or right practice, because its primary
mission (like that of the Religious Book Club in the 1920s and 1930s) was to
sell products.

One Spirit was founded in 1995, featuring what *Publishers Weekly* described as "religion and spirituality books with a New Age/alternative flavor as well as health and self-help titles." It was the fastest-growing specialty book club ever launched by its parent Book-of-the-Month Club. Its editorial director insisted that One Spirit selections were intended to "achieve the broadest possible appeal."[2] One Spirit was responding to some profound changes in American reading and spiritual life. Since the 1990s, growing numbers of Americans reported being more interested in spiritual matters and spiritual growth than they used to be. At the same time, they were increasingly assembling a faith and a set of spiritual practices outside of traditional denominational frameworks.[3] Books and reading played a key role in this process. Religious Studies scholar Robert Fuller argued that since the 1990s, "bookstores have emerged as the most important centers of unchurched spirituality . . . virtual synagogues of spiritual instruction."[4] Because of growing sales of nonfiction religion and spirituality titles, publishers christened the 1990s "the decade of the soul." In the spring of 1994, fully half of the nonfiction bestsellers were about religion/spirituality, and the number of books in print featuring "soul" in the title increased fourfold between 1990 and 1996.[5]

One Spirit is emblematic of a prominent way of being in the world religiously—spiritual seeking. This chapter examines some of the best-selling mainstream religion/spirituality titles of the 1990s in light of increasing numbers of self-reported "spiritual seekers." "Spiritual seeker" is sociologist Wade Clark Roof's term for individuals with fluid, dynamic religious styles who move freely in and out of congregations across the life course, cobbling together a set of spiritual practices by combining elements of various traditions.[6] Many of the bestsellers of the 1990s modeled the formation of alternative, individual spiritual faiths outside of formal religious institutions. They included Thomas Moore's *Care of the Soul* (1992), Karen Armstrong's *A History of God* (1993), Jack Miles's Pulitzer prize–winning *God: A Biography* (1995), and Kathleen Norris's *The Cloister Walk* (1996). Moore's *Care of the Soul* was a self-help book that ruthlessly critiqued psychology but promised fulfillment through disciplined spiritual practice. Armstrong's *A History of God* traced the various ways God was reimagined by Jews, Christians, and Muslims throughout history. Miles's *God: A Biography* discussed the God of the Hebrew Bible not as a supernatural being but as a character in a story. Norris's *The Cloister Walk* was the spiritual memoir of a secular female poet who found a spiritual home in a Benedictine monastery among celibate Catholic men. These books—psychology, history, biography, memoir—nonetheless shared qualities that make them especially useful for seeker spirituality. These included defining themselves against religious conservatism, emphasizing spiritual practice over belief, critiquing consumer culture, and celebrating literary or poetic ways of being in the world.

Seekers and the Literary Marketplace

Scholars from a variety of disciplines concur that since the 1960s Americans have undergone a profound shift in their ways of being in the world religiously. Sociologist Robert Wuthnow characterizes this as a shift from a spirituality centered around dwelling in stable communities—one rooted in homes, neighborhoods, and ethnic communities—to a spirituality centered around seeking—one rooted in individual questing after meaning, knowledge, and wisdom.[7] In the introduction to his 1993 study of baby boomers' religious and spiritual lives, Roof describes this "generation of seekers": "Many within this generation who dropped out of churches and synagogues years ago are now shopping around for a congregation. They move freely in and out, across religious boundaries; many combine elements of various traditions to create their own personal, tailor-made meaning systems. Choice, so much a part of life for this generation, now expresses itself in dynamic and fluid religious styles."[8] Across faiths, interest in mysticism—that is, personal experience of the sacred—grew while trust, faith, and participation in many traditional religious institutions declined. In this remaking of the religious landscape, denominational differences and issues of theology shrank in importance, while the services and support a community could offer people on their individual spiritual journeys became paramount. Many (especially Protestants) drifted in and out of church with the arrival and departure of partners and children and often switched faith traditions or churches for one that better met their needs. Political scientist Alan Wolfe calls this the "circulation of saints," as people—whose beliefs remain essentially unchanged—move in and out of churches and denominations over the life course.[9]

Many scholars look askance at seeker spirituality. They see it as a consumerist way of being in the world colonizing religious faith. People "go shopping" for churches; they try on and discard faiths as the fashions change; they want a religion strictly for instrumental reasons—it provides the comfort, security, or self-esteem that make their everyday lives go more smoothly; and they think of a church as a service provider of weddings, funerals, and religious education for their kids. Sociologist of religion Robert Bellah and his colleagues deplored the growth of individualism and the decline of commitment to larger principles and communities that they found in their 1985 study, *Habits of the Heart*.[10] They offered an especially powerful critique of "Sheilaism"—a kind of religious practice a research subject named "Sheila" put together from the various bits and pieces of traditions she encountered and found useful to her, much as one might shop for furnishings and household items to decorate a room according to one's tastes.

Roof is less critical of these developments, preferring to see them not as self-involved narcissism from the "me generation" but as potential ways of exploring and making deliberate, authentic, and deeply felt choices about spiritual life rather than accepting one's inherited faith without much thought, consideration, or commitment. His scholarly study of these same questions, *Spiritual Marketplace*, recognizes these shifts in religious life and institutions and their connection to consumer capitalism, but he pleads for a closer, more nuanced analysis of how and why spiritual matters are approached and the particular institutional configurations that enable and constrain our religious choices.[11] This chapter is a case study of the literary, commercial, and religious configurations that constrain and enable seeker spirituality.

Although this particular form of spirituality is increasingly prominent and shapes the programs and ministries of many churches and synagogues across the nation, Roof is careful to point out that only roughly 10 to 15 percent of the population is what he would call "highly active seekers"—that is, "people for whom spiritual and metaphysical concerns are a driving force."[12] These seekers primarily live their spiritual lives outside organized institutions, building a faith and spiritual practice from goods and services purchased in the marketplace. Seekers tend to be older, professional, well-educated, and politically liberal. They are concentrated in fields like teaching, nursing, social work, counseling, and arts and crafts, which limits their earnings. They are disproportionately women (two-thirds), less likely than other believers to be married, and they place high value on individualism, personal development, self-fulfillment, and the pursuit of truth. They often blend their religious/spiritual journeys with the study of art, philosophy, science, and psychology—synthesizing language and images from various sources into a distinct worldview.[13]

Disproportionately white, native-born, well-educated, and reasonably well-to-do, they are typical book buyers. Moreover, the literary marketplace meets their spiritual needs far better than most organized religious institutions do. Historically, popular books laypeople read applying faith to the practical problems of contemporary life have been general or nondenominational, and they are usually encountered by individual readers or small reading groups in which interpretations are not closely guided by clerical authorities. Further, the literary marketplace has played an increasing role in the spiritual lives of readers, because more of them have encountered religion outside of traditional denominational frameworks since the 1960s. Roof thinks the increasing sales of religious books are due, in part, to the fact that mainstream publishers have deliberately tailored their offerings to meet the "spiritual vacuums" left by organized religion.[14] Four specific titles from the 1990s have served as resources for spiritual seekers crafting their own religious identity narratives.

Care of the Soul: Spirituality, Consumption, and Self-Help

Thomas Moore's 1992 *Care of the Soul: A Guide for Cultivating Depth and Sacredness in Everyday Life* was a surprise bestseller. The *Los Angeles Times* explained: "It does contradict every billboard image of American values that Moore writes to the broadest audience, uses such words as 'sacred' and 'holy' about life . . . and still climbs his way to the bestseller lists."[15] Moore's previous books were all scholarly texts published by small presses. In 1990, he hired a literary agent, wrote up a book proposal and thirty sample pages, and signed a contract with HarperCollins with a six-figure advance he believed he would not sell enough books to earn. *Care of the Soul* was not widely reviewed, and Moore was invited to do only a few interviews. Nonetheless, the book went through nineteen printings in its first year. More than 400,000 hardcover copies were sold (with total sales of nearly 2 million) by the mid-1990s, and it spent forty-six weeks on the *New York Times* bestseller list. Its sequels, *Soulmates* (1994), *The Re-enchantment of Everyday Life* (1996), and *The Soul of Sex* (1998), became instant bestsellers, but *Care of the Soul* was initially sold primarily through word of mouth, with many consumers purchasing multiple copies to give to their friends and family.[16]

Moore's work was perfect for seekers—spiritual but not tied to any particular faith tradition, concerned with finding sacredness in everyday life but not requiring participation in a particular faith community or set of religious practices. Moore explained in the introduction to *Care of the Soul*: "Although I am borrowing the terminology of Christianity, what I am proposing is not specifically Christian, nor is it tied to any particular religious tradition. It does, however, imply a religious sensibility and recognition of our absolute need for a spiritual life."[17] Moore encourages us to attend religious services, not for theological or moral reasons, but because it gives us regular practice thinking about our lives in mythological or symbolic ways. Although Moore himself is a former monk and still describes himself as an eccentric Catholic, he is much more interested in Greek mythology, Renaissance literature, Jungian psychology, and comparative myths and religions than he is in the sacred texts of the Judeo-Christian tradition. Moreover, he does not mean to suggest that the "soul" in question has anything to do with the immortal souls that concern Christian clergy. Moore writes: " 'Soul' is not a thing, but a quality or a dimension of experiencing life and ourselves. It has to do with depth, value, relatedness, heart, and personal substance" (5). Above all, "soul" is a mediating term—"midway between understanding and unconscious" (xiii), providing "the middle, holding together mind and body, ideas and life, spirituality and the world" (xiv).

Moore's work is perfect for seekers in yet another way. Seekers are disproportionately well-educated professionals, and Moore's books are not an easy read. Even positive reviews concede as much: "Neither pop psychology nor self-help book, it offers no easy answers but it is a thoughtful, eloquent, inspiring, and often vague and frustrating discourse on how we can bring imagination, poetry and yes, soul, back into our lives." And another review: "Despite the book's sometimes obscure references and often circuitous reasoning, Moore's message is simple: Live life with care and thoughtfulness."[18] Readers posting their opinions on Amazon.com are often more pointed: "This is not an easy read" and "There are a great many books out there that are infinitely more accessible to the common reader. I suggest that they be sought out."[19]

Moore comes by his erudition honestly; he is highly and eclectically educated. He spent thirteen years as a member of a Catholic monastic order, leaving just before taking his final vows. He has a bachelor's degree in music from DePaul, a master's degree in musicology from the University of Michigan, a master's degree in theology from the University of Windsor, and a Ph.D. in world religions from Syracuse University. He taught psychology and religion at Southern Methodist University until he was denied tenure. He was a psychotherapist in private practice for seventeen years in New England before *Care of the Soul* launched his career as an author and lecturer.[20]

It is hard to find a category for such a person and even harder to find a category for such books. Is it religion or isn't it? Is it psychology or isn't it? Self-help? New Age? For Moore, this is precisely the point. These divisions are arbitrary, and the way of being in the world such distinctions encourage is part of the reason we live such impoverished, alienated lives. The rationalization of the modern world—its division into rigid categories that encourage efficient living—is what leaves us with this longing for wholeness and transcendence in the first place. Moore writes: "In the modern world we separate religion and psychology, spiritual practice and therapy. There is considerable interest in healing this split, but if it is going to be bridged, our very idea of what we are doing in our psychology has to be radically re-imagined. Psychology and spirituality need to be seen as one. In my view, this new paradigm suggests the end of psychology as we have known it altogether because it is essentially modern, secular, and ego-centered. A new idea, a new language, and new traditions must be developed on which to base our theory and practice" (xv).

Although his books are extraordinarily successful commodities, they are sharply critical of consumer culture and the therapeutic worldview that comes with it. T. J. Jackson Lears made clear that a therapeutic worldview is utterly complicit with consumer capitalism—that the transition from "salvation" to "self-realization" in our way of thinking about selfhood maps almost perfectly onto the transition from notions about character tied to productive work to notions about personality tied to self-presentation and impression management through wise purchase and display of commodities.[21] Moore thinks our sense of malaise arises at least in part from living under the conditions of modern consumer culture. According to Moore, this world is ruthlessly productivist (when are we ever encouraged to do nothing?); does not value the soul; and pursues efficiency, speed, and technology at the expense of our human needs. Working long hours so that we can buy more stuff to fill the emptiness at the center of our lives is just a bad idea, Moore rightly insists.

Moreover, psychology as we know it is part of the problem. Although the first two chapters of *Care of the Soul* are a ruthless critique of conventional psychotherapy that makes clear distinctions between it and care of the soul, Moore saves his best argument for chapter 10. Explaining that psychologists have a catalog of disorders, the DSM-III, that helps doctors and insurance companies more precisely diagnose and standardize emotional and behavioral problems, Moore imagines writing his own DSM-III with a list of "disorders" patients have brought to him: "For example, I would want to include the diagnosis 'psychological modernism,' an uncritical acceptance of the values of the modern world. It includes blind faith in technology, inordinate attachment to material gadgets and conveniences, uncritical acceptance of the march of scientific progress, devotion to the electronic media, and a life-style dictated by advertising. This orientation toward life also tends toward a mechanistic and rationalistic understanding of matters of the heart" (206–7).

Aware that many readers may have encountered his books in psychology or self-help sections, Moore is careful to state up front that his books will not meet reader expectations for the genre: "As you read this book, it might be a good idea to abandon any ideas you may have about living success- fully and properly, and about understanding yourself. The human soul is not meant to be understood. Rather, you might take a more relaxed position and reflect on the way your life has taken shape" (xix). His description of his project is explicitly defined in opposition to conventional therapy: "You can see already that care of the soul is quite different in scope from most modern notions of psychology and psychotherapy. It isn't about curing, fix- ing, changing, adjusting or making healthy, and it isn't about some idea of perfection or even improvement. It doesn't look to the future for an ideal, trouble-free existence. Rather, it remains patiently in the present, close to life as it presents itself day by day, and yet at the same time mindful of religion and spirituality" (xv).

If therapists ought not to conceive of their activities as "cure," what is a better model? Although Moore offers several (parish priests who comfort us in times of trouble, for example), at base, he wants us to be literary critics. He calls care of the soul "an application of poetics to everyday life" (xix). As a "sacred art," it requires "poetic images" provided by "mythology, the fine arts, religions of the world, and dreams" (20). Most profoundly, it involves storytelling—which "helps us see the themes that circle in our lives, the deep themes that tell the myths we live" (13).

As a professional literary critic, I am quite taken by this critique of the therapeutic worldview and the consumerism that enabled it in the name of the transformational effects of stories. However, Moore's spiritually inflected critique of consumer culture is nonetheless thoroughly in keeping with its logic. First, like his Cold War religious self-help predecessors, Moore thinks at the level of the individual, a view that renders invisible the social structures our souls inhabit. Moreover, this individual soul is amazingly unmarked by gender, race, class, sexuality, or nationality. Not once does Moore refer to the structure of social institutions—poverty, colonialism, racism, sexism, or homophobia. For example, although there are feminine archetypes and masculine archetypes, we are not to understand these as having any rela- tionship whatsoever to actual men and women. Here is Moore addressing wealth in the final section of the book, "Care of the World's Soul": "Care for our actual houses, then, however humble, is also care of the soul. No matter how little money we have, we can be mindful of the importance of beauty in our homes. No matter where we live, we live in a neighborhood, and we can cultivate this wider piece of earth, too, as our home, as a place that is integrally bound to the condition of our hearts" (271). This may be quite true, but it is much easier to be mindful of beauty in our $250,000 homes than it is in the projects, and some neighborhoods are just much easier and much safer to cultivate than others. Moreover, most of the maintaining of beautiful homes has historically been done by women, and our culture has placed little value on cleaning and decorating them.

Moreover, like the Cold War religious self-help books discussed in Chapters 5 and 6, Moore's model includes an invisible hand at work. If we all care for our souls, the sum total of these self-nurturing, life-affirming decisions will result in reasoned protection of the environment, and self-acceptance will lead to acceptance and forgiveness of others in ways that will foster global understanding. Moore has been called on this simple-minded view of society before. He defends himself by arguing: "I'm not a political person. . . . I'm trying to present something constructive: a creative way of life that anyone can live. And I think if we did, we would diminish the horrors that are the result of living a mechanistic life that has lost its soul."[22]

More important, however, the subjects hailed by *Care of the Soul* are the subjects of a consumer capitalist society, what Judith Butler calls "performative subjects"—subjects constituted by the behavior/performance/self-presentation in which they are currently engaged, a model of the self that does not incorporate history or depth in any significant way.[23] The key principle is what Moore calls "psychological polytheism,"[24] which means "that psychologically we have many different claims made on us from a deep place. It is not possible, nor is it desirable, to get all of these impulses together under a single focus. Rather than strive for unity of personality, the idea of polytheism suggests living within multiplicity" (66). Although Moore is careful to clarify that he is not suggesting that "anything goes," he is suggesting that the ideal self for a complex, rapidly changing, consumer capitalist society might be many selves, since various selves might be better for various specific occasions.

Finally, Moore's hodgepodge of eclectic and wide-ranging materials is quite postmodern, and in that way complicit with the logic of late capitalism.[25] All of the world's history and legends are at our disposal, to be taken up or discarded as they are helpful to us in narrating our own lives, but in no case does Moore consider the cultures and contexts from which these stories arose.[26] For example, Moore retells Greek myths throughout *Care of the Soul,* but we learn nothing about the culture of the ancient Greeks—slaveholding, the role of women, the Greek legal system, or the wars in which the Greeks were embroiled. Some of those contexts are misogynist and racist and suffer from other troublesome flaws that Moore imports quite uncritically. In *Soul Mates*, Moore discusses the myth of Daphne, who was turned into a tree as she fled from Apollo—who was smitten by her virginal resistance to his seductions. Moore has a great deal to say about "the virgin soul fleeing from the spirit of cultural, Apollonic achievement of intellect, art, and even healing"; "the solitary trying to evade the relational"; "a changing of the sexual impulse into the artistic"; and even "flight from the soul"; but there is not one word about rape.[27]

The choices Moore makes on his historical raiding party are telling, however. The ancient Greeks and Romans, medieval saints and seers, and occasional reference to Eastern religions or the beliefs and practices of indigenous peoples fill most of the pages. The modern, capitalist, industrial world (with the exception of stories about his psychotherapy clients) is absent. In this way, Moore qualifies as what T. J. Jackson Lears, speaking of the turn of the last century (around 1900), calls an "antimodernist"— one who "recoil[s] from 'overcivilized' modern existence to more intense forms of physical or spiritual experience supposedly embodied in medieval or Oriental cultures."[28] All of the practices Moore embraces—closeness to nature, the rituals of sport, the joys of pure aesthetics, handicraft, music, and sacred ritual—were also embraced by WASP elites of the 1890s in their protest against the rationalization and disenchantment of modern life. Like the antimodernism of the 1890s, Moore's book leaves institutional structures unchallenged and consequently suggests that the critical edge of care of the soul will be easily transformed into a recreational activity to be engaged in by the demoralized professional-managerial class in its spare time.

Texts like Moore's *Care of the Soul* are popular because they successfully negotiate some of the contradictions at the center of professional-managerial class life without significantly challenging the structure of the social and economic institutions we inhabit. Our disaffection with alienated labor, the privileging of our identities as individuals rather than as members of larger communities, our sense of emptiness or weightlessness in a world where selves are assembled from the raw materials of consumer culture are all articulated and lent validity by the stamp of an expert. However, this articulation also addresses us as individuals, renders invisible the often exploitative structures of the institutions we inhabit, and reduces history and subjectivity to a set of consumer choices. In this way, Moore's *Care of the*

Soul paradoxically hails us as subjects/consumers in part through criticizing consumerist ways of being in the world.

A History of God: Against Fundamentalisms

Just as Moore's narrative defines itself against and emerges from a critique of conventional psychotherapy, Karen Armstrong wrote *A History of God: The 4,000-Year Quest of Judaism, Christianity, and Islam* in order to contest the increasingly prominent and influential assertions by religious conservatives about the unchanging nature of God and the literal truth of scriptures, assertions Armstrong describes as having detrimental social effects. That is to say that Armstrong's book is the evidence that God is not outside history, and that all our ideas about the divine are provisional and manmade. Armstrong calls fundamentalisms (of the Christian, Jewish, or Islamic variety) a retreat from God into idolatry and insists that such faiths must be "rejected as inauthentic."[29] She explains her project: "This book will not be a history of the ineffable reality of God itself, which is beyond time and change, but a history of the way men and women have perceived him from Abraham to the present day. The human idea of God has a history, since it has always meant something slightly different to each group of people who have used it at various points in time. . . . Had the notion of God not had this flexibility, it would not have survived to become one of the great human ideas" (xx). However critical she is of fundamentalist religion, Armstrong—like Moore—is not by any means antireligion. Indeed, she describes people as "spiritual animals" (xix) and lists the contemporary ills—violence, crime, addiction, despair (398)—that the absence of transcendent meaning creates. Like Moore's vision of a faith for the modern world, Armstrong's is not based on right belief. In her autobiographical introduction to *A History of God*, Armstrong distinguishes between belief in a set of propositions (a catechism) and faith, insisting that her religious movement away from manmade doctrines she accepted unquestioningly in childhood is typical. "Since those days," she argues, "we have put away childish things and have discarded the God of our first years" (xix). Like a latter-day Joshua Loth Liebman, she extrapolates from the personal to the social, suggesting that God seems to some "an aberration, something that the human race had outgrown" (xix). The conclusion of her book is concerned with the God of the future and creating a mature, workable faith for the modern world.

This mature, workable faith involves belief in *something*, but what that something is matters little. Armstrong argues: "Human beings have always created a faith for themselves, to cultivate their sense of the wonder and ineffable significance of life. The aimlessness, alienation, anomie and violence that characterize so much of modern life seem to indicate that now that they are not deliberately creating a faith in 'God' or anything else—it matters little what—many people are falling into despair" (397–98). If one need not embrace particular beliefs in order to imagine oneself as a religious or spiritual person, one does have to cultivate a particular sensibility or way of being in the world. Moreover, cultivating this sensibility requires disciplined spiritual practice. Armstrong calls God "a product of the creative imagination" (xx) and insists that "human beings must deliberately create this sense of God for themselves, with the same degree of care and attention that others devote to artistic creation" (397). Much of the alienation and misery in the world today, she contends, is the result of people failing to make this "imaginative effort," failing "to cultivate their sense of the wonder and ineffable significance of life" (398). In her introduction, Armstrong names this sense of wonder "transcendence" and defines it as "a dimension of the spirit that seems to be beyond the mundane world." Monotheists, she writes, call it "God" (xxi). Moore would call it "soul," and there is certainly a great deal of family resemblance between Moore's and Armstrong's version of being in the world religiously.

First, Armstrong is clear that spirituality requires artistic or literary ways of being in the world rather than scientific ones. "This will not be a history in the usual sense," Armstrong explains in the introduction, "since the idea of God has not evolved from one point and progressed in a linear fashion to a final conception. Scientific notions work like that, but the ideas of art and religion do not. Just as there are only a given number of themes in love poetry, so too people have kept saying the same things about God over and over again" (xxi–xxii). What Armstrong suggests in place of the idol God of fundamentalists is the God of the mystics. "God" here is a subjective experience rooted in mystery. One accesses this God through music, poetry, fiction, stories, dance, painting, sculpture, and architecture, always being careful not to confuse these representations or concepts with the reality beyond them. However, Armstrong is at pains not to suggest that anything goes: "Intelligence, discipline, and self-criticism" are necessary parts of cultivating this sense of the sacred rather than a kind of "indulgent emotionalism" (396–97).

Second, Armstrong's vision of cultivating sacredness in daily life—like Moore's—is profoundly countercultural. One does not passively consume spiritual products; one works at creating sacredness as a spiritual discipline.

"The God of the mystics does not arrive readymade and prepackaged," she argues. "It is not something that is likely to appeal to people in a society which has become used to speedy gratification, fast food and instant communication." Those seeking that kind of easy, "instant ecstasy" should turn not to the God of the mystics but to the God of the "revivalist preacher" (397).

Emphasis on spiritual practice rather than right belief aside, there is a theology emerging from *A History of God* that is humanistic and universal. Armstrong's book does not separate into three parts on Judaism, Christianity, and Islam. Instead, although loosely chronological, most sections examine in detail the parallel developments across these faiths—the rise of mysticism, the search for a scientific, rational faith, and so on—suggesting that in our efforts to reimagine God, we might, in fact, be articulating different versions of a single human experience. At one point, Armstrong insists, "Indeed, we shall find a striking similarity in Jewish, Christian and Muslim ideas of the divine. . . . Each expression of these universal themes is slightly different, however, showing the ingenuity and inventiveness of the human imagination as it struggles to express its sense of 'God'" (xxi–xxii).

Like Moore's notion of psychological polytheism, Armstrong's replacement of the one true God of monotheism with the many one true Gods monotheists have imagined is a way of making sense of postmodern life. As her evolutionary framework makes clear, Armstrong thinks that the idea of a personal God is simply inadequate for the modern world, that it "seems increasingly unacceptable at the present time for all kinds of reasons: moral, intellectual, scientific, and spiritual" (397). If Moore goes out on a historical raiding party for stories/selves to invest our lives with "soul," Armstrong insists that we simply be aware of the many gods we have created for ourselves and be self-aware about the one/ones we are currently creating and to what ends.

Armstrong is the ultimate pragmatist where religion is concerned. She argues: "Despite its otherworldliness, religion is highly pragmatic. We shall see that it is far more important for a particular idea of God to *work* than for it to be logically or scientifically sound. As soon as it ceases to be effective it will be changed—sometimes for something radically different. This did not disturb most monotheists before our own day because they were quite clear that their ideas about God were not sacrosanct but could only be provisional. They were entirely man-made—they could be nothing else—and quite separate from the indescribable Reality they symbolized" (xxi).[30]

Our job then is to cultivate—through spiritual practice and discipline—a sense of the divine in everyday life. Much as art, literature, and music are creative acts that require regular, disciplined practice, so too is creating/imagining God. Moreover, the kinds of God we imagine have everything to do with our social and historical circumstances, and they have profound implications for the kind of world we build. Armstrong's goal is for us to do this mindfully and well. The stakes, she argues, are too high not to do so. "Human beings cannot endure emptiness and desolation," she admonishes. "They will fill the vacuum by creating a new focus of meaning. The idols of fundamentalism are not good substitutes for God; if we are to create a vibrant new faith for the twenty-first century, we should, perhaps, ponder their history of God for some lessons and warnings" (399).

A History of God is a deeply learned book—over 400 pages of densely packed print detailing 4,000 years of monotheism, including an intellectual history of philosophers, mystics, and reformers from all three faith traditions. It has nine pages of maps, a glossary, notes, and suggestions for further reading. It is intellectually challenging. Although many praise its accessible, readable style, a great many readers on Amazon.com described their difficulties getting through the dense historical prose.[31] One review called *A History of God* an "astonishing commercial success," because it was "a straight history of three monotheistic faiths."[32] Indeed, it was a *New York Times* bestseller and an alternate selection of the Book-of-the-Month Club.

Everyone agrees that Armstrong's target audience is seekers. "Like most popular religion books in the secular trade market, *A History of God* is being bought by searchers," explained one review.[33] Readers on Amazon.com held similar convictions. In a review entitled, "A Good Read for the Seeker," one wrote: "WARNING: Reading this book may damage your fundamentalist perception!" Another explained: "This book encourages people to understand that no single person, group, or religious tradition has a monopoly of truth. It also calls people to learn about history to avoid the tragic consequences of claiming human agendas as the will of God."[34]

Armstrong herself is a seeker. She is a British writer and commentator on religion, having written over a dozen books and been part of numerous BBC programs about comparative religion. She was a Roman Catholic nun for seven years (from ages seventeen to twenty-four); she has a degree from Oxford; and she has taught modern literature. She has taught university-level courses at Leo Baeck College for the Study of Judaism in London and is an honorary member of the Association of Muslim Social Sciences. Although she embraced the label of atheist at one point, the process of writing *A History of God* changed her way of describing herself. The "God" she rejected was the anthropomorphic, personal God of the West, and the process of studying and writing about Judaism, Christianity, and Islam (especially their mystic variants) transformed her into a "freelance monotheist," bringing her back to religious faith in ways that surprised her.[35] Her faith is mystical, universalist, and focused on compassion as a force to unite people across faiths and nations.

Ultimately, Armstrong's history of God is much like the images and representations of God she details in its pages—a text emerging from a particular historical moment to address specific cultural and historical needs. If *A History of God* is fairly dense intellectual history, it is nonetheless profoundly *useful* to contemporary readers. Armstrong is firmly rooted in concerns about the rise of the Religious Right in the 1980s and 1990s, and her history is told so that we can get a "take-home lesson" for conducting our social and political lives today. One critic complained: "Her *History of God* is less a history than a tract, as much a product of the 1990s as David Friedrich Strauss's *Das Leben Jesu*, the first secular life of Christ, was of the 1830s. History is about extinguishing present preoccupations in order to rediscover the past. Armstrong's own theological and ecclesiological views shine through on every page: her loathing of fundamentalists, her distrust of authority, her preference for inner illumination over outward observance."[36] Armstrong would say that of course it is—and that it could hardly be anything else. What else is there? Histories of God, like representations of Him, are created by specific historical actors and respond to/participate in specific historical conversations of that moment. Armstrong would simply insist that we be self-aware about this and not confuse one particular socially situated history of God with *the* history of God or with God himself or herself.

God: A Biography: The Triumph of the Literary

The *Washington Times* reviewer called *God: A Biography* "the season's weirdest and most intriguing book."[37] The premise—that Jack Miles (a human being) could write the life story of God (widely held in scriptures to be unknowable)—generated a lot of attention and controversy. The *Times* of London reviewer lamented: "It had to happen. The world's source of potential biography subjects had dwindled to such a thin trickle that it was only a matter of time before someone, staring at the ceiling for inspiration, finally let his thoughts drift further heavenward." The *Jerusalem Report* titled its review "A Wild and Crazy Guy [God]: An Ex-Jesuit Writes the Ultimate Celebrity Bio."[38] Weirdness aside, *God: A Biography* got mostly great reviews—"brilliant, audacious," "a marvel," "dazzling"—and the book won the 1996 Pulitzer Prize for biography.[39]

Like other books for the seeker, Miles's *God: A Biography* sees belief as irrelevant. Miles's project is to write the life story of the God of the Hebrew Bible from Genesis to II Kings (he reads the books in the order found in the Hebrew Bible or Tanakh, not in the order in the Christian Old Testament). His project, then, is a *literary* one, a point he returns to repeatedly. His life of God has a Prelude called "Can God's Life Be Written?" which begins with a discussion of how scholars and critics have discussed the character of Hamlet, and he explicitly uses that framework for talking about God as a character in a work of literature. Miles insists: "Knowledge of God as a literary character neither precludes nor requires belief in God,"[40] and he carefully distinguishes his literary project from that of theology (making statements about God as an extraliterary reality) and of history (discerning the truth about early Jews) (10). "I write here about the life of the Lord God as—and only as—the protagonist of a classic of world literature; namely, the Hebrew Bible or Old Testament. I do not write about (though I certainly do not write against) the Lord God as the object of religious belief" (10). After cataloguing the various roles God has played—Creator, Destroyer, Protector, Family Friend, Liberator, Lawgiver, Conqueror, Father, Counselor, among others—the book concludes with a Postlude that returns to more general musings on the literary, weighing whether the story of God is more like a Greek tragedy or more like a Shakespeare play. Miles argues that because the plot is driven by God's character (He comes to know himself through interactions with people) rather than by fate, God's story is more *Hamlet* than *Oedipus Rex* (397–98).

Although Miles makes no overt religious claims, his way of justifying this literary project as worthwhile gestures toward an audience of seekers. First, the Hebrew Bible is an immensely influential work of literature. Miles explains that "religion—Western religion in particular—may be seen as literature that has succeeded beyond any writer's wildest dreams" (4). Although readers identify with characters and shape their lives in certain ways because they have been inspired or repulsed by characters who "come to life" in books and on the screen, God is different: "No character . . . has ever had the reception that God has had" (5). Miles summarizes: "But whether the ancient writers who wrote the Bible created God or merely wrote down God's revelation of himself, their work has been, in literary terms, a staggering success. It has been read aloud every week for two thousand years to audiences who have received it with utmost seriousness and consciously sought to maximize its influence upon themselves" (5).

Further, Miles insists that knowledge about the God of the Hebrew Bible matters, even if we are not religious, because it is the wellspring of character in the Western world. That is, it is the foundation of the edifice that is Western culture and the key to understanding what makes its individual subjects tick. "Many in the West no longer believe in God, but lost belief, like a lost fortune, has effects that linger," Miles explains (3). If a boy raised in a wealthy family chooses to give his inheritance to the poor and live in humble poverty when he comes of age, his history of wealth nonetheless still shapes his character, Miles insists. Similarly, centuries of building character through *Imitatio Dei*—the imitation of God—create an ideal of human character that persists, even if we no longer believe in that God (3-4). Consequently, whether we are religious or not, the study of the character of God illuminates us in ways that are compelling and relevant. Miles writes: "For non-Westerners, knowledge of the God whom the West has worshiped opens a uniquely direct path to the core and origin of the Western ideal of character. But for Westerners themselves, a deepened knowledge of this God can serve to render conscious and sophisticated what is otherwise typically unconscious and naïve. We are all, in a way, immigrants from the past. And just as an immigrant returning after many years to the land of his birth may see his own face in the faces of strangers, so the modern, Western, secular reader may feel a tremor of self-recognition in the presence of the ancient protagonist of the Bible" (4). There is no reason that orthodox believers cannot appreciate a story about the God of the Hebrew Bible as a literary character, but I suspect few did or will. This is a book that tries to justify the study of God in secular terms that speak directly to seekers' religious needs and desires.

The story that Miles tells about the God of the Hebrew Bible has a trajectory that moves from action to speech to silence (12). That is, God is first acting on the world (creating it and the living things that inhabit it), then speaking to the Hebrew people (who do as he commands, or not), and then falling silent (the laws of Moses speak for him and he no longer acts directly on the world or appears to his people). Although Miles insists that his literary adventuring is not history or theology, the clear implication is that the creator God has been replaced at the close by the Jewish people. That is, the end point of the story is—*us*. "God and his people are beautifully, movingly reconciled as the Hebrew Bible ends," Miles writes, "but it scarcely seems blasphemy to say that his own life is over" (11-12). A humanistic theology is one possible implication of Miles's literary analysis. God has bowed out (at least directly), and the rest of the story is ours to tell or to make.

This does, indeed, seem to be the message many readers took away. "While revealing how the character God has evolved over the millenia [*sic*], Miles really shows how we as people have evolved and how our understanding of God has changed along with our spiritual and religious growth," wrote one Amazon.com reviewer. "In the Tanakh God creates mankind in his own image so that he may have a way to better see himself," explained another. "Miles' interpretation shows us man creating the Tanakh, and God, to do precisely the same thing."[41] Many readers appreciated that the "literary" way of thinking about God gave them new and innovative ways to think about the Bible. "What this book does for me is help me shed some childhood baggage, introduce me to parts of the bible I had forgotten all about or never actually read, and lets me think about the overall meaning of the bible in an exciting new way," explained one appreciative reader.[42] The way of understanding God this reader learned in Sunday school—as an immutable and unknowable Deity that no longer engaged his mind or emotions in a particularly compelling way—gets replaced by a new way of reading/looking at familiar scriptures. Like many books for the seeker, however, *God: A Biography* is not seen as a book for conservative Christians. "I truly enjoyed this book," wrote one Amazon.com reviewer, "and one can only hope that conservative readers will finally loosen up their minds a bit and see the bible as not something fedexed by God to a lucky few, but as an evolving adventure of the human spirit in search of its own cosmic place."[43]

Like other books for the seeker, Miles's biography of God is complicit with the logic of consumer capitalism. As in other texts discussed above, its notions of subjectivity and history are postmodern, part of what Fredric Jameson calls the "cultural logic of late capitalism." Miles argues that what makes the God of the Hebrew Bible such a fascinating character is his multiplicity—"an amalgam of several personalities in one character" (6). Miles concedes that historical analyses of the ancient gods and spirits who were incorporated into the one true God of Judaism might explain away the contradictions God contains, but he insists that it is the tension between multiplicity and unity (the psychological polytheism, so to speak) that makes God a compelling and even addictive character (6).

Similarly, Miles insists that a literary analysis of the God of the Hebrew Bible requires several kinds of "deliberate naïveté" (13). Not only must one read the Hebrew Bible diachronically—as a single story of the development of a single character over time—but one must also ignore distinctions between history and myth, truth and fiction. Because Miles's project is literary rather than historical, he explicitly instructs readers that a different way of reading is called for. Miles is not interested in truth. He explains: "Critical historians of any period or subject are at pains to distinguish what really happened from what did not happen. Even when they are quite certain that they are dealing with a literary invention, their concern is not to appreciate the invention in itself as a work of literary art but to recover from it evidence about some real history, if only the intellectual history of its author. Myth, legend, and history mix endlessly in the Bible, and Bible historians are endlessly sorting them out. Literary criticism, however, not only can but must leave them mixed" (13). This deliberate naiveté is postmodern—collapsing truth and fiction, past and present—and leaving only stories behind, none with any ontological priority over the others. Again, what we are left with is the power of stories to shape and change us and the power of the authors of these books for the seeker to tell them compellingly and well.

Miles's own biography fits the profile of an author of books for the seeker. He calls himself a "pious agnostic" who attends Episcopal services regularly, not because he is without doubts about Christian dogma but because he leaves church feeling inspired to live better—to do unto others, to love his neighbor, for example.[44] Like Moore and Armstrong, he left a religious order (in his case, Jesuit), and turned to a literary life. He has serious academic credentials— having studied religion in Rome and Jerusalem and earned a Ph.D. in Near Eastern languages from Harvard. His research for *God: A Biography* was funded by a Guggenheim Fellowship in 1990. Like Armstrong, Miles has a history as a journalist and media commentator. From 1985 to 1995 he served as literary editor and a member of the board of the *Los Angeles Times*, and he is a former president of the National Book Critics Circle. He is also an occasional writer for the *New York Times*, the *Washington Post*, the *Boston Globe*, and *Commonweal*.[45] Although readers were not without complaints about the difficulty of Miles's prose and the erudition that make the book slow-going in places, Miles shares with other authors of books for the seeker a real gift for popularization, for writing about scholarly ideas in accessible and engaging ways.[46]

The Cloister Walk: Poetry and/as Prayer

The *Christian Century* reviewer wrote in his review of Kathleen Norris's *The Cloister Walk* that "it is astonishing to find a book with chapter headings like 'Celibate Passion,' 'Acedia,' and 'Maria Goretti: Cipher or Saint?' firmly lodged on bestseller lists."[47] *The Cloister Walk*, Norris's account of eighteen (nonconsecutive) months spent at a Benedictine monastery and the musings and meditations this experience inspired, spent eight weeks on the *New York*

Times bestseller list. "I never thought I'd have a bestseller," Norris told *People* magazine, no doubt astonished to find herself being interviewed on the pages of this popular celebrity gossip magazine.[48]

Like *Care of the Soul, The Cloister Walk* is a hard book to categorize. It is a spiritual memoir, but it is also a collection of brief essays about the desert fathers; contemporary society and politics; and debates within and around the Catholic Church about celibacy, sainthood, and the ordination of women, among others. One reviewer described it as "a miscellany of ruminations on the place of religion and poetry in American life in general and Norris's life in particular." One Amazon.com reviewer called it "a combination of a lot of things—a painfully personal journal, a catalog of discoveries and musings, a polished essay on laundry that was published in *The New Yorker*, and several brilliant pieces that stand as academic writing, ready for a feminist publication or academic journal." In an oft-quoted review from the *New York Times Book Review*, Robert Coles describes Norris's writing as "personal, epigrammatic—a series of short takes that ironically address the biggest subject matter possible: how one ought to live a life, with what purposes in mind."[49]

Its genre is difficult to pinpoint, but *The Cloister Walk*'s readers are beyond question seekers. The *Women's Review of Books* classed it with "books that have captured the attention and the imagination of thinking people who take spirituality and faith seriously."[50] One Amazon.com reader loved *The Cloister Walk* because she could share it with all kinds of religious people—Catholics, those alienated from organized religion, and "people on a spiritual quest," but not "people who want an easy spirituality." Another appreciative Amazon.com reviewer wrote, "It reveals a richness in the Christian tradition that I gladly and happily claim as a follower of Jesus. It's not all WWJD bracelets and 'Left Behind' novels."[51] Implied is that readers of *The Cloister Walk*—if they are Christians—are not evangelicals. One reviewer called Norris "one of the true unsung heroes (or heroines, as Norris would prefer) of contemporary Christian writing," but explicitly warned off conservative Christian readers: "Just a word of warning—if you consider yourself a right-wing fundamentalist Christian stay away from this woman, since you will find nothing of value in her work and will likely think her work is 'Biblically unsound' and 'leading to hell.' Your loss. Open your eyes and change your hearts."[52]

The warnings to conservative Christians who embrace biblical inerrancy and "literal" readings of scriptures arise because—like Armstrong—Norris feels compelled to distinguish her brand of religion from that of conservative Christians, who are increasingly prominent in public life. Norris quotes from scripture frequently in *The Cloister Walk* but assures us she does not intend to use the Bible as a weapon against people who disagree with her (as commonly occurs in contemporary media, she asserts).[53] At one point, during a radio interview, she hesitates to call herself a Christian because she feels so many people publicly claiming that label are "jerks about it" (73). Further, she argues that it is a mistake to cede the interpretation of apocalyptic texts to conservatives, because it gives them biblical warrant to pass judgment on other people and creates a "boogey-man God who acts suspiciously like an idol" (213). Finally, the problem with fundamentalism for Norris is a problem of language. The insistence on the literal truth of the Bible impoverishes our spiritual lives, since living words (poetry, prayer) are always metaphoric and connected to our own experience (217). Norris defines herself against another "other," as well. If the rigid dogmatism of fundamentalists is a problem, the "anything goes" looseness of "New Age" religion seems equally problematic for her (64). Norris's spiritual journey is about finding and building a religious faith that is rational, but not rationalized—that is, one that has space for mystery and transcendence.

Like other books for the seeker, *The Cloister Walk* has at its center a deeply felt critique of consumer capitalism and the spiritual ills that come with it— life lived at a frenetic pace, the commodification of just about everything, and a scientific, instrumentalist way of being in the world. Like Moore, Norris is concerned about the cult of efficiency impoverishing our relationships and our lives. She juxtaposes ordinary time—what scholars call "industrial work-time," the notion that time is a currency that can be saved, spent, or wasted—with the monastic "sanctification of time," which insists that every day include work, play, prayer, and study. Norris calls this "poetic time" and insists that it is oriented toward process ("You never really finish anything in life") rather than productivity. In Moore's terms, what Norris is asking is that we live with more soul, weaving ceremony into all the mundane rituals of daily life—eating, sleeping, dressing. Ceremony forces us to slow down, to live thoughtfully and deliberately, sanctifying the ordinary activities of everyday life rather than rocketing along at a frenzied pace in order to dispatch our tasks as efficiently as possible (xix, 267).

The Cloister Walk itself is structured to encourage such deliberate, thoughtful reflection. Norris's goal was to "replicate for the reader the rhythm of saints' days, solemnities, and feasts" (xix–xx) she encountered at St. John's Abbey in Minnesota, so that we would experience the poetic time of the monastery and the repetitions and returns of the liturgical year, as she did. The book is almost completely lacking in narrative drive, and the loosely linked meditations inspired by the liturgical year echo and reflect on one another. Many readers on Amazon.com report that the book did change their ways of thinking about and experiencing time. One described it as "a refreshingly slow read—a tall glass of water in a thirsty world." Another explained that reading it was "like being on a spiritual retreat." One wrote, "As I read, I felt much of my self-generated tension drain away from me. Norris . . . offered me a sense of the peace I so desperately craved."[54] Another Amazon.com reader described it as "one of the most soothing and comforting books I have read in a long time" and pledged to keep it on her "therapy shelf" to reread when she felt "battered by the world." "It's a book to read slowly and savor, and to read again," she advised other readers.[55] Not everyone was so enamored. One suggested that if a reader found patience a challenge, *The Cloister Walk* offered the opportunity to practice this spiritual discipline. Others merely complained that the book seemed tedious or aimless and self-absorbed, or that Norris needed an editor.[56]

Like other books for the seeker, *The Cloister Walk* insists that useful religion is countercultural, that it resists commodification. The Rule of St. Benedict, Norris insists, "does not bow down before the idols of efficiency and the profit motive" (15). People are seeking out monasteries in record numbers precisely because they are not run like corporations. She argues that—paradoxically—monks and poets are necessary, precisely because they are so marginal: "In our relentlessly utilitarian society, structuring a life around writing is as crazy as structuring a life around prayer, yet that is what writers and monks *do*. Deep down, people seem glad to know that monks are praying, that poets are writing poems. This is what others want and expect of us, because if we do our job right, we will express things that others may feel, or know, but can't or won't say" (145). Specifically, what monks and poets give us is language that is profoundly different from that to which we have become accustomed: "In the midst of today's revolution in 'instant communication,' I find it a blessing that monks still respect the slow way that words work on the human psyche. They take the time to sing, chant, and read the psalms aloud, leaving plenty of room for silence, showing a respect for words that is remarkable in this culture, which goes for the fast talk of the hard sell, the deceptive masks of jargon, the chatter of television 'personalities'" (145). Because they are so spectacularly unproductive, Norris calls both praying and writing poetry "absurd acts," "useless, if not irresponsible," when considered within a consumer capitalist framework (146). By placing themselves outside the cult of efficiency, poetry and liturgy maintain our connection to those intangibles (humility, solitude, peace) that cannot be commodified and that allow us to imagine worlds beyond or outside capitalism and political ideologies (22).

As has already become clear, Norris connects the ills of consumer capitalist society with literal, impoverished ways with words. She asks: "I wonder if the pace of modern life, along with our bizarre propensity for turning everything into a commodity, erodes our ability to think symbolically, to value symbols for their transformative power. . . . It reminds me that ritual and symbol are as necessary to human beings as air and water. They mark us as human, and give us identity" (316). Norris's story in *The Cloister Walk* is both a spiritual journey and a poet's bildungsroman. In her twenties, Norris had taken what one of her teachers called the "artist's road to redemption," finding salvation through writing, but during her year in residence at St. John's Abbey, she begins to understand her apprenticeship as a poet as an incomplete "religious quest" (xviii). What her year immersed in liturgy teaches her is that poetry and prayer, the writing life and the spiritual life, are one and the same. Poetry and prayer alike, she finds, are "a dialogue with the sacred" (64). Much of her meditation on this topic centers around *lectio divina*, translated as holy reading or spiritual reading. She describes it: "*Lectio* is an attempt to read more with the heart than with the head. One does not try to 'cover' a certain amount of material so much as surrender to whatever word or phrase catches the attention. A slow, meditative reading, primarily of the scriptures, *lectio* respects the power of words to resonate with the full range of human experience" (xx).

This experience of just "being with words" (93) is both countercultural (that is, spectacularly inefficient and unproductive) and radically open to mystery, ambiguity, and multiplicity of meaning (that is, a challenge to literal, fundamentalist ways with words). She explains: "Every day you recite the psalms, and you listen, as powerful biblical images, stories, and poems are allowed to flow freely, to wash over you. Doctrine and dogma are effectively submerged; present, but not the point" (xxi). Norris comes to understand her poetry as a form of active *lectio*, a meditation on the scriptures that grows to include larger existential questions about the world and her place in it (144). By the end of her year at St. John's Abbey, Norris experiences a coming together of poetry and faith in the choir loft of the monastery: "I had just experienced a healing, a joining together of what had been pulled apart in me for many years, when I thought I had to choose *between* literature and religion. It was my encounter with the Benedictines, after I had apprenticed as a writer for many years, that taught me otherwise. Much to my surprise, their daily liturgy and *lectio* profoundly intensified my sense of metaphor as essential to our capacity to hope, and to dream" (220).[57] Like Moore, Norris believes that what we need to be religious in a healthy way are not ideas or doctrines but stories. "Poetry's function is not to explain but to offer images and stories that resonate with our lives," she argues, in a line that could very well have come from *Care of the Soul* (95).

Norris also shares with Moore and Armstrong the sense that religion is less a matter of belief than spiritual practice. She repeatedly returns to the idea that writing and faith are both disciplines, ways of life continually (re) created through regular practice.

> I told the monks that I had come to see both writing and monasti-
> cism as vocations that require periods of apprenticeship and
> formation. . . . Related to this, I said, was recognizing the dynamic
> nature of both disciplines; they are not so much subjects to be mas-
> tered as ways of life that require continual conversion. For example,
> no matter how much I've written or published, I always return to
> the blank page; and even more important, from a monastic point of
> view, I return to the blankness within, the fears, laziness and cow-
> ardice that, without fail, will mess up whatever I'm currently writing
> and, in turn, require me to revise it. The spiritual dimension of this
> process is humility, not a quality often associated with writers, but
> lurking there, in our nagging sense of the need to revise, to weed out
> the lies you've told yourself and get real. As I put it to the monks,
> when you realize that anything good you write comes *despite* your
> weaknesses, writing becomes a profoundly humbling activity. (142)

Moreover, like Moore, Norris is dubious about the idea that there is a "right" way to live or to be in the world religiously. There are no ten easy steps or guidebooks to point the way: "The hard work of writing has taught me that in matters of the heart, such as writing, or faith, there is no right or wrong way to do it, but only the way of your life. Just paying attention will teach you what bears fruit and what doesn't. But it will be necessary to revise—to doodle, scratch out, erase, even make a mess of things—in order to make it come out right" (62).

The Cloister Walk is like *Care of the Soul* in another way as well. Norris's notions of identity, like Moore's, are postmodern. Her biography is an illus-tration of "psychological polytheism." Norris is both an oblate of a Roman Catholic Benedictine monastery, trying to live the rule of St. Benedict in her Dakota home, and a member and lay leader at her grandmother's

Presbyterian Church. *The Cloister Walk* suggests that these identities are not in conflict—that is, one can inhabit both of these religious identities without experiencing them as contradictory. One reviewer described this as her "oddly ecumenical approach to life."[58] Another argued that "Norris is unabashedly clear about her religious roots—they are Presbyterian, Methodist and Roman Catholic (as sifted through the Benedictine sensibility)." He argues: "Norris does not explain away, apologize for or abjure the theological convictions that underlie her spiritual insights. Rather, she tries to ground these spiritual reflections in the doctrinal history and worship life of the community of faith."[59] Norris, then, fully embraces specific institutional religious identities; she just embraces more than one at a time.

Moreover, Norris's way of being in the world historically is quite postmodern. She celebrates a way of reading that detaches scriptures from their historical context. For example, although she concedes that the Psalms are "angry and often violent poems from an ancient warrior culture" that seem hopelessly patriarchal and vengeful, she insists that the practice of singing them in community transforms them (93–100). Benedictine women, in particular, find an outlet for anger in these poems, which don't explain away or theologize rage. One reads aloud as a way of bringing stories into our own world: "One benefit of *lectio continua* is that it enables a person to hear the human voices of biblical authors. . . . A human voice is speaking, that of an apostle, or a prophet, and the concerns critical to biblical interpretation— authorship of texts, interpolation of material, redaction of manuscript sources—recede into the background. One doesn't forget what one knows, and the process of listening may well inform one's scholarship. But in communal *lectio*, the fact that the Book of Jeremiah has several authors matters far less than that a human voice is speaking, and speaking to you. Even whether or not you believe that this voice speaks the word of God is less important than the sense of being sought out, personally engaged, making it possible, even necessary, to respond personally, to take the scriptures to heart" (33). Although she is deeply concerned with contemporary gender and sexual politics and community building, Norris nonetheless suggests that the (submerged) historicity of these stories matters much less than an individual's personal, emotional engagement with them.[60] Norris's meditations range widely across history, making sisters of Emily Dickinson and Hildegard of Bingen, for example (221–22).

One could also characterize Norris, writing from a monastery run according to the sixth-century Rule of St. Benedict, as an antimodernist. Although others dismiss these cloistered monks as "an anachronism" or "an object of romantic illusion," Norris calls them "admirable bearers of tradition" and insists on the necessity of the silence, humility, and stability they carry into the modern world (311). Nonetheless, Norris finds herself a little at sea trying to live out her sixth-century commitments in her twentieth-century home: "My nine months' immersion in the slow, steady rhythms of monastic life was a kind of gestation. But now that I'm back 'in the world,' now that my husband and I have come home from Minnesota, I'm not sure what I'm giving birth to. At times I'm homesick for a place [or a time?] that isn't mine, homesick for two hundred monks and their liturgy. . . . What do I do now for ceremony and community?" (267). Norris's vision is profoundly social. She ends her account of a liturgical year spent at the Benedictine monastery in Minnesota with a meditation on the ways monks create the divine in community, weaving transcendence from collective worship and care for one another.

Conclusion

Sociologist of religion Nancy Ammerman describes the making of religious identity narratives that invoke an experience of transcendence or a sense of connection with a "Sacred Other." Although many of these narratives locate the teller as part of a traditional religious institution—a church or temple or mosque—they need not do so. These narratives emerge in conversation as people distinguish themselves from others, connect their present choices and circumstances with their individual and collective histories, and seek to reconcile their behavior with their ideal selves.[61] Books are one source of religious narrative a reader might use to create his or her own story.

Books for the seeker provide some of the raw materials from which liberal religious identity narratives are made. These books suggest that the conservative Christians who insist that seekers are heretics who will burn in hell are immature, inauthentic believers whose faith is really a form of idolatry. They suggest that belief is far less important than dedicated spiritual practice at finding transcendence and symbolic meaning in our lives. They respond to the human misery created by consumer capitalist culture—industrial work-time, alienated labor, commodification—by offering a spiritually inflected critique that derives from antimodern practices. Most of all, they offer us new ways with words—open, mysterious, ambiguous, and metaphoric.

Roof explains the prominence of seeker spirituality by arguing that it just makes sense, given contemporary social conditions. The global media expose us to a variety of religious idioms that accumulate layers of meanings.

The privileging of scientific-technical knowledge and the rationalization of modern life fuel a longing for transcendence and wholeness. Ideas about American individualism and therapeutic notions of the self encourage the cultivation of many spiritual paths. Roof calls the seeker a "*bricoleur*"—one who "cobble[s] together a religious world from available images, symbols, moral codes and doctrines, thereby exercising considerable agency in defining and shaping what is considered to be religiously meaningful."[62]

Books for the seeker offer models of *bricolage* to religious liberals and provide the justification for it. Miles suggests that God's story is more important than any particular truth about Him. Moore urges us to think about our lives in terms of myths and sacred stories (*any* myths and sacred stories). Norris argues that poetry and prayer are indistinguishable. Armstrong insists that, since the time of Abraham, Christians, Muslims, and Jews have told different stories about God, depending on their needs and circumstances, and suggests that we could/should do nothing else. These books respond to the ills of consumer culture by promising that dedicated spiritual practice, deliberate cultivation of a sense of the sacred, and the adoption of new ways with words will re-enchant everyday life. Ironically, these critiques of late capitalism embrace postmodern (that is, late capitalist) notions of subjectivity and history, suggesting that both can be imagined as consumer choices.[63]

However, these books are also tools for creating what Roof calls a "reflexive spirituality"—a deliberately and self-consciously constructed faith that is aware of itself as situated, as one of many possible views arising from a believer's biography, history, and social and economic location.[64] These books for the seeker are part of a largely overlooked liberal religious culture in America—what Leigh Eric Schmidt calls the "spiritual left," a community of memory based in religious liberalism whose origins lie in a cosmopolitan alliance of nineteenth-century nonconformists, including Quakers, Reform Jews, Transcendentalists, Spiritualists, Vedantists, and sundry other fellow travelers. Like their spiritual ancestors, contemporary seekers embrace religious liberty, sympathy for diverse faiths, universal brother/sisterhood, and the importance of personal spiritual practice.[65] Moreover, they find support for these values and narratives to orient and inspire them spiritually in these best-selling books for the seeker. I discovered all of these titles while participating in services and programs at a Unitarian Universalist church. In the next chapter, I talk specifically about the ways a spirituality reading group associated with this church took up these and other similar titles as resources for creating individual and collective religious identity narratives.

TEN

The New Gnosticism

Gender, Heresy, and Religious Community

And if the sale of books is any indication, the gender and semantic devices of
American god-talk will be firmly established as feminine before they are done.

—PHYLLIS TICKLE

In the Gnostics, . . . modern-day seekers saw their reflection, or at least
the most hopeful believed they did.

—PHILIP JENKINS

In the last chapter, I discussed selected "books for the seeker," mainstream
religion/spirituality titles from the 1990s that model the formation of liberal
religious identity narratives through *bricolage*. These books share a family resemblance: they define themselves against conservative Christianity;
emphasize spiritual practice over right belief; critique consumer culture;
and celebrate literary or poetic ways of being in the world. In this chapter, I
discuss my experience as a participant-observer with a single religious reading group affiliated with a Unitarian Universalist (UU) church in a major
Sunbelt city. Chapter 9 was primarily concerned with books for the seeker
as texts; this chapter is concerned with readers of texts like these. It examines the ways readers take up mass-marketed books as resources for forming spiritual communities and for (re)creating class, gender, and religious
identities. Specifically, I investigate how discussion of titles related to "the
new Gnosticism"—Elaine Pagels's *Beyond Belief* (2003) and Dan Brown's
The Da Vinci Code (2003)—allow readers to create religious identity narratives, individually and collectively. Through these texts, readers explore
what it means to be women in a patriarchal religious culture and what it
means to be embattled religious liberals in the Bible Belt. UU readers easily
connect their own sense of being a religious/intellectual aristocracy to the
early Christian heretics we know as the Gnostics. Readings of the Gnostic

gospels (re)create Christian tradition in ways that reclaim "heresy" as a profoundly ethical position of reasoned dissent from irrational, absolutist creeds. These ways of creating a usable religious past involve differentiating themselves from a conservative Christian "other." Nevertheless, although reading these books (re)creates oppositional, liberal religious identities for UUs and sometimes motivates progressive political action, their ways of reading and their engagement with therapeutic culture bear a striking family resemblance to evangelical ways with words.

I had originally imagined *What Would Jesus Read?* as a historical study. As I began my reading and research in 2000, I joined the Spirituality Book Discussion Group at this particular church for two reasons. First, I thought being engaged on a regular basis with serious religious readers was a way to keep me intellectually honest, since it is more difficult to oversimplify the complex reading practices of living, breathing readers to whom one has a relationship than dead readers who have left only sketchy traces in the historical record. Second, academic work is isolating, often painfully so, and the fellowship of people who took religious reading seriously was important to me, especially since my own institutional location was much more focused on traditionally literary topics. I told members of the reading group when I joined the group at the beginning of the school year that I was working on an academic book on the history of religious reading in America.

A few years into the study, when I had informally been talking with editors about the project, several encouraged me to include contemporary reading as part of *What Would Jesus Read?* I thought about this for about six months and decided it was something I wanted to do. I got Internal Review Board approval for the research through my university. It included participation in the group, which was open to the public, and individual interviews with volunteers about their religious reading and what I called their spiritual autobiographies. I officially marked my change in status to participant-observer in the first few minutes of the next meeting and asked for volunteers who would be willing to be interviewed about their reading and religious life. I conducted three such interviews. Although I had to drop in and out of the group due to teaching schedules and research leaves, I participated in monthly meetings from 2000 through 2006. Members of this group were immensely generous and supportive, if a little bemused that this could count as academic work. In part, they chose to participate because they had an existing relationship with me as an active member of this group and considered it an act of kindness to help me (as did I). They were extraordinarily busy people, juggling careers, families, work for social justice, and dedicated spiritual lives. If volunteers did not return phone calls to schedule interviews or to offer specific reactions to the draft chapter I sent them, I did not push. Three members read early drafts of this chapter; one offered a specific, detailed critique and extended conversation about it.

As I have presented versions of this work-in-progress to audiences of scholars, students, and community members over the years, I have been astonished at the controversy it has engendered. Because I am talking about heresies that have real consequences for contemporary cultural politics, listeners tend to bring intense feelings to the topic. In addition, I encountered what I call disciplinary fundamentalisms. As an American Studies scholar, I am using a number of methodologies to examine how readers make meaning from texts—ethnography, literary analysis, sociology of religion, and literary and cultural history. I do this intentionally. Meaning emerges from the interaction of readers' personal histories with the structure of texts. In addition, what we read and how we read are profoundly conditioned by the kinds of communities we as readers participate in and the social framing and infrastructure through which books are made available to us. What follows, then, is neither religion, literary criticism, history, nor sociology, but a strategic deployment of a number of methods to answer an interdisciplinary question about how reading shapes religious identity and community for one group of readers at the turn of the twenty-first century.

I also need to say a word about how truth or Truth functions in these "heretical" narratives. I am not arguing that the claims made by Elaine Pagels in *The Gnostic Gospels* and *Beyond Belief* or that parts Dan Brown claims to be based on truth in *The Da Vinci Code* are true in either historical or theological terms. I am not concerned about whether the Gnostics are or are not genuine Christians (there is a huge and contentious literature on this already). I am not concerned about whether "Gnosticism" is even a meaningful term, given the vast variety of texts and the great variety of historical actors who have been lumped together (probably incorrectly) under this term. I am also not concerned about whether the Gnostic Gospels actually say what Pagels says they do, or if she is interpreting them correctly. Nor am I interested in either defending or attacking the books UU readers chose to read or the ways they chose to read them. That is to say that I am making no claims to theological correctness or historical accuracy or scholarly soundness of the *popular* understanding of Gnosticism these UU readers embraced. As a literary and cultural historian of twentieth-century America, I am concerned about the way these narratives about Gnosticism and other popular heresies were appropriated by this group of liberal religious readers to craft individual and collective religious identity narratives that make sense of their place in contemporary American culture. Mine is a popular reading project about the contemporary United States, not a project about Gnosticism per se or about what religious readers ought to read and how they ought to do it. Whether these narratives are (historically or theologically) true or not, the belief that they are, or that they might be, has real, material consequences for the way these readers imagine themselves and for the way they participate in public religious life. I am reminded of Karen Armstrong's assertion that it is much less important that the stories we tell about God be true than that they be useful. This is a case study of how this set of narratives was immensely useful to one set of liberal religious people.

In the discussion to follow, I often use the pronoun "we" to describe members of this reading group, including myself as a participant-observer. In many places, I felt entirely included in the community and the conversation. For example, I often felt that secular or religiously liberal people were outnumbered and marginalized by conservative Christians in this part of the world and valued the support and solidarity this progressive religious community offered. At other times, I was either uncomfortable with, or unable to participate in, certain ways of thinking about religious life. I have done my best to make these moments clear in the text and to include the comments of members in places where my interpretations seemed controversial to them.

This chapter is divided into four parts. First, I characterize UU readers as spiritual seekers and examine the institutional structures and traditions that shaped their ways of reading. Next I examine the content of book discussions, explicating the cultural work performed at group meetings. I then look closely at the discussion of a single text, Dan Brown's *The Da Vinci Code*, in the context of contemporary cultural politics. Finally, I explore the common ground between evangelicals and these religious liberals that emerges in the way they use shared texts to (re)create religious community and in their engagement with therapeutic discourse.

Readers as Spiritual Seekers

Members of this reading group were spiritual seekers. That is, they were people who were creating a dynamic spiritual life by combining elements of various traditions, moving in and out of religious institutions according to their needs. As discussed in the last chapter, seekers tend to be well-educated, professional, liberal-leaning, older, and disproportionately female. Their spiritual practices are often informed by art, philosophy, science, and psychology.[1] For example, I did three "spiritual autobiography" interviews with members of this reading group, all of whom had complicated religious histories. One member was raised a Methodist, had attended UU churches for many years, but had considered joining a Catholic church after she became involved with the community through her children's school. Another was a daughter of Presbyterian missionaries who had married into Catholicism in young adulthood. At the time of the interview, she was a member of this church and an oblate at a Benedictine monastery and had an active Buddhist meditation/study practice with a local community. The third was raised a Methodist and had been deeply involved with interfaith dialogue and action as a member of this church. However, she narrated her spiritual history primarily through her involvement with social and political action and with the arts community. Courses taken in college and involvement in struggles for social justice in the 1960s and 1970s shaped all of the spiritual autobiographies.

Unitarian Universalism—a creedless religion—is, in many ways, the institutionalization of seeker spirituality.[2] Although historically it arises from liberal Christian roots, it is a denomination that currently includes Christians and Jews, Buddhists and Wiccans, theists and atheists, agnostics and humanists. UUs pride themselves on their democratic governance and the openness of their communities. In part, they imagine themselves as endlessly engaged in reconsidering and redefining their spiritual beliefs and practices in community with one another. A small denomination of 223,000 members, it was formed in 1961 from the merger of two denominations with a history of oppositional viewpoints—the Unitarians (who opposed the doctrine of the trinity) and the Universalists (who believed in salvation for all), although by the time of the merger neither Christianity nor belief in God was required of members.[3] They are part of what Leigh Eric Schmidt calls the "spiritual left," a cosmopolitan community of memory based in religious liberalism.[4] Robert Fuller argues that Unitarians and Universalists have particular prominence in the history of spiritual seeking in America. The Unitarians, for example, sponsored the first visitors from India to bring Hindu beliefs to the United States in the 1840s (which gave Emerson and Thoreau their introduction to Eastern philosophies and religion). Fuller describes nineteenth-century Unitarians as "in the forefront of almost every progressive intellectual and social cause" and points out the particular appeal of this free-thinking denomination to affluent, urban New Englanders and other progressives.[5]

UUs are intensely involved in the spiritual and literary marketplaces.[6] According to Unitarian Universalist Association figures, UUs are over-whelmingly white (95 percent), and they have the highest level of educational achievement and the second-highest income level of any major American religious group.[7] Their race, class, and cultural privilege make them typical book-buyers. For this group of readers, a particular class of best-selling titles related to the Gnostic gospels served as a resource for creating individual and collective religious identity narratives. The Gnostic gospels, which include a suppressed set of accounts of Jesus' life and teachings deemed heretical by early church fathers, were unearthed at Nag Hammadi, in Egypt, in 1945, and were first made widely available in English translation in 1977.[8] What matters for my purposes here is not scholarly understandings of these texts, but *popular* understandings and the cultural work they do in the lives of this particular set of readers. This group's understanding is derived largely from two books for popular audiences: Elaine Pagels's *The Gnostic Gospels* (1979) and *Beyond Belief* (2003), both selections of the reading group. These texts served readers in a number of interlocking ways. First, the gospels and books about them were a resource for creating a usable spiritual/religious past for people largely alienated from the faiths of their youth. Second, it allowed many to build a sustaining spiritual community (that is, a support group) imagined as an intellectual aristocracy. Third, it authorized a systematic revaluation of women's roles and of the sacred feminine.

The Cultural Work of Book Discussions

The Spirituality Book Discussion Group was begun in 1999 by one highly motivated member in her forties who wanted to read important books about religion for her own benefit and thought it would be nice to have a commu-nity to do it with.[9] She spoke to the director of adult religious education and got an announcement put in the bulletin with the church's other religious education offerings. Imagined as a place "to discuss books that chronicle religious journeys and trace explorations of faith," meetings—typically the last Monday of the month from 7 to 9 P.M. during the academic year—were expected to be "both a literary and a spiritual exercise."[10] The initial list of readings was chosen from recommended titles from the minister and the director of adult religious education, although members subsequently sug-gested titles that they had read, heard about, or discussed with book groups elsewhere. Scheduling was by consensus. Some years, there was a volunteer discussion leader for each meeting; other years, the organizer introduced the book or everyone brought in a question or passage to share. Typically, the discussion leader shared some biographical information about the author and a few reviews of the title, sometimes bringing in printouts or addresses of related websites. The year's inaugural meeting in September was usually a discussion of a popular novel related to religion or spirituality, which drew particularly large attendance (for example, Barbara Kingsolver's *The Poisonwood Bible* and Dan Brown's *The Da Vinci Code*). Although there was a core group of four to eight people who attended almost every time, many other church members came when they could, brought friends or family members, or dropped in only when a title was of particular interest. Although participants included men and women in their twenties through their seventies, most regular attendees were middle-class, professional white women in their forties and fifties.

The role of ministers or church staff as opinion leaders was immensely important. Not only were they frequent recommenders of titles, but they were often invited to attend or lead discussion on particular books they had suggested. Often the discussion facilitator's research included an e-mail to a minister or staff member with three or four questions related to the title. Moreover, the weekly sermons at worship services and the conversations taking place in other parts of the church overseen by church staff formed a framework for talking about these issues. Members were on occasion frustrated by their lack of formal training in theology or church history and welcomed short versions of lectures or classes other members had attended on related topics and were willing to recapitulate for the group. The meetings on Elaine Pagels's *Beyond Belief* (January 2004) and Dan Brown's *The Da Vinci Code* (September 2003) were among the best-attended discussions, drawing fifteen to twenty people who engaged in lively debate and exchange.

What was most noteworthy about these book discussions for me—a trained literary critic—was that we spent very little time engaging the text in literary ways—looking closely at particular passages or evaluating the claims and evidence in the text, for example. Most of the time we were talking about *us*, and the book was the site for us to engage with one another and issues of faith and spirituality central to our lives.[11] I spent the early meetings waiting for the book discussion to begin before I finally realized that everyone else was having it. For this group, the author's biography, the critical reviews of the book, and accounts of conversations with others about it were the discussion of the book rather than (as I had assumed) the "warm up" for the discussion.

For example, the discussion of Elaine Pagels's *Beyond Belief* (which compares the Gnostic gospel of Thomas favorably with the canonical gospel of John) began with one member declaring that it "reeked of Unitarianism."[12] These early Christians had gone their own ways, followed their own paths. It was, another insisted, "like reading Unitarian history" and resembled more than anything else "conversations we have here every week." Conversation quickly turned to practical matters. How did people like us get turned into a heretical minority when this hallowed tradition of pursuing enlightenment through spiritual discipline rather than externally enforced right belief had been present from Christianity's beginnings? The slippage from early Christians to twenty-first-century religious liberals was effortless. Among other things, these books were occasions to discuss us as heretics in a conservative Christian city, as a community of spiritual seekers surrounded by much more powerful orthodox institutions.

This discussion of texts that come from worlds historically, economically, and socially distant from our own as if they were written explicitly for us is characteristic of contemporary evangelicals as well. In his comparative ethnographic study of evangelical Bible study groups, James Bielo argues that the most common way of reading was to apply the biblical text to readers' everyday lives.[13] Similarly, in her ethnography of Vineyard Christian Fellowship churches, T. M. Luhrmann describes this as both a common way of reading in evangelical churches and characteristic of her own house Bible study group: "People spoke like this in the house group. They took these sentences written hundreds and hundreds of years ago and turned them into admonishments or encouragements about what had happened to them that afternoon."[14]

These ways of reading also intersect with "middlebrow" practices I have discussed throughout this book. That is to say that, as readers, we were not interested in the aesthetics or form of the texts but instead in how they were useful to us. Readers drew no line between art and life but instead read their lives into these books and these books into their lives. Readers identified with characters; told stories about their spouses, children, colleagues, and friends that reading the book aroused; and used the book as a site for discussing their own concerns and for finding spiritual and moral support for their daily struggles.[15] Perhaps the best way of describing these conversations is as a form of "spiritual consciousness-raising."[16] I use this term to suggest both the intimacy of personal disclosure and the potential for remade vision and inspiration to political or social action. Book group members were sharing their thoughts and experiences as spiritual beings in the world in order to build—together—an understanding of the larger social and political framework in which these spiritual lives played out.

Also like many evangelical Bible study groups, the "us" emerging from these conversations was of primary concern.[17] Self-definition takes up a great deal of time in most UU churches. In part because Unitarian Universalism is a creedless religion, individual members are responsible for defining their own beliefs and spiritual practices to an extraordinary degree. In addition, most feel compelled to work hard at explaining their faith to (often scandalized) kin and co-workers who attend more conventional churches. This emphasis on self-definition receives institutional support. For example, the bimonthly UU periodical includes a section for "elevator speeches" readers wrote in to share—brief explanations of Unitarian Universalism members could give to people with whom they might share an elevator for three minutes or so.[18]

Whoever we were, we were certainly *not* the creed-bound conservatives who unquestioningly believed what they were told. UUs in this congregation defined themselves against an evangelical Christian "other" that was perceived as holding a great deal of control over social and political life in this part of the world. Media scholar Lynn Schofield Clark suggests that the need to define one's self in relation to the increasingly prominent evangelicalism in America is prominent among many social and religious groups: "I found that it was impossible to talk about anyone's interest in or rejection of religion without recognizing the extent to which evangelicalism has permeated U.S. culture and the way that people experience and identify with religion today, which is surprising given the increasing religious pluralism of U.S. society."[19] Clark argues that evangelicalism increasingly serves as the normative religion in the United States—that is, it defines "what it means to be religious and to be moral."[20] This was true of the UU readers I observed, who—to a person—put a great deal of energy into defining themselves in opposition to conservative Christians. For example, many discussions dealt with readers' difficulties relating to fundamentalist or evangelical colleagues and family members, who were sometimes convinced that UUs were bound straight for hell. Discussions of several titles—Marcus Borg's *The God We Never Knew* and John Shelby Spong's *Why Christianity Must Change or Die*—centered around the question of whether it was possible to be Christian or to be religious without also being bigoted, small-minded, or intolerant. Part of the project of these books and the discussion of them, then, was to "save" Jesus and/or the Bible from fundamentalists and conservative evangelicals. The book group and sometimes the church more generally functioned for members as a support group. They came to church not because they were churchgoers (or at least they weren't when they lived in more progressive places), but because they felt a real need for the support and solidarity provided by this progressive church community in this particular city. Many described it as a "haven" in interviews undertaken for a self-study.

For many readers, part of the appeal of Pagels's *Beyond Belief* was her argument that the creation of Christian orthodoxy impoverished our religious heritage by replacing open, supportive faith communities with creed-bound cliques. The relevant chapter was entitled "From the Feast of Agape to the Nicene Creed," a title one reader glossed as "From the sublime to the ridiculous." UUs easily saw themselves as members of loving communities and their evangelical sisters and brothers as members of creed-bound cliques. Members laughingly shared their memories of learning and reciting the Nicene Creed or the Apostle's Creed (which the facilitator had brought copies of) in the Methodist, Presbyterian, and Lutheran churches in which many had grown up.

As may have already become clear, the "us" that emerged from these conversations was also an intellectual aristocracy. Many group members held that most people needed to be told what to believe and how to practice. Orthodoxy was necessary for the masses, most of whom did not welcome the hard work of critically evaluating faith traditions, weighing the ethical and moral implications of various belief systems, and examining which practices built a better world. At two different discussions, one member invoked the statistic that only a tiny percentage of the population were abstract thinkers, according to the Myers-Briggs personality inventory many of us had been exposed to at work, as civic volunteers, or (years ago) as part of a church leadership retreat. In this telling, "we" were the abstract thinkers and everyone else embraced orthodox religion, simply because it was easier.

For example, Pagels discusses the ritual of a "second baptism" practiced by an early Gnostic sect called the Valentinians in *Beyond Belief.*[21] These second baptisms recognized that a disciple had progressed to a new, higher level of spirituality through study and discipline than that marked by the first baptism at his or her conversion. Having achieved a higher level of enlightenment which the second baptism marked, these believers nonetheless still considered themselves Christians (albeit ones further along the path). Orthodox bishops would have none of this, branding these early Gnostics heretics and placing them beyond the pale. Discussion easily slid from the second baptism of second-century heretics to the spiritual practices of contemporary UUs. While many readers recognized the historical forces at work (the political power of a single, unified Christian church for the Roman Empire), they nonetheless felt sympathy for individuals who needed the "crutch" of orthodoxy on their spiritual journeys. Fearless spiritual seeking was apparently for the few—people like us.

This characterization of us as a "chosen few" always made me uncomfortable, and I was not alone. Although this theme came up repeatedly in book discussions, someone usually challenged the person making elitist assertions of this kind. Most often, a person involved in interfaith service and study simply stated that she or he knew smart, independent thinkers who came from other faith traditions. One member who believed in the spiritual superiority of UUs conceded that he was being elitist but maintained that—anecdotal exceptions aside—it was true. Another member simply recast the spiritual hierarchy as a matter of individual differences when challenged. She explained that her sister-in-law was musically gifted but that she herself could not carry a tune. Similarly, some people were just "spiritually gifted" in ways that others were not.[22]

UUs also saw their own ideals mirrored in Gnostic communities. According to our popular understanding, Gnostics were less concerned with a single, unified church than with pursuing their inner light, seeking wisdom through study and spiritual discipline, and following the dictates of their own consciences. They are, in fact, named for the secret knowledge (*gnosis*) they claimed to possess. Many communities made no distinctions between men and women, between clergy and laity. Many Gnostic gospels read Jesus through Greek philosophy, providing a rational faith that resonated with self-described free thinkers like us.[23]

There are very few born-and-raised Unitarian Universalists (roughly 10 percent of members nationwide).[24] For the most part, those participating in this congregation had fled the (mostly Christian) religious traditions of their youth—Presbyterians, Methodists, Catholics, Baptists, Pentecostals, among others. Many were disgusted by their tradition's positions with respect to women or gays and lesbians or just realized one day that they did not, in fact, believe the creeds they recited together each week. Many others were what sociologists describe as the "unchurched"—those who grew up without a religious background but who experienced the lack of a religious community profoundly in middle age. People in both groups had stories to tell about exploration of other religious traditions and spiritual practices (transcendental meditation, yoga, Zen Buddhism), many dating back to the 1960s and 1970s. In some ways, what members were doing here—those lacking a tradition, those fleeing their tradition, and those who had taken bits and pieces of many traditions—was building a usable past together. This need to anchor oneself in a specific place and a specific historical tradition might be experienced as especially pressing, because these readers were rootless in so many other ways—geographically mobile, highly educated professionals living in fairly new suburban developments.

The influence of Buddhism and other Eastern religions encountered during the Viet Nam War era was immense, as it was for baby boomers generally.[25] The church offered an adult education class on Buddhism twice during 2003–4, which filled to capacity, with a waiting list, months before it began. Our spirituality book group had read Thich Nhat Hanh's *Living Buddha, Living Christ* (October 2000) on the recommendation of the senior minister, Karen Armstrong's *Buddha* and Walpola Rahula's *What the Buddha Taught* (November 2003), Cheri Hubler's *Suffering Is Optional* (April 2004), and Sharon Salzberg's *Faith* (May 2006) in an effort to educate ourselves about Buddhist history and practice. Some members had read titles by the Dalai Lama or other widely circulated Buddhist scholars on their own. Some had returned to look again at their own (abandoned) Christian heritage after these and other Buddhist thinkers had sent them back to contemplate their inherited tradition.[26]

The Gnostic gospels were incredibly useful in this context, because they offered a counter-tradition to the Christian orthodoxy from which many readers were alienated. Orthodoxy gave us Christ as the only son of God and exclusive source of salvation, but some Gnostic gospels suggested that the Divine was not external to, superior to, or different from us in fundamental ways, but that it inhabited us all as it had inhabited Jesus. The orthodox language of sin and salvation is replaced in many Gnostic gospels with the language of ignorance and enlightenment. This was a Christianity that offered us a place in Christian heritage and explained our own invalid exclusion from the spiritual community. Moreover, the Christianity of "Thomas Christians" (so named for the Gnostic Gospel of Thomas) sounded an awful lot like Buddhism to many readers.[27] One member specifically invoked and agreed with a passage from *Beyond Belief* in which an American follower of a Zen master declared, "Had I known the Gospel of Thomas, I wouldn't have had to become a Buddhist!"[28] Presumably, if this reader had been taught a different version of Christianity, she too would not have had to seek so far afield for a workable spiritual practice.[29]

Feminism was an important part of the spiritual worldviews of many members of the reading group and the larger congregation. Of UU ministers,

51 percent are women, and UUs have long ordained women and performed commitment ceremonies for gay couples.[30] Many members came to this church specifically because the minister was a woman who spoke about feminist concerns on a regular basis. In addition to recognizing sacred days from various faith traditions—Easter and Yom Kippur, for example—this church marked Susan B. Anthony's one hundredth birthday. Many members had come to this church in the first place because it "celebrated women."

From the start, feminist concerns shaped the Spirituality Book Discussion Group.[31] Like most reading groups that gather for any purpose, women were in the majority.[32] Some evenings there were no men at all. Several readers who attended regularly had been activists in the 1970s and 1980s around feminist issues—domestic violence, abortion, gay rights, or women's health—and continued to pursue social justice work. Some titles explicitly invoked discussion of feminist theology and/or women's lives under patriarchal religious institutions—Carol Lee Flinders's *At the Root of This Longing*, Anita Diamant's *The Red Tent*, Margaret Starbird's *Woman with the Alabaster Jar*, and several works by Kathleen Norris. Starbird's study suggested that Mary Magdalene was not a prostitute but instead Jesus' wife who carried his child (and his bloodline) to the royal Merovingian family in France, a story she argued was passed on in a coded way through legends about the Holy Grail. If Jesus was not a celibate man but a married one whose most trusted and beloved disciple was not Peter but Mary Magdalene, then we inherit a Christian tradition that is not phobic about sex and hostile to women but one that welcomes women—body and soul—into the faith. Diamant's *The Red Tent* is a rewriting of the Hebrew Bible story of Dinah's rape and her brothers' vengeance from Dinah's point of view—as a story of passionate, forbidden love. It is also a celebration of sisterhood and women's culture, a culture that the reading group agreed was increasingly kept alive in single-sex book groups like our own that evening.

The Gnostic gospels were also useful in (re)creating a feminine/feminist spiritual identity for many readers. First, many had come to this religious tradition fleeing misogyny or homophobia in their own. That many Gnostic gospels openly advocated the spiritual equality of men and women (at least in our popular understanding of them) was a refreshing change of pace. For example, the Gospel of Mary Magdalene suggested that Peter's jealousy and the unwillingness of the twelve disciples to believe that Jesus had entrusted sacred wisdom to a woman (instead of to them) was what had resulted in her marginalization in the canonical gospels.

If orthodoxy provided only a patriarchal lineage and a trinity of men—Father, Son, and Holy Spirit—some Gnostic gospels offered a sacred feminine spirit of wisdom that partook of the divine. Women had held sacredness and power in early Christianity, but jealous, imperfect men who won the war of words over which of Jesus' sacred teachings would survive and which interpretations of them would be accepted suppressed this history. In part, then, our investigations of early Christian heretics were intended to unearth a past that offered the hope, justice, and equality that we longed for in our own world rather than justifications for injustice, intolerance, and hatred that we had all heard too much of.

There is some controversy about Pagels's reading of Gnosticism as a more equitable religious tradition for women than orthodox Christianity. For example, in a review of Pagels's *The Gnostic Gospels* for *Theology Today*, Kathleen McVey challenges Pagels's evidence that Gnostic communities had a more inclusive image of God, that they emphasized the version of the creation story that granted men and women more parity, and that their social practices were based on equality rather than on women's subordination.[33] McVey argues that "heresy and feminism were not such good bedfellows as either Pagels or the modern Christian misogynists would have us believe." Similarly, Philip Jenkins argues that "feminist interpretations of the hidden gospels represent a triumph of hope over judgment."[34] Whether correct or not, however, this aspect of Pagels's argument about the Gnostics held immense appeal for these UU readers.

For some alienated Christians, the importance of the Gnostic gospels in reclaiming their heritage cannot be exaggerated. One reader described the finding of the Nag Hammadi texts in 1945 as a "second Reformation." She explained that what the Gnostic gospels did for her was to "redeem Christianity"—offering her a vision of the divine within, a (suppressed) sacred feminine, inspiration, and a road map for continuing spiritual growth—all of which she felt lacking in her orthodox Christian upbringing. She chose to describe herself not as a Christian but as someone who was ready to let Jesus be her teacher—the enlightened Jesus of the gospel of Thomas, not the divine Christ of John. Gnosticism, then, was a way to achieve rapprochement with her Christian heritage without making the kinds of exclusivist claims about being the one true religion that many readers had fled.

What these readers are doing on the last Monday evening of the month, then, is hashing out what Ammerman calls religious identity narratives, discussed at length in the last chapter.[35] In the reading, discussion, and debate over numerous religion and spirituality titles, readers are assembling their own narratives of spiritual life, individually and collectively. Lynn Schofield Clark, elaborating on Ammerman's model of religious identity, explains: "Identity construction is an ongoing process guided by the need each of us have to consciously make sense of our choices, and the often unconscious ways in which these choices create a form of social solidarity with (or distinct from) others."[36] These individual and collective identities emerge in conversation as people define allies and enemies, locate their current choices and situation in history, and seek to reconcile their behavior and circumstances with their ideals.[37]

In many ways, Pagels's work was made-to-order for these readers. In her review of Pagels's *The Gnostic Gospels*, McVey argues: "Elaine Pagels' *Gnostic Gospels* is a book calculated to appeal to the liberal intellectual Christian who feels personally religious but who dislikes 'institutional religion.' In the midst of the resurgence of antiscientific and anti-intellectual currents throughout American Christianity, Pagels has presented us with an appealing portrayal of the gnostic Christians as a beleaguered minority of creative persons deprived of their rightful historical role by a well-organized but ignorant lot of literalists."[38] It is an appealing portrayal, indeed, and easily invites identifications by contemporary UUs in the Bible Belt with those Gnostic Christians from the second century who were victims of orthodox church historiography.

Discussing *The Da Vinci Code*: Creating Religious Identity and Community

Having looked closely at who these readers are and how their ways of reading participate in (re)creating religious identities, I'd like to look more closely at the discussion of a single book, Dan Brown's *The Da Vinci Code*, and do some reflecting on ethnographic practice. In the novel, Harvard symbologist Robert Langdon is called in by the French police after a curator at the Louvre with whom he had an appointment is found murdered in the galleries. In the final moments of his life, the curator has left a bizarre series of clues involving the works of Leonardo da Vinci. The curator's granddaughter Sophie (a professional cryptographer) and Langdon must solve the mystery in order to clear Langdon's name (he is suspected of the murder) and figure out who has killed the curator and three other leading members of an ancient secret society, the Priory of Sion. The investigation sends them off on their own latter-day Grail quest, seeking the suppressed evidence that Jesus had married Mary Magdalene and left her pregnant, so that his bloodline continued through a family of French nobles into the present day. The leading members of the Priory of Sion were presumably murdered because they knew where to find proof that the heresy was true and that the Catholic Church had suppressed the evidence for centuries. Although it initially appears that the Vatican and a sect of ascetics known as Opus Dei are implicated in the murders, in actuality, Leigh Teabing—a secular scholar whose monomaniacal pursuit of truth drives him to kill—is responsible for the deaths.[39]

The first hardcover edition was packaged as a thriller, with blurbs on the back cover from best-selling action, adventure, and mystery novelists, but no theologians or ministers. The discussion about *The Da Vinci Code* in the larger culture, however, centered on the religious implications of this ancient heresy represented in modern garb. *The Da Vinci Code* discussion (September 2003) was one of the best-attended sessions in our book group's history, with seventeen people in attendance. This was not surprising, because discussions of novels were typically better attended and because the book affirmed a kind of feminist, religiously liberal worldview that celebrated heretics as heroes.[40] For me, it was a book that made clear that contemporary spirituality was *about* narrative and metaphor, that the "truth" mattered less than the power and resonance of sacred stories in all of our lives. I was most interested in the way Brown chose to end the book. Once the murders are solved, Langdon and Sophie continue their pursuit of the documents that prove that Jesus and Mary Magdalene had a child and that the church had knowingly suppressed this evidence for centuries. They find the remnants of Sophie's family (believed dead) in hiding at Rosslyn Chapel, in Scotland, where they believe the final clue has led them. At this point, Langdon is frantic to find the hidden evidence, arguing that if it is not made public, the truth about Mary Magdalene and the sacred feminine will be lost forever. Sophie's grandmother disagrees, asking in mock exasperation, "Why is it that men simply *cannot* let the Grail rest?" She patiently explains both the nature of the Grail (metaphorical) and the truth about it (present in art and literature versus science). Explaining that the Priory of Sion never intended to unveil the Grail, she argues: "It is the mystery and wonderment that serve our souls, not the Grail itself. The beauty of the Grail lies in her ethereal nature. . . . For some, the Grail is a chalice that will bring them everlasting life. For others, it is the quest for lost documents and secret history. And for most, I suspect the Holy Grail is simply a grand idea . . . a glorious unattainable treasure that somehow, even in today's world of chaos, inspires us" (444). Further, she insists that making public the documents held in trust by the Priory of Sion (proof that the heresy is true) is unnecessary and will change absolutely nothing: "Look around you. Her story is being told in art, music, and books. More so every day. The pendulum is swinging. We are starting to sense the dangers of our history . . . and of our destructive paths. We are beginning to sense the need to restore the sacred feminine" (444). The wise, elderly woman lecturing the scientifically trained Harvard symbologist about truth, evidence, and narrative is a powerful image, and Brown makes clear that Langdon (unlike the murderously obsessed Teabing) learns his lesson.

In an Epilogue, Langdon realizes he has misread the final clue, which does not—in fact—point to Rosslyn Chapel in Scotland, but instead to the pyramid in the 1993 addition to the Louvre, where he becomes convinced the Holy Grail rests. Instead of arranging to have the pyramid opened up to reveal the secret chamber he believes is hidden underneath, Langdon falls to his knees in awe and worship. The final lines of the novel read as follows: "With a sudden upwelling of reverence, Robert Langdon fell to his knees. For a moment, he thought he heard a woman's voice . . . the wisdom of the ages . . . whispering up from the chasms of the earth" (454). Brown is clear here that it matters little whether the Mary Magdalene heresy is true or not—what matters is that the story has the power to move and inspire us. Sophie's grandmother did not send Langdon out to find the Holy Grail, having told him it was not at Rosslyn Chapel. Nor did she order him to cease and desist all that questing, but instead she trusted him to behave appropriately when he figured it out. Ascertaining that he was at work on a book about symbols of the sacred feminine, she urged him in parting: "Finish it, Mr. Langdon. Sing her song. The world needs modern troubadours" (444).

Brown could have definitively answered for us whether the Grail was, in fact, hidden in the Louvre addition, but he didn't. He could have presented us with "the truth" (at least within the confines of this fiction), but instead he chose to preserve the mystery. What was important was not what actually happened, but the powerful survival in art, myth, and legend of the sacred feminine. Whether or not Jesus really married Mary Magdalene, the centuries-long survival of stories about the sacred feminine in the face of formidable official suppression testified to its continuing life and relevance to believers everywhere.

What I liked about the book was the way it included us, as readers, as part of that tradition. Having read this book, we were now part of carrying on the sacred feminine and its traditions into the present, part of keeping it alive outside of patriarchal and oppressive religious structures. If Sophie and her brother were Jesus' descendants (part of the Merovingian line of

French nobility), then the divine still dwells in human form, is (literally and metaphorically) living among us still. If the secret is buried in the architecturally controversial addition to the Louvre that Francois Mitterand planned and implemented, then the sacred feminine dwells not in a vault in some medieval castle but instead inhabits and continues to shape contemporary life and politics.

Moreover, Langdon's position—when asked by Sophie if he thinks they ought to make public the proof of Jesus' marriage and the church's suppression of those facts—takes for granted that nonliteral readers are the ones who truly understand religious *Truth*. Langdon explains: "Sophie, *every* faith in the world is based on fabrication. That is the definition of *faith*—acceptance of that which we imagine to be true, that which we cannot prove. Every religion describes God through metaphor, allegory, and exaggeration, from the early Egyptians through modern Sunday school. Metaphors are a way to help our minds process the unprocessible. The problems arise when we begin to believe literally in our own metaphors" (342). Here are echoes of countless book discussions from which we—UUs—had emerged as an intellectual and spiritual aristocracy beset by literal-minded folks incapable of or unwilling to engage in independent thought. Still, Langdon is no Leigh Teabing, sure that the historical record must be corrected and superstitious notions purged from the world. He continues: "The Bible represents a fundamental guidepost for millions of people on the planet, in much the same way the Koran, Torah, and Pali Canon offer guidance to people of other religions. If you and I could dig up documentation that contradicted the holy stories of Islamic belief, Judaic belief, Buddhist belief, pagan belief, should we do that? Should we wave a flag and tell the Buddhists that we have proof the Buddha did not come from a lotus blossom? Or that Jesus was not born of a *literal* virgin birth? *Those who truly understand their faiths understand the stories are metaphorical*" (341–42, emphasis added).

After several years with this reading group, I was quite sure I knew what we would talk about—the costs of suppressing the sacred feminine and the resulting world full of social and environmental injustice, the superiority of liberal faiths like our own that understood the historical and cultural specificity of sacred stories, the irrelevance of literal truths to spiritual life, and the enduring importance of mystery and transcendence in a scientific, rationalized world. I was wrong.[41]

No one actually disagreed with me; members just had no interest in discussing Brown's rhetorical choices. My colleagues were interested in only one question—"Is it true?" To judge from the massive onslaught of popular coverage—network television specials, newspaper and magazine cover stories, books rushed to press from liberals and conservatives alike—that promised to separate fact from fiction in *The Da Vinci Code*, this was what most readers desired to know. Dan Brown's preface promised that the historical events represented in the novel were real, and millions of readers wanted to know if this claim was true.[42] The group facilitator had done her research, poring over websites, bringing in printouts of reproductions of Da Vinci's works, investigating the parts of the text with factual existence, including Opus Dei (which had a sharply worded objection to its depiction in the novel on its website). All of our energy was poured into establishing which parts of the novel were "true" and which were made up.

When I raised the issue that Brown had chosen not to definitively answer that question for us, and—in fact—made rhetorical choices to suggest that "Is it true?" was the wrong question to be asking in the first place, I didn't get very far. When I suggested that placing the Holy Grail in the 1990s addition to the Louvre made us part of the tradition of art and literature celebrating the suppressed sacred feminine, one member suggested that that was a part Brown made up (the hidden vault in the Louvre) and joked that the sequel would feature them bringing excavators to the museum. When I pointed out that the book was not anti–Catholic Church in the sense that although it initially casts suspicion on Opus Dei and the Vatican, the bad guy is a secular scholar monomaniacally and murderously obsessed with publishing the truth, nobody was slowed in the least in our pursuit of truth. If Langdon was content to leave the mystery and transcendence of the sacred feminine intact—asking himself if the decision to reveal it or not was even his to make—we had no such scruples.

I seldom fought this hard to be heard about a book, and I was seldom this frustrated with the direction of the discussion. In the torrent of debate engendered by this book, my few contributions—interjected at irregular intervals over the course of two hours—failed to generate much interest. At first, this surprised me. As a group, we had read about the Mary Magdalene heresy and discussed it in the past, and the "reading" I did of Dan Brown's ideas about the nature of the sacred seemed entirely in line with the discussions we had been developing together for many months. In part, my frustration arose from the fact that this was a novel—which I was trained to read professionally in a way I was not trained to read (for example) Karen Armstrong's *A History of God*. The group read fiction no differently from nonfiction, mining both for useful truths without much attention to authors' rhetorical and formal choices, which continue to structure much literary criticism. I do not mean to suggest that these were bad book discussions or that all book discussions should resemble those in the literature class-room. I do mean to suggest that the rules for reading and discussing books in spiritual communities are different from those in the classroom, and in this case, I was clearly reading as a literature professor. My interpretation of *The Da Vinci Code* emphasized the power of stories and the centrality of the people (like me) who interpret them.

What the direction of the discussion told me was that this book was not about the transformative power of stories in all of our lives (a self-interested literary critic's reading), but instead it was a story about the persecution of free thinkers by religious conservatives (a self-interested religious liberal's reading). There is a relationship between who we are and what we know, and the religious liberal's narrative was much more available and compelling to these readers than the one I saw clearly from my own unique subject position. Part of the appeal of the book for these readers was that it prominently featured a conspiracy.[43] Orthodox bishops and other religious authorities had conspired in the past to police the version of history and sacred scripture that would be available to us, and reading books like *The Da Vinci Code*, *The Gnostic Gospels*, *Beyond Belief*, *The Woman with the Alabaster Jar*, and others, cast us in the role of heroic questers after Truth (even if that Truth was that there are many truths). These books hailed us as crusaders seeking the truth behind orthodoxy, heretics like our spiritual ancestors, which was a flattering portrait of one's self to be handed (much more flattering than the burning-in-hell portraits we'd all heard too much of).

"Heresy" and "heretic" are powerful words at this church. Unitarians opposed the doctrine of the trinity made orthodoxy at the Council at Nicaea in 393 C.E. Universalists believed in universal salvation rather than in original sin and the doctrine of the elect. Although ours is a creedless religion, our spiritual ancestors were nonetheless heretics, and we prided ourselves on being free thinkers like them. What was most fascinating to me about the orientation classes at this church was the existence of a UU structural equivalent of saints and martyrs. For example, Michael Servetus, burned at the stake for heresy in 1553 for challenging the doctrines of the trinity and of predestination, took a starring role. The book group read his biography, by Lawrence and Nancy Goldstone, *Out of the Flames: The Remarkable Story of a Fearless Scholar, a Fatal Heresy, and One of the Rarest Books in the World* (2002), which celebrated the power of printing, books, and free intellectual inquiry as much as it celebrated Servetus himself.

Conspiracy was invoked by members in a different context as well. In September 2003, many were concerned about the absence of mass media attention to the religious claims made in the book. Reviews (many of which the facilitator had examined) discussed the book as a thriller but made little mention of it as a spiritual or religious document. Many were angry about this, seeing a hesitance on the part of the mass media to challenge conservative religious leaders. Why weren't these issues on talk shows, on NPR, on talk radio in the same way that (for example) the *Left Behind* books were examined as religious or spiritual documents making theological claims? Dan Brown became *our* voice, the voice of religious liberalism in the media—the one who could reach a much larger audience through this popular thriller than the Jesus Seminar ever could. Readers easily projected their own sense of feeling embattled and silenced onto Dan Brown, whom they perceived as a victim of a media conspiracy of silence to keep him out of the public eye.[44] According to this narrative, reporters were held in thrall by despotic conservative religious leaders whose power to silence dissenting views was no less than that of the proto-orthodox bishops in Nicaea with whom readers easily identified them.

The nature of public discourse about religion and spirituality came up frequently in book discussions. In some ways, members were attending this book group (and, arguably, this church) in order to better equip themselves for conversations about politics, economics, and morality in the Bible Belt, conversations profoundly shaped by the Bible and by evangelical understandings of the relationship between religion and public life.[45] The group read John Buehrens's *Understanding the Bible: An Introduction for Skeptics, Seekers, and Religious Liberals* (2004), which argues (among other things) that we should know our Bible whether we consider it a sacred book or not in order to better engage rhetorically with those who use biblical warrant for political and social action. Several members of the group had recommended books to others that they found to be useful tools for engaging in discussion about the Bible with people from other faiths.[46] On some level, these conversations were about our roles as citizens of the world and supported individuals who felt religiously motivated to be political and social activists in their neighborhoods. These conversations took place all over the church—which offered opportunities to be involved in interfaith community action, voter registration, AIDS patient care, environmental action, and the struggle for racial justice, among others. Although individual members need not embrace any of these causes, the church as a community educated and supported members in their struggles to live their values.[47]

Liberals and Conservatives Reading: Religious Identity and Community

I have argued here that Gnosticism—*as popularly understood*—has particular appeal to these UU readers, who experience themselves as an embattled intellectual aristocracy in an evangelical wasteland. These texts provide readers with a usable past—connection to an alternative Christian tradition, access to a suppressed history of women as spiritual agents, and a road map for seeking enlightenment through spiritual practice. Ironically, there is a contradiction at the center of this process of individual and collective self-definition. Although these UUs define themselves against an evangelical Christian "other" whose unquestioning embrace of orthodoxy serves as a foil for their own courageous spiritual seeking, their ways of reading, the therapeutic worldview that structures their discourses, and the ways they (re)create religious communities overlap significantly. In his comparative ethnography of evangelical group Bible studies, Bielo argues that readers most often apply the texts they read directly to their everyday lives, that they explicitly seek to cultivate intimacy, that they practice with each other how to have effective conversations about faith with outsiders ("witnessing"), and that they negotiate their religious identities and often (re)establish their own superiority in the process. All of this was true of UU readers as well. As political scientist Alan Wolfe argues of contemporary religious life in America, "There is . . . a sense in which we are all evangelicals now."[48]

Wolfe argues that religious life in America across the spectrum has a therapeutic rather than a doctrinal emphasis. Americans are a profoundly religious people, but he characterizes their religion as quite "thin." Attending a Bible study for many years, he argues, does not necessarily mean you have either read much of the Bible or understand much about the historical or theological scholarship on it. He characterizes these groups as support groups or therapeutic communities that frequently use a single Bible verse or chapter as a jumping-off point to discuss their own emotional and spiritual challenges.[49] Luhrmann found that the Vineyard Fellowship congregations she studied were profoundly shaped by psychotherapeutic practices. She summarizes: "The evangelical Christianity that emerged out of the 1960s is fundamentally psychotherapeutic. God is about relationship, not explanation, and the goal of the relationship is to convince congregants that their lives have a purpose and that they are loved."[50]

Certainly, this UU book group functioned as a support group as well. A "good" discussion was one in which people engaged in some personal disclosure about their struggles with religious faith and doubt, their mystical experiences, or particular "dark nights of the soul" (divorce, deaths of parents, a soul-destroying job, family tensions). A bad discussion—that is, one where conversation lagged and readers were not particularly engaged—was inevitably one that was "safe," that was only about the book and not about us.[51] In the course of learning about early Christian heretics, we inevitably sought support from each other for our own heretical beliefs. Although few relationships were pursued outside the group, those who attended regularly got to know each other not only as readers and thinkers, but also as struggling human beings. The group provided emotional, intellectual, and spiritual support for religious exploration, questioning, and doubt and for building alternative faiths. Similarly, Bielo found that one of the key roles of evangelical group Bible study was cultivating intimacy. Such "sharing" involved being open, vulnerable, and trusting of one another. Auditors were expected to offer not judgment and critique, but love and support.[52]

Just as a therapeutic language of healing characterizes many evangelical small-group ministries, therapeutic language was prominent in UU book discussions.[53] For example, the group spent a great deal of time in the discussion of Pagels's *Beyond Belief* addressing one woman's question: "How do we recover from orthodoxy? How do we recover from 1,600 years of religious abuse?" Her phrasing of the question, which cast us (and our spiritual ancestors) as victims of abusive church fathers, immediately reinvigorated a conversation that had begun to lag. This way of framing the question resonated with many there, who could easily explain much of the (social and political) evil in the world as the result of violence done to individual psyches. That said, these were book discussions, not therapy groups or prayer circles or dinner clubs (all of which were available at this church). The book was important as a source of authority, a provider of knowledge, ideas, and frameworks, and a bridge to the larger world. As educated professionals who valued higher education, the image of ourselves as critical readers of serious books that engaged our minds was an important part of why we were there.[54]

As previously discussed, Amy Johnson Frykholm argues that this way of reading characterized by porous boundaries between texts and lives describes readers of the best-selling novels of the rapture, *Left Behind*, as well.[55] This end-times prophecy is dressed up as a high-tech adventure story in which a small band of newly converted (post-rapture) Christians does battle with the Antichrist, who is taking over the world under the auspices of a successor body to the United Nations. Nonetheless, evangelical readers see this fiction as having immediate relevance to their daily lives. Frykholm writes: "Readers of *Left Behind* narrate the rapture and its particular manifestation in the *Left Behind* series as provoking for them thoughts about ultimate meaning and the ultimate nature of reality. It conjures up fears about their own salvation and the salvation of loved ones while providing a lens through which contemporary life can be understood. Often readers narrate their own interaction with the novels as a spiritual turning point where they realize how pressing and significant God's plan for history is, how imminent the end may be. They feel compelled to share this concern with others, with unsaved or religiously marginal people in their own lives who need to know that the rapture is imminent and also with fellow believers who need to share the message."[56] There is an easy slippage here between the fictional characters, whose lacking or inauthentic Christianity results in their being left behind at the rapture, and the readers, who fear for the fates of their own immortal souls. Just as contemporary UUs see themselves and their lives in the trials of early Christian heretics, evangelical readers see themselves in the fictional "Tribulation Force" in *Left Behind*.

Similarly, part of the appeal of the *Left Behind* novels is the accessible and engaging ways they interpret coded or cryptic passages of biblical prophecy—especially the Book of Revelation. What becoming an "insider" to biblical prophecy does is assure evangelical readers that God is in charge, that all the chaos in the world is part of His plan, and that they have a privileged place in that history (among those who will be raptured). Frykholm argues that prophecy is a tool for "world-making," that is, it provides a framework that organizes the random confusion of world events into meaningful patterns and locates ordinary people in sacred history.[57]

One could make a similar argument about the function of *The Da Vinci Code* for religious liberals. It is an engaging and accessible guide to the Mary Magdalene heresy and the complicated history of mythmaking about the Holy Grail.[58] What becoming an "insider" to Grail mythology does is assure liberal readers that orthodox history has been carefully and duplicitously shaped by powerful conservative institutions, that they will be persecuted for their pursuit of the truth, and that there is heroism in their free thinking. If prophecy "makes a world" (that is, a meaningful world) by providing an organizing framework (God's plan) through which to view it, then heretical texts similarly "make a world" centered on spiritual seeking, free thought, and questioning authority, a worldview easily imported into contemporary cultural debates.

In each case—*Left Behind* and *The Da Vinci Code*—readers have their religious beliefs confirmed and their religious identities affirmed. In each case, people like them—true believers in Christ or heretical free thinkers, respectively—emerge victorious. The band of Christians battling the Antichrist in *Left Behind* are the sole possessors of the Truth, given discernment and strength through the power of God to ultimately triumph over their enemies (who long ago claimed the secular world for their own). Similarly, *The Da Vinci Code* offers a world in which heretics hold the intellectual and moral high ground—not the corrupt Catholic bishops nor the religious fanatics at Opus Dei nor the utterly secular scholars like Teabing. Langdon and Sophie—the seekers in the novel—possess both secret knowledge about codes and symbols that allows them to unravel the Truth behind the conspiracy of silence about Jesus' marriage *and* the capacity of mystics to experience the transcendent power of the sacred feminine. In *The Da Vinci Code* and in popular books about the Gnostic gospels, the highest calling is to be both a free thinker and a believer—that is, a religious liberal.

It is also useful to think of this UU reading group as a de facto women's group, since it was always predominantly—and often entirely—women.[59] There is a considerable body of work on evangelical women, and here, too, there is surprising overlap. For example, Lynn Neal argues that Christian romance novels perform three different kinds of cultural work for evangelical women: (1) they distinguish evangelical women from the mainstream (sex-saturated, secular) culture, thus allowing them to demonstrate and maintain their religious identities; (2) the novels move women from the margins to the center of evangelical life (that is, they move the emphasis from the male leader in the pulpit to the Christian wife and mother in the home); and (3) they elicit women's devotion by placing human love stories within the larger narrative of God's love for humanity throughout history.[60] Although there is a thirty-year-old tradition of evangelical feminism, Neal's evangelical women (and those in studies not specifically focused on reading by Griffith, Brasher, and others) largely reject the label of "feminism" in place of the biblical doctrine of wifely submission to men's sacred headship.[61] Although there is considerable evidence to suggest that this submission is largely symbolic and that a pragmatic egalitarianism prevails in many evangelical homes, these romance novels make clear that the work of Christian women as wives and mothers is the central drama of evangelical life.

Although many UUs in this group were self-described feminists who were or had been social activists, their religious reading functioned in remarkably similar ways. Just as reading a Christian romance novel marked an evangelical woman as different from and separate from a sinful, secular mainstream and allowed her to identify with a victorious, Christian heroine, reading heretical books set off UU readers from many of their more traditionally religious friends and neighbors. Every time they were seen with such a book, it marked them in the same way that those buttons that say "I read banned books" mark people as free thinkers. In addition, every time they read one, they were reminded of the nobility of heresy and were able to identify with heroes like Sophie and Langdon or the early Christian Gnostics in *Beyond Belief*.

Certainly much of the appeal of the Gnostic gospels and other readings about women's spirituality the UU group read was that they moved women from the margins to the center of stories about Christian faith. If Jesus was married to Mary Magdalene and she was his most beloved and trusted disciple, then Peter and the succession of popes tracing their authority to him look a great deal less important. Moreover, replacing a celibate Jesus with a married, reproducing Jesus places heterosexual love, women, and the family in a much more prominent place.[62]

Finally, if Christian romance novels place evangelical women in history, in a central position as wives and mothers founding a Christian country, Gnostic gospels place UU women in history as well, as the spiritual daughters of church leaders, leading disciples, and possessors of sacred power and wisdom, a history left untold in most orthodox churches. Neal argues that the world of the Christian romance novel is a source of hope for evangelical women. In these worlds, God's control remains constant, evangelicals emerge triumphant, and America is Christian.[63] The "happy ending," then, is not just that the girl gets the boy, but that they both get the world that—as evangelicals—they have hoped and prayed for. Similarly, books casting free thinkers as heroes inspire UU readers in their struggles for spiritual discernment and invigorate them for the often dispiriting task of working for social justice here on earth.

Although cast as opponents in cultural debates, religious liberals and evangelicals appear to read (different) books for similar reasons—to (re)create their religious identities, to restore women to the center of religious life, and to place themselves in history as important spiritual/religious actors. These books *remind* readers of their beliefs and values and help them (re) construct their faith in the face of daily challenges and disappointments.[64] What is most striking is that actors believed to be at opposite ends of the religious and political spectrum—conservatives versus progressives, literal readers versus metaphoric readers, believers in the Truth versus believers in many truths—nonetheless share a culture of religious reading. Whatever our religious beliefs (or lack thereof), we inhabit the same world shaped in often competing ways by patriarchal Judeo-Christian traditions, therapeutic culture, consumerism, and the ideology of literacy (the belief that reading offers economic, spiritual, and social uplift).

In the last decade, a wealth of wonderful studies of religious ways with words have appeared.[65] However, these studies are almost without exception focused on evangelical reading and writing practices, either historically or in contemporary conservative Christian communities.[66] In its current state, the discipline has replicated the popular tendency to treat evangelicalism as normative, to have much to say about conservative Christian reading and writing and little to say about other religious ways with words (even other Christian ways with words). In this chapter, I traced the ways one set of white, professional liberal religious women used reading and book discussion to craft individual and collective religious identity narratives. This illuminates both the ways UU readers distinguish themselves from the normative evangelicalism in America and their shared motivations for and practices of religious reading. Since the disciplinary structures we inhabit encourage us to study conservatives and liberals, evangelicals and seekers, as distinct literary and faith communities, it is useful to be reminded of these common cultural threads.

Conclusion

─◆─

In idealizing an autonomous, difficult art as the only source of resistance
to . . . repressive regimes, [we] also shortchange the heterogeneous,
and politically variable, uses of literary texts in daily life.

There is no compelling reason why the practice of theory requires us to go
behind the backs of ordinary persons in order to expose their beliefs as deluded or
delinquent. . . . What would it mean to take this idea and place it as the heart of
literary theory? Among other things, it calls on us to engage seriously with ordinary
motives of reading—such as the desire for knowledge or the longing for
escape—that are either overlooked or undervalued in literary scholarship

—RITA FELSKI

Why do these much-maligned and much-loved popular religious books
matter? First, many of them are still around—decades after their initial
publication—shaping Americans' ways of being in the world. *In His Steps* is
available in countless paperback editions, the latest published in July 2012.
Readers on Amazon.com report that they still find it inspiring and thought
provoking, and many have purchased multiple copies to give to friends and
family. In the run-up to the 2000 U.S. presidential election, George W. Bush
claimed that Jesus was his favorite philosopher. Not to be outdone, Al Gore
insisted that he solved every ethical dilemma by asking, "What would Jesus
do?"[1] In recent years, Sheldon's question has structured debates over what
contemporary Christians should drive (not SUVs) and their diets (there is a
diet plan and cookbook called *What Would Jesus Eat?*).

The Man Nobody Knows is still in print. One of my editions has a blurb
on the back from James L. S. Collins, president and CEO of Chick-fil-A
(a self-proclaimed Christian company), who reports rereading the book
every year. He estimates he has given away hundreds of copies and recommended the book to thousands more.[2] Although I frame *The Man*
as a cultural document of the 1920s, some of my students in American

Studies courses easily read Barton's Jesus into their own lives. One glossed the book: "Jesus, my homeboy." Others connected Barton's fusion of commerce and Christianity with the programming at a nearby mega-church they described as "Six Flags over Jesus." Presumably, the consumer pleasures that enticed congregants to the church—coffee bar, state-of-the-art gym, movie theater, for example—rivaled those at Six Flags over Texas, a popular amusement park in the area.

Norman Vincent Peale's *The Power of Positive Thinking* still sells. In teaching this book as part of a course on Cold War popular cultures, I discovered that several of my students had an edition in which Peale's admonition "Do not comment that the Communists will soon destroy the country" had been altered to read "Do not comment that the terrorists will soon destroy the country," presumably all that was required to update this classic volume for contemporary readers.[3] *The Late Great Planet Earth* is still in print, and many readers returned to their copies in the wake of the September 11 terrorist attacks and found new meaning in it. These are clearly enduring texts. Generations of readers have appropriated them as what Kenneth Burke calls "equipment for living."[4] For many readers, these books still *work*—give them specific guidance for taking action in the world; make them feel less anxious, empty, and sad; sanctify their (often dull and poorly remunerated) daily labors; and give them a place in a larger historical narrative.

Further, books like these (and controversies about them) are still around. Bruce Barton's attempt to sanctify business has spawned a whole industry of Christian business books, *Jesus, CEO* (1995) among them.[5] Much like *The Power of Positive Thinking*, Bruce Wilkinson's best-selling *The Prayer of Jabez* (2000) taught readers how to pray in order to achieve prosperity. Critics—like those in the 1950s—were appalled by this "prosperity gospel" and the reduction of faith to a means to an end. Stories about the end times still sell, most prominently the *Left Behind* series (1995–2007) by Tim LaHaye and Jerry B. Jenkins. *The Gospel of Judas* (2006) created anew the firestorm of debate over which ancient texts Christians should embrace to place themselves in history and shape their vision for the future.

Moreover, these books and these readers still hold rather low status in the academy. For example, another religion fellow at the National Humanities Center, where I spent a year during the early stages of this project, teased me about the "penitential reading" I was doing. What bad thing had I done, that I was required to spend my days in my study with texts like these? Another colleague cheered me on in my study of popular religious books, because she assumed that I must be writing an exposé about how stupid the people who read them must be. Inspired by the Norman Vincent Peale I had been reading, I cultivated gratitude that conversations like this kept me just angry enough to keep reading and writing, when nothing else would do the trick.

Although studies of religion have placed less emphasis on social class in recent years, my investigations of twentieth-century religious bestsellers place education and cultural capital at the center of many controversies over books.[6] Scholars and intellectuals focus on the theological errors contained in many popular books and the aesthetic failings of their language and style. Ordinary readers often concede the limitations of these texts but assert that they do useful work in the world, nonetheless. This is to say that lay readers and professional readers do not so much oppose each other as they talk past each other about these books. Intellectuals worry over what these texts *say*, but ordinary readers focus—quite pragmatically—on what they *do*.

That said, relationships to these books are much more complicated than the simple binary of grateful popular embrace or scornful intellectual critique might indicate. Even incisive critics of these books can sometimes find them useful. That is, ideology critique and pragmatic appropriation of these books for practical help are by no means mutually exclusive. Professional readers are often "ordinary" or "popular" readers in other contexts. For example, when I teach *The Power of Positive Thinking* as a cultural document of the Cold War to students in American Studies courses, most usually respond with contempt for the book. They find this book embarrassing, they tell me, much more embarrassing than the 1950s lesbian pulp novel with the lurid cover they also read for this class. They report efforts to hide the book's cover when reading it in public, and many proactively tell their friends that they are reading this book *for a class*. With little prompting from me, they can come up with the communitarian critique—that Peale is focused so resolutely on the happiness and success of individuals that social injustice is rendered invisible. Some—following Reinhold Niebuhr— are pretty horrified by the idea that one would turn religion into a means to an end. Others—following Barbara Ehrenreich—suggest that failure to consider possible negative outcomes could compromise the quality of our thinking in pretty shocking ways.[7] Nevertheless, these same students sometimes find Peale useful. If I ask if anyone actually tried out Peale's techniques, some students—in their reading journals or (sheepishly) in class—will own up to having done so. One had miserable Thursdays that semester—twelve straight hours of class, lab, and student teaching. The Thursday after she read *The Power of Positive Thinking*, she engaged in some affirmations—it would be a great day, she was young and healthy and energetic, everything would go fine, and so on. It went better! Another student, anxious about flying, had a trip home scheduled over the weekend. She tried out Peale's techniques and was much less distressed by her flight as a consequence. One student just loved Peale from the get-go, comparing him to Stephen Covey, whose *Seven Habits of Highly Effective People* (1989) had made him a more effective person. My point here is that individual readers can read the same book in different ways, depending on institutional context and the mission and goals with which they approach the text. As part of a Cold War American Studies course, students saw this text as part of "containment culture" and traced out family resemblances with David Riesman's "other-directed" men and Betty Friedan's women entrapped by domesticity. As stressed-out students, anxious flyers, and people who just wanted to be better and feel better, they could see it as useful for everyday life, fully fifty or sixty years after its initial publication. The ability to critique the intellectual and theological limitations of the book in no way undermined their ability to appreciate that—whatever its limitations—it *worked*.

Indeed, scholars have begun to investigate the diversity of reading practices surrounding a single text. Eve Sedgwick compares the motivations of scholars and ordinary readers/seekers learning about Buddhism. She explains: "To put it crudely, academic scholars of Buddhism are vocationally aimed at finding a path, however asymptotic, toward a knowledge of their subject(s) that would be ever less distorted by ignorance, imperialist presumption, and wishful thinking, or by characteristic thought patterns of Western culture. On the other hand, the attachment of the nonacademic reader to the truth value of readings on Buddhism may rest on a good deal more pragmatic base. The question Is this (account) accurate or misleading? may give way for these readers to the question Will this (practice) work or won't it?"[8] Moreover, Sedgwick—as a literary scholar and a practicing Buddhist—would have found herself occupying both positions or toggling between the two. Most scholars of popular reading are also popular readers, and the lines between the two are sometimes muddy.

As my references to Felski and Sedgwick suggest, *What Would Jesus Read?* is informed by a crisis in literary studies. Scholars trained in the 1980s and 1990s spent a great deal of time learning how to do "symptomatic" reading or ideology critique. That is, we read texts for the hidden meanings—for what was silenced or repressed or obfuscated by its language. Both psychoanalysis and Marxism encouraged critics to read with a hermeneutic of suspicion, to get past the manifest meaning to the latent meaning or past the illusion of "realism" to the machinery that made capitalist ways of being in the world seem natural or inevitable or "commonsensical." Increasingly, literary scholars have begun to talk about alternatives to symptomatic reading. The options are innumerable—surface reading, Sharon Marcus's "just reading," Eve Sedgwick's "reparative reading," Rita Felski's "historical phenomenology," Franco Moretti's "distant reading," Bruno LaTour's "actor network theory," to name a few.[9] Such attempts to reimagine literary studies suggest that there is increasing awareness of different ways of reading in the academy and increasing interest in their implications. There is not, however, a corresponding interest among literary scholars in the historically situated reading practices of ordinary people. If our canons are considerably less impoverished than they used to be since the 1980s, our notions of who "we" are continue to be troublingly narrow. "We"—academics, literary scholars, historians, theologians, intellectuals—continue to focus on our own ways of reading as *right*, as the best or most valid ways of making sense of texts rather than one among many ways with words. This both impoverishes our literary history and dampens our ability to be politically effective as we engage the larger world.

My goal is to suggest that these alternative ways of reading—these alternative cultures of letters—are alive and well and have been flourishing in plain sight for the last hundred-odd years, but that we have dismissed them as unworthy of our notice or as just flat-out wrong and politically misguided. Religious ways of reading have both shaped literary culture and provided a foil against which literary studies defined itself. In providing thick descriptions of many religious cultures of letters in twentieth-century America, my goal has been to broaden our notions of what American literary history is and appreciate anew the power of reading and writing to transform lives.

This is—as one of my colleagues quipped—a purpose-driven book. *What Would Jesus Read?* is concerned with elucidating nonliterary ways of reading and addressing the place of right and wrong ways of reading in literary and religious studies, but—at base—it is concerned with the place of the humanities in the larger world. As a scholar and an advocate for public humanities, I think we do ourselves a disservice by accepting historically specific definitions of literature that literary studies and religious studies have offered. Popular religious books provide a great deal of evidence that reading and writing matter deeply to people who do not define themselves as intellectuals and suggest that books have the power to transform lives and change the world, an argument I take seriously. In part, I am suggesting that it has been so difficult to advocate effectively for funding and attention to the humanities because scholars have dismissed as invalid so many of the books and ways of reading that many nonprofessional readers find genuinely transformative.

What Would Jesus Read? also participates in the ongoing process of reimagining what religious studies might look like. At the end of a presentation on this project to a working group of history colleagues, one of them asked, "So—what's religious about this?" I found this question almost unanswerable, since its assumptions about what "religion" was seemed so utterly at odds with my own. "Lived religion" scholarship from the 1990s and beyond exists in part to interrogate the assumptions behind questions like this. In his overview essay for the founding collection, *Lived Religion in America*, Robert Orsi explains that these essays—together—establish that "to study lived religion entails a fundamental rethinking of what religion is and of what it means to be 'religious.' Religion is not only not *sui generis*, distinct from other dimensions of experience called 'profane.' Religion comes into being in an ongoing, dynamic relationship with the realities of everyday life."[10] These popular religious texts did not seem much interested in faith as some kind of transcendent realm, but in usefulness for everyday life, in freely mingling the sacred and the profane. Moreover, as discussed in the Introduction, I have come to understand nominally secular cultural categories like "the middlebrow" as always already shaped by religious ways with words.

This question does point to two others about popular religious reading that seem worth examining. The first is, "How is this different from (secular) middlebrow reading?" The second is, "How is this different from therapy?" These questions are related. From the project's beginnings, I repeatedly asked myself some version of the first question. As I sat in on reading groups and book discussions affiliated with various different kinds of churches, I kept thinking to myself, "How is this different from secular reading groups?" Especially if groups were reading novels with only minimal overtly religious content, often I could not tell the difference. Although Ann Ruggles Gere, Barbara Sicherman, and Elizabeth Long had explicitly excluded religious readers from their historical and contemporary studies of reading groups, I sometimes saw little to distinguish them.[11] Secular and religious readers eschewed the dispassionate scrutiny that is required in the academy and took a pragmatic, practical approach to these books—how could they engage in rather immediate ways with our daily lives? Books were an invitation to create a community and to talk about readers' own concerns and preoccupations through it. In his 1994 study of support groups and community building in contemporary America, Robert Wuthnow made a similar argument about small-group Bible study: "What counts is less the studying of specific lessons (And certainly not religious worship), but activities that people enjoy, that allow them to interact informally with a few other people, and that, in many ways, are not decidedly different from the activities that other people who are not in such groups do in their leisure time."[12] Although his intention was to challenge assertions like Wuthnow's and insist on the distinctiveness of evangelical Bible studies, James Bielo found that some of the groups he studied were driven by quite secular shared concerns. For example, one group was preoccupied with "history," and they understood their Bible study as an activity similar to watching the History Channel or going to museums.[13] In this way, much of what goes on in religious reading groups is not significantly different than what goes on in nonreligious reading groups.

However, sometimes religious reading is explicitly *about* articulating a religious identity. Social Gospel novels labored to distinguish religious reading from both academic and commercial/leisure reading. Religious readers read in order to take social action, not to escape into a self-contained world of ideas or to divert themselves for a few hours. Contemporary UUs read primarily to create—individually and collectively—religious identity narratives that distinguish them from their evangelical brothers and sisters and provide space to think about what it means to be religious liberals in the Bible Belt and women in patriarchal religious institutions. The evangelical reading groups described by Bielo similarly spent a lot of time differentiating themselves from others—Lutherans from Methodists and Pentecostals, for example—and establishing their own superiority to these others.[14]

Undoubtedly, religious reading is often therapeutic. Readers acquire, read, and discuss these books because they are seeking reassurance and guidance in navigating a world that they experience as overwhelming and bewildering. Readers are trying to make/find meaning, and these religious books offer narratives and models of narrative-making that enable them to do this. Matthew Hedstrom argues that the liberal religious middlebrow culture of the 1920s, 1930s, and 1940s was focused on psychology and mysticism because this therapeutic focus transcended sectarianism and allowed readers to reconcile science and religious belief.[15] Religious readers during World War II and its Cold War aftermath snapped up religious self-help books promising them peace of mind, peace of soul, and peace with God from a variety of different religious viewpoints. The idea was that in this anxious age, God could quell your anxieties, give you energy, help you forgive yourself, and guide you to manage your grief and disappointments. T. M. Luhrmann argues that contemporary evangelical practices are "fundamentally psychotherapeutic." Prayer leaders resemble empathetic psychotherapists, and congregants come to church—in part—to practice imagining what it would feel like to be loved unconditionally.[16] UU reading groups are—among other things—support groups for embattled religious liberals in the Bible Belt. People read these popular religious books, alone and together, to make themselves feel better—less alone, less embattled, less sick with anxiety about their individual and collective fates.

The connections of popular religious reading to middlebrow reading and to therapy are related. As Timothy Aubry argues, middlebrow reading in contemporary America *is* therapeutic reading: "Many readers in the United States today treat novels less as a source of aesthetic satisfaction than as a practical dispenser of advice or a form of therapy. They choose books that will offer strategies for confronting, understanding, and managing their personal problems. They want to encounter characters who remind them of themselves, their family members, or their friends. In search of comfort and companionship, they also expect novels to validate their grievances, insecurities, and anxieties while confirming their sense of themselves as deep, complicated, emotionally responsive human beings."[17] Much of this is true of readers of twentieth-century religious bestsellers, contemporary and historical. Businessmen in the 1920s loved Bruce Barton's Jesus because he was someone like them. UUs liked to read about Gnosticism because they saw themselves in the religious/intellectual aristocracy that second-century Gnostic communities imagined themselves to be. Young, conservative Christians in the 1970s embraced *The Late Great Planet Earth* because it offered bedrock certainty about their salvation in a world that looked increasingly precarious and placed them among the chosen people on the right side of history. Readers bring many of the same therapeutic purposes and goals to religious reading and to novels they read for pleasure and uplift in their leisure time.

Popular religious reading, then, is engaged with the relationship between humans and the divine, but it is also therapeutic and pragmatically useful for navigating daily life. It is intimately enmeshed with gender, race, class, education, age, privilege, and emotional styles as well. Religious identity narratives are also about these other identities. Readers of melodramatic Social Gospel novels by Harold Bell Wright and Charles Sheldon embraced not only a kind of liberal Protestantism, but also emotional styles that many literary scholars found/find embarrassing. Wright's readers, in particular, were encouraged to see God's plan as inextricably linked to a sexist and racist social order. Bruce Barton's Jesus embodied "practical Christianity," but he was also virile and manly. Popular readings of the Gnostic gospels are not just heretical; they are also feminist and shaped by the cultural capital their privileged readers possess. *The Late Great Planet Earth* is not just premillennial dispensationalism; it is also anti-institutional and explicitly targeted at young, disenchanted readers.

If the boundaries between religious reading and middlebrow or therapeutic reading are sometimes muddy, boundaries between different communities of popular religious readers sometimes blur as well. Because we have only begun the immense scholarly task of mapping the field of religious print culture, I can only raise tentative questions based on the examples in *What Would Jesus Read?* at this point. Nonetheless, it is clear that Cold War readers enthusiastically read religious self-help books promising them peace of mind from Catholic, Jewish, conservative, and liberal Protestant writers, often across faith lines. Moreover, these books shared a set of assumptions about what religion was good for and how religious reading participated in furthering "the American way" at home and abroad. Although they read different books and defined themselves against each other, contemporary UU readers and conservative Christian readers appear to share motivations for reading and ways of reading popular books. Evangelical women and UU women are engaged in (re)creating their religious identities through reading, distinguishing themselves from others through their embrace of these texts. Their books often move women and their concerns to the center of religious life from the margins of their patriarchal churches. As they discuss books, they are placing themselves in history, creating a "usable past" that will reinspire them for their often dispiriting daily work. The "lived religion" enacted through popular reading suggests that there is some common ground between the practices of liberal and conservative Protestants, even in a bitterly divided era.

Similarly, readers of Lindsey's (fundamentalist) *The Late Great Planet Earth*, like readers of Barton's (liberal Protestant) *The Man Nobody Knows*, were much less concerned with theological correctness than scholars and ministers were. They wrenched relevant texts out of their historical contexts and read them into contemporary life and politics, treating these texts as though they had been written expressly to address personal concerns. In both cases, the importance of institutional religion diminished and the individual soul took center stage. The focus on psychology and mysticism at the Religious Book Club in the 1920s and 1930s echoed this shift in emphasis from institutions to individuals. Certainly, books for the seeker emphasize individual spiritual journeys over building religious institutions, as well.

Moreover, religious reading instruction across faiths invites readers to collapse the distance between the worlds of sacred books and their own worlds. Here is Luhrmann describing guidance she received from the leader of her contemporary, evangelical Vineyard Fellowship Bible study: "She wanted us to enter the passage as participants and to imagine that we were there as the story unfolded. She told us that Jesus was a storyteller, and she thought that what mattered was that his stories became so real for us, it was as if they had happened in our own lives."[18] Here is Orsi describing how the imaginations of Catholic children in the United States had been trained in the 1940s and 1950s: "Children were encouraged to imagine themselves in scenes from the lives of Jesus, Mary and the saints, to interact with these figures, and to experience the emotions (sad, frightening, joyful) of a particular episode from scripture or hagiography. . . . Through their imaginations, children became the contemporaries of holy figures, literally entering into the iconography and narratives of the tradition."[19] Finally, for good measure, here is high praise from the pages of the *Religious Book Club Bulletin* for a novel called *Armor of Light* from 1930: "To be transported in imagination across the chasm of nearly nineteen centuries and live vividly in the world of the first century Christians is the experience of the readers of this beautiful narrative."[20] These instructions—evangelical, Catholic, and liberal Protestant—suggest some overlap in ways of reading. Moreover, all bear some resemblance to what Gregory Jackson calls an "aesthetics of immediacy," which he identifies as distinctly American and distinctly Protestant, a vivid, visual homiletic tradition that powerfully places readers/viewers in the world of the text and calls them to take moral action.[21] I am not suggesting that these moments describe a single, transdenominational, transhistorical way of reading. Across faiths and across different time periods, this way of collapsing the distance between religious texts and contemporary readers was turned to quite distinct ends and with quite distinct outcomes. I am suggesting that the academic structure of departments scholars occupy predispose us to find what is distinctive about liberals and conservatives, Protestants, Catholics, and Jews, and to underplay common threads—a therapeutic emphasis, pragmatic help for everyday life, engagement with consumer culture, a belief in the power of reading to shape souls and character. Indeed, much lived religion scholarship moves in this direction. Orsi argues that what scholarship on lived religion does is to "invite a redirection of religious scholarship away from traditions—the great hypostasized constructs of 'Protestantism,' 'Catholicism,' and so on—and likewise away from the denominational focus that has so preoccupied scholars of American religions, toward a study of how particular people, in particular places and times, live in, with, through, and against the religious idioms available to them in culture—*all* the idioms, including (often enough) those not explicitly their 'own.'"[22]

What Would Jesus Read? reminds us as scholars that different kinds of reading and writing emerge from different social and historical circumstances to meet the needs of differently situated readers and writers. These popular twentieth-century religious cultures of letters illuminate nonliterary, often *anti*-literary, ways with words. They suggest that much religious reading urges an immediate connection between reading and social action rather than emphasizing intertextual connections. Many popular religious books are much less concerned with theological correctness and historical accuracy than they are with offering practical guidance for readers' daily lives. Such books are often therapeutic in their emphasis, offering readers reassurance and hope and providing models for (re)creating religious identity and community through narrative. Moreover, the "politics" of these texts arise not only from their language, but also from the material books in which that language appears and the social and historical circumstances of the readers who take them up as equipment for living. *What Would Jesus Read?* also reminds us that our own reading and writing practices—like those of "popular" or nonprofessional readers—are shaped by the social structures we inhabit while we undertake that work. It is my hope that this book has illuminated these neglected popular religious cultures of letters, and that it also invites literary and religious studies scholars to look again—critically—at our own ways of reading and writing.

APPENDIX A

Survey Materials for *The Late Great Planet Earth* Readers

I solicited readers from Theolog (a *Christian Century* blog) and H-Amrel, an online discussion group on the history of American Religion.

Solicitation materials:
Do you remember Hal Lindsey's *Late Great Planet Earth*? I'd like to hear about it. I am an American Studies professor, and I am collecting narratives about the experience of reading Hal Lindsey's *Late Great Planet Earth* for a book I am writing about religious bestsellers and their readers in the twentieth-century United States. For more information, please go to my website www.utdallas.edu/~erins and click on "*Late Great Planet Earth* survey."

Text on website:
I am collecting narratives about the experience of reading Hal Lindsey's *Late Great Planet Earth* for a book I am writing about religious bestsellers and their readers in the twentieth-century United States. I am interested in all kinds of memories related to the book, in whatever form seems best to tell them. However, I have included a few prompts below:

1. When/how did you hear about the book? What convinced you that you wanted to read it?

2. Did you talk about it with anyone? If so, whom? In what ways?

3. What do you remember about the book or your discussions of it? Did it change your way of thinking or your way of being in the world? What did you think/feel while you were reading and talking about this book?

4. Did reading or talking about this book have any short-term or long-term impact on your religious life? Do you think about it differently now than when you first encountered the book?

5. Demographic information
   Gender
   Age
   Race
   Occupation
   Religious affiliation (if any)

6. Would you be willing to be contacted for a follow-up survey or interview? If so, please provide your contact information.

Please email narratives to erins@utdallas.edu with "LGPE memories" in the subject line. No attachments, please.

Erin A. Smith
Associate Professor of American Studies & Literature
University of Texas at Dallas
www.utdallas.edu/~erins
For more information, please contact erins@utdallas.edu

APPENDIX B

Questions to Frame Spiritual Autobiography Interviews

1. Would you tell me the story of your religious/spiritual development over the course of your life? Were there important turning points? If so, what precipitated them?

2. Are there particular texts that have been important to your spiritual development (books, films, lectures, courses, art works, etc.)?

3. What religious or spiritual communities have you belonged to? What did they provide for you? Do you belong to one now?

4. Is your life's work or occupation related to your religious faith? If so, how?

5. Does your religious faith shape your community or social activism? If so, how?

NOTES

Abbreviations

BU   Joshua Loth Liebman Collection, Howard Gotlieb Archival Research Center, Boston University, Boston, Mass.

IU   Lilly Library, Indiana University, Bloomington, Ind.

KSHS   Center for Historical Research, Kansas State Historical Society, Topeka, Kans.

LC   *Religious Book Club Bulletin*, Library of Congress, Washington, D.C.

SU   Norman Vincent Peale Papers, Special Collections Research Center, Syracuse University, Syracuse, N.Y.

UA   Harold Bell Wright Papers, Special Collections at the University of Arizona Libraries, Tucson, Ariz.

UTS   Harry Emerson Fosdick Papers, UTS Collection, Burke Library at Union Theological Seminary, Columbia University Libraries, New York, N.Y.

WHS   Bruce Barton Papers, Wisconsin Historical Society Archives, Madison, Wis.

Introduction

1. Marty, "Preface" and "The Protestant Press: Limitations and Possibilities," vii, 8–11.

2. "Output of Religious Books."

3. On the size and growth of religious publishing since 1945 and the difficulties of measuring its scope, see Gutjahr, "The Perseverance of Print-Bound Saints."

4. See, for example, Gere, *Intimate Practices*; Elizabeth Long, *Book Clubs*; and Sicherman, *Well-Read Lives*.

5. David D. Hall, *Worlds of Wonder, Days of Judgment*; Matthew J. Brown, *Pilgrim and the Bee*; Tompkins, *Sensational Designs*; Reynolds, *Faith in Fiction*; Jackson, *Word and Its Witness*. Some notable recent exceptions include Frykholm, *Rapture Culture*; Neal, *Romancing God*; and Hedstrom, *Rise of Liberal Religion*.

6. David D. Hall, *Lived Religion in America*; see especially Orsi's essay in this volume, "Everyday Miracles: The Study of Lived Religion."

7. Gordon, *Norman Vincent Peale*, chap. 15.

8. Schmidt, *Consumer Rites*, 13.

9. "Amazing Novelty in Book Advertising," 1145; "Appleton Wins First Prize at Advertising Convention," 1664.

10. G. W. Freeman to Bruce Barton, 25 August 1925, Bobbs-Merrill Manuscripts, IU.

11. Schmidt, *Consumer Rites*; McDannell, *Material Christianity*; Morgan, *Visual Piety*.

12. Fessenden, *Culture and Redemption*; Modern, *Secularism in Antebellum America*.

13. Chartier, *Order of Books*, 5; Felski, *Uses of Literature*, 11.

14. De Certeau, *Practice of Everyday Life*, chap. 12; Chartier, "Culture as Appropriation," 233.

15. I use the terms "popular readers" or "ordinary readers" (or sometimes "lay readers," if the distinction between clergy and laity is most important) to name what Jonathan Rose calls

"non-professional" readers—that is, "readers who did not read and write for a living" (51). Previous generations of scholars most often referred to such readers as "common readers." See Rose, "Rereading the English Common Reader."

16. On the institutional framework for literary reading in the academy, see Guillory, "The Ethical Practice of Modernity."

17. The term is Richard Brodhead's. His reconstruction of the institutionalized literary worlds of nineteenth-century America and their differential availability to writers of different races, genders, regions, and social classes allowed me to rethink these twentieth-century popular religious books not as literary failures but as books that were *differently* literary—that emerged from different social grounds and had different social purposes. Although Brodhead's cultures of letters are largely structured by class, education, and cultural capital, I extend his insights to consider explicitly religious cultures of letters, cultures he did not discuss. See Brodhead, *Cultures of Letters*.

18. In a 2007 piece revisiting his influential *Order of Books*, Chartier specifically addressed this widespread misunderstanding of his discussion of popular reading. At no point did he suggest that readers were limitlessly creative and socially unbounded as they made meaning from texts. With de Certeau—whose idea of "poaching" he sought to flesh out historically—Chartier meant to challenge semiotic accounts of reading that argued that meaning was determined by the structure of language alone (and—consequently—that one could determine its "politics" from the text alone). Chartier substituted a triangle in which meaning arises from the interaction among language, material text, and reader. Chartier's work—and my own—is to take ideas like "interpretive community" (from Stanley Fish) and "appropriation" (from Foucault) and deploy them in historically and sociologically informed ways. See Chartier, "*The Order of Books* Revisited." This is part of a symposium, "What Was the History of the Book?"

19. "Thick description" is Clifford Geertz's phrase. See Geertz, "Thick Description."

20. Lears, "From Salvation to Self-Realization," 31.

21. The term comes from Charles Sheldon's biographer. See Timothy Miller, *Following in His Steps*, 15.

22. Rubin, *Making of Middlebrow Culture*.

23. Radway, *Feeling for Books*. More recent work on middlebrow and middle-class reading includes Botshon and Goldsmith, *Middlebrow Moderns*; Harker, *America the Middlebrow*; Harker, *Middlebrow Queer*; Ehrhardt, *Writers of Conviction*; Hutner, *What America Read*; and Blair, *Reading Up*.

24. Bourdieu, *Distinction*, 4, 28–44. For a compelling update of Bourdieu's work on cultural capital for the contemporary British context, see Bennett, Savage, and Bortolaia, *Culture, Class, Distinction*.

25. Radway, *Feeling for Books*, 152.

26. Rubin, *Making of Middlebrow Culture*, chap. 4, especially 174, 158.

27. Frykholm, *Rapture Culture*, 114–15.

28. In *Word and Its Witness*, Gregory Jackson argues that the "homiletic" roots of realism and naturalism in early twentieth-century America lie in Puritan sermon conventions. The rhetorical and stylistic forms are old, but they have been repurposed for secular life and taken out of a context that required Christian action from readers. Conversely, I am arguing here that although middlebrow reading practices have been taken out of their religious context, the intimate link between reading and action persists.

29. Rubin, *Making of Middlebrow Culture*, xvii.

30. Ibid., xviii.

31. Ibid., 5.

32. In her map of contemporary literary criticism, Felski identifies what she calls "theological styles of reading," which emphasize that literary ways with words are fundamentally different from everyday language. That is, they are valuable precisely because of their "originality, singularity, alterity, untranslatability, or negativity" (*Uses of Literature*, 4).

33. Hedstrom, *Rise of Liberal Religion*.

Chapter 1

1. Mott, *Golden Multitudes*, 226.

2. For a discussion of the Social Gospel more generally, see Curtis, *A Consuming Faith*; Ferré, *A Social Gospel for Millions*; William C. Graham, *Half-Finished Heaven*; Luker, *The Social Gospel in Black and White*; and Bederman, "The Women Have Had Charge of the Church Work Long Enough."

3. Ferré, *Social Gospel for Millions*, 8.

4. The phrase "equipment for living" comes from Burke, "Literature as Equipment for Living."

5. The term comes from Sheldon's biographer. See Timothy Miller, *Following in His Steps*, 15.

6. For example, articles on the topic without exception deal centrally with Sheldon's *In His Steps*, the most popular of these novels and the most frequently cited in surveys of American religion (see Lindley, "Women and the Social Gospel Novel"). In his monograph on Social Gospel literature, William C. Graham claims that *Inside of the Cup* is the best example of a Social Gospel novel (*Half-Finished Heaven*, 159).

7. Ward, the niece of Matthew Arnold, was the author of twenty-five novels, publishing *Robert Elsmere*, her most popular work, at the age of thirty-six. For publication history, see Rosemary Ashton's introduction to the Oxford University Press edition, vii. See also Ramsey, "Books and Bookmakers," 11. My inclusion of this British novel with American Social Gospel novels is based on its American readership (all of these were popular books about religion and reading in the United States during this period), but also suggests that the ways of reading they represent and advocate for were part of a transatlantic culture of liberal Protestantism. I am challenging here Gregory Jackson's suggestion that the link between religious reading and social action in the homiletic novels he discusses was uniquely American. See Jackson, *Word and Its Witness*, 4–5.

8. Mrs. Humphry Ward, *Robert Elsmere*, 53.

9. Ibid., 59.

10. Ibid., 197.

11. Ibid., 384.

12. Ibid.

13. Ibid.

14. Ibid., 507.

15. Ibid.

16. Ibid., 473.

17. Ibid., 475.

18. Ibid., 518.

19. Sales figures and rankings are available from Hackett and Burke, *80 Years of Best Sellers*, 78, 80. William Graham details the links between Churchill and the leading lights of the Social Gospel movement. Churchill's publisher sent him Rauschenbusch's *Christianity and the Social Crisis*, and Rauschenbusch read *Inside of the Cup* and liked it (William C. Graham, *Half-Finished Heaven*, 159, 155).

20. Churchill, *Inside of the Cup*, 136.

21. Ibid., 270.

22. Ibid., 268.

23. Timothy Miller, *Following in His Steps*, 15.

24. Historians of reading have long distinguished between the intensive reading of a single, important volume—usually the Bible—and the extensive reading—usually of novels—of many different books, none possessing any extraordinary significance to the reader. The distinction originally comes from Rolf Engelsing, who called the transition from intensive to extensive reading part of a "reading revolution" that occurred in the late eighteenth century. The distinction has been challenged and complicated by many subsequent scholars. See, for example, Davidson, *Revolution and the Word*, 69–79. Nonetheless, the distinction continues to structure discussions of religious reading. For example, Paul Griffiths distinguishes between religious reading, which is attentive to the text as lovers are to their beloved, and consumerist reading, which is fast, frantic, and seeks only to find the interesting or necessary parts of the text for one's purposes. Griffiths, like his nineteenth-century predecessors, intends to divide "good" ways of reading from "bad." Good ways of reading are intensive, prayerful, and powerful in their effects. See Griffiths, *Religious Reading*.

25. Sheldon, *Charles M. Sheldon: His Life Story*, 269.

26. Ibid., 269–70.

27. Ibid., 268–69.

28. Ibid., 296–97.

29. For a psychoanalytically inflected discussion of reading in nineteenth-century America as a form of communion with authors and characters, see Silverman, *Bodies and Books*. See also Hochman, *Getting at the Author*, on "friendly reading," which imagined reading in the nineteenth century as a conversation with the author.

30. Sheldon, *Charles M. Sheldon: His Life Story*, 298.

31. See Candy Gunther Brown, *Word in the World*, 116; and Nord, *Faith in Reading*, 114, 124–25.

32. See Timothy Miller, *Following in His Steps*, chap. 4; and Ripley, "The Strange Story of Charles M. Sheldon's *In His Steps*," 241.

33. Sheldon, *Charles M. Sheldon: His Life Story*, 196–97. On nineteenth-century female writers of evangelical fiction, see Tompkins, *Sensational Designs*.

34. Sheldon, *Charles M. Sheldon: His Life Story*, viii.

35. Jackson, *Word and Its Witness*, 196. For a fuller definition of the homiletic novel, see ibid., 158–59.

36. Ibid., 162–63. See also Jackson, "What Would Jesus Do?," 643. Contemporary literary scholars might describe Sheldon's worldview as deeply informed by what Pierre Bourdieu calls "the popular ethos." See Bourdieu, *Distinction*, 28–44. Although Jackson argues that the homiletic novel transcended class, inviting working- and middle-class readers to identify—as Christ did—with the poor and down-trodden, this way of reading—what Jackson calls an "aesthetic of immediacy"—lost institutional support as modernist aesthetics became dominant in the academy (*Word and Its Witness*, 184–87, 5). Readers with a great deal of education might have a larger number of reading protocols to draw on, depending on their goals and circumstances (that is, homiletic reading was one among many modes of literacy), but homiletic reading might be one of the few protocols available to those lacking education. In this way, modes of reading that emerged from Protestant scripture reading (that is, they were "religious" ways of reading that crossed class lines) might come to be mapped onto social class. Homiletic reading

might be especially likely to become "popular" reading in the late nineteenth and early twentieth centuries, when intellectuals were at pains to consolidate their own power by challenging the cultural authority once wielded by religious institutions.

37. George T. B. Davis, "Charles M. Sheldon, Novelist," 75–76.

38. The publishing history of *In His Steps* is rife with myths and inaccuracies, some of them perpetrated by Sheldon himself. See, for example, Sheldon, *History of "In His Steps,"* copy in Charles Monroe Sheldon/Central Congregational Church collection, #222, KSHS. For an untangling of the myths, see Ripley, "The Strange Story of Charles M. Sheldon's *In His Steps*"; Mott, *Golden Multitudes*, 193–97; and Timothy Miller, *Following in His Steps*, chap. 4.

39. The most influential analysis is Boyer, "In His Steps: A Reappraisal." See also Elzey, "What Would Jesus Do?"

40. Although there is evidence that working- and middle-class congregations and white and black readers took up Sheldon's challenge to live as Jesus would, we shall see that other Social Gospel novels illustrated that religious ways of reading were intimately enmeshed with gender and social class, and not always in progressive ways. On homiletic novels as transcending class, race, and (in some ways) gender, see Jackson, *Word and Its Witness*, 184–87.

41. Ava Baron argues that high unemployment brought on by economic recession and the arrival of the linotype machine in the 1890s destroyed printers' job security. Conservative estimates claim that each new machine put two printers out of work. On the history of the de-skilling (and demasculinization) of printers' work, see Baron, "An 'Other' Side of Gender Antagonism at Work," 56.

42. See, for example, Sheldon, *In His Steps*, 111–12, 155.

43. Ibid., 81–82.

44. Ibid., 140.

45. Ibid., 140–41.

46. Ibid., 54, 56.

47. Ibid., 89, 91.

48. Sheldon, "The Ethics of Some Publishers." On his gratitude for the defective copyright, see Sheldon, "Foreword," v–vi. As Candy Gunther Brown argues, such piracy was not an unusual part of religious print culture in nineteenth-century America: "Evangelicals assumed that texts did not belong to their authors but to the Christian community, and members of this community could appropriate any printed matter for particular purposes. The understanding of texts contributed to the fluidity of the canon and the disregard of copyrights" (*Word in the World*, 7–8).

49. Jackson, *Word and Its Witness*, 4, 94.

50. Frykholm, *Rapture Culture*, 115. Christian publisher Tyndale House publishes a series of *Life Application Study Bibles*, which include notes and guides demonstrating the contemporary relevance of the Bible. That is to say that this way of reading receives significant institutional support in the packaging and marketing of Bibles. In his ethnography of contemporary evangelical small-group Bible studies, James Bielo similarly argues that the most common way of reading is to apply Bible verses to readers' everyday lives. Moreover, he finds an extremely close relationship between text and action in these groups (Bielo, *Words upon the Word*, 50).

51. On *Robert Elsmere* as the inspiration for social action that became the kernel of *In His Steps*, see Timothy Miller, *Following in His Steps*, 70. Mott calls *In His Steps* a "naïve *Robert Elsmere*" (*Golden Multitudes*, 195). The other inspiration for *In His Steps* was W. T. Stead's 1894 *If Christ Came to Chicago*, an influence Sheldon only acknowledged after some controversy in an 1899 edition.

52. The best source on "the Jesus newspaper" is Ripley, "Another Look at the Rev. Mr. Charles M. Sheldon's Christian Daily Newspaper." See also Michael Ray Smith, *The Jesus Newspaper*; and Timothy Miller, *Following in His Steps*, chap. 5. A Christian daily newspaper was a long-time dream of Sheldon's. In 1895, he published a two-part article in the Social Gospel paper, *The Kingdom*, laying out his plans (Sheldon, "A Plea for a Christian Daily Newspaper"). In July 1899, his address to the Christian Endeavor Society convention in Detroit was on this topic. In March 1899, he told *Our Day* of his plans for a Christian metropolitan daily newspaper; see George T. B. Davis, "Charles M. Sheldon, Novelist."

53. Quotation from Ripley, "Another Look at the Rev. Mr. Charles M. Sheldon's Christian Daily Newspaper," 19. My narrative here is drawn primarily from Ripley's account.

54. Ibid.

55. See *Topeka Daily Capital*, 13 March 1900, 2.

56. See "Starving India."

57. See Sheldon, *Charles M. Sheldon: His Life Story*, 126–28. The postmortem on the Sheldon edition was generally negative. Most important, there was not a whole lot of news in it. The local competitor, the *Topeka State Journal*, had its circulation increase 40 percent that week, since the *Capital* subscribers learned a great deal about the evils of military force and demon rum, various not-so-timely human disasters, and Christian social work, but not much about the week's current events (Ripley, "Another Look at the Rev. Mr. Charles M. Sheldon's Christian Daily Newspaper," 28). Other critics claimed that censoring the news was not the only way to present it from a Christian perspective. Many newsmen resented the implied critique of their moral character in Sheldon's weeklong experiment. Others pointed out that religious and denominational periodicals were flourishing and questioned the need for a daily paper such as Sheldon's.

58. Sheldon, "The Topeka Capital This Week."

59. See Gladstone, "'Robert Elsmere' and the Battle of Belief"; and Mrs. Humphry Ward, "The New Reformation, a Dialogue." They also had significant correspondence on the topic. See Peterson, "Gladstone's Review of *Robert Elsmere*." Both are discussed in Ashton's introduction.

60. See Ashton, "Introduction," xv.

61. Ibid., xvii.

62. Gregory Jackson argues that homiletic novels created powerful, personal identifications with the oppressed that had the potential to transcend gender, or at least narrow nineteenth-century notions of womanhood (*Word and Its Witness*, 187). This section and the section on Harold Bell Wright's fusion of social Darwinism and evangelical Christianity in Chapter 2 suggest this was not always the case.

63. For a survey of the representations of women in thirty-seven Social Gospel novels and a comparison of the images of women in male-authored versus female-authored texts, see Lindley, "Women and the Social Gospel Novel."

64. Sheldon, *In His Steps*, 243, 222.

65. Mrs. Humphry Ward, *Robert Elsmere*, 323.

66. Ibid., 510.

67. Ibid., 530.

68. Churchill, *Inside of the Cup*, 1.

69. Churchill presents many such characters' stories in *Inside of the Cup*. Phil Goodrich narrates a typical story of how the failure of one teacher to acknowledge the contradiction between traditional faith and reason turns an entire class of boys into agnostics (415–16). Evelyn Waring complains, "We should like to believe, but . . . all our education contradicts the doctrines that are most insisted upon. We don't know where to turn. We have the choice of going to

people . . . who know a great deal and don't believe anything, or to clergy men like Mr. Hodder, who demand that we shall violate the reason in us which has been so carefully trained" (10).

70. Ibid., 7.

71. Ibid., 59–66, 69–79, 176–83.

72. Ibid., 137.

73. Ibid., 510.

74. Ibid., 457–61.

75. Ibid., 454, 456.

76. In this way, the fate of *In His Steps* supports the narrative of declension from intellectually vigorous theology to mass-produced but intellectually vacuous piety by the close of the nineteenth century, described by Ann Douglas, T. J. Jackson Lears, and David Reynolds. See Douglas, *Feminization of American Culture*; Lears, "From Salvation to Self-Realization"; and Reynolds, *Faith in Fiction*.

77. Nord, *Faith in Reading*, 119.

78. Candy Gunther Brown, *Word in the World*, 1, 4.

79. Ibid., 7.

80. Gregory Jackson calls these widely shared story structures "homiletic templates." The pilgrimage template shaped homiletic fiction and provided a structure whereby readers could "textualize" their own lives, imposing order on their daily struggles through these master plots. Enabled by the allegorical or typological structure of these texts, readers (like characters in the novels) could learn to see their individual lives as particular iterations of eternal, divine plots. See Jackson, *Word and Its Witness*, 23. His discussion of the pilgrimage template is in chapter 2.

81. Sheldon's biographer calls *In His Steps* "overly sentimental, theologically sloppy, literarily forgettable." See Timothy Miller, *Following in His Steps*, 69.

82. Gregory Jackson compellingly argues a different case—that realism and naturalism, which have been discussed in secular frames in literary studies, are, in fact, intimately enmeshed with homiletic plots and conventions. The interplay between reading and social action is often missing in literary realism and naturalism, however. He discusses the implications for literary studies in his introduction and epilogue (*Word and Its Witness*, 23–24, 282). See also Jackson, "What Would Jesus Do?" 641–61.

83. The phrase is Richard Brodhead's. Brodhead, *Cultures of Letters*, especially 1–12.

84. For a discussion of these questions in the career of Harold Bell Wright, see Erin A. Smith, "Melodrama, Popular Religion, and Literary Value." My discussion of the institutionalization of literature is informed by Guillory, *Cultural Capital*.

85. See Eliot, "Tradition and the Individual Talent."

86. John Guillory (among others) explicitly links New Critical literary practice to religious ways with words. It is no coincidence, he argues, that New Criticism arrived on the scene just as there was increasing investment in universities as institutions taking over some of the cultural functions of churches (*Cultural Capital*, 140).

Chapter 2

1. Ronald Reagan to Jean B. Wright, 13 March 1984, personal collection of Susan Cline. Reagan talked about his experience of reading *That Printer of Udell's* throughout his life. See Reagan, *Ronald Reagan*, 32; and Kengor, *God and Ronald Reagan*, chap. 2. See also Morris, *Dutch*, 40–42; and Cannon, *Governor Reagan*, 19.

2. According to Nye, the other four best-selling novelists are Winston Churchill (discussed in Chapter 1), Gene Stratton-Porter, Owen Wister, and Mary Roberts Rhinehart. See Nye, *Unembarrassed Muse*, 40; and Dickinson, *Best Books of Our Time*, 334. In 1947, Frank Luther Mott, distinguished historian of bestsellers in America, compiled a list of bestsellers from 1665 onward, defining "bestseller" as a book whose sales equaled at least 1 percent of the U.S. population in the decade of its publication. Wright wrote five such books (Mott, *Golden Multitudes*, 7, 312–13, 225–33).

3. Tompkins, *Sensational Designs*, especially chaps. 5 and 6.

4. Wright, *To My Sons*, 252.

5. Mencken, *Prejudices*, 38–39; Cooper, "Popularity of Harold Bell Wright," 498.

6. On the relationship between women writers and their publishers in the nineteenth century, see Kelley, *Private Woman, Public Stage*; and Coultrap-McQuin, *Doing Literary Business*.

7. Wright, *To My Sons* manuscript, 220, UA.

8. On "muscular Christianity," see Putney, *Muscular Christianity*.

9. Bederman, "The Women Have Had Charge of the Church Work Long Enough," 435–40.

10. Wright, *That Printer of Udell's*, 83–84.

11. Wright, *Calling of Dan Matthews*, 186–87.

12. Wright also took his version of muscular Christianity to other media. Most of Wright's novels were made into Hollywood films (fifteen between 1916 and 1949), including *The Winning of Barbara Worth* (1926) starring Gary Cooper and *The Shepherd of the Hills* (1941) with John Wayne (see Tagg, *Harold Bell Wright*, 189–90). Wright wrote not only for *Christian Century* and *Ladies' Home Journal*, but also for *Physical Culture*, a popular muscle magazine.

13. Wright, *To My Sons*, 10.

14. See Cosulich, "Crumbs from the Table of Success"; Cosulich, "Methods of Harold Bell Wright"; and Cosulich, "Mr. Wright Builds a Boat."

15. Wright, *To My Sons*, 254.

16. Frank, "Pseudo-Literature"; Hart, "One Hundred Leading Authors." See also Cooper, "Popularity of Harold Bell Wright," 498.

17. Mencken, *Prejudices*, 32–33, 38. Even booksellers, who stood to profit from Wright's popular works, got on the bandwagon. One witness at the 1921 annual American Booksellers Association convention testified to "a tendency to sneer at the mention of such names as Zane Grey, Joe Lincoln, Gene Stratton-Porter, and Harold Bell Wright, despite the well-known fact that the mere announcement of a new book by one of these authors means an immediate immense sale" ("Why the Common People Do Not Buy More Books").

18. Wright, *To My Sons*, 253–54.

19. "Wright Confesses He Is 'at Sea' in Literary Circles."

20. "Harold Bell Wright Admits He Is Not a Literary Man."

21. "Dear Sir" Specimen Ads, D. Appleton & Company, 1922, 4, Appleton-Century Manuscripts, IU.

22. Mott, *Golden Multitudes*, 233.

23. Bourdieu, *Distinction*, 28–44.

24. Kenamore, "A Curiosity in Best-Seller Technique." Some critics understood that Wright's work was intended for nonliterary audiences and reading in nonliterary ways. Like voices crying in the wilderness, they repeatedly insisted that Wright's popularity told us absolutely nothing about the state of American literature or about literary taste more generally. One *New York Times Book Review* columnist asked in 1921, "But do people interested in American literature read Harold Bell Wright? And if they do, do they read him for any literary reasons at all?" See "Why Is Harold Bell Wright?"

25. Quoted in the Book Supply Company 1918 Illustrated Catalog of Books, 17, 16 (also 12), UA. See also "Harold Bell Wright Admits He Is Not a Literary Man."

26. Wright, *To My Sons*, 106; see also ibid., 190.

27. Wright, *When a Man's a Man*, 220.

28. Wright, *To My Sons*, 187–88.

29. Ibid., 189.

30. Hofstadter, *Anti-intellectualism in American Life*, 33–34. Wright's anti-intellectualism had religious roots. He was saved by an itinerant Disciples of Christ minister in 1893. Disciples practiced a revivalistic style of religion based on scripture alone. They tended to be anti-institutional, anti-creedal, and action-oriented. All governance was local, and they opposed "denominationalism" (that is, divisions among Protestants), espousing "applied Christianity" instead. There was more emphasis on Christ's moral example than on his atoning death. See Ketchell, *Holy Hills of the Ozarks*, 4–9.

31. "Making Best Sellers with Newspaper Space."

32. Karetzky, *Reading Research and Librarianship*, 18, 99.

33. Tebbel, *Between Covers*, 88.

34. See Hilkey, *Character Is Capital*, chap. 1, especially 23. In this light, the similarity of Wright's (mostly mail-order) books to the turn-of-the-century success manuals that Hilkey studies is striking. Both were didactic, offered moralizing inspiration, and emphasized individual virtue and personal character, and both were written by teachers or ministers to help readers achieve success.

35. Estabrook, "The Undeveloped Side of the Book Business."

36. Of the more than 320 pages in the 1918 catalog, only 6 were given over to fiction.

37. The Book Supply Company 1918 Illustrated Catalog of Books, 7, UA.

38. After the publication of his third novel, *Calling of Dan Matthews* (1909), the Book Supply Company contracted with the firm of Reilly & Lee to distribute Wright's novels through regular book-trade channels. See Mott, *Golden Multitudes*, 229.

39. One industry commentator in 1924 explained: "When a Wright novel is published the orders pile in from stores and places with which a publisher has ordinarily no contact; and the order from a hamlet in North Carolina is likely to exceed the order from Brentano's in New York" (Overton, *Authors of the Day*, 93). Five years after Wright left the Book Supply Company for D. Appleton & Company, an old New York publishing house, *Publishers Weekly* noted that Wright's work was still selling disproportionately at outlets outside the mainstream. Although there were only 1,500 retail bookshops in the United States in 1925, orders for Wright's books came from over 10,000 places—presumably general stores, stationers, and drugstores in small towns and rural areas, revealing that Wright's books—widely advertised in newspapers across the country—created "retail outlets" where there were none before ("Making Best Sellers with Newspaper Space").

40. John Ferré argues that readers of Social Gospel novels were mostly middle- and upper-class, disproportionately female, young or middle-aged, high school–educated, mainline Protestants. While I think Ferré might be right about the readers of Social Gospel theology by Gladden, Ely, and Rauschenbusch, Wright's readers seem to occupy a different social location. See Ferré, *Social Gospel for Millions*, 12.

41. See "Report of a Meeting between Robert H. Poole and Elsbury Reynolds at the Office of Frank Belcher and Robert Jannings, 318 Security Building," Appleton-Century Manuscripts, IU. The divorce was industry-wide news. Appleton bought a two-page ad in *Publishers Weekly* announcing the new alliance, and it garnered a rather long article as well. See "Harold Bell Wright Goes to Appleton."

42. Harold Bell Wright to William H. Briggs, 3 March 1933, UA.

43. Hawthorne, "The Wright American," 111; see also Farrar, "Clean Fiction."

44. Phelps, "The Why of the Best Seller."

45. Jacket copy, *Helen of the Old House*, Appleton-Century Manuscripts, IU; Baker and Taylor Co. Catalog, ibid. Wright's unconventional audience also made serializing his later work in mass-market magazines a mixed blessing. Trade publishers frequently used prior publication as a serial in newspapers and mass-market magazines as a way to boost sales, since it kept the author and the title in the public eye and introduced new readers to the author's work. Since Wright thought most of his readers spent more time with farm journals and denominational religious papers than with slick weekly or monthly magazines like *Cosmopolitan*, he did not think the increased visibility did him much good. In addition, many of his readers wrote to him—outraged—that he would allow his work to appear in periodicals published by William Randolph Hearst, whose less-than-spotless record in ethics and morality was well known in the 1930s. See Harold Bell Wright to William H. Briggs, 3 March 1933, UA.

46. For examples, see Wister, "Quack-Novels and Democracy"; Ford, "Three Rousing Cheers"; and Hastings, "Fiction Is Stranger Than Truth."

47. "Harold Bell Wright—His Books"; Hawthorne, "The Wright American," 112.

48. Overton, *Authors of the Day*, 94.

49. Harold Bell Wright to William H. Briggs, 3 March 1933, UA.

50. See Mott, *Golden Multitudes*, 226.

51. Cooper, "Popularity of Harold Bell Wright," 498. See also "Manufactured Popularity," *Detroit News*, 28 August 1921, clipping, Appleton-Century Manuscripts, IU.

52. "Telling It to the World," Pamphlet, 1921, Appleton-Century Manuscripts, IU.

53. "Advertisement for *Helen of the Old House*."

54. "Amazing Novelty in Book Advertising"; "Appleton Wins First Prize at Advertising Convention."

55. "What Heredity Has Done for Successful Men and Women," Proof Sheets, 1925, Appleton-Century Manuscripts, IU.

56. Baker and Taylor Co. Catalog, 1925, ibid.

57. On the marketing of modernism in the 1920s and 1930s, see Turner, *Marketing Modernism between the Two World Wars*. As Turner details, modernist writers and their publishers did engage in advertising and promotion, but the scale of Wright's campaigns and the unapologetic embrace of books as commodities are qualitatively different.

58. Wright, *To My Sons*, 40; see also "Do You Believe the America of Our Ideals Really Exists?" The feature discusses Wright's wholesome, optimistic philosophy through a write-up of notable Americans' responses to the query, "What do you think . . . of the present day tendency of many of our literary critics to praise only the sordid, grim and mean interpretations of life as being 'art,' while they consign to outer darkness, as being falsely sentimental, the novel that holds a positive message of cheer and hope for mankind? Is it not time to cease praising the unceasing flow of destructive fiction now parading in the guise of realism?"

59. Wright, *Eyes of the World*, 42.

60. Ibid., 37.

61. Ibid., 209.

62. See ibid., 74: "That his stories are identical in material and motive with the vile yarns that are permitted only in the lowest class barber shops and in disreputable barrooms, in no way detracts from the admiring praise of his critics, the generosity of his publishers, or the appreciation of those for whom he writes."

63. Wister, "Quack-Novels and Democracy"; quotation from "Dear Sir" Specimen Ads, D. Appleton & Company, 1922, 4, Appleton-Century Manuscripts, IU.

64. Peter Brooks, *Melodramatic Imagination*, xiii, 15–16.

65. Peter Brooks is concerned specifically with nineteenth-century novelists whose work follows the French "golden age" of melodrama (1800–1830), but his formulation is particularly useful for the liberal, Protestant United States in the late nineteenth and early twentieth centuries. Richard Wightman Fox argues that the decline of liberal Protestant hegemony began after World War I when the validation of secularism pushed many would-be liberal Protestants into pure secularism and the absence of miracles and talk of transcendence in liberal Protestantism pushed others into evangelical religion. See Fox, "Experience and Explanation in Twentieth-Century American Religious History."

66. Aaron Ketchell places Wright in the conservative wing of the Social Gospel because of his emphasis on individuals rather than social transformation (*Holy Hills of the Ozarks*, xiv).

67. On theater as religious pedagogy in the nineteenth century, see Jackson, *Word and Its Witness*, 197. The play version of *Shepherd* is still performed nightly in Branson, Missouri, every summer. On Wright's other major literary influences—Hiawatha legends, the King James Bible, Shakespeare, *Pilgrim's Progress*—see Overton, *Authors of the Day*, 91.

68. Nye, *Unembarrassed Muse*, 40. Wright's 1932 novel *Exit* was a novel about a play and also a novel about life as a stage and people as actors with roles.

69. Wright, *To My Sons*, 115.

70. Ibid., 114.

71. Ibid., 115.

72. Owen Wister said of *Eyes of the World* that almost all of its characters were "taken, without a change in so much as a hair of their heads, from the closet where melodrama keeps its most battered and shop-worn puppets" ("Quack-Novels and Democracy," 729). Frederic Cooper argues that "the real reason that Mr. Wright sounds so often familiar is that his situations are the common property of melodrama the world over. You do not find them in current fiction, but you do find them on New York's East Side stage and its equivalents, and in the moving picture" ("Popularity of Harold Bell Wright," 500).

73. *Bookman* ran articles on both the role of Wright's books in creating a tourism industry in the Ozarks and the real-life "originals" for *Shepherd*'s characters. See Hendrickson, "Book People Come True"; and Milstead, "Harold Bell Wright, Press Agent." For a brilliant analysis of Wright's influence on tourism in Branson, see Ketchell, *Holy Hills of the Ozarks*.

74. Singer, *Melodrama and Modernity*, 44–46.

75. See, for example, the flattering descriptions of Sammy and Matt's perfect appearances (Wright, *Shepherd*, 26, 29) and the distinctly unflattering descriptions of Wash Gibbs and Ollie Stewart (ibid., 68, 170).

76. Peter Brooks, *Melodramatic Imagination*, 45.

77. Ibid., 46.

78. Wright, *Shepherd*, 301–2.

79. Ibid., 280.

80. Ibid., 302.

81. Ibid., 202–3, emphasis in original.

82. Singer, *Melodrama and Modernity*, 134.

83. Wright, *Shepherd*, 13.

84. Several of Wright's other novels are similarly set in places that explicitly stand for any place or every place. See the opening pages of Wright, *Calling of Dan Matthews*; and Wright, *Their Yesterdays*.

85. Jackson, *Word and Its Witness*, 33, 144; see especially "Bifurcated Time,"143–51.

86. Denning, *Mechanic Accents*, 72; see also Habegger, *Gender, Fantasy, and Realism in American Literature*, 111–12.

87. Quoted in Singer, *Melodrama and Modernity*, 146; see also ibid., 33, 153; and Walkowitz, *City of Dreadful Delight*.

88. See especially Baldwin, *Men Who Make Our Novels*, 196–97; and Overton, *Authors of the Day*, 82. Gregory Jackson argues that *Pilgrim's Progress* is "America's *ur* homiletic text" (*Word and Its Witness*, 105), providing the master plot or template that allowed readers to emplot their spiritual lives (104–16). See also Machor, *Reading Fiction in Antebellum America* (62), for a discussion of how reviews in popular periodicals testify to the continuing presence of allegorical modes of reading.

89. Wright, *Shepherd*, 144–45.

90. See Durant, *Darwinism and Divinity*, 14.

91. Wright, *Shepherd*, 292.

92. Ibid., 302.

93. Peter Brooks, *Melodramatic Imagination*, 15–16.

94. Ibid., 5.

95. Wright, *Shepherd*, 303.

96. Bederman, *Manliness and Civilization*.

97. See Ketchell, *Holy Hills of the Ozarks*, 194–201, especially 195, 197.

98. Wright, *Shepherd*, 24.

99. Ibid., 297.

100. Ibid., 259.

101. Ibid., 68, 145.

102. Wright, *Calling of Dan Matthews*, 32.

103. Ibid., 65.

104. Wright, *Winning of Barbara Worth*, 85.

105. Ibid., 101.

106. Ibid., 476.

107. Ibid., 290.

108. For an intelligent discussion of the problematic ways white women were empowered by evolutionary theories of race, see Newman, *White Women's Rights*.

109. Indeed, women have a distinct role to play in service of the race in all of Wright's novels. For example, *Their Yesterdays* includes a tirade against women who refuse to reproduce, since their selfishness will bring about the destruction of the race. Success at a job, for a woman, Wright maintained, is not success at all, because only in marriage and motherhood can she find true fulfillment (Wright, *Their Yesterdays*, 59, 88, 93–94). In *When a Man's a Man*, Wright makes clear that men and women are to be judged not on their humanity but on their distinctly different "manhood" and "womanhood" (117–18).

110. See Durant, *Darwinism and Divinity*, 21.

111. On this process as a function of popular texts more generally, see Cawelti, *Adventure, Mystery, and Romance*, 290.

112. This bears some resemblance to the nineteenth-century dime novels aimed at working-class women; see Enstad, *Ladies of Labor, Girls of Adventure*; and Denning, *Mechanic Accents*. Such reconciliations are everywhere in Wright's novels. In *Ma Cinderella*, wealthy artist Diane marries the penniless but educated backwoods boy John (a clear inversion of the "natural" gendered order), but only after he has inherited enough money to buy her house from her and made a grand speech about there having been just about enough petticoat management. In *Helen of the Old House*, the son of a wealthy industrialist and the daughter of a workman

get married, but this hardly counts as class rapprochement. The industrialist dies, leaving half his fortune to his own children and half to the children of the workman, since the workman actually invented the process he stole in order to make himself rich. Not only are they financial equals at the time of the wedding, but they started life as next-door neighbors.

113. In his discussion of homiletic novels, Gregory Jackson emphasizes their potential to transcend race, class, and gender and the progressive action for social justice they motivated. Although some readers of these books did create cross-class and cross-race alliances, Wright's fictions maintained that God's laws were inextricably intertwined with racial and gender hierarchies.

114. According to Richard Wightman Fox, liberal Protestants focused, in part, on sanctifying the secular, finding the divinity in the natural world through human efforts. See Fox, "Experience and Explanation in Twentieth-Century American Religious History," 400.

115. Wright, *To My Sons*, 245.

116. Ibid., emphasis added.

117. Ibid., 251–52.

118. On the complicity of the personalization or individualization of the sacred with the values of the modern marketplace, see Curtis, *A Consuming Faith*, 228–78. Wright's reconciliation of science and religion, his individual remaking of the sacred, stakes out a quite common theological position called "immanentism." Because modern science revealed physical causes for much of what was formerly thought of as supernatural, notions of the divine shrank. Immanentists like Wright countered this disenchantment by locating God in the natural world, seeing his designing hand in the unfolding of life according to biological principles. See Roberts, *Darwinism and the Divine in America*, 239–40.

119. Chinese cooks and servants, black janitors, and unskilled Hispanic workmen fill the pages of Wright's novels. Wing Foo and Yee Kee, effeminate Chinese house servants, provide comic relief by making horrible linguistic gaffes and giggling indiscriminately. See Wright, *Eyes of the World*; and Wright, *When a Man's a Man*. In *God and the Groceryman*, Uncle Zac is a simpleminded but cheerful black janitor, who is only too pleased to be told that his soul is white as snow. The Hispanic workmen employed by Jefferson Worth are angry, violent, ungrateful, and largely unmoved even by the pleas of Barbara's beautiful, white womanhood when Worth is late paying their wages.

120. Lears, "From Salvation to Self-Realization"; Douglas, *Feminization of American Culture*.

Chapter 3

1. "New Interest in Religious Books."

2. See, for example, "Religious Renaissance"; see also "New Interest in Religious Books"; "The Religious Book Season"; "Bibles and Best Sellers"; and Newton, "Religious Books."

3. Most in the industry believed that sales of religious books had dramatically increased; see, for example, "New Interest in Religious Books"; "Religious Renaissance"; and "Religious Books as Best Sellers." But there were those who disagreed. Grant Overton argued that large, steady sales of religious books dated back at least as far as 1900 (Overton, "Twentieth Century Book Buying Habits").

4. "Two New Religious Departments"; "Why Harpers Have Entered the Field of Religious Books"; Hedstrom, *Rise of Liberal Religion*, 84; "Religious Books of the Month." The Religious Book Club was founded in November 1927 with 980 members. Fifteen months later, it had 7,500 members in all fifty states and thirty-two foreign countries. See Cavert, "What Religious Books Are Read." In 1930, it merged with the Christian Century Book Service conducted by the

periodical *Christian Century* when its editor, Dr. Charles Clayton Morrison, joined the Editorial Committee. See *RBC Bulletin*, July 1929. An extensive (but not complete) collection of the *RBC Bulletin* is in the Library of Congress. It was subsequently owned by Book Club Associates, Meredith Corporation, Iverson-Norman Associates, and (since 1988) Crossroad/Continuum Publishing Group, where it continues to function as a separate operating unit. See "Crossroad Acquires Two Religious Book Clubs." In 1988, it had 6,000 members, mostly mainline Protestant clergy. See "Religious Book Clubs 1988."

5. See "Output of Religious Books." The totals excluded pamphlet material—a format particularly common for religious material. On the overlap between denominational or self-identified religious houses and general trade ventures in the early twentieth century, see Rubin, "Boundaries of American Religious Publishing."

6. "Religious Book Week," *Publishers Weekly*, 15 January 1921; "Selling an Idea"; "Religious Book Week and After."

7. "New Interest in Religious Books."

8. "Why Harpers Have Entered the Field of Religious Books."

9. "New Interest in Religious Books."

10. Munson, "Selling Religious Books."

11. "Religious Book Week," *Publishers Weekly*, 15 January 1921.

12. "'Religious Bookshelf' to Be Published in October."

13. Hedstrom, *Rise of Liberal Religion*, 22. In chapter 1, Hedstrom profiles many of the leaders of the campaign and the institutions that enabled it.

14. See, for example, Hunting, "What Is a Religious Book?"; "What Is a Religious Book? (An Editorial in the Rock Island *Argus* April 1, 1922)"; "What Is a Religious Book?," *Publishers Weekly*, 29 March 1924; and "What Is a Religious Book?," *Publishers Weekly*, 2 April 1927.

15. Hunting, "What Is a Religious Book?"; Newton, "Religious Books," 2003; "Religious Book Week," *Publishers Weekly*, 15 January 1921.

16. "Output of Religious Books."

17. Loveland, "Laymen's Interest in Religious Books," 754; Hunting, "What Is a Religious Book?"; Newton, "Religious Books," 2003.

18. Hedstrom, *Rise of Liberal Religion*, 27.

19. "What Is a Religious Book?," *Publishers Weekly*, 2 April 1927.

20. R. Laurence Moore, *Selling God*, 5.

21. Weber, "Religious Books Deserve Attention from the Newspapers Every Week."

22. Religious Book Week poster illustration, *Publishers Weekly*, 5 February 1921; Religious Book Week poster illustration, *Publishers Weekly*, 17 February 1923; "Religious Book Week and the Press." See also "New Religious Book Poster"; "Religious Book Season," 667; Davies, "Selling Religious Books"; "Suggestions for Booksellers for Religious Book Week"; and "Year-Round Bookselling Campaign Bulletins." For a brilliant discussion of the publicity posters for Religious Book Week in the 1920s, see Hedstrom, *Rise of Liberal Religion*, 39–49.

23. Quoted in Melcher, "Great Books Are Life Teachers."

24. "Religious Book Week," *Publishers Weekly*, 26 February 1921.

25. "President Harding's Letter to the Religious Book Week Committee."

26. W. J. Smith, "A Progressive Religious Book Store."

27. Kelly, "More Religious Books in the Home"; "A Proper Pulpit Theme."

28. Murray, "The Market for Religious Books."

29. Stidger, "New Era in Religious Books."

30. See "Religious Books as Bestsellers"; Loveland, "Laymen's Interest in Religious Books," 753; and Potter, "Spring-Religion-Books."

31. "Program for Religious Reading."

32. See, for example, "Religious Book Week Plans"; and "Ministers as Reviewers."

33. See, for example, "Books for the Minister"; and "More Books for Ministers."

34. Bradley, "A Lending Library in the Church."

35. "Creating Religious Book Interest"; Myers, "Inter-Church Reading Program."

36. "Religious Book Week and After." Hedstrom offers a more complete list of periodical coverage of the first year's campaign (*Rise of Liberal Religion*, 32).

37. Hedstrom, *Rise of Liberal Religion*, 28–29.

38. Ibid., 31.

39. One 1929 account claimed that 40 percent of members were ordinary laypeople, neither ministers nor professors. See Whipple, "Books on the Belt," 182; quotation from Hedstrom, *Rise of Liberal Religion*, 65. However, at least 80 percent of the correspondence published from readers in the *RBC Bulletin* came from ministers, and in the 1940s helpful reminders appeared around tax time that those volumes purchased for professional improvement could be written off on one's taxes (*RBC Bulletin*, March 1947, 6, LC).

40. "Religious Books of the Month."

41. See review of *Love and Marriage*, by Winfield Scott Hall (*RBC Bulletin*, December 1929, 5, LC).

42. See, for example, *RBC Bulletin*, February 1929, 4, LC. Selections included the Lynds' *Middletown*, Stephen Vincent Benet's "John Brown's Body," Mark Van Doren's *Anthology of World Poetry*, Franz Boas's *Anthropology and Modern Life*, Charles and Mary Beard's *Rise of American Civilization*, and Countee Cullen's "The Black Christ," among others. These "general interest" books appeared irregularly and disappeared from the *RBC Bulletin* soon after, suggesting that the experiment was a failure. On the porousness of the category of "religious publishing" in the early twentieth century, see Rubin, "Boundaries of American Religious Publishing," 210–11.

43. "Religious Books of the Month."

44. Ibid.; see also Tebbel, *The Golden Age between Two Wars*, 299.

45. Hedstrom, *Rise of Liberal Religion*, 67.

46. Darnton, *Forbidden Bestsellers of Pre-Revolutionary France*, 184.

47. Loveland, "Laymen's Interest in Religious Books," 755.

48. This deeply felt conflict is apparent not only in the *RBC Bulletin* copy but also in the writings of both ordinary laypeople and religious intellectuals. See the discussion of letters written to Bruce Barton, author of the best-selling 1925 life of Christ, *The Man Nobody Knows*, in Chapter 4. Quaker mystic and best-selling author Rufus Jones explained this early twentieth-century conflict (which the Quakers experienced earlier than most other religious communities) as follows: "There are few crises to compare with that which appears when the simple, childhood religion, imbibed at mother's knee and absorbed from early home and church environment, comes into collision with a scientific, solidly reasoned system" (Rufus M. Jones, *Social Law in the Spiritual World*, 9–10).

49. *RBC Bulletin*, December 1927, 3, LC.

50. The phrase "living at the same time in two separate worlds" comes from a review of Dwight Bradley's *The Recovery of Religion*, which sought to reconcile science and religion through a "separate realms" argument: " 'Science and religion are sovereign each in its own realm, the realm of the former being that of objective research, the realm of the latter being that of subjective experience.' A keen appreciation of this dilemma of living at the same time in two

separate worlds, the objective and the subjective, is felt to be necessary to the recovery of vital religion" (*RBC Bulletin*, December 1929, 5, LC).

51. See Cavert, "A Year's Additions to the Church Library"; and Cavert, "What Religious Books Are Read."

52. Mather also helped Clarence Darrow prepare his famous interrogation of William Jennings Bryan by playing the part of Bryan during a weekend rehearsal before the final day of the trial.

53. Members could return a selection for full credit within ten days of receipt if they were not satisfied with it. They automatically received the main selection unless they returned a form requesting one of the month's alternate selections or a past selection in its place. Members could also purchase alternates or past selections in addition to a month's main selection.

54. Loveland, "Laymen's Interest in Religious Books," 755.

55. Mather was uniquely qualified to offer Religious Book Club readers this kind of reassurance. As a Harvard geologist, he was "unhesitatingly accepted as an authority in his field," and he wrote this book for laymen not in order to debunk religion, but as "interpreter of the spiritual meaning of the universe" and as "champion of religious faith." See *RBC Bulletin*, August 1928, 1, LC. Born into a devout family of Baptists, Mather's faith was deeply influenced by Social Gospel thinkers, who focused attention on bringing about a just order here on earth by transforming social institutions according to Christian principles (see Bork, *Cracking Rocks and Defending Democracy*, chap. 16).

56. *RBC Bulletin*, December 1929, 5, LC; *RBC Bulletin*, August 1929, 4, LC.

57. All brief reviews from *RBC Bulletin*, May 1929, 6, LC.

58. Note the continuities here between the Religious Book Club and the cultural work of Harold Bell Wright's novels, discussed in Chapter 2.

59. Howard Schweber calls this approach to the natural sciences "Protestant Baconianism," which he describes as the marriage of Francis Bacon's inductive scientific method and the theology/epistemology of Scottish Common Sense. Protestant Baconianism had four core tenets: (1) commitment to natural theology (that is, the study of nature provided evidence of religious truths); (2) an understanding of science as an exercise in taxonomy; (3) belief in a grand synthesis of all knowledge into a single system; and (4) an understanding of science as public endeavor that would yield moral and civic uplift. See Schweber, "The 'Science' of Legal Science." On nineteenth- and twentieth-century beliefs about the relationship between religion and science, see Roberts, *Darwinism and the Divine in America*; and Durant, *Darwinism and Divinity*. Roberts argues that evolution did not significantly disturb theology until the last quarter of the nineteenth century, when intellectuals were forced to either reject Darwin's theories or achieve some kind of rapprochement between biblical truths and modern science.

60. See Rubin, *Making of Middlebrow Culture*, xvii, xvi–xviii, 10–15.

61. Hedstrom argues that the Religious Book Club's emphasis on psychology, mysticism, and spirituality was the most important part of its enduring legacy, inspiring the "spiritual seekers" who have preoccupied sociologists of religion from the 1960s onward (*Rise of Liberal Religion*, 71–78).

62. *RBC Bulletin*, July 1932, 1, LC. See also Review of *The Bearing of Psychology upon Religion*, by Harrison Sacket Elliott (*RBC Bulletin*, February 1928, 3–4, LC); and Review of *Psychology and Religious Experience*, by W. Fearson Halliday (*RBC Bulletin*, April 1930, 4, LC).

63. *RBC Bulletin*, October 1930, 3, LC.

64. "Religious Books of the Month."

65. *RBC Bulletin*, February 1928, 6, LC.

66. See also Review of *Gospel for Asia: A Study of Three Religious Masterpieces, Gita, Lotus, and Fourth Gospel*, by Kenneth Saunders (*RBC Bulletin*, April 1928, 4, LC). Saunders's book is

characterized as "breathing appreciation more than criticism" for other faiths, but the review is quick to affirm that the author is "an ardent Christian himself," however much he might admire these other faiths. The November 1928 *RBC Bulletin* featured a review of the alternate title, *The Christian Life and Message in Relation to Non-Christian Systems of Life and Thought*. It reads: "The Relation of Christianity to each of the major non-Christian religions is briefly and lucidly surveyed, with special reference to the best elements in those religions. . . . The argument of Archbishop Temple is a masterful setting forth of the claim of Christianity to uniqueness and universality" (4–5).

67. *RBC Bulletin*, October 1928, 2, LC.

68. *RBC Bulletin*, October 1928, 1, LC. The review of *The Pilgrimage of Buddhism* additionally described Pratt's conclusion that Christian missionaries must not seek to destroy or supersede Buddhism as "the point at which there is most room for differing with some of the author's conclusions" (2).

69. Review of *What We Live By*, by Abbe Ernest Dimnet (*RBC Bulletin*, June 1932, 1, LC).

70. *RBC Bulletin*, April 1929, 2, LC. See also Review of *How the Reformation Happened*, by Hillaire Belloc (*RBC Bulletin*, May 1928, 3, LC): "It may doubtless be taken as representative of the view of many liberal-minded members of the Roman Church."

71. *RBC Bulletin*, June 1932, 2, LC.

72. See "Another Book Club"; and "Catholic Book Club Names Directors." At the same time, the Catholic Book Club was careful to assert that it was not a sectarian organization. Any author, regardless of his/her faith tradition, could be featured, if the work had adequate literary merit and did not violate Catholic teachings.

73. See, for example, Review of *Lausanne: The Will to Understand*, by Edmund Davison Soper (*RBC Bulletin*, March 1928, 3, LC); Review of *The Scandal of Christianity*, by Peter Ainsle (*RBC Bulletin*, April 1929, 5, LC); and Review of *Christian Unity*, by Gaius Jackson Slosser (*RBC Bulletin*, May 1929, 4, LC), which provided a historical overview of movements for Christian unity in order to provide context for contemporary debates.

74. *RBC Bulletin*, February 1928, 5, LC.

75. See *RBC Bulletin*, April 1929, 4, LC; and *RBC Bulletin*, May 1929, 3, LC.

76. *RBC Bulletin*, February 1928, 4–5, LC.

77. Warner, *Letters of the Republic*.

78. Radway, *Feeling for Books*, 284–85.

79. Cavert, "What Religious Books Are Read."

80. *RBC Bulletin*, August 1928, 3, LC. This double reassurance about the soundness of scholarship and accessibility of presentation was characteristic of the *Bulletin*. C. S. Woodward's *Christ in the Common Ways of Life*, for example, was described as "written on the level of the layman" "from the first page to the last," but "this never means any sacrifice of depth or solidity" (*RBC Bulletin*, July 1928, 3).

81. *RBC Bulletin*, February 1928, 2–3, LC. See also Review of *The Dilemma of Protestantism*, by William E. Hammond (*RBC Bulletin*, August 1929, 4–5, LC). Hammond's discussion is praised particularly for its focus on local, specific, concrete, everyday problems. He takes the viewpoint of a practicing pastor versus a theoretical or abstract approach.

82. Frykholm, *Rapture Culture*, 111.

83. On the pure aesthetic versus the popular ethos, see Bourdieu, *Distinction*, 28–44.

84. Radway, *Feeling for Books*, chap. 8.

85. William H. Leach's *Church Finance* was introduced as "a book full of practical suggestiveness for the minister and officers who are charged with responsibility for the financial administration of the local church" (*RBC Bulletin*, February 1929, 4, LC).

86. *RBC Bulletin*, February 1928, 1, LC.

87. *RBC Bulletin*, March 1928, 5, LC.

88. Radway, *Feeling for Books*, 284–85. For incarnations of this idea in nineteenth-century America, see Hochman, *Getting at the Author*; and Silverman, *Bodies and Books*.

89. *RBC Bulletin*, February 1928, 3, LC.

90. *RBC Bulletin*, April 1930, 4, LC.

91. See Review of *The Romance of the English Bible*, by Laura H. Wild (*RBC Bulletin*, August 1929, 5, LC).

92. *RBC Bulletin*, October 1930, 2, LC.

93. *RBC Bulletin*, June 1928, 8, LC; *RBC Bulletin*, June 1928, 8, LC; *RBC Bulletin*, March 1929, 8, LC.

94. *RBC Bulletin*, March 1928, 7, LC.

95. Hedstrom places the Religious Book Club in the larger context of efforts to help overwhelmed readers/consumers navigate the immense marketplace of religious literature in the 1920s and 1930s. There were many book lists and reading programs, including those put out by the Religious Books Round Table of the American Library Association. See *Rise of Liberal Religion*, chap. 2, especially 56–61.

96. Quoted in *RBC Bulletin*, December 1927, 6, LC; *RBC Bulletin*, October 1928, 5, LC.

97. *RBC Bulletin*, December 1927, 6, LC; *RBC Bulletin*, October 1928, 5, LC.

98. Lears, "From Salvation to Self-Realization."

99. *RBC Bulletin*, March 1928, 3–4, LC.

100. Ibid.

101. Ibid., 7.

102. *RBC Bulletin*, April 1928, 3–4, LC.

103. *RBC Bulletin*, April 1929, 1, LC.

104. Ibid.

105. Ibid., 3.

106. *RBC Bulletin*, April 1930, 2, 4, LC.

107. Hedstrom, *Rise of Liberal Religion*, 70.

108. *RBC Bulletin*, July 1928, 2, LC.

109. Hedstrom, *Rise of Liberal Religion*, 68.

110. See McDannell, *Material Christianity*, 6.

111. See ibid.; Schmidt, *Consumer Rites*; and Morgan, *Visual Piety*.

Chapter 4

1. Bruce Barton's correspondence is found in two places. Some letters are located in the Bruce Barton Papers, Wisconsin Historical Society, Madison, Wis. Literary correspondence is found in boxes 82–124. Some correspondence is located in the Bobbs-Merrill Manuscripts at Indiana University. The letters quoted as epigraphs are from the WHS. See Eva Coombs to Bruce Barton, 11 November 1926, WHS; J. Paul Maynard to Bruce Barton, 15 November 1926, WHS; and Allen Rice to Bruce Barton, 4 May 1926, WHS. For a methodological critique of how scholars have used the Barton archive, see Ryan, "Teasing Out Clues, Not Kooks."

2. "Prophets of sanctified commercialism" is a phrase from Rev. C. Everett Wagner, who saw Barton's work as representative of a larger movement to cheapen religion and justify material excesses in the 1920s. See Wagner, "Religion Rings the Cash Register."

3. Some of the best analyses of Barton's work include Fried, *Man Everybody Knew*, chap. 4; Susman, "Piety, Profits, and Play: The 1920s"; Meyer, *Positive Thinkers*, 177–80; Ribuffo, "Jesus Christ as Business Statesman"; and Simone Weil Davis, *Living Up to the Ads*, chap. 2.

4. Lears, "From Salvation to Self-Realization," 31. Lears's complete argument is more sophisticated. He characterizes Barton as "confused and ambivalent" (5), torn between the new therapeutic ethos and an older emphasis on character.

5. "Mr. Barton Makes a Success Story of the Life of Christ"; Seldes, "The Living Christ"; Herring, "The Rotarian Nobody Knows." See also Potter, "Present Day Portraits of Jesus." Potter maintains that Barton's representation of Jesus as a "supersalesman" is "repulsive, except to Rotarians and Babbitts" (590). Fried summarizes the early, more positive notices about the book (*Man Everybody Knew*, 96–97).

6. "Jesus as Efficiency Expert"; "Booming Religion as a Business Proposition." See also Untitled review, in *Living Church*. The unnamed author of "Jesus as Efficiency Expert" was Reinhold Niebuhr (Fried, *Man Everybody Knew*, 100).

7. For sales figures, see Hackett and Burke, *80 Years of Best Sellers*, 99–102.

8. The phrase is Kenneth Burke's; see Burke, "Literature as Equipment for Living."

9. Fried, *Man Everybody Knew*, 229; ibid., 52; see also ibid., x, 121, 231, 235; and Susman, "Piety, Profits, and Play: The 1920s," 192.

10. Ray Long to Bruce Barton, 2 November 1923, WHS.

11. "Text of Bruce Barton's Radio Talk Given Sunday, 6 November, at 9 P.M. EST," Bobbs-Merrill Manuscripts, IU.

12. Quoted in Marsden, *Fundamentalism and American Culture*, 3.

13. Charles W. Koller to Bruce Barton, 3 September 1927, WHS.

14. Perceptions of Barton and others aside, this was not the case. On the commodification of religion and its implication with the mass media and the capitalist marketplace in nineteenth-century America, see R. Laurence Moore, *Selling God*.

15. Barton, *The Man Nobody Knows: A Discovery of the Real Jesus* (Chicago: Ivan R. Dee, 2000). Subsequent page references are in the text.

16. The picture is somewhat more complicated. Barton sold the ideal of self-sacrificing "service" to businessmen, urging them to put customers and coworkers first. Barton seemed quite sincere in his desire to Christianize business (versus merely using Christianity to justify capitalist practices). I am in agreement with Richard Fried, Barton's biographer, here (see Fried, *Man Everybody Knew*, 107, 226, 233). It is important to note, however, that the self-sacrificing businessman in Barton's narrative is always rewarded in this world with material success.

17. W. Brooks Brown to Bruce Barton, 9 June 1926, WHS; J. V. Clarke to Herbert S. Baker, 21 October 1925, WHS.

18. On "muscular Christianity," see Putney, *Muscular Christianity*; and Bederman, "The Women Have Had Charge of the Church Work Long Enough." For an earlier example of an attempt to place businessmen (rather than praying mothers) at the center of Christian life, see Kathryn T. Long, "Turning . . . Piety into Hard Cash." Long analyzes press coverage of the 1857–58 "businessmen's revival."

19. Walter S. Lewis to Bruce Barton, 22 September 1926, WHS.

20. Hewitt H. Howland to Bruce Barton, 18 January 1924, WHS.

21. Seldes, "Service."

22. Barton, *Book Nobody Knows*, 51–52.

23. Barton, *What Can a Man Believe?*, chap. 5.

24. Barton, *Book Nobody Knows*, 27. Similarly, Barton's life of Paul, *He Upset the World*, was about finding a point of identification with this distant church father rather than understanding him in his historical context: "You and I are neither archeologists nor students of comparative religion. We are just weak human beings, full of problems and well versed in combats with the devil. Unless Paul was like ourselves we care little about him. The purpose of this book is to show that he WAS like ourselves" (Barton, *He Upset the World*, 54).

25. Lears, *Fables of Abundance*, 154.

26. Marchand, *Advertising the American Dream*, chap. 2, 341. My descriptions of advertising in the 1920s are deeply influenced by Marchand's work.

27. Mrs. Stanley A. Swanson to Bruce Barton, 5 June 1931, WHS. See also Edna A. Wilmot to Bruce Barton, 27 January 1925, WHS, for a description of "that period in which every creed of the college student is torn to bits." For a parent's views about the secularizing influence of schools, see Henry B. Stryker to Bruce Barton, 22 September 1933, WHS.

28. Bruce Barton to Herbert S. Baker, 3 October 1925, WHS.

29. "Barton, Bruce, The Man Nobody Knows Promotional Material," Bobbs-Merrill Manuscripts, IU.

30. Ibid.

31. James Angell to Bruce Barton, 29 September 1925, WHS.

32. M. P. Hanford to Bruce Barton, 25 May 1925, WHS. See also Anne C. Norris to Bruce Barton, 17 January 1926, Bobbs-Merrill Manuscripts, IU; and Horace Notte to Bruce Barton, 3 April 1950, WHS.

33. William V. Morgan to Bruce Barton, 14 January 1955, WHS.

34. Aaron Bradbury to Bruce Barton, 2 January 1930, WHS; Bruce Barton to Aaron Bradbury, 6 January 1930, WHS; Aaron Bradbury to Bruce Barton, 14 January 1930, WHS. For similar advice from Barton to another reader seeking to get ahead, see Robert Cornell to Bruce Barton, 25 May 1925, WHS; Bruce Barton to Robert Cornell, 28 May 1925, WHS; and Robert Cornell to Bruce Barton, 8 June 1925, WHS.

35. "Just His Girl" to Bruce Barton, 29 June 1934, WHS. See also D. L. Palmer to Bruce Barton, 19 September 1932, WHS; and Louis D. Pettit to Bruce Barton, 27 June 1932, WHS.

36. Mary Bissell McIver to Bruce Barton, 11 December 1929, WHS; Bruce Barton to Mary McIver, 19 December 1929, WHS.

37. Fried, *Man Everybody Knew*, 230.

38. Ibid., 78.

39. Orsi, *Thank You, St. Jude*.

40. Pease, "Bruce Barton," 62–63. The story is actually more complicated. Edrene Montgomery argues that Betty Crocker was created by men promoting Gold Medal flour for a company called Washburn Crosby Co., which was later absorbed by General Mills. Barton's company merely popularized Betty Crocker as an advertising icon when it acquired the General Mills account. See Montgomery, "Bruce Barton and the Twentieth Century Menace of Unreality," 227–31. Barton's biographer, Richard Fried, calls the idea that Barton created Betty Crocker a "myth" (*Man Everybody Knew*, 63), although he concedes that BBD&O subsequently shaped and promoted her image.

41. Marchand, *Advertising the American Dream*, 16, 353–54.

42. Ibid., xxi.

43. Fried, *Man Everybody Knew*, 227; see also ibid., x.

44. E. P. West to D. L. Chambers, 6 April 1925, WHS.

45. Charles E. Adams to D. L. Chambers, 14 April 1925, WHS; Howell E. Rees to Bruce Barton, 12 February 1926, WHS. See also Eva Coombs to Bruce Barton, 11 November 1926, WHS. Many

reviewers had special praise for the accessibility and ordinariness of Barton's Jesus. In the *Indianapolis Times*, for example, Walter Hickman explained, "Bruce Barton has done a strikingly human thing—he brings Jesus into your home" ("More Comments on *The Man Nobody Knows* by Bruce Barton," in "Miscellaneous Publicity Materials for *Man Nobody Knows*," box 107, WHS).

46. Marchand, *Advertising the American Dream*, 14.

47. Radway, *Feeling for Books*, 284–85.

48. J. Dan Dunaway to Bruce Barton, 5 September 1927, WHS.

49. Hazel Wangsness to Bruce Barton, 19 August 1951, WHS.

50. See, for example, Henry Ward Beecher, *The Life of Jesus Christ* (1871), which represents Jesus as a sympathetic companion, particularly for women.

51. For example, see (illegible) Heath Sale to the Editor of the Woman's Home Companion, 21 August 1925, WHS; Gaddie Bolton Allbritain to Bruce Barton, 17 April 1926, WHS; Lucy A. Jones to Bruce Barton, 10 September 1926, WHS; and Mrs. F. E. Gendron to Bruce Barton, 3 May 1948, WHS.

52. See Amos Parrish to Bruce Barton, 18 January 1926, WHS; and Mrs. Henry Buck to Bruce Barton, 4 September 1926, WHS.

53. For example, see Arthur Hamil to Bruce Barton, 7 March 1938, WHS; Vernon Biddle to Bruce Barton, 8 March 1953, WHS; and Mrs. Cecile Knott Tucker to Bruce Barton, 7 September 1941, WHS.

54. Tim Grande to Bruce Barton, 17 February 1942, WHS.

55. W. J. Bryan to W. C. Bobbs, 29 April 1925, WHS; Campbell Morgan to D. L. Chambers, 4 May 1925, WHS. See also D. L. Chambers to Bruce Barton, 4 February 1927, WHS. Before landing at Bobbs-Merrill, *The Man Nobody Knows* was rejected by Maxwell Perkins at Scribner's because he feared it would be "a shock" to many of the Scribner's readers who came to Scribner's because of its large religious books department and history as a publisher of pious books. Editors at Bobbs-Merrill, however, urged Barton to not revise the book in any way that would reduce its shock value, desiring that whatever changes he made for magazine serialization not make the book manuscript "any less daring, any less picturesque, any less related to modern business and its terminology." See Maxwell E. Perkins to Bruce Barton, 8 April 1924, WHS; and Hewitt H. Howland to Bruce Barton, 22 January 1924, WHS.

56. J. V. Clarke to H. S. Baker, 21 October 1925, WHS.

57. Radway, *Feeling for Books*, 278.

58. Mrs. William Audas to Bruce Barton, 14 January 1955, WHS.

59. Barton, *Book Nobody Knows*, 15.

60. Quoted in promotional material in "Barton, Bruce, The Man Nobody Knows Promotional Material," Bobbs-Merrill Manuscripts, IU.

61. *Buffalo News*, 7 September 1935.

62. Mrs. William Audas to Bruce Barton, 14 January 1955, WHS. See also Miss A. E. Schultz to Bruce Barton, n.d. (1928), WHS; and Bill Martin to Bruce Barton, 11 May 1925, WHS

63. See Radway, *Feeling for Books*, 152, 259, 277.

64. Quoted in D. L. Chambers to Bruce Barton, 25 February 1927, WHS.

65. Francis L. Palmer to Bruce Barton, 20 February 1926, WHS. In some ways, this eliding of historical and cultural context resembles ways of reading encouraged by the middlebrow Great Books programs of the 1920s and 1930s, which offered readers only the primary text. Readers were to read all of Western literature as though the texts were contemporary and addressed the dilemmas of everyday life. Barton was a student at Amherst College, where he studied with John Erskine, one of the founders of the Great Books movement (Rubin, *Making of Middlebrow Culture*, chap. 4, especially 174, 158).

66. Bruce Barton to D. L. Chambers, 8 February 1927, WHS.

67. Matthew Stinson to the Editor of the *Boston Herald*, 18 January 1926, enclosed in a letter from F. W. Buxton (of the *Boston Herald*) to Bruce Barton, 18 January 1926, WHS.

68. For an example of one such review, see Dwyer, "Books." The reviewer calls *The Man Nobody Knows* an "astounding book." He alleges that Barton distorts history to suit his purposes and that the book is characterized by a "general recklessness where facts are concerned."

69. J. A. Rondthaler to Bobbs-Merrill, 27 April 1926, WHS.

70. Arnold F. Normanberg to Bruce Barton, 20 July 1926, WHS.

71. I am disagreeing here with Richard Wightman Fox, who calls Barton's book "profoundly emblematic of liberal Protestantism," although lacking in commitment to the Social Gospel (*Jesus in America*, 319). Although Barton's theology was liberal, I am arguing that the appeal of his books was that they insisted that theology actually mattered little. Edrene Montgomery claims that Barton's work freed readers from the "tyranny of limited alternatives" (liberal or fundamentalist) and restored a sense of Christian community where churches failed to do so. My position here is closer to that of Stephen Prothero, who argues that readers were far less moved by Jesus the businessman than they were by Jesus the struggling human being, and that Barton successfully sidestepped divisive issues such as evolution and biblical criticism. See Montgomery, "Bruce Barton and the Twentieth Century Menace of Unreality," 131; see also Montgomery, "Bruce Barton's *The Man Nobody Knows*"; and Prothero, *American Jesus*, 98–108.

72. Douglas, *Feminization of American Culture*; Lears, "From Salvation to Self-Realization."

73. See David D. Hall, *Worlds of Wonder, Days of Judgment*; and Anne S. Brown and David D. Hall, "Family Strategies and Religious Practice."

74. Ammerman, "Golden Rule Christianity," 196.

75. Barton, *Book Nobody Knows*, 277.

76. Ibid., 290.

77. Barton, *What Can a Man Believe?*, v–vi.

78. See clippings and advertisements in "Barton, Bruce, What Can a Man Believe? Promotional Material," and "Barton, Bruce, The Man Nobody Knows Promotional Material," Bobbs-Merrill Manuscripts, IU.

79. See Bruce Barton to Mary Converse, 19 January 1925, WHS; Gertrude Lane to Bruce Barton, 30 December 1924, WHS; Gertrude Lane to Bruce Barton, 30 January 1925, WHS; Rev. Michael Andrew Chapman to Edward Anthony (*Woman's Home Companion*), 15 December 1924, WHS.

80. See D. L. Chambers to Bruce Barton, 14 January 1927, WHS. Barton wrote to one Catholic reader who had praised *The Man Nobody Knows* that his letter was particularly welcome for this reason (Bruce Barton to Horace Notte, 18 April 1950, WHS).

81. See Bruce Barton to Herbert S. Baker, 3 October 1925, WHS. Nonetheless, Fried characterizes fundamentalist reactions to *The Man Nobody Knows* as "savage" (*Man Everybody Knew*, 99).

82. See Abrams, *Selling the Old-Time Religion*, 40–47.

83. D. L. Chambers to Bruce Barton, 14 May 1924, WHS.

84. Bruce Barton to D. L. Chambers, 16 January 1926, WHS; Bruce Barton to D. L. Chambers, 28 August 1926, WHS.

85. The initial mailing was more than 500 complimentary copies. D. L. Chambers to Bruce Barton, 18 April 1925, WHS.

86. Bruce Barton to D. L. Chambers, 12 February 1925, Bobbs-Merrill Manuscripts, IU.

87. Bruce Barton to Herbert S. Baker, 3 October 1925, WHS.

88. D. L. Chambers to Bruce Barton, 29 April 1925, WHS; Bruce Barton to D. L. Chambers, 7 September 1926, WHS; M. Louise MacLeod to Herbert Baker, 3 December 1925, WHS.

89. Bobbs-Merrill, an Indiana publishing house, was a good fit. It made its name with popular fiction. It was the first firm to create bestsellers through mass advertising and the first to use full-page ads in national newspapers. It used illustration in its ads, used color on dust jackets, and did single title advertising long before it was common. See O'Bar, "A History of the Bobbs-Merrill Company."

90. D. L. Chambers to Bruce Barton, 21 August 1925, WHS.

91. "To the Trade," in "The Man Nobody Knows Promotional Materials," Bobbs-Merrill Manuscripts, IU.

92. Christopher Grauer, Letter to Fellow Book Merchants, "Barton, Bruce, The Man Nobody Knows Promotional Material," Bobbs-Merrill Manuscripts, IU.

93. Osborn, "Will Dealers Follow the Leader?"

94. Miriam S. Lewis to Bruce Barton, 1 March 1931, WHS.

95. H. Strong Smith to Bruce Barton, 23 November 1925, WHS; G. W. Freeman to Bruce Barton, 25 August 1925, Bobbs-Merrill Manuscripts, IU.

96. David D. Hall, *Lived Religion in America*, vii–ix.

Chapter 5

1. McLoughlin, *Revivals, Awakenings, and Reform*, chap. 6. See also Niebuhr, "Is There a Revival of Religion?"; "Religion and the Intellectuals"; and H.S., "The Novel Goes to Church."

2. Luccock, "Religion in the Bookstore."

3. Hutchinson, "Have We a 'New' Religion?," 140.

4. "Phenomenal Interest in Religious Books"; Luccock, "Religion in the Bookstore."

5. Hutchinson, "Have We a 'New' Religion?," 138. Reinhold Niebuhr similarly maps the class-fractured religious scene in his "Is There a Revival of Religion?"

6. Hutchinson, "Have We a 'New' Religion?" 140.

7. Ibid., 143.

8. Ibid., 148.

9. *New York Sunday News*, 11 December 1955; quotation from George, *God's Salesman*, 128. For discussions of Peale and comparisons with Sheen and Liebman, see Edmund Fuller, "Pitchmen in the Pulpit," 29; and William Lee Miller, "Some Negative Thinking," 20.

10. William Lee Miller, "Some Negative Thinking," 19–20.

11. George, *God's Salesman*, 140.

12. Gordon, *Norman Vincent Peale*, chap. 15; see also George, *God's Salesman*, 129, 140–50.

13. See Peters, "Case against 'Easy' Religion," 22. For the response/defense of Peale, see Gordon, "Case for 'Positive' Faith." For examples invoking Sheen and Liebman, see Edmund Fuller, "Pitchmen in the Pulpit," 29; and William Lee Miller, "Some Negative Thinking," 20.

14. Peters, "Case against 'Easy' Religion," 92, 93, 94.

15. Ibid., 92–93.

16. Edmund Fuller, "Pitchmen in the Pulpit," 29.

17. Peters, "Case against 'Easy' Religion," 92. See also Edmund Fuller, "Pitchmen in the Pulpit," 29; and Cate, "God and Success," 75. Niebuhr insisted in other places that he and Peale had nothing in common (George, *God's Salesman*, 141).

18. Peters, "Case against 'Easy' Religion," 93. Paul Tillich similarly thought it was dangerous to use religion for utilitarian purposes, especially the achievement of business success, and he and Peale had repeated exchanges on the topic (George, *God's Salesman*, 152).

19. Edmund Fuller, "Pitchmen in the Pulpit," 29.

20. Peters, "Case against 'Easy' Religion," 94.

21. William Lee Miller, "Some Negative Thinking," 23.

22. Cate, "God and Success," 74.

23. See William Lee Miller, "Some Negative Thinking," 20.

24. Ibid., 23.

25. Ibid., 19.

26. Ibid., 22–23.

27. Ibid., 20.

28. A number of executives bought copies of *The Power of Positive Thinking* in bulk to distribute to their employees and managers and wrote Peale to describe the resulting increase in morale and profits. See, for example, Chauncey Beeman to Norman Vincent Peale, 26 February 1953, SU; Norman Vincent Peale to Myron Boardman, 7 December 1951, SU; and Norman Vincent Peale to Myron Boardman, 20 November 1951, SU.

29. William Lee Miller, "Some Negative Thinking," 24.

30. Ibid.

31. Niebuhr, "How Adventurous Is Dr. Fosdick?," review in *Christian Century*, quotation from Robert Moats Miller, *Harry Emerson Fosdick*, 275. See also Meyer, *Positive Thinkers*, chap. 16, especially 213–16. In later life, Niebuhr did find some common ground with Fosdick and regretted the fervor of his youthful critique. See Reinhold Niebuhr to Harry Emerson Fosdick, 12 September 1956, UTS.

32. See Dorrien, *Making of American Liberal Theology*, 384.

33. In looking back over his life and the work of liberal theologians and ministers, Fosdick accepted some of the critique of liberalism from Niebuhr and other neo-orthodox thinkers. "We were adjusting Christian thought to a secular culture," he conceded, pointing out that the purpose of Christianity was to question and challenge secular culture, not to accommodate or adapt the gospel to it (Fosdick, *Living of These Days*, 245–46). Fosdick himself actively supported work for social justice.

34. Quoted in Heinze, *Jews and the American Soul*, 231; see also Heinze, "*Peace of Mind* (1946)," 48.

35. Quoted in Heinze, *Jews and the American Soul*, 231, 233.

36. Billy Graham, *Peace with God*, 7

37. Martin, *Prophet with Honor*, 163.

38. See ibid., 186.

39. "Cultural dopes" is Stuart Hall's term. See Stuart Hall, "Notes on Deconstructing 'the Popular,'" 232.

40. Rev. E. Marcellus Nesbitt, DD, to Harry Emerson Fosdick, 20 November 1956, UTS. See also Taylor E. Roth to Harry Emerson Fosdick, 7 June 1949, UTS.

41. Quoted in Robert Moats Miller, *Harry Emerson Fosdick*, 275.

42. Peale collected many of the anecdotes from these letters and the new applications of his ideas that his readers shared with him in a 1959 volume, *Amazing Results of Positive Thinking*. Peale described these letters as coming from "Catholics, Protestants, and Jews alike, and [they] told how God had become a living reality" (viii).

43. Mrs. Fergus Easton to Norman Vincent Peale, 15 January 1960, SU.

44. Mr. R. E. Ault to Norman Vincent Peale, 15 January 1960, SU.

45. Luccock, "Religion in the Bookstore," 993.

46. Radway, *Feeling for Books*, 284–85.

47. Elsie F. Sewell to Norman Vincent Peale, quotation from "Excerpts from Thank-You Letters & Testimonials, Summer of 1959," SU.

48. Glenn C. McGee to Harry Emerson Fosdick, 1 June 1961, UTS. See also Mr. W. N. Blachly to Harry Emerson Fosdick, 3 March 1944, UTS.

49. Harry Emerson Fosdick to Doris Waugh, 21 May 1951, UTS.

50. See, for example, Marguerite Cronan to Joshua Loth Liebman, 5 October 1947, BU.

51. Jack Stenbuck, "A Modern Joshua in the Book Stalls," 4, draft of a profile of Joshua Loth Liebman, box 43, BU.

52. Mrs. Izma (unclear) Byram to Joshua Loth Liebman, 12 February 1948, BU. See also Jeannette Cain to Joshua Loth Liebman, 24 July 1947, BU.

53. Walter Hasting to Joshua Loth Liebman, 5 January 1948, BU; see also Mrs. Samuel Goodman (Jessie) to Joshua Loth Liebman, 12 January 1948, BU.

54. See, for example, Mrs. Anne Fine to Joshua Loth Liebman, 11 August 1947, BU.

55. See, for example, "Liebman, Joshua Loth, Rabbi," *Current Biography*, October 1946, 26–28, clipping in box 34, BU.

56. All quotations from an advertisement for *Peace of Mind*, by Joshua Loth Liebman, "MARCH 22 WILL SEE THE PUBLICATION OF A BOOK WHICH MAY WELL PROVE TO BE A VITAL INFLUENCE IN AMERICAN LIFE," box 78, BU.

57. "This book may help you find the greatest gift in all the world . . . PEACE OF MIND," ad poster, box 78, BU; quoted on two advertising posters for *Peace of Mind*: "PEACE OF MIND: A Magnificent Book!" and "PEACE OF MIND, Joshua Liebman, OVER ONE MILLION COPIES SOLD," box 78, BU.

58. See, for example, Patricia B. Kurland to Joshua Loth Liebman, 8 March 1948, BU.

59. See, for example, Mrs. May Kinberg to Joshua Loth Liebman, 29 September 1947, BU; and Lucile L. Le Sourd to Joshua Loth Liebman, 14 November 1947, BU. Liebman cited the sections on managing grief as among the most compelling to readers in a 1947 "Meet the Author" radio interview. See "MEET THE AUTHOR: Rabbi Joshua Loth Liebman, 11–11:15 A.M., 29 December 1947," box 73, "Dr. Liebman's Book Material 'Peace of Mind' Pamphlets, Magazines, etc., Publicity" Folder, BU.

60. Heinze, *Jews and the American Soul*, 210–13; Hedstrom, "Psychology and Mysticism in 1940s Religion," 254.

61. Hofstadter, *Anti-intellectualism in American Life*, 394; Maddocks, "Field Trips among the Intellectuals," 570; quotation from Cooney, *Rise of the New York Intellectuals*, 4, 3. My account of the history of *Partisan Review* is largely drawn from Cooney and Jumonville, *New York Intellectuals Reader*.

62. This definition of the group comes from Jumonville, *New York Intellectuals Reader*, 3. Many were neo-conservatives by the 1980s.

63. Howe, "New York Intellectuals: A Chronicle and a Critique," 29.

64. Cooney, *Rise of the New York Intellectuals*, 58.

65. Wald, *New York Intellectuals*, 28.

66. Jumonville, *New York Intellectuals Reader*, 1–4.

67. "Religion and the Intellectuals." Subsequent page references are in the text.

68. H.S., "The Novel Goes to Church," 22–23.

69. See also Parkes (327); Schapiro (225); and Rahv (240) in "Religion and the Intellectuals."

70. See also Howe (471–72); Farrell (320); and Macdonald (478) in ibid.

71. See also Hook (230); and Schapiro (335) in ibid.

72. Irving Howe similarly situated himself as an unreconstructed socialist (472) in ibid.

73. All quotations from Cooney, *Rise of the New York Intellectuals*, 194.

74. Ibid., 196, 200. The quote is from Jumonville, *New York Intellectuals Reader*, 5.

75. Christian Smith, "Introduction: Rethinking the Secularization of American Public Life," 33.

76. Ibid., 44–45.

77. Ibid., 39–41.

78. Ibid., 46.

79. Ibid., 48, 51, 52.

80. Ibid., 47.

81. See, for example, Davis (313–14); Schapiro (334); Auden (126); and Greenberg (466–67) in "Religion and the Intellectuals."

82. See, for example, Howe (470) and Phillips (481) in ibid.

83. See, for example, Graves (134); Howe (471); and Phillips (481) in ibid.

84. H.S., "The Novel Goes to Church," 22.

85. Ibid.

86. Ibid.

87. "If People Ever Required Religious Faith, It's Now."

88. H.S., "The Novel Goes to Church," 22–23.

89. A significant minority of the *Partisan Review* contributors were sympathetic to religion or even confessional in their pieces. See, for example, Allen Tate, Jacques Maritain, Paul Tillich, and Dwight Macdonald.

90. Luccock, "Religion in the Bookstore," 993.

91. H.S., "The Novel Goes to Church," 22–23.

92. William Lee Miller, "Some Negative Thinking," 24.

Chapter 6

1. Mrs. F. A. (Mildred) Lehner to Joshua Loth Liebman, 18 June 1947, BU; Joshua Loth Liebman to Mildred Lehner, 14 July 1947, BU. Liebman recommended Fosdick to many readers, citing the similarities of their ideas and approaches. See, for example, Joshua Loth Liebman to Mrs. Charles D. Cook, 16 July 1947, BU.

2. "Phenomenal Interest in Religious Books"; Luccock, "Religion in the Bookstore."

3. See Massa, *Catholicism and American Culture*, 90.

4. See Heinze, *Jews and the American Soul*, 205.

5. In his follow-up volume, *Amazing Results of Positive Thinking*, Peale related the story of a golfer—infamous for his bad sportsmanship—who turned over a new leaf after reading books by Peale and Sheen. Mrs. John E. Elsing (Elvira Elsing) to Norman Vincent Peale, 2 November 1959, SU; see also G. E. Hon to Norman Vincent Peale, 8 April 1959, SU; and Peale, *Amazing Results of Positive Thinking*, 51.

6. Liebman declined to provide a blurb for the book, citing other pressing obligations that left him too busy to do so. See Hedstrom, "Psychology and Mysticism in 1940s Religion," 252; Heinze, *Jews and the American Soul*, 235; K. S. Giniger to Joshua Loth Liebman, 4 February 1948, BU; and Joshua Loth Liebman to K. S. Giniger, 3 February 1948, BU.

7. Marty, *Pilgrims in Their Own Land*, 414; quotation from Massa, *Catholicism and American Culture*, 85. There were limits to this ecumenism, however. While liberals might easily embrace the work of Fosdick and Liebman, to read the work of Sheen and Graham alongside these earlier texts was more difficult.

8. For a detailed account of these institutional factors, see Hedstrom, *Rise of Liberal Religion*, chaps. 4 and 5.

9. Ibid., 146.

10. Much like mind-cure in the nineteenth century, whose meetings tended to be on Sunday afternoons so that practitioners could attend church in the morning, the practices were understood by most as complementary. For example, Carol George, Peale's most recent biographer, argues that positive thinking was a "revitalization" movement and that followers founded interest groups that transcended denominational lines while still attending mainstream churches (George, *God's Salesman*, 130).

11. See, for example, Peale, *Power of Positive Thinking* (New York: Fawcett, 1996), viii; and Billy Graham, *Peace with God*, 7.

12. Fosdick, *On Being a Real Person*, 28, 191; Liebman, *Peace of Mind*, 186; Sheen, *Peace of Soul*, 7–8.

13. Fosdick, *On Being a Real Person*, 33; Sheen, *Peace of Soul*, 140.

14. Liebman, *Peace of Mind*, xi; Sheen, *Peace of Soul*, 1.

15. Liebman did address the social justice question in the preface to his book, conceding that "there is no question about it—a more just social order will cure vast numbers of people of their present inner conflicts and maladjustments," but he suggested that we are all faced with universal psychological tasks—death and dying, living in families, facing personal failure—that require psychological attention nevertheless (*Peace of Mind*, xii–xiii). In addition, it is clear that Liebman's well-adjusted, mature people were necessary to build a more just world. Similarly, while Fosdick conceded that caring about genetics and social reform was necessary, he maintained that there was too little emphasis on personal agency in 1940s America and too much emphasis on social and genetic determinism (*On Being a Real Person*, 4–8, 11).

16. Herberg, *Protestant-Catholic-Jew*, 80–81.

17. See ibid., chaps. 2 and 3.

18. Ibid., 57.

19. McLoughlin, *Revivals, Awakenings, and Reform*, 186; Meyer, *Positive Thinkers*; quotation from Massa, *Catholicism and American Culture*, 85, 247.

20. Biographical material is largely drawn from Robert Moats Miller, *Harry Emerson Fosdick*.

21. Fosdick, *Living of These Days*, vii.

22. Ibid., 78.

23. Quoted in Robert Moats Miller, *Harry Emerson Fosdick*, 104.

24. Fosdick, *Living of These Days*, 214–15. On Fosdick and counseling, see Robert Moats Miller, *Harry Emerson Fosdick*, chap. 15; and Meyer, *Positive Thinkers*, chap. 16.

25. Robert Moats Miller, *Harry Emerson Fosdick*, 275.

26. Harry Emerson Fosdick to Richard M. Elliott, 6 January 1944, UTS.

27. Fosdick, *On Being a Real Person*, x, xii. Subsequent page references are in the text.

28. In his history of mind-cure, Donald Meyer calls this concept "Supply" and defines it as the belief that knowledge, peace, happiness, and power are available to us on demand (*Positive Thinkers*, 75).

29. Ibid., 212.

30. Meyer argues: "Fosdick refused technical theological disputation; basically, he wanted theology itself played down, insisting, with William James, that the life of religion lay in action, not logic" (212).

31. Fosdick, *Living of These Days*, 231.

32. "Fosdick's Last Year"; quotation from Hedstrom, "Psychology and Mysticism in 1940s Religion," 251.

33. Harry Emerson Fosdick to Joshua Loth Liebman, 9 April 1947, BU. Liebman had earlier preached a sermon on *On Being a Real Person* and publicly praised Fosdick's volume for the

rare skill with which he had used psychological insights. For further links between Liebman and Fosdick, see Heinze, *Jews and the American Soul*, 234–35; and Hedstrom, "Psychology and Religion in 1940s Mysticism," 251–52.

34. Heinze, *Jews and the American Soul*, 205.

35. Biographical material is largely drawn from ibid., chap. 9.

36. Clemenko, "The Man behind 'Peace of Mind.'"

37. "MEET THE AUTHOR: Rabbi Joshua Loth Liebman, 11–11:15 A.M., 29 December 1947," in box 73, "Dr. Liebman's Book Material, 'Peace of Mind' Pamphlets, Magazines, etc., Publicity" Folder, BU.

38. Liebman, *Peace of Mind*, 152. Subsequent page references are in the text.

39. Jason Stevens argues that the "master-narrative" of the Cold War was that the United States had to relinquish illusions about innocence (read: immaturity) and accept responsibility in a fallen world. Liebman's representation of "mature" faith fits into that master narrative. See Stevens, *God-Fearing and Free*, xi.

40. Radio address, "'Peace of Mind,' 16 March 1947," typescript, p. 2, BU.

41. Liebman, "The Art of Happiness."

42. Advertising poster, "March 22 Will See the Publication of a Book," box 78, BU. Not everyone was convinced by this argument for liberal Jewish-Christian solidarity. A minority of Catholic readers protested that Liebman had written an anti-Christian book. Liebman made one reference to Jesus in the book, and although some wrote to him saying they loved this reference, others took him to task for only referencing Jesus once and demanded to know his position on Jesus. See, for example, Mrs. F. A. (Mildred) Lehner to Joshua Loth Liebman, 18 June 1947, BU; and Stanley P. Kirn to Joshua Loth Liebman, 21 August 1947, BU. Others criticized him for stubborn blindness to the sacrificial death and resurrection of Jesus and his failure to speak meaningfully to anything but the most superficial fears and anxieties as a consequence. See Dr. N. A. Moore to Joshua Loth Liebman, 30 November 1947, BU. Several mailed evangelizing pamphlets to him in the hope that they might bring him to see the light. For example, M. N. Bonbrake to Joshua Loth Liebman, 2 December 1947, BU; and Mr. D. M. Pinkham to Simon and Schuster, 27 May 1947, BU.

43. Heinze, *Jews and the American Soul*, 218, 225.

44. Ibid., 225–27; see also Heinze, "*Peace of Mind* (1946)."

45. Many letters and tributes in the Liebman papers try to distinguish him from his fellow travelers in the "cult of reassurance" by insisting on his prophetic Jewishness and his intellectualism. See, for example, Stephen Wise to Mrs. Joshua Loth Liebman, 11 June 1948, BU.

46. "Microphone Missionary."

47. Biographies of Sheen include Reeves, *America's Bishop*; and Riley, *Fulton J. Sheen*. See also Sheen's autobiography, *Treasure in Clay*.

48. Quoted in Massa, *Catholicism and American Culture*, 83.

49. Ibid., 91; Reeves, *America's Bishop*, 2.

50. Riley, *Fulton J. Sheen*, 200.

51. "Microphone Missionary."

52. Sheen, *Peace of Soul*, 6. Subsequent page references are in the text.

53. He also needed the book to extricate him from a public controversy over psychoanalysis that made headlines in the *New York Times* for six months in 1947. He had offered a scathing and (many argued) unfair critique of psychoanalysis during a sermon he preached in March 1947, and *Peace of Soul* was designed, in part, to clarify publicly Sheen's position vis-à-vis psychoanalysis and to make amends to the many Catholic psychiatrists he had offended. Both Riley (*Fulton J. Sheen*, 198–200) and Reeves (*America's Bishop*, 198–201) include discussion of the controversy.

54. O'Brien, *Renewal of American Catholicism*, 138; quotation from Massa, *Catholicism and American Culture*, 91.

55. See Herberg, *Protestant-Catholic-Jew*, chaps. 3 and 7.

56. Massa, *Catholicism and American Culture*, 85.

57. Ibid., 96–97.

58. Riley, *Fulton J. Sheen*, 205. Conversely, Anthony Burke Smith argues that Sheen's show was a vehicle for achieving Cold War consensus and that it aided and abetted the shift from a Catholic identity based on communalism to an "American" identity based in mass consumption and centered in private life. See Anthony Burke Smith, *The Look of Catholics*, chap. 5.

59. Massa, *Catholicism and American Culture*, 97.

60. In his discussion of Fosdick's *On Being a Real Person*, Liebman's *Peace of Mind*, and Thomas Merton's *Seven Storey Mountain*, Hedstrom argues similarly that although these books had large, interfaith readerships, "each book remained distinctively *of* its own tradition," a challenge to Herberg's anxieties about lost religious rigor (*Rise of Liberal Religion*, 175).

61. Quoted in Robert Moats Miller, *Harry Emerson Fosdick*, 273.

62. Ahlstrom, *Religious History of the American People*, 56; quotation from George, *God's Salesman*, 146.

63. The list comes from George, *God's Salesman*, 131. Biographical information comes from George's account.

64. See ibid., 135, 146, 163–64; see also Meyer, *Positive Thinkers*, 282–83.

65. Meyer, *Positive Thinkers*, 259–60.

66. Quoted in George, *God's Salesman*, 152.

67. Meyer, *Positive Thinkers*, 260; George, *God's Salesman*, 141–42.

68. George, *God's Salesman*, viii.

69. Quoted in ibid., 136. His first bestseller was *A Guide to Confident Living* (1948).

70. Peale, *Power of Positive Thinking*, xii. Subsequent page references are in the text.

71. "The best-loved inspirational book of our time reaches its 2,000,000th copy anniversary," poster, reprinted from the *New York Times Book Review*, 8 April 1956, in "Norman Vincent Peale–Special–Power of Positive Thinking Publicity" Folder, SU.

72. May, *Homeward Bound*.

73. Nadel, *Containment Culture*, 4.

74. Others have remarked on Peale's individualistic view of the world. See, for example, George, *God's Salesman*, 138; and Meyer, *Positive Thinkers*, 261, 284.

75. Edmund Fuller, "Pitchmen in the Pulpit," 28.

76. James Gilbert estimates that seventy-five out of the ninety anecdotes are about businessmen, military leaders, or sports figures who succeed through positive thinking. See Gilbert, *Men in the Middle*, 111.

77. Meyer points out that Peale's books teach you to play "the game" but do not question the rules of the game, which are taken for granted (*Positive Thinkers*, 284).

78. Gilbert, *Men in the Middle*, 111.

79. Ibid., 110–13.

80. See May, *Homeward Bound*, 19–22.

81. The figure is from the *New York Times Book Review* ad, "The best-loved inspirational book of our time reaches its 2,000,000th copy anniversary," reprinted from the *New York Times Book Review*, 8 April 1956, in "Norman Vincent Peale–Special–Power of Positive Thinking Publicity" Folder, SU.

82. Women apparently identified easily with failed, ineffectual men in *Power of Positive Thinking*, suggesting that women more easily related to men's stories than vice versa. Although

Peale tailored his book for men, most of its readers were probably women. Peale's critics did not recognize any explicit or implicit gendering of "positive thinking" at all. The figures come from George, *God's Salesman*, 120. A more inclusive count of supporters estimates majorities of up to 75 percent women (ibid., 155). On the appeal of New Thought to women more generally, see ibid., 7–8; and Meyer, *Positive Thinkers*, chap. 3.

83. Mrs. Luther E. Robinson to Norman Vincent Peale, 16 February 1960, SU.

84. Mrs. J. L. Barnett to Norman Vincent Peale, 23 July 1949, SU; see also Ann C. Jones to Norman Vincent Peale, 8 July 1949, SU.

85. Finding Aid, SU.

86. Meyer, *Positive Thinkers*, chap. 3.

87. Reviews of Peale in the 1950s suggested as much. See William Lee Miller, "Some Negative Thinking," 21; and Peters, "Case against 'Easy' Religion," in which Reinhold Niebuhr is quoted on this question.

88. Martin, *Prophet with Honor*, 130.

89. Ibid., 152.

90. George, *God's Salesman*, 148.

91. Ibid.

92. See Edmund Fuller, "Pitchmen in the Pulpit," 20. Many of the critics of the cult of reassurance compared Peale and Graham. One called Peale "the wealthy man's Billy Graham," since he promised the well-to-do the same kinds of spiritual gifts that Graham promised to ordinary people. Both were preoccupied with saving the souls of American men, as well, and used the example of their own masculinity to attempt to reach converts.

93. Graham, *Secret of Happiness*, v.

94. Ibid., 3; see also Heinze, *Jews and the American Soul*, 235.

95. Graham, *Secret of Happiness*, 73.

96. Ibid.

97. Graham, *Peace with God*, 21. Subsequent page references are in the text.

98. Graham, *Secret of Happiness*, 87.

99. Boston Public Library, "Celebrities' Choices," box 4, BU.

100. Nadel, *Containment Culture*, 3.

101. "Communism's Public Enemy Number One"; quotation from Martin, *Prophet with Honor*, 167.

102. Martin, *Prophet with Honor*, 165.

103. Graham's position changed significantly over time. For example, by 1980, he had renounced his earlier conflation of Christianity and patriotism (ibid., 472).

104. Ibid., 593.

105. Graham, *Secret of Happiness*, 52; see also ibid., 66–67, on the importance of Christian belief and practice behind the form of democratic government the United States was exporting to the developing world.

106. See William Lee Miller, "Some Negative Thinking," 19.

107. Quoted in George, *God's Salesman*, 108. The author discusses Peale's politics in chaps. 6 and 7.

108. Crosby, *God, Church, and Flag*, xi, 5, 13; quotation from Riley, *Fulton J. Sheen*, 55, 132. On Sheen and anticommunism, see Riley, *Fulton J. Sheen*, chap. 5. Reeves talks about Sheen's anticommunism throughout. See Reeves, *America's Bishop*, 86–92, 99–100, 126–28, 131–34, 203–10, 233–35, 243–47, 260.

109. See Reeves, *America's Bishop*, 206–8.

110. Ibid.; Riley, *Fulton J. Sheen*, 243–47.

111. See Riley, *Fulton J. Sheen*, 189; and Massa, *Catholicism and American Culture*, 90–91.

112. "Microphone Missionary."

113. Reeves, *America's Bishop*, 143.

114. Sheen, *Freedom under God*, 167; see also Riley, *Fulton J. Sheen*, 52–53.

115. This is the title of the final section of chapter 8 of Liebman, *Peace of Mind*.

116. Ibid., 173–74.

117. Liebman, "Hope for Human Brotherhood."

118. Hedstrom, *Rise of Liberal Religion*, 193.

119. Fosdick, *Living of These Days*, 310.

120. Burford, untitled review; quotation from Hedstrom, *Rise of Liberal Religion*, 205.

121. See untitled excerpts from letters in "Fosdick–Correspondence–Books–On Being a Real Person–1943–49" Folder, UTS; Francis Geddes to Harry Emerson Fosdick, 29 April 1949, UTS; Jean Roblyer to Harry Emerson Fosdick, n.d., UTS; Charles Boynton to Harry Emerson Fosdick, 5 October 1956, UTS; and Lt. Denton Lotz to Harry Emerson Fosdick, 20 May 1962, UTS.

122. See Hedstrom, "Psychology and Mysticism in 1940s Religion," 254.

123. See Paul Buralli to Norman Vincent Peale, 14 March 1962, SU; Paul Buralli to Norman Vincent Peale, 9 March 1962, SU; ad from *New York Times Book Review*, 8 April 1956, "*Power of Positive Thinking* Publicity" Folder, SU; Heinze, "*Peace of Mind* (1946)," 32; Martin, *Prophet with Honor*, 152; Harry Emerson Fosdick to Mr. L. K. Hall, 20 November 1949, UTS; and untitled clipping (1962) in "Fosdick–Correspondence–Books–On Being a Real Person–1950–60" Folder, UTS.

124. Mrs. E. B. Robertson to Harry Emerson Fosdick, 23 September 1957, UTS.

125. See Martin, *Prophet with Honor*, 476.

126. See ibid., 505.

127. Pollock, *Billy Graham*, 5, 100–101, 210.

128. See Harry Emerson Fosdick to Helen L. Bailey, 1 May 1956, UTS.

129. Erdman Harris to Harry Emerson Fosdick, 9 January 1927, UTS.

130. Harry E. Campbell to Harry Emerson Fosdick, 5 March 1924, UTS.

131. Wilbert B. Smith to Harry Emerson Fosdick, 5 April 1946, UTS; see also W. B. Smith to Harry Emerson Fosdick, 29 September 1923, UTS.

132. Klein, *Cold War Orientalism*, 13.

133. See Marchand, *Advertising the American Dream*, chaps. 2 and 3.

134. McAlister, *Epic Encounters*, chap. 1.

135. See "Introduction," in "Fosdick–Correspondence–Books–On Being a Real Person—1950–60" Folder, UTS. Fosdick always approved requests to translate his works, specifying only that it should be done intelligently, that it be done as missionary work rather than as a commercial undertaking, and that he receive copies of the finished work. For historical context on the publishing/circulation of books in post–World War II Japan, see Hench, *Books as Weapons*, chap. 12.

136. This is yet another characteristic of Cold War Orientalism. See Klein, *Cold War Orientalism*, 65.

137. Radway, *Feeling for Books*, 284–85.

138. Laugesen, "Books for the World," 127–28. Laugesen is clear that "modernization" was often merely a more acceptable term for "Americanizing" emerging nations, which cloaked the process with an aura of objectivity and inevitability rather than casting it as a political and economic contest over developing nations with the Soviets (136).

139. Ibid., 137, 140.

140. Ibid., 129.

141. See ibid., 137–38.

142. Ibid., 139.

143. Ibid., 130, 138.

144. On ethnicity, pluralism, religion, and national character studies, see Gleason, *Speaking of Diversity*, chap. 7.

Chapter 7

1. *Publishers Weekly*, 9 March 1970, 50.

2. "What's Selling on the Religious Books Scene," 55, 58.

3. Krauthammer, "Where's the 2000 Buzz?"

4. C.B.G., "'Hidden' Best Sellers among Religious Books," 45.

5. For an excellent history of evangelical publishing, see Blodgett, *Protestant Evangelical Literary Culture and Contemporary Society*, especially chap. 2.

6. Marty, "Religious Publishing: A Decline but Not a Demise," 524–25.

7. "Religious Publishers Seek Ways to Meet a Crisis."

8. C.B.G., "Religious Publishing: In Transition to What?"; Marty, "Religious Publishing: A Decline but Not a Demise," 525.

9. Marty, "Religious Publishing: A Decline but Not a Demise," 525; see also Patterson, "Broad-Based Publishing Philosophy."

10. C.B.G., "Religious Publishing: In Transition to What?"

11. "Religious Publishers Seek Ways to Meet a Crisis"; "Currents: Religious Publishers Study Their Market."

12. "Currents: Interest in Religion, Crisis in the Market"; see also *Publishers Weekly* special religious books issue of 8 March 1971.

13. "Currents."

14. C.B.G., "Religious Publishers Confident They Can Keep Pace with the 70s."

15. Freilich, "ABA: The Convention Goes West."

16. Marty, "Religious Publishing: A Decline but Not a Demise," 527. This conviction was widely held among booksellers and publishers. See Grannis, "Taste and Trends, 1972, in Religious Books," 37, 38; Marty, "A Spiritual Revival, a Commercial Boom, and Yet"; and Delloff, "ABCs of the CBA," 841.

17. Marty, "Religious Publishing: A Decline but Not a Demise," 526.

18. Grannis, "Taste and Trends, 1972, in Religious Books," 37.

19. Marty, "Religious Publishing: A Decline but Not a Demise," 526.

20. B.A.B., "Review of the ABA Panels."

21. Kirsch, "Interviews: Hal Lindsey," 30.

22. Sanders, "Apocalypse Then"; Silk, "Religious Books: Seven That Made a Difference"; Boyer, "John Darby Meets Saddam Hussein."

23. "Religious Publishing and the 'Mainstream.'"

24. C.B.G., "Religious Books: The Season's Top Titles."

25. Leach, "Paradox of Religious Books," 40; Leach, "We Are What We Read," 1089.

26. Leach, "We Are What We Read," 1089.

27. Holt, "Brisk Sales and High Attendance Mark Christian Booksellers Meeting," 49; see also Hewitt, "Religion Publishers Note Expanding Trade Sales," 42, 44.

28. Holt, "Brisk Sales and High Attendance Mark Christian Booksellers Meeting," 47; Hewitt, "Record Attendance at 28th Annual Booksellers Convention."

29. D.M., "Religious Backlist: The Strongest Category," 79.

30. C.B.G., "Religion Publishers View Mass Market Paperbacks."

31. Kirsch, "Interviews: Hal Lindsey," 31.

32. "Views on Publishing," 55; see also Holt, "CBA Convention in Anaheim," 32.

33. "Views on Publishing," 55.

34. Kirsch, "Interviews: Hal Lindsey," 31; Ruark, "Meeting the Evangelical Needs." See also C.B.G., "Religion Publishers Cite Growing Trend to Paperbacks," 24, 26.

35. Ruark, "Meeting the Evangelical Needs."

36. B.A.B., "Review of the ABA Panels," 81; Holt, "Brisk Sales and High Attendance Mark Christian Booksellers Meeting," 46.

37. Holt, "Brisk Sales and High Attendance Mark Christian Booksellers Meeting," 46.

38. Forbes, "Unlisted Bestsellers," 40.

39. Leach, "We Are What We Read," 1090.

40. Ibid., 1092.

41. Man, "Religious Books Booming."

42. Grannis, "Taste and Trends, 1972, in Religious Books," 37.

43. McDowell, "Publishers: A Matter of Faith"; McDowell, "Religious Publishing: Going Skyward." On the rapid growth of evangelical publishing, see also "Phenomenon of the Religious Best Seller," 46; Montagno, Monroe, and Abramson, "Holy Writ," 58; and Donadio, "Faith-Based Publishing."

44. Dillon, "Christian Booksellers Have Cause to Celebrate," 41.

45. Griffin, "Christian Booksellers in Washington."

46. "Views on Publishing," 56.

47. Montagno, Monroe, and Abramson, "Holy Writ," 58.

48. Krauthammer, "Where's the 2000 Buzz?"

49. Silk, "Religious Books: Seven That Made a Difference."

50. "Phenomenon of the Religious Best-Seller," 47.

51. 1972 trends in book sales demonstrated strongest sales for evangelical books, although sales of Eastern religion and mysticism books held their own. See Grannis, "Taste and Trends, 1972, in Religious Books," 37.

52. C.B.G., "Religious Books: The Season's Top Titles."

53. Woodward, Barnes, and Lisle, "Born Again," 68. Looking back on 1976, Gary Wharton (who had left Zondervan to head the Christian News Service's parent company by this time) pointed out that all the major presidential candidates—Jimmy Carter, Gerald Ford, and Ronald Reagan—claimed some kind of born-again experience. He could cite cover stories and major features in all the major news magazines—*Time*, *Newsweek*, and *U.S. News and World Report*—on evangelicals (Wharton, "Continuing Phenomenon of the Religious Best Seller," 82).

54. Holt, "Brisk Sales and High Attendance Mark Christian Booksellers Meeting," 47.

55. Ibid.

56. R.D., "ABA: The Smoothest Convention Ever," 48.

57. Donadio, "Faith-Based Publishing."

58. R.D., "ABA: The Smoothest Convention Ever," 48; see also Man, "Religious Books Booming."

59. Adams, "Moving Religion Market," 44; Ruark, "Meeting the Evangelical Needs."

60. Liepa, "Serving the Christian Booksellers," 64.

61. "Reaching Out for a Growing Market of Readers."

62. Man, "Religious Books Booming."

63. Leach, "Paradox of Religious Books," 41.

64. D.M., "Religious Backlist: The Strongest Category," 78. See also "Phenomenon of the Religious Best Seller," 45; and Montagno, Monroe, and Abramson, "Holy Writ," 58.

65. Grannis, "Taste and Trends, 1972, in Religious Books," 42, 37; Holt, "Western Religious Publishers See 'Phenomenal Growth Period,'" 73.

66. Maryles and Holt, "CBA in Dallas," 39.

67. Kirsch, "Interviews: Hal Lindsey," 30.

68. L.F., "Selling Evangelical Books," 48.

69. Holt, "Brisk Sales and High Attendance Mark Christian Booksellers Meeting," 47; Griffin, "Christian Booksellers Find Optimism in a Slow Economy," 42.

70. "Phenomenon of the Religious Best Seller," 45.

71. Dillon, "Christian Booksellers Have Cause to Celebrate," 40.

72. C.B.G., "Religious Publishers Confident They Can Keep Pace with the 70s," 33. See also C.B.G., "Religion Publishers View Grim Teen Attitudes," 46. The model for reaching a youth audience was Logos Books, which opened its first store in Ann Arbor just down the street from the University of Michigan in 1970. This "crazy" endeavor of opening religious bookstores near college campuses was extraordinarily successful. See L.F., "Selling Evangelical Books," 48; Carlson, "A New Generation Christian Bookstore," 28–29; and Shank, "A Word about Logos."

73. Grannis, "Taste and Trends, 1972, in Religious Books," 38.

74. Kirsch, "Interviews: Hal Lindsey," 31.

75. Ibid.

76. "Phenomenon of the Religious Best Seller," 47.

77. "Religion: The New Rebel Cry."

78. Howard, "Groovy Christians of Rye, NY," 80.

79. Ellwood, *One Way*, 8.

80. Sometimes Lindsey does not appear in books from the 1970s about the Jesus movement at all. Other times, he has brief mentions or appears in a chapter about those on the margins of the movement. See Hiley H. Ward, *Far-Out Saints of the Jesus Communes*, 109; and Enroth, Ericson, and Peters, *Jesus People*, chap. 7.

81. Jorstad, *That New-Time Religion*, 68.

82. Enroth, Ericson, and Peters, *Jesus People*, 141.

83. There were about a dozen books that appeared in 1971 and 1972 about the Jesus People, mostly from denominational publishers. See Ellwood, *One Way*, 89; see also Enroth, Ericson, and Peters, *Jesus People*, 127; McFadden, *Jesus Revolution*, 43; and Jorstad, *That New-Time Religion*, 75.

84. See, "Speaking for the Evangelical Publishers"; see also Roshevsky, "RPG: What It Is and What It Does."

85. Stobbe, "Religious Publishing," Letters to the Editor, 9.

86. See also Delloff, "ABCs of the CBA"; and "Fervor and Froth."

87. Peckham, "Retailing: Religion Is Big Business as Christian Booksellers Meet in Denver," 47.

88. See two appreciative letters to the editor about coverage of the 1977 Christian Booksellers Association annual convention from the executive vice president and an evangelical publisher who exhibited there praising the breadth and fairness of the coverage ("Two Comments on PW's CBA Convention Coverage," Letters to the Editor, 49–50).

89. Leach, "We Are What We Read," 1092.

90. Marty, "Religious Publishing: A Decline but Not a Demise," 528. Marty made a similar argument in "A Spiritual Revival, a Commercial Boom, and Yet," in which he lamented the decline from the democratic interaction, consensus-building, and civic virtue of "the city" to the narrow parochialism of "the tribe" (84).

91. "Religious Publishing's Solomons and Shebas."

92. Lyles, "Abingdon, Don't Abdicate."

93. "Religious Publishing's Second Spring." Eating metaphors were common. Werner Linz of Episcopalian publisher Seabury agreed that there was a growing audience of people interested in "real religious books." "They have graduated from evangelical snacking," he explained. See Montagno, Monroe, and Abramson, "Holy Writ," 58.

94. "Editorial Comment: Publishing in an Age of Mergers."

95. In addition to tensions between religious publishers and general booksellers, who did not take religious books seriously or bother to include them on industry bestseller lists, there were tensions among religious publishers and booksellers. One presenter read the national religious bestseller list issued by the Christian News Service at a panel presentation. At the close, some of the panelists expressed doubt as to whether some of these books (Lindsey, Pat Boone, "I'm Ok, You're Ok") actually belonged in a "serious religious bookstore." See "Religious Books in the Mainstream."

96. "Editorial Comment: Religious Books and the Critic's Task."

97. Marty, "You'll Never Get Rich," 1119.

98. Marty, "Updating the List," 575.

99. Thatcher, "Welcome to a New Breed of Religious Writers," 46.

100. Kirsch, "Interviews: Hal Lindsey," 30.

101. Orsi, *Between Heaven and Earth*, 188–90.

102. The figure comes from Frum, "Best-Seller Lists Need Repair."

103. "A Phenomenal Bestseller You Won't Find Listed on the Opposite Page"; quotation from Forbes, "Unlisted Bestsellers," 40.

104. Ibid.

105. Frum, "Best-Seller Lists Need Repair."

106. Thompson, "Checking It Twice"; Shaw, "Lists Flawed."

107. Thompson, "Checking It Twice."

108. Ibid.; quotation from Heer, "Battle of the Lists"; see Truitt, "Culturebox: Apocalypse Soon."

109. All quotations from Thompson, "Checking It Twice."

110. "Fervor and Froth"; see also Wharton, "Continuing Phenomenon of the Religious Best Seller," 82.

111. Montagno, Monroe, and Abramson, "Holy Writ," 58.

112. "Editorial Comment: Publishing in an Age of Mergers."

113. Kirsch, "Interviews: Hal Lindsey," 32.

114. Forbes, "Unlisted Bestsellers," 42.

115. "Phenomenon of the Religious Best Seller," 45.

116. Leach, "Paradox of Religious Books," 41.

117. Quotation from Montagno, Monroe, and Abramson, "Holy Writ," 58.

118. "Phenomenon of the Religious Best Seller," 46.

119. Ibid.

120. Ibid.

121. Ibid.; Lisa See, "Speaking for the Evangelical Publishers," 59.

122. "Phenomenon of the Religious Best Seller," 46; D.M., "Religious Backlist: The Strongest Category," 79.

123. Lisa See, "Speaking for the Evangelical Publishers," 59.

124. McDowell, "Publishers: A Matter of Faith." One article on building a strong backlist of religious books came with a list of twenty-five all-time (and still selling) bestsellers. *The Late Great Planet Earth* was in the top category, with more than 9 million copies sold, the only book not a Bible in the top-selling category ("Religious Best Sellers," 88).

125. D.M., "Religious Backlist: The Strongest Category," 78.

Chapter 8

1. Boyer, *When Time Shall Be No More*, ix, xii; see also Boyer, "John Darby Meets Saddam Hussein."

2. McAlister, *Epic Encounters*, 167–68; see also McAlister, "Prophecy, Politics, and the Popular," 779.

3. McAlister, *Epic Encounters*, 166.

4. Although neither Boyer nor McAlister spends much time on it, both concede that readers might not agree entirely with the authors and creators of prophecy texts. Their primary concern is textual analysis rather than audience or reception studies.

5. Stuart Hall, "Notes on Deconstructing 'the Popular,'" 232.

6. I received Internal Review Board approval to solicit individuals' memories of reading *The Late Great Planet Earth* through these sources. I offered drafts of this chapter to all nine personal respondents. Three requested to see it. One sent comments. I had initially hoped to place ads in evangelical periodicals such as *Christianity Today* as well. This proved prohibitively expensive, and many readers reached through Theolog and H-Amrel asserted that they had read the book so long ago that they could not remember it very well. The Amazon.com reviews were available from a cross-section of differently religious readers who did remember the book well enough to review it. For examples of Amazon.com reviews as a source of reader response, see Gutjahr, "No Longer Left Behind"; and Aubry, *Reading as Therapy*.

7. There is some disagreement about sales figures. The oft-repeated 10 million figure comes from McDowell, "Publishers: A Matter of Faith," 18. The 7.5 million figure for the 1970s comes from Walters, "Paperback Talk," 27. Later sales figures come from Boyer, *When Time Shall Be No More*, 5–6; and Chris Hall, "What Hal Lindsey Taught Me about the Second Coming," 83.

8. Quotation from Gribben, *Writing the Rapture*, 8; Chris Hall, "What Hal Lindsey Taught Me about the Second Coming," 83.

9. McAlister, *Epic Encounters*, 167, 338.

10. Lindsey's editor at Zondervan initially warned him to keep his expectations for sales low because the Christian market was already saturated with Bible prophecy books (Kirsch, "Interviews: Hal Lindsey," 30).

11. Ibid., 31.

12. McAlister, *Epic Encounters*, 167.

13. M.H., email message to the author, 18 September 2008.

14. Christopher B. Jonnes, "Interesting Fiction," Review of *The Late Great Planet Earth*, Amazon.com, 21 December 2000, Web, accessed 8 October 2008; Christian Book Reviews, "Oops . . . I Did It Again," Review of *The Late Great Planet Earth*, Amazon.com, 25 August 2006, Web, accessed 8 October 2008.

15. Kirsch, "Interviews: Hal Lindsey," 31.

16. T.L., email message to the author, 18 September 2008.

17. Mark J. Koenig, "Mindless and Pathetic," Review of *The Late Great Planet Earth*, Amazon.com, 16 May 2000, Web, accessed 8 October 2008; Thomas H. Griffith, "What a Load of Baloney," Review of *The Late Great Planet Earth*, Amazon.com, 21 January 2006, Web, accessed 8 October 2008.

18. A Customer, "Horrible Scholarship but Entertaining," Review of *The Late Great Planet Earth*, Amazon.com, 1 July 1999, Web, accessed 8 October 2008.

19. J.G., email message to the author, 6 October 2008. Gribben distinguishes between prophecy novels and prophetic nonfiction, arguing that the eclipse of the latter in the late 1990s by the *Left Behind* novels marks a sea change in "popular prophetic consciousness." Gribben argues that nonfiction is prescriptive rather than descriptive and tends to be more emphatic about its claims. Fiction, on the other hand, allows for free play of the reader's imagination, engages in speculative versus falsifiable claims, and enables readers to enjoy the text without necessarily embracing the author's worldview (*Writing the Rapture*, 15–16). As its packaging and the reports of its readers make clear, all of these things were true of Lindsey's readers as well. Many of them read without accepting its truth claims or embracing Lindsey's point of view. Some enjoyed it specifically because of its imaginative, speculative nature. Gribben's insistence that there is a great divide between how fiction and nonfiction function aside, he does concede that *The Late Great Planet Earth* "blurred the line between fact and fiction," between "prophetic entertainment and biblical interpretation" (9).

20. For an example from contemporary scholarship, see McAlister, *Epic Encounters*, 177. For examples from reviews, see Tinder, "Future Fact? Future Fiction?," 40; and Christian Book Reviews, "Oops . . . I Did It Again."

21. See Chapter 7, section headed "Mencken Redux: Conservative Christians in the Mainstream Media."

22. Marty, "Varieties of Religious Publishing," 55. Gribben argues that this is how evangelical fiction functions more generally: "Prophecy novels, like other evangelical novels, are stories that believers 'tell themselves about themselves.' Their primary purpose is to build a defined community by recruiting and instructing adherents" (*Writing the Rapture*, 15).

23. See, for example, W. Foley, "Biblical Terrorism," Review of *The Late Great Planet Earth*, Amazon.com, 11 October 2002, Web, accessed 8 October 2008; Mike Burns, "To Those Who Sing This Book's Praises," Review of *The Late Great Planet Earth*, Amazon.com, 21 January 2007, Web, accessed 8 October 2008; Lois, 'Why Is There No ZERO Star Option??," Review of *The Late Great Planet Earth*, Amazon.com, 16 February 2006, Web, accessed 8 October 2008; Quiltz "aznurse," "Would the Average Intelligent Adult Really Believe This?" Review of *The Late Great Planet Earth*, Amazon.com, 27 December 1999, Web, accessed 8 October 2008; David Haggith, "Do Yourself a Favor and Dig Deeper," Review of *The Late Great Planet Earth*, Amazon.com, 16 December 1999, Web, accessed 8 October 2008; and Gary, "One Star—but Only Because Negative Numbers Aren't a Choice," Review of *The Late Great Planet Earth*, Amazon.com, 21 September 2000, Web, accessed 8 October 2008.

24. See, for example, S.K., email message to the author, 13 August 2008.

25. Richard D. Cappetto "RickDC," "A Classic on Biblical Prophecy," Review of *The Late Great Planet Earth*, Amazon.com, 5 December 2003, Web, accessed 8 October 2008; Nathan627, "Is the Earth Rushing toward Catastrophe?," Review of *The Late Great Planet Earth*, Amazon.com, 11 August 2003, Web, accessed 8 October 2008; P. Wiseman, "This Book Is Magnificent," Review of *The Late Great Planet Earth*, Amazon.com, 1 August 2003, Web, accessed 8 October 2008.

26. Shirley Priscilla Johnson, "Midwest Book Review," Review of *The Late Great Planet Earth*, Amazon.com, 4 July 2004, Web, accessed 8 October 2008.

27. See Volkert Volkersz, "It's Time to Take a Second Look at Lindsey," Review of *The Late Great Planet Earth*, Amazon.com, 13 February 2001, Web, accessed 8 October 2008; Raul R. Ibarra, "The Ultimate in a Reading Experience," Review of *The Late Great Planet Earth*, Amazon.com, 18 September 2001, Web, accessed 8 October 2008; and David D. Williams, "A Life Saver," Review of *The Late Great Planet Earth*, Amazon.com, 14 December 2007, Web, accessed 8 October 2008.

28. Volkert Volkersz, "It's Time to Take a Second Look at Lindsey"; see also Dean Duerkop, "He Who Wins Souls Is Wise," Review of *The Late Great Planet Earth*, Amazon.com, 24 October 2007, Web, accessed 8 October 2008.

29. W. F. Giuliano, "Sheer Idiocy," Review of *The Late Great Planet Earth*, Amazon.com, 30 September 2003, Web, accessed 8 October 2008; Maksutov "mahlerite1," "Pure Bunk," Review of *The Late Great Planet Earth*, Amazon.com, 6 July 2005, Web, accessed 8 October 2008.

30. A Customer, "Fundamentalist Nonsense for the Ignorant and the Stupid," Review of *The Late Great Planet Earth*, Amazon.com, 15 April 1999, Web, accessed 8 October 2008.

31. Reverend Raven "Brainiac at Large," "Lindsay's Cottage Industry," Review of *The Late Great Planet Earth*, Amazon.com, 4 January 2005, Web, accessed 8 October 2008; Ellie Reasoner, "Not EVEN Good for a Laugh," Review of *The Late Great Planet Earth*, Amazon.com, 15 September 2005, Web, accessed 8 October 2008.

32. "king-ludd," "I Can't Believe Anyone Takes This Seriously," Review of *The Late Great Planet Earth*, Amazon.com, 29 November 2003, Web, accessed 8 October 2008.

33. John D. Wagner "jwagner4," "Vacuous and Outdated," Review of *The Late Great Planet Earth*, Amazon.com, 21 March 2005, Web, accessed 8 October 2008; Mark H. Drought, "I Love This Stuff," Review of *The Late Great Planet Earth*, Amazon.com, 29 April 2004, Web, accessed 8 October 2008.

34. FrKurt Messick, "To Everything There Is a Season," Review of *The Late Great Planet Earth*, Amazon.com, 28 January 2004, Web, accessed 8 October 2008; Mark J. Koenig, "Mindless and Pathetic," Review of *The Late Great Planet Earth*, Amazon.com, 16 March 2000, Web, accessed 8 October 2008; Novel Reader, "Just a Review," "PLEASE . . . Buy Something Else," Review of *The Late Great Planet Earth*, Amazon.com, 3 November 2005, Web, accessed 8 October 2008. Other reviewers split their rating—saying they would have given it five stars when they read it as teenagers, but had since changed their minds: see Volkert Volkersz, "It's Time to Take a Second Look at Lindsey"; and Ed "Prophecy Reader," "There Are Better Books Out There Today," Review of *The Late Great Planet Earth*, Amazon.com, 18 June 2008, Web, accessed 8 October 2008.

35. Gary, "One Star—but Only Because Negative Numbers Aren't a Choice." See also A Customer, "It'd Be Funny If It Weren't for All the Destroyed Lives," Review of *The Late Great Planet Earth*, Amazon.com, 12 June 2001, Web, accessed 8 October 2008.

36. W. Foley, "Biblical Terrorism"; J. Golden, "Illegitimate Interpretation," Review of *The Late Great Planet Earth*, Amazon.com, 23 September 2007, Web, accessed 8 October 2008; Reverend Raven "Brainiac at Large," "Lindsay's Cottage Industry."

37. Tribolumen, "Fascinating Like a Car Crash," Review of *The Late Great Planet Earth*, Amazon.com, 3 February 2007, Web, accessed 8 October 2008; Mike Burns, "To Those Who Sing This Book's Praises"; FBRobertson, "fbrobertson2," "Concerning Ol' Hal," Review of *The Late Great Planet Earth*, Amazon.com, 24 March 2003, Web, accessed 8 October 2008; Volkert Volkersz, "It's Time to Take a Second Look at Lindsey." Most such reviews were sincere.

Others were sarcastic: "Save your ten bucks for something more worthwhile, like a couple of Spider-Man comics or something" (Lois, 'Why Is There No ZERO Star Option?").

38. kb in Washington, "Boy Have Some Reviewers Got It Wrong," Review of *The Late Great Planet Earth*, Amazon.com, 29 September 2008, Web, accessed 8 October 2008; Phillip Withers, "PapaGuk," "Naturally, Most People Just Don't Get It," Review of *The Late Great Planet Earth*, Amazon.com, 5 December 2006, Web, accessed 8 October 2008.

39. Knight, "snipurl.com/bookshoppe," "'FEAR THE ONE WHO CAN DESTROY BOTH BODY AND SOUL IN HELL'—JESUS," Review of *The Late Great Planet Earth*, Amazon.com, 25 April 2006, Web, accessed 8 October 2008; Lizzeedee, "Skin Care Store Owner," "Pay No Mind to the Scoffers," Review of *The Late Great Planet Earth*, Amazon.com, 23 July 2006, Web, accessed 8 October 2008; Brianna Lauren, "Tomorrow's Headlines Today," Review of *The Late Great Planet Earth*, Amazon.com, 22 January 2004, Web, accessed 8 October 2008; Joseph Conklin, "Wow, All the Negative Reviews," Review of *The Late Great Planet Earth*, Amazon.com, 4 November 2006, Web, accessed 8 October 2008; A Customer, "Chilling, Exciting, & Accurate!" Review of *The Late Great Planet Earth*, Amazon.com, 6 October 1997, Web, accessed 8 October 2008.

40. Lindsey and Carlson, *The Late Great Planet Earth*, 131.

41. Ibid., 114.

42. A Customer, "Ooops," Review of *The Late Great Planet Earth*, Amazon.com, 9 December 1998, Web, accessed 8 October 2008; see also J.G., email message to the author, 6 October 2008; and Marcia L. Dietrich, "Paranoia, Fear and Inaccuracy," Review of *The Late Great Planet Earth*, Amazon.com, 6 December 2002, Web, accessed 8 October 2008.

43. Mark Grindell, "Looks Just Like the Real Thing," Review of *The Late Great Planet Earth*, Amazon.com, 4 April 2003, Web, accessed 8 October 2008.

44. K.C., Interview with the author, 11 January 2003.

45. Lindsey and Carlson, *The Late Great Planet Earth*, 129.

46. Ibid., 130.

47. Ibid., 67.

48. Ibid., 127, 183, 134, 128. Lindsey's anti-institutionalism was not lost on his critics. One explained: "The fact of the matter is that Darbyist dispensationalism contains a hidden element of hostility toward the church" (Vanderwaal, *Hal Lindsey and Biblical Prophecy*, 32).

49. Lindsey and Carlson, *The Late Great Planet Earth*, 182–83.

50. Ibid., 183. Cornelius Vanderwaal, a critic of Lindsey, concedes that Lindsey is right about this: "We must recognize that not just young people but Christians of all ages are fed up with churches that preach little more than middle-class values, churches that conceal a great deal of uncertainty and uneasiness behind the inertia with which they resist change" (*Hal Lindsey and Biblical Prophecy*, 88).

51. Chris Hall, "What Hal Lindsey Taught Me about the Second Coming," 84.

52. Ibid.

53. See Krauthammer, "Where's the 2000 Buzz?"

54. P. Wiseman, "This Book Is Magnificent," Review of *The Late Great Planet Earth*, Amazon. com, 1 August 2003, Web, accessed 8 October 2008.

55. Heather Hendershot argues that this is one of apocalyptic media's three goals: (1) instruct readers in prophecy theology; (2) frighten people into conversion; and (3) convert those left behind. See Hendershot, *Shaking the World for Jesus*, chap. 6, 179–80; see also Bivins, *Religion of Fear*, chap. 6.

56. W. Foley, "Biblical Terrorism"; A Customer, "100% Pure Apocalyptic Drivel," Review of *The Late Great Planet Earth*, Amazon.com, 4 April 1999, Web, accessed 8 October 2008.

57. A Customer, "A Dazzling Persuasive Failure," Review of *The Late Great Planet Earth*, Amazon.com, 14 October 2002, Web, accessed 8 October 2008. See also W. Foley, "Biblical Terrorism"; Ellie Reasoner, "Not EVEN Good for a Laugh"; Gary, "One Star—but Only Because Negative Numbers Aren't a Choice."

58. FrKurt Messick, "To Everything There Is a Season."

59. kb in Washington, "Boy Have Some Reviewers Got It Wrong."

60. Knight, "snipurl.com/bookshoppe," "'FEAR THE ONE WHO CAN DESTROY BOTH BODY AND SOUL IN HELL'—JESUS."

61. J.G., email message to the author, 6 October 2008; Lois, 'Why Is There No ZERO Star Option??"

62. Marcia L. Dietrich, "Paranoia, Fear and Inaccuracy."

63. S.W., email message to the author, 13 August 2008; M.H., email message to the author, 18 September 2008.

64. J.G., email message to the author, 6 October 2008; S.W., email message to the author, 15 August 2008.

65. John Pittaway, "After September 11, a Must Read," Review of *The Late Great Planet Earth*, Amazon.com, 1 November 2001, Web, accessed 8 October 2008; Raul R. Ibarra, "The Ultimate in a Reading Experience." This contradicts what Frykholm found in her study of *Left Behind* readers. *Left Behind* was about hope and being reunited with dead friends and family members, not about fear and destruction. See Frykholm, *Rapture Culture*, chap. 8.

66. Chris Hall, "What Hal Lindsey Taught Me about the Second Coming," 83–84.

67. S.W., email message to the author, 15 August 2008.

68. Ellwood, *One Way*, 92–93.

69. Jorstad, *That New-Time Religion*, 75.

70. Lindsey and Carlson, *The Late Great Planet Earth*, 164–66.

71. McAlister, *Epic Encounters*, 177; Boyer, *When Time Shall Be No More*, 128. One critic characterized Lindsey's book as "dispen-sensationalism" (quoted in Gribben, *Writing the Rapture*, 9).

72. Johns, "Hell Awaits," Review of *The Late Great Planet Earth*, Amazon.com, 15 September 2006, Web, accessed 8 October 2008.

73. See Boyer, "From Tracts to Mass-Market Paperbacks," 29.

74. For a brief and clear account, see McAlister, "Prophecy, Politics, and the Popular," 778–79.

75. See, for example, John D. Wagner "jwagner4," "Vacuous and Outdated," Review of *The Late Great Planet Earth*, Amazon.com, 21 March 2005, Web, accessed 8 October 2008; A Customer, "Rather Sticky Subject," Review of *The Late Great Planet Earth*, Amazon.com, 28 November 2003, Web, accessed 8 October 2008.

76. Two of these were emailed to me by a reader who saw my call for readers' recollections of reading *The Late Great Planet Earth* in the 1970s and early 1980s.

77. Boersma, *Is the Bible a Jigsaw Puzzle*, 7.

78. Vanderwaal, *Hal Lindsey and Biblical Prophecy*, 55, 15.

79. J.G., email message to the author, 6 October 2008.

80. Avid Reader, "Rapture Cult at Its Finest," Review of *The Late Great Planet Earth*, Amazon.com, 18 September 2007, Web, accessed 8 October 2008; see also Bill Newcomer, "Please Spare Us," Review of *The Late Great Planet Earth*, Amazon.com, 22 January 2000, Web, accessed 8 October 2008: "Do yourself a favor. . . . Take the money you were going to use to buy this book, and use it to feed starving third world children. Then read your Bible, without the Schofield [*sic*] notes, and let it speak for itself."

81. S.W., email message to the author, 15 August 2008.

82. Ibid.

83. Frykholm characterizes conversion as a change in language that shifts one's understanding of the world (*Rapture Culture*, 165–67). Clearly, this reader had found new language to make sense of his life and his place in an anxious world.

84. Luhrmann, *When God Talks Back*, 299, 268. In chapter 1, Luhrmann traces the roots of Vineyard Fellowship back to the Jesus movement in California in the 1960s and 1970s.

85. Dean Duerkop, "He Who Wins Souls Is Wise"; see also Knight, "snipurl.com/bookshoppe," "'FEAR THE ONE WHO CAN DESTROY BOTH BODY AND SOUL IN HELL'—JESUS"; Blue Jay "Jason," "I Can See Why," Review of *The Late Great Planet Earth*, Amazon.com, 30 March 2003, Web, accessed 8 October 2008; and Mark Nelson, "A Classic," Review of *The Late Great Planet Earth*, Amazon.com, 13 December 2004, Web, accessed 8 October 2008.

86. In this way, Lindsey's 1970s and 1980s readers resemble the nineteenth-century evangelicals described by Candy Gunther Brown, whose readers judged a book by its effects. If it brought readers closer to God, then it was a good book (Candy Gunther Brown, *Word in the World*, 4, 7); see also Nord, *Faith in Reading*, chaps. 6 and 7.

87. Chris Hall, "What Hal Lindsey Taught Me about the Second Coming," 83.

88. T.L., email message to the author, 18 September 2008; Boyer, *When Time Shall Be No More*, 126–27; McAlister, *Epic Encounters*, 165.

89. Chris Hall, "What Hal Lindsey Taught Me about the Second Coming," 84.

90. On the history of prophecy fiction, see Gribben, *Writing the Rapture*. For his study of end-times prophecies, Boyer read over 100 pre-1945 prophecy books and over 200 published since 1945, in addition to the proceedings of eight conferences and about twenty-five prophecy newsletters and magazines (*When Time Shall Be No More*, xiii). The number of prophecy titles accelerated after World War II and the founding of Israel in 1948.

91. McAlister, *Epic Encounters*, 165.

92. Kirsch, "Interviews: Hal Lindsey," 30.

93. Ibid., 30–31.

94. Lindsey and Carlson, *The Late Great Planet Earth*, 7.

95. Ibid., chap. 1, 18.

96. Vanderwaal, *Hal Lindsey and Biblical Prophecy*, 53.

97. Radway, *Feeling for Books*, 278.

98. Lindsey and Carlson, *The Late Great Planet Earth*, 135.

99. Ibid., 64.

100. Mark Nelson, "A Classic"; Shirley Priscilla Johnson, "Midwest Book Review."

101. Vanderwaal, *Hal Lindsey and Biblical Prophecy*, 13.

102. Ibid., 15–16.

103. See, for example, Tinder, "Future Fact? Future Fiction?," 40: "The problem with the evangelicals who turn the Bible into a kind of crystal ball is that they show very little historical awareness."

104. Chris Hall, "What Hal Lindsey Taught Me about the Second Coming," 84. Ellwood argues that evangelicals think about Bible time as both past and continuously present. They— like first-century Christians—live in a world of miracles, expect the end of the world in this generation, and feel that Christ is a real, material presence in their lives. The version of this world they inhabit is permeated with the New Testament and was—they believe—foreordained by God in the scriptures. Evangelicals thus place themselves outside history by simultaneously inhabiting the world of today and the world of the New Testament (Ellwood, *One Way*, 31–32,

72–73). This way of reading texts—as both part of the past in which they were written and par-ticipating in/foretelling current events—resonates with what Michael Denning calls allegorical or typological reading, a way of reading associated with popular or working-class audiences (Denning, *Mechanic Accents*, 71–72).

105. Frykholm, *Rapture Culture*, 115.

106. Vanderwaal, *Hal Lindsey and Biblical Prophecy*, 88.

107. Ibid., 89.

108. See Radway, *Feeling for Books*, 152, 259, 277.

109. See Marsden, *Evangelicalism and Modern America*, x; and Boyer, *When Time Shall Be No More*, 304–11.

110. Gribben, *Writing the Rapture*, 3–4.

111. Quotation from Frykholm, *Rapture Culture*, 9. The body of theoretical writings on the history of the book addressing this issue is large. See, for example, de Certeau, *Practice of Everyday Life*, 165–76; Chartier, *Order of Books*, chap. 1; and Darnton, *Forbidden Bestsellers of Pre-Revolutionary France*, chap. 7.

112. The exception is *Rapture Culture*, Frykholm's study of *Left Behind* readers. Boyer addresses the question of his methodology in the preface to his book—he reads texts, because he is an intellectual historian and not a social scientist (*When Time Shall Be No More*, xii). Glenn Shuck addresses the creativity of readers as poachers only briefly in an epilogue (Shuck, *Marks of the Beast*, 206). Gribben thinks we need studies of readers of prophecy fiction, espe-cially since these readers are mostly white and male and American and may hold a great deal of cultural influence (*Writing the Rapture*, 24).

113. Luhrmann, *When God Talks Back*, 295.

Chapter 9

1. Gift, "One Spirit: Resources for the Spirit, Mind, and Body."

2. Kimberly Winston, "Religion Update: Opening New Pathways to Consumers."

3. For an overview of 1990s scholarship and polls related to religious belief, see Diane Winston, "Gallup Says America Has a Shallow Faith."

4. Robert Fuller, *Spiritual, but Not Religious*, 157; see also Tickle, *God Talk in America*, 33.

5. See Wuthnow, *After Heaven*, 123, 229; and Evenson, "Soulful Books Give Readers Insight."

6. Roof, *Generation of Seekers*, 5; see also Wuthnow, *After Heaven*, chap. 1.

7. Wuthnow, *After Heaven*, chap. 1, especially 3, 15.

8. Roof, *Generation of Seekers*, 5.

9. Wolfe, *Transformation of American Religion*, 44.

10. Bellah et al., *Habits of the Heart*; on "Sheilaism," see ibid., 221, 235.

11. Roof, *Spiritual Marketplace*, 10.

12. Roof, *Generation of Seekers*, 79. However, Alan Wolfe suggests that the "spiritual but not religious" category might be the new majority in the United States (*Transformation of American Religion*, 183). A 2012 Pew Research Center Religion and Public Life survey showed that one in five Americans (and one in three under the age of thirty) claimed no religious affiliation (researchers call them "the nones"), although many believed in God, prayed, or had other reli-gious/spiritual practices ("'Nones' on the Rise").

13. Roof, *Generation of Seekers*, 80.

14. Roof, *Spiritual Marketplace*, 98.

15. Rourke, "The Intimate Achievement."

16. The story of *Care of the Soul*'s publication is most completely told in Yoffe, "How the Soul Is Sold"; and Coughlin, "Best Seller That Can Touch the Soul."

17. Moore, *Care of the Soul*, xv. Subsequent page references are in the text.

18. Madrigal, "Finding the Soul of Life."

19. "A Deep, Caring Treatment of an Important Subject," Review of *Care of the Soul*, Amazon. com, 22 April 1999, Web, accessed 5 June 2001; "Pretentious, Dry and BORING!" Review of *Care of the Soul*, Amazon.com, 26 April 1998, Web, accessed 5 June 2001. See also "Very Little to Do with Care of the Soul," Review of *Care of the Soul*, Amazon.com, 19 February 1998, Web, accessed 5 June 2001.

20. McClurg, "Baby Boomers Become Sold on Souls"; Moriwaki, "Filling Deep Spring of Life."

21. See Lears, "From Salvation to Self-Realization"; and Lears, *No Place of Grace*.

22. Lieblich, "Nurture Your Soul with Enchantment."

23. See Butler, *Gender Trouble*; and Butler, *Bodies That Matter*.

24. Wuthnow's critique of Moore's "psychological polytheism" (*After Heaven*, 157–64) has influenced my discussion here.

25. See Jameson, *Postmodernism*.

26. Michael Kimmel offers a similar criticism. See Kimmel, "Thomas Moore's Bestselling Books Speak to an Age Hungry for Simpler Living."

27. Thomas Moore, *Soul Mates*, 13–14.

28. Lears, *No Place of Grace*, xv.

29. Armstrong, *History of God*, 391. Subsequent page references are in the text.

30. Some critics called her to task for just this pragmatism: "One cannot avoid the impression sometimes that Ms. Armstrong is much more concerned that our ideas of God be 'workable' and subjectively meaningful than that they in fact be true." See Haught, "Search for Higher Reality."

31. On readability, see Missing in Action, "If This Won't Shake Your Thinking, Nothing Will," Review of *A History of God*, Amazon.com, 18 April 2000, Web, accessed 11 August 2011. On its scholarliness or the difficulty of its prose, see Carmine Puleo, "HISTORY OF GOD," Review of *A History of God*, Amazon.com, 8 June 2009, Web, accessed 11 August 2011; Jimmy, "Not for the Casual Reader," Review of *A History of God*, Amazon.com, 13 April 2009, Web, accessed 11 August 2011; Darvish Shadravan "bigd," "Not What I Hoped For," Review of *A History of God*, Amazon.com, 22 December 2007, Web, accessed 11 August 2011; J. Wurzelmann, "Informative," Review of *A History of God*, Amazon.com, 21 May 2005, Web, accessed 11 August 2011; Tom Venman, "Superb Scholarship," Review of *A History of God*, 10 April 2005, Web, accessed 11 August 2011; Christopher Wingo, "A+ Read," Review of *A History of God*, Amazon.com, 4 January 2005, Web, accessed 11 August 2011; and JD in Rochester, "Good Book but Long Read," Review of *A History of God*, Amazon.com, 29 December 2004, Web, accessed 11 August 2011.

32. Witham, "God Is Now a Celebrity."

33. Ibid.

34. Lewis Chamberlain, "A Good Read for the Seeker," Review of *A History of God*, Amazon. com, 10 October 2001, Web, accessed 11 August 2011; Michael D. Sterken, "A True Work of Scholarship," Review of *A History of God*, Amazon.com, 12 October 2008, Web, accessed 11 August 2011. See also Richard Crist, "For Freethinkers Only," Review of *A History of God*, Amazon.com, 9 December 2004, Web, accessed 11 August 2011.

35. "Writing 'A History of God'"; Mason, "Tracing Three Religions, All with One God."

36. Johnson, "Immortal Longings."

37. Adelman, "Biography of God Like Nothing Else."

38. Shone, "Holy Unconvincing"; Gorenberg, "A Wild and Crazy Guy."

39. O'Reilly, "The Man Who Took a Close Look at God."

40. Miles, *God: A Biography*, 4. Subsequent page references are in the text.

41. Linda Thornton, "Scholarly with Room for Belief," Review of *God: A Biography*, Amazon.com, 19 April 2003, Web, accessed 11 August 2011; schapmock, "New Look at the Old Testament," Review of *God: A Biography*, 19 January 2002, Web, accessed 11 August 2011.

42. Book Sleuth, "A Very Refreshing Take on God," Review of *God: A Biography*, Amazon.com, 29 September 2009, Web, accessed 11 August 2011.

43. Reason, "A Fabulous Read," Review of *God: A Biography*, Amazon.com, 24 December 2001, Web, accessed 11 August 2011.

44. O'Reilly, "A 'Pious Agnostic' Puts Love of Neighbor First."

45. Biographical material is from the front matter of Miles, *God: A Biography*.

46. See Gregory Bascom, "Unquestionably Worth the Effort," Review of *God: A Biography*, Amazon.com, 5 May 2003, Web, accessed 11 August 2011; Edward J. Barton, "The Bible as Literature—God as the Protagonist," Review of *God: A Biography*, Amazon.com, 9 August 2011, Web, accessed 11 August 2011; Do-It-Yourself-Guy "Jake," "A Bit Scholarly at Times, but Mostly Interesting and Fun," Review of *God: A Biography*, Amazon.com, 15 December 2009, Web, accessed 11 August 2011; Lillian C. Harrison, "Well Intentioned, Perhaps," Review of *God: A Biography*, Amazon.com, 13 March 2009, Web, accessed 11 August 2011; L. Leeder, "Worthwhile but Heavy," Review of *God: A Biography*, Amazon.com, 24 November 2007, Web, accessed 11 August 2011; and Pingchung Chan, "God: A Biography," Review of *God: A Biography*, Amazon.com, 8 October 2005, Web, accessed 11 August 2011.

47. Spangler, Review of *The Cloister Walk*.

48. Mitchell and Nelson, "Place of the Spirit," 77–78.

49. Jacobs, Review of *The Cloister Walk*, 146–47; Willie Krischke, "Wisdom and Doubt," Review of *The Cloister Walk*, Amazon.com, 12 November 2000, Web, accessed 11 October 2001; Coles, "A School for Love."

50. Stroud, "Words of Wisdom," 17–18.

51. Timothy Kearney, "Take Notice Spiritual Journeyers," Review of *The Cloister Walk*, Amazon.com, 11 June 2003, Web, accessed 11 August 2011; Krischke, "Wisdom and Doubt."

52. A Customer, "LECTIO DIVINA, Indeed!," Review of *The Cloister Walk*, Amazon.com, 1 February 2000, Web, accessed 11 August 2011.

53. Norris, *The Cloister Walk*, xx. Subsequent page references are in the text.

54. Daphne.stevens@att.net, "Poetry and Liturgy," Review of *The Cloister Walk*, Amazon.com, 18 June 2000, Web, accessed 11 August 2011; A Customer, "Poetic, Pensive, and Thought-Provoking," Review of *The Cloister Walk*, Amazon.com, 15 May 1998, Web, accessed 11 August 2011; Angela Belt, "Glimpse of Peace," Review of *Cloister Walk*, Amazon.com, 8 June 2000, Web, accessed 11 August 2011.

55. A Customer, "A Soothing Book for Upsetting Times," Review of *The Cloister Walk*, Amazon.com, 2 July 1998, Web, accessed 11 August 2011.

56. Shawn Mc Elhinney, "An Excellent Book," Review of *The Cloister Walk*, Amazon.com, 7 April 2001, Web, accessed 11 October 2001; A Customer, "Aimless and Self-Absorbed," Review of *The Cloister Walk*, Amazon.com, 24 April 1998, Web, accessed 11 August 2011; Whimsy Taylor, "Self-Absorbed, Rambling, Scattered, Disjointed," Review of *The Cloister Walk*, Amazon.com, 1 October 2008, Web, accessed 11 August 2011.

57. Metaphor is at the center of Norris's spirituality. She argues that both fundamentalists and enforcers of "political correctness" have declared war on metaphor (*Cloister Walk*, 155).

58. Cunningham, "Monasticism, Newly Seen."

59. Michael Higgins, "Sources of Faith Need Not Be Disguised."

60. This way of reading is middlebrow in that it eschews distanced, aesthetic, or scholarly contemplation in favor of emotional engagement with texts that are imagined to be continuous with life. Great Books study groups of the early twentieth century insisted that students should read and discuss all the great works of Western civilization without any interpretive apparatus, as though each were written specifically to speak to our own condition. Norris is suggesting that collectively reading the Bible aloud is very much the same experience.

61. Ammerman, "Religious Identities and Religious Institutions."

62. Roof, *Spiritual Marketplace*, 75.

63. In this way, books for the seeker are very much like New Age literature and discourse. Paul Heelas argues that New Age ideas both arise from modern consumer capitalist culture and critique it. See Heelas, *New Age Movement*, chaps. 5 and 6.

64. Roof, *Spiritual Marketplace*, 75.

65. Schmidt, *Restless Souls*, 2, 6–7, 9.

Chapter 10

1. Roof, *Generation of Seekers*, 5, 80.

2. Members do embrace a set of shared principles. The Unitarian Universalist Association lists them: "The inherent worth and dignity of every person; justice, equity and compassion in human religions; the free and responsible search for truth and meaning; the right of conscience and the use of the democratic process within our congregations and in society at large; the goal of world community with peace, liberty and justice for all; respect for the interdependent web of all existence of which we are a part." See "Our Unitarian Universalist Principles."

3. Paulson, "'Words of Reverence' Roil a Church." On the history of Unitarians and Universalists, see Robinson, *The Unitarians and the Universalists*; Bumbaugh, *Unitarian Universalism*; Jacoby, *Freethinkers*; and Schmidt, *Restless Souls*.

4. Schmidt, *Restless Souls*, 2, 6–7, 9.

5. Robert Fuller, *Spiritual, but Not Religious*, 22.

6. Philip Jenkins argues that the flourishing market for books on the "hidden gospels" and the historical Jesus owes a great deal to small-group discussions at liberal mainline churches, especially Methodist, Presbyterian, United Church of Christ, and Unitarian Universalist (*Hidden Gospels*, 159–60).

7. Paulson, "'Words of Reverence' Roil a Church." The enthusiasm of these UU readers for Gnosticism may be related to their class privilege. David Brooks describes the spiritual life of what he calls the new ruling class, bourgeois bohemians ("Bobos"), as characterized by "individualistic pluralism," which resonates with UU spiritual seeking and its acceptance of divergent views (*Bobos in Paradise*, 234). Similarly, Robert Bellah argues that mysticism (that is, personal experience of the sacred) "is found most often among prosperous, well-educated people" (Bellah et al., *Habits of the Heart*, 246). In a more nuanced analysis of the place of social class in religious practices, Sean McCloud argues that "religious omnivores" are present across the class spectrum, although he concedes that this way of being in the world requires a kind of aesthetic distancing more characteristic of privileged people and that less-privileged religious omnivores often draw from a more restricted range of materials. See McCloud, *Divine Hierarchies*, 26–27.

8. There is a rich contemporary scholarship on the Gnostic gospels, much of it calling into question the unity or coherence of the Nag Hammadi texts and the usefulness of the term

"Gnostic" at all. See, for example, King, *What Is Gnosticism?*; and Ehrman, *Lost Christianities*. Less sympathetic readings of the Gnostic gospels include Jenkins, *Hidden Gospels*; and Groothuis, *Jesus in an Age of Controversy*, especially chaps. 5 and 6. What matters for my purposes here is not scholarly understandings of these texts, but the effects of sometimes incorrect *popular* understandings in readers' everyday lives. For an overview of the scholarly debates about Gnosticism, see Byrne, "End of Gnosticism?" For an examination of the tensions between scholarly and popular understandings of Gnosticism, see Byrne, "'Code' Breakers."

9. The group focused on Christian spirituality its first year but was reimagined to include books emerging from many faith traditions. Though many UUs have a Christian or Jewish or Buddhist practice, others practice a this-worldly humanist faith or agnosticism. There were sometimes tensions over what shared worship ought to look like. One reader described some members of the church as "fundamentalist atheists," who had no patience with God or God language and saw such traditional religious belief as backward. Another reader—a Christian— explained that she felt "in the closet" about Jesus and her prayer life, a vocabulary available to church members because of the large LGBT community at the church. The congregation had, in fact, been engaged in a conversation about the use of religious language—"God" versus "a higher power," "prayer" versus "meditation" or "contemplation"—as part of a denomination-wide consideration of the issue at the urging of the president of the Unitarian Universalist Association. See Sinkford, "Our Calling."

10. *Adult Religious Education Bulletin*, Fall 2001.

11. Megan Sweeney argues in her study of women's reading in prison that books serve a similar purpose for many incarcerated women. As her research progressed, Sweeney realized that the specific book read mattered less than the quality of discussion about it: "The books served as a kind of connective tissue; they enabled interaction and dialogue, and they fostered women's engagements with characters, with other readers, with the outside world, and with developing versions of themselves" (*Reading Is My Window*, 228).

12. Unless otherwise specified, all quotations are from the monthly meetings of the Spirituality Book Discussion Group. This research is based on participation in the book group, observation/participation in larger church activities, and three unstructured interviews with members of the reading group focusing on their "spiritual autobiographies" in 2004 and 2005, which lasted, on average, two hours.

13. Bielo, *Words upon the Word*, 50.

14. Luhrmann, *When God Talks Back*, 91; see also ibid., 12, 89.

15. On the middlebrow, see Radway, *Feeling for Books*, especially chaps. 3 and 8; and Rubin, *Making of Middlebrow Culture*.

16. I thank Elizabeth Turner, who heard an early presentation of this material, for suggesting the term. Megan Sweeney similarly found that "discussing books with others also served as a kind of 'consciousness-raising process' that enabled women to validate their own views as legitimate or understandable" (*Reading Is My Window*, 238). Alan Wolfe suggests that conservative Christian women's Bible studies are like consciousness-raising groups (*Transformation of American Religion*, 131–32).

17. James Bielo identifies negotiating religious identity as one of the key roles of evangelical group Bible study, including the emphasis on distinguishing one's own religious community from other, less worthy ones (*Words upon the Word*, chap. 6).

18. Unitarian Universalist Association president William G. Sinkford called for readers to write in with their "elevator speeches" in his "Our Calling" column of March/April 2003. Responses were published in several subsequent issues. See, for example, "Affirmations: Elevator Speeches."

19. Clark, *From Angels to Aliens*, 45; see also Eck, *New Religious America*.

20. Clark, *From Angels to Aliens*, 45.

21. Pagels, *Beyond Belief*, 136–42.

22. This part of this chapter about UUs as a spiritual/intellectual aristocracy also made some members who read it in draft form uncomfortable. One did not disagree with my account and conceded she had encountered similar attitudes elsewhere in the church but did not think the term "intellectual aristocracy" was accurate. "Do we really sound that patronizing?" she asked. There is some evidence that a similar dynamic functions in UU communities nationwide. In a 1997 denomination-wide survey, the most commonly selected multiple choice answer to "What tickles your spiritual funny bone?" was, "UUs claim to be seekers at the same time we act like we have the answers" (31.3 percent). See "Fulfilling the Promise: The 1997 Unitarian Universalism Needs and Aspirations Survey."

23. In these ways, UUs participated in all three major target audiences for books on the hidden gospels, according to Philip Jenkins, who identifies women, seekers, and those with commitments to Eastern religion and philosophies as particularly engaged by this scholarship (*Hidden Gospels*, 17).

24. See "Fulfilling the Promise: The 1997 Unitarian Universalism Needs and Aspirations Survey." Although most respondents came to UU churches because the UU faith "made sense" to them, Christians were more likely to cite dissatisfaction with another church as a reason to join a UU congregation.

25. See Porterfield, *Transformation of American Religion*, chap. 4; Tickle, *God-Talk in America*; and Tickle, *Re-discovering the Sacred*.

26. This was true of one reader with whom I conducted an in-depth interview. At the time of the interview, she was having difficulty juggling her religious commitments to this church and those to her Buddhist community, wondering whether she ought to maintain her ties to the UU church at all.

27. The Thomas for whom the Gnostic Gospel of Thomas is incorrectly named (it is attributed to him by legend only) was a missionary to India (suggesting one possible avenue through which Hinduism or Buddhism may have influenced this scripture). See Pagels, *Gnostic Gospels*, 27.

28. Pagels, *Beyond Belief*, 74.

29. The appeal of the Gnostic gospels extended to the larger church community. In May 2006, a "UU Christians" group began meeting on Thursday nights. One of their early topics was "Lost Christianities: Christian Scriptures and the Battles over Authentication," which examined the social construction of orthodoxy and heresy in the early church (Church Bulletin, 11, 18 June 2006).

30. On the numerous nineteenth-century feminists whose commitment to gender equity arose from Unitarian and Universalist backgrounds (including Margaret Fuller, Elizabeth Palmer Peabody, Judith Sargent Murray, and Olympia Brown), see Robinson, *The Unitarians and the Universalists*, 126–32.

31. Feminism or "the feminine" is widely held to be a critical and growing component of American spirituality more broadly. See especially Tickle, *God-Talk in America*, 115.

32. Scholarship on historical and contemporary women's reading groups includes Elizabeth Long, *Book Clubs*; Hartley, *Reading Groups*; Gere, *Intimate Practices*; and Sicherman, *Well-Read Lives*. Most studies suggest that 65 to 70 percent of reading groups are women's groups and that in mixed-gender groups women are usually in the majority.

33. McVey, "Gnosticism, Feminism, and Elaine Pagels."

34. Ibid., 499; Jenkins, *Hidden Gospels*, 146.

35. See Ammerman, "Religious Identities and Religious Institutions."

36. Clark, *From Angels to Aliens*, 11.

37. The kinds of identity narratives UU readers created resemble those created in the actively interfaith "Common Ground" adult education courses studied by Kelly Besecke, in which "the language of reflexive spirituality" became a cultural resource members shared in their discussion of meaning. Besecke rethinks reflexive spirituality for a group or community context, arguing that this language is committed to both modern rationality and transcendent meaning. Common Ground readers share a language of metaphoric interpretation, mysticism (an experiential way of making meaning), pluralism, and reflexivity (taking a critical distance on spirituality and revising in light of new knowledge). See Besecke, "Speaking of Meaning in Modernity."

38. McVey, "Gnosticism, Feminism, and Elaine Pagels." 499. Similarly, Philip Jenkins argues: "Despite its dubious sources and controversial methods, the new Jesus scholarship of the 1980s and 1990s gained such a following because it told a lay audience what it wanted to hear. . . . Generally the hidden gospels offer wonderful news for liberals, feminists, and radicals within the churches, who challenge what they view as outdated institutions and prejudices" (*Hidden Gospels*, 16). For a critique for a general audience, see Douthat, *Bad Religion*, chap. 5. Douthat is focused on the way these books undermine religious institutions.

39. Dan Brown, *The Da Vinci Code*. Subsequent page references are in the text.

40. In October 2004 (a year after the book discussion), the head minister preached a sermon entitled, "The Da Vinci Code: It's Just a Novel! Or Is It?" At an annual church auction, she had offered up a sermon to be preached on a topic chosen by the highest bidder. The highest bidder wanted to hear about *The Da Vinci Code*. She confirmed my sense that this was a book for us, one that brought up issues we had long been concerned with—the humanity of Jesus, feminism and spirituality, the metaphorical-versus-literal truth of scriptures—and that it was nice to finally have some company in the larger culture to talk about these issues with. In addition, shortly before the film opened in May 2006, the adult religious education program ran a series of lectures on the sacred feminine, the first of which was called "Decoding *The Da Vinci Code*."

41. T. M. Luhrmann, a psychological anthropologist, similarly found that her "scholars' questions" ("I wanted to know about the text, its history, and its construction") were at odds with the ways of reading characteristic of the Vineyard Christian Fellowship members she was studying (*When God Talks Back*, 91–92).

42. *The Da Vinci Code* sold 46 million copies in forty countries before the release of the film version in May 2006. For one representative example of popular coverage focusing on its truth claims, see "Untangling Novels' Facts from Fiction." In 2006, there were forty-four books from Amazon.com that promised to separate truth from fiction in *The Da Vinci Code* (see Weiss, "Ripping 'The Da Vinci Code.'"). For a thorough debunking of Brown's truth claims, see chap. 6, "Holy Blood, Holy Grail, Holy Shit," in Aaronovitch, *Voodoo Histories*. This emphasis on truth resonates with the aesthetic/ethos that Ted Striphas argues characterized Oprah's Book Club, in which the emphasis on the reality of books (novels, memoirs, autobiographies) rendered these genre distinctions irrelevant to readers (*Late Age of Print*, chap. 4, especially 125–30).

43. Aaronovitch argues that conspiracy theories—stereotypes aside—are largely circulated among educated, middle-class people. Moreover, belief in the conspiracy is presumed to grant an individual membership in an intellectual aristocracy that sees through the official version of events (*Voodoo Histories*, 338–39, 11).

44. Fuel was added to the fire when ABC ran an hour-long prime-time special on 3 November 2003 (in most markets), "Jesus, Mary, and Da Vinci," which sought (what else?) to

investigate the truth of the claims made by Brown in the novel. The prime-time special was preempted in this market, however, by a celebration for a departing local newscaster and moved to the wee hours of the morning until protests from viewers gave it an early Sunday morning run.

45. This function—to prepare readers to engage publicly with people of other faiths—is in line with James Bielo's argument that one of the functions of evangelical group Bible study is as backstage "practice" for witnessing to nonbelievers whom participants might encounter in daily life (*Words upon the Word*, chap. 5).

46. One reader, who called herself "a great skimmer," seldom finished any of the books, preferring to read for the gist to equip herself for discussion and argument with the "values voters" who were her neighbors and colleagues. A member of a number of activist churches in the past, this reader was impatient with much of the focus on developing a personal spiritual practice at this church, which she saw as a distraction from the social justice issues that were the backbone of her faith.

47. Readers in the group thought of reading in several—sometimes competing—ways. For some, reading was a spiritual practice, a time for quiet contemplation and centering oneself (that might or might not shape political or social action). For others, reading was a way to equip oneself for activist citizenship. Because of these different orientations, readers had divergent opinions about the best kinds of books to read—novels, social/political commentary, theology, and so on. To some extent, these (sometimes competing) orientations—spiritual practice versus social activism—were present in the larger church community.

48. Wolfe, *Transformation of American Religion*, 36.

49. Ibid., 74.

50. Luhrmann, *When God Talks Back*, 296; see also ibid., 3, 101. "These [faith] practices share a good deal with psychotherapy, and they have a great side benefit. They enable churches like the Vineyard to deliver emotionally to their congregants—to make their congregants feel better about themselves—even when the faith of those congregants is weak" (101).

51. The adult religious education director, who facilitated discussion on one book she had recommended, made a point to thank everyone for being so open and generous about their own struggles. Readers sometimes thanked each other for being particularly good listeners or for being particularly forthcoming.

52. See Bielo, *Words upon the Word*, chap. 3.

53. See especially Griffith, *God's Daughters*, chaps. 1 and 3.

54. Reading and study are held in such high regard that congregants were sometimes urged by their leaders to stop reading and start living/doing/acting. For example, when small-group fellowship groups were being organized, participants were explicitly discouraged from reading together at their regular meetings. The founding facilitator of the Spirituality Book Group stepped down when she reached a place where she felt it was time to "stop reading and start praying."

55. Frykholm, *Rapture Culture*, 115. See also Luhrmann, *When God Talks Back*, 89: "The form of Bible study that dominates small house groups in most evangelical churches and in campus ministry is a method that turns a sometimes obscure text into a story that is personally specific to the reader. In this method, you take a passage . . . and you talk about what the passage says, what it means, and how it applies to your life. This is not about scholarship. You do not, in this method, learn about when the scripture was written or which other scriptures it cites—not that there would be anything wrong with that, but it simply isn't the goal of the method." Christian publisher Tyndale House publishes a series, *Life Application Study Bibles*, which include notes

and guides demonstrating the contemporary relevance of the Bible. That is to say that this way of reading receives significant institutional support in the packaging and marketing of Bibles. Although I would characterize the UU readers in this group as "life-application method" readers, many also participated in religious education classes that did center on historical scholarship—the Jesus Seminar, the canonization of the books of the New Testament, ancient Greek philosophy, the history of early Christianity, and so on. Wolfe argues that classes such as these are usually found in liberal or mainline churches. The assumption in such churches is that a highly educated clerical elite has tutorial responsibilities to less-learned congregants (*Transformation of American Religion*, 84, 93). The therapeutic (life-application) model and the education model coexisted in this reading group, although the life-application method of reading was dominant.

56. Frykholm, *Rapture Culture*, 11.

57. Ibid., 132, 16.

58. Citing its emphasis on secret knowledge (*gnosis*), Timothy Beal calls *The Da Vinci Code* "a book of revelation in thriller form." Since the *Left Behind* books are arguably *the* Book of Revelation in thriller form, the parallel I am drawing between the two seems fitting. See Beal, "Opinion: Just a Closer Walk."

59. There were two long-standing women's groups at the church—one that met during the day (designed for homemakers) and one that met at night (for women who worked outside the home).

60. Neal, *Romancing God*, 13.

61. On evangelical feminism, see Cochrane, *Evangelical Feminism*. Studies that address wifely submission in theory and in practice include Griffith, *God's Daughters*, especially 4–5, 44–45, chap. 6; Brasher, *Godly Women*; Gallagher, *Evangelical Identity and Gendered Family Life*; and Stacey, *Brave New Families*.

62. There are (quite necessary) feminist critiques of the ways contemporary discourse emphasizes Mary Magdalene's role as a wife/mother, rather than as a disciple or apostle possessing intellectual and spiritual equality with men. See, for example, the scholars quoted in Darman and Underwood, "An Inconvenient Woman."

63. Neal, *Romancing God*, 178.

64. That readers tend to read books that confirm their beliefs and affirm their identities is supported by a 2006 Baylor University study of America's religious landscape. Sociologists surveyed 1,700 American adults about their religious beliefs and practices, including the reading of sacred texts and popular books. The survey confirmed that "people mostly read within their own religious affiliation" and identified two main "camps": evangelicals (*Left Behind*, *Purpose-Driven Life*) and New Age (*Celestine Prophecy*). Of respondents, 19 percent reported reading a *Left Behind* book and 19 percent reported reading *Purpose-Driven Life*. The most popular book was *The Da Vinci Code* (28.5 percent of respondents reported reading it), although the more often a respondent attended church, the less likely she or he was to have read it. See Hilliard, "Baylor Study Offers Data on Reading Habits."

65. Contemporary ethnographies include Bielo, *Words upon the Word*; Luhrmann, *When God Talks Back*; Frykholm, *Rapture Culture*; and Neal, *Romancing God*. On the history of evangelical reading and writing practices in America, see Candy Gunther Brown, *Word in the World*; and Nord, *Faith in Reading*.

66. The predominance of work on evangelicals is recent. As Robert Orsi explains, liberal or mainline Protestant churches were normative in the early years of religious studies in the United States and structured the graduate training of scholars (*Between Heaven and Earth*, 188–90).

Conclusion

1. Richard Higgins, "Sold on Spirituality," 19.

2. Barton, *Man Nobody Knows* (Stone Mountain, Georgia: GA Publishing, 1998).

3. The "terrorist" edition is Peale, *Power of Positive Thinking* (New York: Fireside, 2003), 21.

4. Burke, "Literature as Equipment for Living."

5. Laurie Beth Jones, *Jesus, CEO.*

6. For an overview of the history of social class as a category in religious studies scholarship, see McCloud, *Divine Hierarchies.*

7. See Ehrenreich, *Bright-Sided.*

8. Sedgwick, *Touching Feeling*, 155. See also Felski, *Uses of Literature*, 12: "That one person immerses herself in the joys of *Jane Eyre*, while another views it as a symptomatic expression of Victorian imperialism, often has less to do with the political beliefs of those involved than their position in different scenes of readings."

9. See, for example, Felski, *Uses of Literature*; Sedgwick, *Touching Feeling*, especially chap. 4; Marcus, *Between Women*; and Moretti, *Graphs, Maps, Trees.* For an overview of this literature, see the fall 2009 special issue of *Representations* titled "The Way We Read Now," edited by Sharon Marcus and Stephen Best with Emily Apter and Elaine Freedgood. See especially Best and Marcus, "Surface Reading: An Introduction." See also the 2010 special issue of *New Literary History* on "New Sociologies of Literature," edited by James English and Rita Felski; see especially English, "Everywhere and Nowhere."

10. Orsi, "Everyday Miracles," 7.

11. Gere, *Intimate Practices*; Elizabeth Long, *Book Clubs*; Sicherman, *Well-Read Lives.*

12. Wuthnow, *Sharing the Journey*, 148.

13. James Bielo argues that Bible study is where religion happens, that the kind of self-reflexive, active consideration of religious belief and practice that Bible study provides is like nothing else (*Words upon the Word*, 7). Chapter 4 addresses how readers' outside interests shaped group discussions.

14. Ibid., chap. 6.

15. Hedstrom, *Rise of Liberal Religion*, 7.

16. Luhrmann, *When God Talks Back*, 296; see also ibid., 3, 101.

17. Aubry, *Reading as Therapy*, 1.

18. Luhrmann, *When God Talks Back*, 2.

19. Orsi, "Sacred Superheroes." I am grateful to Orsi for sending me a copy of his paper.

20. *RBC Bulletin*, April 1930, 4, LC.

21. Jackson, *Word and Its Witness*, 163.

22. Orsi, "Everyday Miracles," 7.

BIBLIOGRAPHY

Archival Collections

Bloomington, Indiana
    Lilly Library, Indiana University
        Appleton-Century Manuscripts
        Bobbs-Merrill Manuscripts
Boston, Massachusetts
    Howard Gotlieb Archival Research Center, Boston University
        Joshua Loth Liebman Collection
Madison, Wisconsin
    Wisconsin Historical Society Archives
        Bruce Barton Papers
New York, New York
    Burke Library at Union Theological Seminary, Columbia University Libraries
        UTS Collection
            Harry Emerson Fosdick Papers
Syracuse, New York
    Special Collections Research Center, Syracuse University
        Norman Vincent Peale Papers
Topeka, Kansas
    Center for Historical Research, Kansas State Historical Society
        Charles Monroe Sheldon/Central Congregational Church Manuscript Collection
Tucson, Arizona
    Special Collections at the University of Arizona Libraries
        Harold Bell Wright Papers
Washington, D.C.
    Library of Congress
        Religious Book Club Bulletin

Books, Articles, and Theses

Aaronovitch, David. *Voodoo Histories: The Role of the Conspiracy Theory in Shaping Modern History*. New York: Riverhead Books, 2010.

Abrams, Douglas Carl. *Selling the Old-Time Religion: American Fundamentalists and Mass Culture, 1920–1940*. Athens: University of Georgia Press, 2001.

Adams, James L. "Moving Religion Markct." *Christianity Today*, 25 August 1972, 44.

Adelman, Ken. "Biography of God Like Nothing Else." *Washington Times*, 28 July 1995, A21.

Advertisement for *Helen of the Old House*. *Publishers Weekly*, 29 January 1921, front cover.

"Affirmations: Elevator Speeches." *UU World: The Magazine of the Unitarian Universalist Association* 17, no. 5 (September/October 2003), http://www.uuworld.org/2003/05/

affirmations.html, and 17, no. 6 (November/December 2003), http://www.uuworld
.org/2003/06/affirmations.html. Accessed 26 August 2006.

Ahlstrom, Sydney. *A Religious History of the American People*. New Haven: Yale University
Press, 1972.

"Amazing Novelty in Book Advertising." *Publishers Weekly*, 1 October 1921, 1145.

Ammerman, Nancy T. "Golden Rule Christianity: Lived Religion in the American Mainstream."
In *Lived Religion in America: Toward a History of Practice*, edited by David D. Hall, 196–216.
Princeton: Princeton University Press, 1997.

———. "Religious Identities and Religious Institutions." In *Handbook for the Sociology of
Religion*, edited by Michele Dillon, 207–24. Cambridge: Cambridge University Press,
2003.

"Another Book Club." *Publishers Weekly*, 14 April 1928, 1624.

"Appleton Wins First Prize at Advertising Convention." *Publishers Weekly*, 12 November 1921,
1664.

Armstrong, Karen. *A History of God: The 4,000-Year Quest of Judaism, Christianity, and Islam*.
New York: Ballantine, 1993.

Ashton, Rosemary. "Introduction." In *Robert Elsmere*, by Mrs. Humphry Ward. New York:
Oxford University Press, 1987.

Aubry, Timothy. *Reading as Therapy: What Contemporary Fiction Does for Middle-Class
Americans*. Iowa City: University of Iowa Press, 2011.

B.A.B. "A Review of the ABA Panels: Religious Market and Beyond." *Publishers Weekly*, 26 June
1978, 81.

Baldwin, Charles C. *The Men Who Make Our Novels*. New York: Moffat Yard, 1919.

Baron, Ava. "An 'Other' Side of Gender Antagonism at Work: Men, Boys, and the
Remasculinization of Printers' Work, 1830–1920." In *Work Engendered: Toward a New History
of American Labor*, edited by Ava Baron, 47–69. Ithaca: Cornell University Press, 1991.

Barton, Bruce. *The Book Nobody Knows*. Indianapolis: Bobbs-Merrill, 1926.

———. *He Upset the World*. Indianapolis: Bobbs-Merrill, 1931, 1932.

———. *The Man Nobody Knows*. Stone Mountain, Georgia: GA Publishing, 1998.

———. *The Man Nobody Knows: A Discovery of the Real Jesus*. 1925. Chicago: Ivan R. Dee, 2000.

———. *What Can a Man Believe?* Indianapolis: Bobbs-Merrill, 1928.

Beal, Timothy K. "Opinion: Just a Closer Walk with 'The Da Vinci Code.' " *Chronicle of Higher
Education*, 25 May 2006, 7.

Bederman, Gail. *Manliness and Civilization: A Cultural History of Gender and Race in the
United States, 1880–1917*. Chicago: University of Chicago Press, 1995.

———. " 'The Women Have Had Charge of the Church Work Long Enough': The Men
and Religion Forward Movement of 1911–1912 and the Masculinization of Middle-Class
Protestantism." *American Quarterly* 41, no. 3 (September 1989): 432–65.

Bellah, Robert N., Richard Madsen, William M. Sullivan, Ann Swidler, and Steven M. Tipton.
Habits of the Heart: Individualism and Commitment in American Life. Berkeley: University of
California Press, 1985, 1996.

Bennett, Tony, Mike Savage, and Elizabeth Bortolaia. *Culture, Class, Distinction*. Hoboken:
Taylor and Francis, 2008.

Besecke, Kelly. "Speaking of Meaning in Modernity: Reflexive Spirituality as a Cultural
Resource." *Sociology of Religion* 62, no. 3 (2001): 365–81.

Best, Stephen, and Sharon Marcus. "Surface Reading: An Introduction." *Representations* 108
(Fall 2009): 1–21.

"Bibles and Best Sellers." *Publishers Weekly*, 6 October 1923, 1219.

Bielo, James S. *Words upon the Word: An Ethnography of Evangelical Group Bible Study*. New York: New York University Press, 2009.

Bivins, Jason C. *Religion of Fear: The Politics of Horror in Conservative Evangelicalism*. New York: Oxford University Press, 2008.

Blair, Amy. *Reading Up: Middle-Class Readers and the Culture of Success in the Early Twentieth-Century United States*. Philadelphia: Temple University Press, 2011.

Blodgett, Jan. *Protestant Evangelical Literary Culture and Contemporary Society*. Westport, Conn.: Greenwood Press, 1997.

Boersma, T. *Is the Bible a Jigsaw Puzzle . . . An Evaluation of Hal Lindsey's Writings*. St. Catherines, Ontario: Paideia Press, 1978.

"Books for the Minister." *Publishers Weekly*, 16 February 1929, 760.

"Booming Religion as a Business Proposition." *Christian Century*, 21 May 1925, 658.

Bork, Kennard Baker. *Cracking Rocks and Defending Democracy: Kirtley Fletcher Mather, Scientist, Teacher, Social Activist, 1888–1978*. San Francisco: Pacific Division AAAS, 1994.

Botshon, Lisa, and Meredith Goldsmith, eds. *Middlebrow Moderns: Popular American Women Writers of the 1920s*. Boston: Northeastern University Press, 2003.

Bourdieu, Pierre. *Distinction: A Social Critique of the Judgment of Taste*, translated by Richard Nice. Cambridge: Harvard University Press, 1984.

Boyer, Paul S. "From Tracts to Mass-Market Paperbacks: Spreading the Word via the Printed Page in America from the Early National Era to the Present." In *Religion and the Culture of Print in Modern America*, edited by Charles L. Cohen and Paul S. Boyer, 14–38. Madison: University of Wisconsin Press, 2008.

———. "In His Steps: A Reappraisal." *American Quarterly* 23, no. 1 (Spring 1971): 60–78.

———. "John Darby Meets Saddam Hussein: Foreign Policy and Bible Prophecy." *Chronicle of Higher Education*, 14 February 2003, B12.

———. *When Time Shall Be No More: Prophecy Belief in Modern American Culture*. Cambridge: Harvard University Press, 1992.

Bradley, Dwight. "A Lending Library in the Church." *Publishers Weekly*, 18 March 1922, 847.

Brasher, Brenda E. *Godly Women: Fundamentalism and Female Power*. New Brunswick: Rutgers University Press, 1998.

Brodhead, Richard. *Cultures of Letters: Scenes of Reading and Writing in Nineteenth-Century America*. Chicago: University of Chicago Press, 1993.

Brooks, David. *Bobos in Paradise: The New Upper Class and How They Got There*. New York: Simon and Schuster, 2000.

Brooks, Peter. *The Melodramatic Imagination: Balzac, Henry James, Melodrama, and the Mode of Excess*. New Haven: Yale University Press, 1976.

Brown, Anne S., and David D. Hall. "Family Strategies and Religious Practice: Baptism and the Lord's Supper in Early New England." In *Lived Religion in America: Toward a History of Practice*, edited by David D. Hall, 41–68. Princeton: Princeton University Press, 1997.

Brown, Candy Gunther. *The Word in the World: Evangelical Writing, Publishing, and Reading in America, 1789–1880*. Chapel Hill: University of North Carolina Press, 2004.

Brown, Dan. *The Da Vinci Code*. New York: Doubleday, 2003.

Brown, Matthew J. *The Pilgrim and the Bee: Reading Rituals and Book Culture in Early New England*. Philadelphia: University of Pennsylvania Press, 2007.

Bumbaugh, David E. *Unitarian Universalism: A Narrative History*. Chicago: Meadville Lombard Press, 2000.

Burford, C. C. Untitled review of *On Being a Real Person. Champaign (Ill.) News-Gazette*, 25 April 1943.

Burke, Kenneth. "Literature as Equipment for Living." In *The Philosophy of Literary Form*, 3rd ed., 293–304. Berkeley: University of California Press, 1973.

Butler, Judith. *Bodies That Matter: On the Discursive Limits of "Sex."* New York: Routledge, 1993.

———. *Gender Trouble: Feminism and the Subversion of Identity.* New York: Routledge, 1990.

Byrne, Richard. "'Code' Breakers." *Chronicle of Higher Education*, 5 May 2006, A21.

———. "The End of Gnosticism?" *Chronicle of Higher Education*, 5 May 2006, A18.

C.B.G. "'Hidden' Best Sellers among Religious Books." *Publishers Weekly*, 28 February 1972, 45.

———. "Religion Publishers Cite Growing Trend to Paperbacks." *Publishers Weekly*, 18 October 1976, 24, 26.

———. "Religion Publishers View Grim Teen Attitudes." *Publishers Weekly*, 14 April 1975, 46.

———. "Religion Publishers View Mass Market Paperbacks." *Publishers Weekly*, 18 February 1974, 45.

———. "Religious Books: The Season's Top Titles." *Publishers Weekly*, 13 September 1976, 61.

———. "Religious Publishers Confident They Can Keep Pace with the 70s." *Publishers Weekly*, 8 March 1971, 33, 34.

———. "Religious Publishing: In Transition to What?" *Publishers Weekly*, 9 March 1970, 61.

Cannon, Lou. *Governor Reagan: His Rise to Power.* New York: Public Affairs, 2003.

Carlson, James. "A New Generation Christian Bookstore." *Publishers Weekly*, 30 November 1970, 28–29.

Cate, Curtis. "God and Success." *Atlantic Monthly*, April 1957, 75.

"Catholic Book Club Names Directors." *Publishers Weekly*, 5 May 1928, 1856.

Cavert, Samuel McCrea. "What Religious Books Are Read." *Publishers Weekly*, 16 February 1929, 752.

———. "A Year's Additions to the Church Library." *Publishers Weekly*, 18 February 1928, 663.

Cawelti, John G. *Adventure, Mystery, and Romance: Formula Stories as Art and Popular Culture.* Chicago: University of Chicago Press, 1976.

Chartier, Roger. "Culture as Appropriation: Popular Cultural Uses in Early Modern France." In *Understanding Popular Culture: Europe from the Middle Ages to the Nineteenth Century*, edited by Steven Kaplan, 229–54. New York: Mouton, 1984.

———. *The Order of Books: Readers, Authors, and Libraries in Europe between the Fourteenth and Eighteenth Centuries*, translated by Lydia G. Cochrane. Stanford, Calif.: Stanford University Press, 1994.

———. "*The Order of Books* Revisited." *Modern Intellectual History* 4, no. 3 (2007): 509–19.

Churchill, Winston. *The Inside of the Cup.* New York: Macmillan, 1913.

Clark, Lynn Schofield. *From Angels to Aliens: Teenagers, the Media, and the Supernatural.* New York: Oxford University Press, 2003.

Clemenko, Harold B. "The Man behind 'Peace of Mind.'" *Look*, 6 January 1948, 15.

Cochrane, Pamela D. H. *Evangelical Feminism: A History.* New York: New York University Press, 2005.

Coles, Robert. "A School for Love." *New York Times*, 5 May 1996, section 7, p. 12.

"Communism's Public Enemy Number One." *Chicago Daily News*, 11 June 1955, 1.

Cooney, Terry A. *The Rise of the New York Intellectuals:* Partisan Review *and Its Circle.* Madison: University of Wisconsin Press, 1986.

Cooper, Fredric Taber. "The Popularity of Harold Bell Wright." *Bookman*, January 1915, 498–500.

Cosulich, Bernice. "Crumbs from the Table of Success: An Interview with Harold Bell Wright." *Writer's Monthly*, December 1925, 503–5.

———. "The Methods of Harold Bell Wright." *Editor*, 16 August 1924, 55–57.

———. "Mr. Wright Builds a Boat." *Sunset Magazine*, August 1927, 66.

Coughlin, Ruth. "A Best Seller That Can Touch the Soul." *Chicago Sun-Times*, 24 October 1993, 14.

Coultrap-McQuin, Susan Margaret. *Doing Literary Business: American Women Writers in the Nineteenth Century*. Chapel Hill: University of North Carolina Press, 1990.

"Creating Religious Book Interest." *Publishers Weekly*, 10 November 1928, 1985.

Crosby, Donald. *God, Church, and Flag: Senator Joseph R. McCarthy and the Catholic Church, 1950–1957*. Chapel Hill: University of North Carolina Press, 1978.

"Crossroad Acquires Two Religious Book Clubs." *Publishers Weekly*, 11 November 1988, 14.

Cunningham, Lawrence. "Monasticism, Newly Seen." *Commonweal*, 1 May 1996, 26.

"Currents." *Publishers Weekly*, 28 September 1970, 39–40.

"Currents: Interest in Religion, Crisis in the Market." *Publishers Weekly*, 9 March 1970, 33.

"Currents: Religious Publishers Study Their Market." *Publishers Weekly*, 9 March 1970, 33.

Curtis, Susan. *A Consuming Faith: The Social Gospel and Modern American Culture*. Baltimore: Johns Hopkins University Press, 1991.

Darman, Jonathan, and Anne Underwood. "An Inconvenient Woman." *Newsweek* (Pacific Edition), 29 May 2006, 44–53.

Darnton, Robert. *The Forbidden Bestsellers of Pre-Revolutionary France*. New York: Norton, 1995.

Davidson, Cathy N. *Revolution and the Word: The Rise of the Novel in America*. New York: Oxford University Press, 1986.

Davies, Wilbur High. "Selling Religious Books." *Publishers Weekly*, 16 February 1929, 751.

Davis, George T. B. "Charles M. Sheldon, Novelist." *Our Day* 18, no. 3 (March 1899), 74–77.

Davis, Simone Weil. *Living Up to the Ads: Gender Fictions of the 1920s*. Durham: Duke University Press, 2000.

De Certeau, Michel. *The Practice of Everyday Life*, translated by Steven R. Rendell. Berkeley: University of California Press, 1984.

Delloff, Linda Marie. "ABCs of the CBA." *Christian Century*, 12 September 1979, 840–41.

Denning, Michael. *Mechanic Accents: Dime Novels and Working-Class Culture in America*. Rev. ed. New York: Verso, 1998.

Dickinson, Asa. *Best Books of Our Time, 1901–1925*. New York: H. W. Wilson, 1931.

Dillon, Kay Putnam. "Christian Booksellers Have Cause to Celebrate." *Publishers Weekly*, 12 August 1974, 40–41.

D.M. "Religious Backlist: The Strongest Category." *Publishers Weekly*, 13 September 1976, 78–79.

Donadio, Rachel. "Faith-Based Publishing." *New York Times*, 28 November 2004, BR35.

Dorrien, Gary. *The Making of American Liberal Theology: Idealism, Realism, and Modernity, 1900–1950*. Louisville: Westminster John Knox Press, 2003.

Douglas, Ann. *The Feminization of American Culture*. New York: Knopf, 1977.

Douthat, Ross. *Bad Religion: How We Became a Nation of Heretics*. New York: Free Press, 2012.

"Do You Believe the America of Our Ideals Really Exists?" *McCall's Magazine*, June 1925, 4.

Durant, John, ed. *Darwinism and Divinity: Essays on Evolution and Religious Belief*. New York: Blackwell, 1985.

Dwyer, James. "Books." *Commonweal*, 1 July 1925, 214.

Eck, Diana L. *A New Religious America: How a "Christian Country" Has Now Become the World's Most Religiously Diverse Nation*. San Francisco: HarperSanFrancisco, 2001.

"Editorial Comment: Publishing in an Age of Mergers." *Christian Century*, 16 November 1977, 1051.

"Editorial Comment: Religious Books and the Critic's Task." *Christian Century*, 17 May 1978, 523.

Ehrenreich, Barbara. *Bright-Sided: How Positive Thinking Is Undermining America*. New York: Metropolitan, 2009.

Ehrhardt, Julia. *Writers of Conviction: The Personal Politics of Zona Gale, Dorothy Canfield Fisher, Josephine Herbst, and Rose Wilder Lane*. Columbia: University of Missouri Press, 2004.

Ehrman, Bart D. *Lost Christianities: The Battles for Scripture and the Faiths We Never Knew*. New York: Oxford University Press, 2003.

Eliot, T. S. "Tradition and the Individual Talent." In *Selected Essays, 1917–1932*, 3–11. New York: Harcourt, 1932.

Ellwood, Robert S., Jr. *One Way: The Jesus Movement and Its Meaning*. Englewood Cliffs, N.J.: Prentice Hall, 1973.

Elzey, Wayne. "'What Would Jesus Do?' *In His Steps* and the Moral Codes of the Middle Class." *Soundings* 58, no. 4 (Winter 1975): 463–89.

English, James F. "Everywhere and Nowhere: The Sociology of Literature after 'the Sociology of Literature.'" *New Literary History* 41, no. 2 (Spring 2010): v–xxiii.

Enroth, Ronald M., Edward E. Ericson Jr., and C. Breckinridge Peters. *The Jesus People: Old-Time Religion in the Age of Aquarius*. Grand Rapids, Mich.: Eerdman's, 1972.

Enstad, Nan. *Ladies of Labor, Girls of Adventure: Working Women, Popular Culture, and Labor Politics at the Turn of the Twentieth Century*. New York: Columbia University Press, 1999.

Estabrook, J. Joseph. "The Undeveloped Side of the Book Business." *Publishers Weekly*, 26 May 1923, 1617.

Evenson, Laura. "Soulful Books Give Readers Insight, Make Best-Sellers." *San Francisco Chronicle*, 25 December 1996, A1.

Farrar, John. "Clean Fiction." *Independent*, 5 December 1925, 637–38.

Felski, Rita. *Uses of Literature*. Malden, Mass.: Blackwell, 2008.

Ferré, John P. *A Social Gospel for Millions: The Religious Bestsellers of Charles Sheldon, Charles Gordon, and Harold Bell Wright*. Bowling Green, Ohio: Bowling Green University Popular Press, 1988.

"Fervor and Froth." *Time*, 26 July 1976, online article. Accessed 28 June 2011.

Fessenden, Tracy. *Culture and Redemption: Religion, the Secular, and American Literature*. Princeton: Princeton University Press, 2007.

Forbes, Cheryl. "Unlisted Bestsellers." *Christianity Today*, 23 June 1972, 40–42.

Ford, Corey. "Three Rousing Cheers!!! The Parody Adventures of Our Youthful Heroes iii: When a Rollo Boy's a Rollo Boy or, Virtue Triumphant in Three Weeks." *Bookman*, November 1925, 254–58.

Fosdick, Harry Emerson. *The Living of These Days: An Autobiography*. New York: Harper, 1956.

———. *On Being a Real Person*. New York: Harper, 1943.

"Fosdick's Last Year." *Time*, 18 June 1946, 56.

Fox, Richard Wightman. "Experience and Explanation in Twentieth-Century American Religious History." In *New Directions in American Religious History*, edited by Harry S. Stout and D. G. Hart, 394–413. New York: Oxford University Press, 1997.

———. *Jesus in America: Personal Savior, Cultural Hero, National Obsession*. San Francisco: HarperSanFrancisco, 2004.

Frank, Waldo. "Pseudo-Literature." *New Republic*, 2 December 1925, 46–47.

Freilich, Leila. "ABA: The Convention Goes West." *Publishers Weekly*, 9 July 1973, 23.

Fried, Richard M. *The Man Everybody Knew: Bruce Barton and the Making of Modern America*. Chicago: Ivan R. Dee, 2005.

Frum, David. "Best-Seller Lists Need Repair." *Toronto Star*, 20 July 1996, 11.

Frykholm, Amy Johnson. *Rapture Culture: Left Behind in Evangelical America*. New York: Oxford University Press, 2004.

"Fulfilling the Promise: The 1997 Unitarian Universalism Needs and Aspirations Survey." http://www.uua.org/archive/promise/results.html. Accessed 26 August 2006.

Fuller, Edmund. "Pitchmen in the Pulpit." *Saturday Review*, 9 March 1957, 28–30.

Fuller, Robert. *Spiritual, but Not Religious: Understanding Unchurched America*. New York: Oxford University Press, 2001.

Gallagher, Sally K. *Evangelical Identity and Gendered Family Life*. New Brunswick, N.J.: Rutgers University Press, 2003.

Geertz, Clifford. "Thick Description: Toward an Interpretive Theory of Culture." In *The Interpretation of Cultures: Selected Essays*, 3–30. New York: Basic Books, 1973.

George, Carol V. R. *God's Salesman: Norman Vincent Peale and the Power of Positive Thinking*. New York: Oxford University Press, 1993.

Gere, Ann Ruggles. *Intimate Practices: Literacy and Cultural Work in U.S. Women's Clubs, 1880–1920*. Urbana: University of Illinois Press, 1997.

Gift, Patricia A. "One Spirit: Resources for the Spirit, Mind, and Body." Web. Accessed 11 October 2001.

Gilbert, James. *Men in the Middle: Searching for Masculinity in the 1950s*. Chicago: University of Chicago Press, 2005.

Gladstone, W. E. "'Robert Elsmere' and the Battle of Belief." *Nineteenth Century* 23 (May 1888): 769.

Gleason, Philip. *Speaking of Diversity: Language and Ethnicity in Twentieth-Century America*. Baltimore: Johns Hopkins University Press, 1992.

Gordon, Arthur. "The Case for 'Positive' Faith." *Redbook*, September 1955, 25.

——. *Norman Vincent Peale, Minister to Millions: A Biography*. Englewood Cliffs, N.J.: Prentice-Hall, 1958.

Gorenberg, Gershom. "A Wild and Crazy Guy." *Jerusalem Report*, 7 September 1995, 42.

Graham, Billy. *Peace with God*. New York, Doubleday, 1953.

——. *The Secret of Happiness: Jesus' Teaching on Happiness as Expressed in the Beatitudes*. New York: Doubleday, 1955.

Graham, William C. *Half-Finished Heaven: The Social Gospel in American Literature*. New York: University Press of America, 1995.

Grannis, Chandler. "Taste and Trends, 1972, in Religious Books." *Publishers Weekly*, 28 February 1972, 37–42.

Gribben, Crawford. *Writing the Rapture: Prophecy Fiction in Evangelical America*. New York: Oxford University Press, 2009.

Griffin, William. "Christian Booksellers Find Optimism in a Slow Economy." *Publishers Weekly*, 20 August 1982, 42.

——. "Christian Booksellers in Washington: Bibles Bigger Than Ever as Christian Book Sales Hit Billion-Dollar Mark." *Publishers Weekly*, 26 August 1983, 363.

Griffith, R. Marie. *God's Daughters: Evangelical Women and the Power of Submission*. Berkeley: University of California Press, 1997.

Griffiths, Paul J. *Religious Reading: The Place of Reading in the Practice of Religion*. New York: Oxford University Press, 1999.

Groothuis, Douglas. *Jesus in an Age of Controversy*. Eugene, Ore.: Wipf and Tock, 2002.

Guillory, John. *Cultural Capital: The Problem of Literary Canon Formation*. Chicago: University of Chicago Press, 1993.

———. "The Ethical Practice of Modernity: The Example of Reading." In *The Turn to Ethics*, edited by Marjorie Garber, Beatrice Hanssen, and Rebecca L. Walkowitz, 29–46. New York: Routledge, 2000.

Gutjahr, Paul C. "No Longer Left Behind: Amazon.com, Reader-Response, and the Changing Fortunes of the Christian Novel in America." *Book History* 5 (2002): 209–36.

———. "The Perseverance of Print-Bound Saints: Protestant Book Publishing." In *The Enduring Book: Print Culture in Postwar America*. Vol. 5 of *A History of the Book in America*, edited by David Paul Nord, Joan Shelley Rubin, and Michael Schudson, 376–88. Chapel Hill: University of North Carolina Press, 2009.

Habegger, Alfred. *Gender, Fantasy, and Realism in American Literature: The Rise of American Literary Realism in W. D. Howells and Henry James*. New York: Columbia University Press, 1982.

Hackett, Alice Payne, and James Henry Burke. *80 Years of Best Sellers, 1895–1975*. New York: Bowker, 1977.

Hall, Chris. "What Hal Lindsey Taught Me about the Second Coming." *Christianity Today*, 25 October 1999, 82–85.

Hall, David D. *Worlds of Wonder, Days of Judgment: Popular Religious Belief in Early New England*. New York: Knopf, 1989.

———, ed. *Lived Religion in America: Toward a History of Practice*. Princeton: Princeton University Press, 1997.

Hall, Stuart. "Notes on Deconstructing 'the Popular.'" In *People's History and Socialist Theory*, edited by Raphael Samuel, 227–39. Boston: Routledge, 1981.

Harker, Jaime. *America the Middlebrow: Women's Novels, Progressivism, and Middlebrow Authorship between the Wars*. Amherst: University of Massachusetts Press, 2007.

———. *Middlebrow Queer: Christopher Isherwood in America*. Minneapolis: University of Minnesota Press, 2013.

"Harold Bell Wright Admits He Is Not a Literary Man! Noted Novelist Whose Books Lead as Best Sellers Confesses He's 'at Sea' in Literary Circles; He Is Tired of Being Criticized!" *Douglas (Ariz.) International*, 10 September 1921, 1588.

"Harold Bell Wright Goes to Appleton." *Publishers Weekly*, 30 October 1920, 1308.

"Harold Bell Wright—His Books." *New York Times Book Review*, 10 August 1913, 3.

Hart, Irving Harlow. "The One Hundred Leading Authors of Best Sellers in Fiction from 1895 to 1944." *Publishers Weekly*, 19 January 1946, 287.

Hartley, Jenny. *Reading Groups*. New York: Oxford University Press, 2001.

Hastings, Milo. "Fiction Is Stranger Than Truth." *New Republic*, 21 July 1920, 227–28.

Haught, John F. "Search for Higher Reality: 'History of God' Carries Lessons Worth Pondering." *Washington Times*, 24 October 1993, B8.

Hawthorne, Hildegarde. "The Wright American." In *Bookman Anthology of Essays*, edited by John Farrar, 710–13. New York: Doran, 1923.

Hedstrom, Matthew S. "Psychology and Mysticism in 1940s Religion: Reading the Readers of Fosdick, Liebman, and Merton." In *Religion and the Culture of Print in Modern America*, edited by Charles L. Cohen and Paul S. Boyer, 343–67. Madison: University of Wisconsin Press, 2008.

———. *The Rise of Liberal Religion: Book Culture and American Spirituality in the Twentieth Century*. New York: Oxford University Press, 2013.

Heelas, Paul. *The New Age Movement.* Cambridge: Blackwell, 1996.

Heer, Jeet. "Battle of the Lists: A Country's Best-Seller Lists Confirm Certain National Stereotypes—Dieting Americans, for Example." *National Post* (Canada), 10 January 2004, RB07.

Heinze, Andrew R. *Jews and the American Soul: Human Nature in the Twentieth Century.* Princeton: Princeton University Press, 2004.

———. "*Peace of Mind* (1946): Judaism and the Therapeutic Polemics of Postwar America." *Religion and American Culture* 12, no. 1 (2002): 31–58.

Hench, John B. *Books as Weapons: Propaganda, Publishing, and the Battle for Global Markets in the Era of World War II.* Ithaca: Cornell University Press, 2010.

Hendershot, Heather. *Shaking the World for Jesus: Media and Conservative Evangelical Culture.* Chicago: University of Chicago Press, 2004.

Hendrickson, James. "Book People Come True." *Bookman,* October 1925, 192–93.

Herberg, Will. *Protestant-Catholic-Jew: An Essay in American Religious Sociology.* New York: Doubleday, 1960.

Herring, Hubert C. "The Rotarian Nobody Knows." *World Tomorrow,* December 1925, 382.

Hewitt, Peter F. "Record Attendance at 28th Annual Booksellers Convention." *Publishers Weekly,* 15 August 1977, 51.

———. "Religion Publishers Note Expanding Trade Sales." *Publishers Weekly,* 23 October 1978, 42–44.

Higgins, Michael. "Sources of Faith Need Not Be Disguised." *Toronto Star,* 17 April 1999, Life, n.p.

Higgins, Richard. "Sold on Spirituality Religion Is Everywhere in America These Days; but Is Faith Really Deepening, or Is It Just Being Marketed Better?" *Boston Globe* magazine, 3 December 2000, 19.

Hilkey, Judy Arlene. *Character Is Capital: Success Manuals and Manhood in Gilded Age America.* Chapel Hill: University of North Carolina Press, 1997.

Hilliard, Juli Cragg. "Baylor Study Offers Data on Reading Habits." *Religion Bookline—Publishers Weekly,* 6 September 2006.

Hochman, Barbara. *Getting at the Author: Reimagining Books and Reading in the Age of American Realism.* Amherst: University of Massachusetts Press, 2001.

Hofstadter, Richard. *Anti-intellectualism in American Life.* New York: Knopf, 1963.

Holt, Patricia. "Brisk Sales and High Attendance Mark Christian Booksellers Meeting." *Publishers Weekly,* 14 August 1978, 46–49.

———. "CBA Convention in Anaheim: Substantive Books Get Center Stage at Well-Attended Annual Meeting; Christian Publishers, Sensing a More Hospitable Climate, Are Eschewing 'Fluff' and Are Returning to the Basics." *Publishers Weekly,* 21 August 1981, 32.

———. "Western Religious Publishers See 'Phenomenal Growth Period.'" *Publishers Weekly,* 26 September 1977, 73.

Howard, Jane. "The Groovy Christians of Rye, NY: Youngsters Go on a Religion Trip and Leave Many Parents Baffled." *Life,* 14 May 1971, 78.

Howe, Irving. "The New York Intellectuals: A Chronicle and a Critique." *Commentary* 46, no. 4 (October 1968): 29–50.

H.S. "The Novel Goes to Church." *Saturday Review,* 24 June 1950, 22–23.

Hunting, Harold B. "What Is a Religious Book?" *Publishers Weekly,* 18 March 1922, 843–44.

Hutchinson, Paul. "Have We a 'New' Religion?" *Life,* 11 April 1955, 140.

Hutner, Gordon. *What America Read: Taste, Class, and the Novel, 1920–1960.* Chapel Hill: University of North Carolina Press, 2008.

"If People Ever Required Religious Faith, It's Now." *Saturday Evening Post*, 11 November 1950, 10–11.

Jackson, Gregory S. "What Would Jesus Do? Practical Christianity, Social Gospel Realism, and the Homiletic Novel." *PMLA* 121, no. 3 (May 2006): 641–61.

———. *The Word and Its Witness: The Spiritualization of American Realism*. Chicago: University of Chicago Press, 2009.

Jacobs, Dale. Review of *The Cloister Walk* by Kathleen Norris. *Journal of Popular Culture* 32, no. 4 (Spring 1999): 146–47.

Jacoby, Susan. *Freethinkers: A History of American Secularism*. New York: Holt, 2004.

Jameson, Fredric. *Postmodernism, or the Cultural Logic of Late Capitalism*. Durham: Duke University Press, 1991.

Jenkins, Philip. *Hidden Gospels: How the Search for Jesus Lost Its Way*. New York: Oxford University Press, 2001.

"Jesus as Efficiency Expert." *Christian Century*, 2 July 1925, 851.

Johnson, Daniel. "Immortal Longings." *The Times (London)*, 4 March 1993, Features, n.p.

Jones, Laurie Beth. *Jesus, CEO: Using Ancient Wisdom for Visionary Leadership*. New York: Hyperion, 1995.

Jones, Rufus M. *Social Law in the Spiritual World: Studies in Human and Divine Inter-Relationships*. Philadelphia: John C. Winston, 1904.

Jorstad, Erling. *That New-Time Religion: The Jesus Revival in America*. Minneapolis: Augsburg, 1972.

Jumonville, Neil. *The New York Intellectuals Reader*. New York: Routledge, 2007.

Karetzky, Stephen. *Reading Research and Librarianship: A History and Analysis*. Westport, Conn.: Greenwood Press, 1982.

Kelley, Mary. *Private Woman, Public Stage: Literary Domesticity in Nineteenth-Century America*. New York: Oxford University Press, 1984.

Kelly, Irving. "More Religious Books in the Home." *Publishers Weekly*, 15 March 1924, 973.

Kenamore, Clair. "A Curiosity in Best-Seller Technique." *Bookman*, July 1918, 541.

Kengor, Paul. *God and Ronald Reagan: A Spiritual Life*. New York: HarperCollins, 2004.

Ketchell, Aaron. *Holy Hills of the Ozarks: Religion and Tourism in Branson, MO*. Baltimore: Johns Hopkins University Press, 2007.

Kimmel, Michael S. "Thomas Moore's Bestselling Books Speak to an Age Hungry for Simpler Living." *Los Angeles Times*, 27 March 1994, Book Review, 1.

King, Karen L. *What Is Gnosticism?* Cambridge: Harvard University Press, 2003.

Kirsch, Jonathan. "PW Interviews: Hal Lindsey." *Publishers Weekly*, 14 March 1977, 30–32.

Klein, Christina. *Cold War Orientalism: Asia in the Middlebrow Imagination, 1945–61*. Berkeley: University of California Press, 2003.

Krauthammer, Charles. "Where's the 2000 Buzz?" *Washington Post*, 19 November 1999, A45.

Laugesen, Amanda. "Books for the World: American Book Programs in the Developing World, 1948–1968." In *Pressing the Fight: Print, Propaganda, and the Cold War*, edited by Greg Barnhisel and Catherine Turner, 126–44. Boston: University of Massachusetts Press, 2010.

Leach, Michael. "The Paradox of Religious Books: Rising Sales and Declining Faith: Bibles, and Books That Offer Comfort and Guidance on a Personal Level, Are the Mainstays of a Vigorous Market." *Publishers Weekly*, 9 September 1974, 40–41.

———. "We Are What We Read." *Christian Century*, 20 November 1974, 1089–92.

Lears, T. J. Jackson. *Fables of Abundance: A Cultural History of Advertising in America*. New York: Basic, 1994.

———. "From Salvation to Self-Realization: Advertising and the Therapeutic Roots of the Consumer Culture, 1880–1930." In *The Culture of Consumption: Critical Essays in American History, 1880–1980*, edited by Richard Wightman Fox and T. J. Jackson Lears, 3–38. New York: Pantheon, 1983.

———. *No Place of Grace: Antimodernism and the Transformation of American Culture, 1880–1920*. Chicago: University of Chicago Press, 1981.

L.F. "Selling Evangelical Books." *Publishers Weekly*, 23 June 1975, 48.

Lieblich, Julia. "Nurture Your Soul with Enchantment, Author Says." *Cleveland Plain Dealer*, 30 June 1996, Arts & Living, 1F.

Liebman, Joshua Loth. "The Art of Happiness." *Cosmopolitan*, September 1948, 38.

———. "Hope for Human Brotherhood." *Ladies' Home Journal*, January 1948, 132.

———. *Peace of Mind*. New York: Simon and Schuster, 1946.

Liepa, Alex. "Serving the Christian Booksellers." *Publishers Weekly*, 26 September 1977, 64.

Lindley, Susan H. "Women and the Social Gospel Novel." *Church History* 54 (1985): 56–73.

Lindsey, Hal, with C. C. Carlson. *The Late Great Planet Earth*. Grand Rapids, Mich.: Zondervan, 1970.

Lipsitz, George. "The Struggle for Hegemony." *Journal of American History* 75, no. 1 (June 1988): 146–50.

Long, Elizabeth. *Book Clubs: Women and the Uses of Reading in Everyday Life*. Chicago: University of Chicago Press, 2003.

Long, Kathryn T. "'Turning . . . Piety into Hard Cash': The Marketing of Nineteenth-Century Revivalism." In *God and Mammon: Protestants, Money, and the Market, 1790–1860*, edited by Mark A. Noll, 236–64. New York: Oxford University Press, 2002.

Loveland, Gilbert. "Laymen's Interest in Religious Books." *Publishers Weekly*, 16 February 1929, 753–56.

Luccock, Halford E. "Religion in the Bookstore: An Old Alliance Stouter Than Ever." *Publishers Weekly*, 18 February 1950, 990–93.

Luhrmann, T. M. *When God Talks Back: Understanding the American Evangelical Relationship with God*. New York: Knopf, 2012.

Luker, Ralph E. *The Social Gospel in Black and White: American Racial Reform, 1885–1912*. Chapel Hill: University of North Carolina Press, 1991.

Lyles, Jean Caffey. "Abingdon, Don't Abdicate." *Christian Century*, 18 May 1977, 470–71.

Machor, James L. *Reading Fiction in Antebellum America: Informed Response and Reception Histories, 1820–1865*. Baltimore: Johns Hopkins University Press, 2011.

Maddocks, Melvin. "Field Trips among the Intellectuals." *Sewanee Review* 90 (1982): 570.

Madrigal, Alix. "Finding the Soul of Life." *San Francisco Chronicle*, 7 June 1992, Sunday Review, 4.

"Making Best Sellers with Newspaper Space." *Publishers Weekly*, 15 August 1925, 549–50.

Man, Martha. "Religious Books Booming, CBA Conference Hears." *Publishers Weekly*, 10 September 1973, 38.

Marchand, Roland. *Advertising the American Dream: Making Way for Modernity, 1920–1940*. Berkeley: University of California Press, 1985.

Marcus, Sharon. *Between Women: Friendship, Desire, and Marriage in Victorian England*. Princeton: Princeton University Press, 2007.

Marsden, George M. *Fundamentalism and American Culture: The Shaping of Twentieth-Century Evangelicalism, 1870–1925*. New York: Oxford University Press, 1980.

———, ed. *Evangelicalism and Modern America*. Grand Rapids, Mich.: Eerdman's, 1984.

Martin, William. *A Prophet with Honor: The Billy Graham Story*. New York: Morrow, 1991.

Marty, Martin E. *Pilgrims in Their Own Land*. Boston: Little, Brown, 1984.

———. "Preface" and "The Protestant Press: Limitations and Possibilities." In *The Religious Press in America*, edited by Martin E. Marty, John G. Deedy Jr., David Wolf Silverman, and Robert Lekachman. vii–viii and 3–63. New York: Holt, Rinehart, and Winston, 1963.

———. "Religious Publishing: A Decline but Not a Demise." *Christian Century*, 28 April 1971, 524–28.

———. "A Spiritual Revival, a Commercial Boom, and Yet." *Publishers Weekly*, 13 February 1978, 83.

———. "Updating the List." *Christian Century*, 16 May 1979, 575.

———. "Varieties of Religious Publishing." *Publishers Weekly*, 13 September 1976, 55.

———. "You'll Never Get Rich." *Christian Century*, 15 November 1978, 1119.

Maryles, Daisy, and Patricia Holt. "CBA in Dallas: Sharing Ministry in a Heat Wave; a Bullish Outlook and New Book Trends Brighten Christian Bookseller Meeting." *Publishers Weekly*, 15 August 1980, 39.

Mason, M. S. "Tracing Three Religions, All with One God." *Christian Science Monitor*, 18 May 2001, 19.

Massa, Mark D. *Catholicism and American Culture: Fulton Sheen, Dorothy Day, and the Notre Dame Football Team*. New York: Crossroad, 1999.

May, Elaine Tyler. *Homeward Bound: American Families in the Cold War Era*. 20th anniversary edition. New York: Basic, 2008.

McAlister, Melani. *Epic Encounters: Culture, Media, and U.S. Interests in the Middle East since 1945*. Berkeley: University of California Press, 2001, 2005.

———. "Prophecy, Politics, and the Popular: The *Left Behind* Series and Christian Fundamentalism's New World Order." *South Atlantic Quarterly* 102, no. 4 (Fall 2003): 773–98.

McCloud, Sean. *Divine Hierarchies: Class in American Religion and Religious Studies*. Chapel Hill: University of North Carolina Press, 2007.

McClurg, Jocelyn. "Baby Boomers Become Sold on Souls: Writer Reworks Concept in Pair of Best Sellers." *Hartford Courant*, 21 January 1995, B5.

McDannell, Colleen. *Material Christianity: Religion and Popular Culture in America*. New Haven: Yale University Press, 1995.

McDowell, Edwin. "Publishers: A Matter of Faith." *New York Times*, 6 April 1980, BR2.

———. "Religious Publishing: Going Skyward." *New York Times*, 12 May 1981, C10.

McFadden, Michael. *The Jesus Revolution*. New York: Harper and Row, 1972.

McLoughlin, William G. *Revivals, Awakenings, and Reform: An Essay on Religion and Social Change in America, 1607–1977*. Chicago: University of Chicago Press, 1978.

McVey, Kathleen. "Gnosticism, Feminism, and Elaine Pagels." Review of *The Gnostic Gospels* by Elaine Pagels. *Theology Today* 37, no. 4 (January 1981): 498–501.

Melcher, Frederic G. "Great Books Are Life Teachers." *Publishers Weekly*, 8 April 1922, 1037.

Mencken, H. L. *Prejudices: Second Series*. New York: Farrar, 1977.

Meyer, Donald. *The Positive Thinkers: Popular Religious Psychology from Mary Baker Eddy to Norman Vincent Peale and Ronald Reagan*. Rev. ed. Middletown, Conn.: Wesleyan University Press, 1988.

"Microphone Missionary." *Time*, 14 April 1952, 73.

Miles, Jack. *God: A Biography*. New York: Vintage, 1995.

Miller, Robert Moats. *Harry Emerson Fosdick: Preacher, Pastor, Prophet*. New York: Oxford University Press, 1985.

Miller, Timothy. *Following in His Steps: A Biography of Charles M. Sheldon*. Knoxville: University of Tennessee Press, 1987.

Miller, William Lee. "Some Negative Thinking about Norman Vincent Peale." *Reporter*, 13 January 1955, 19–24.

Milstead, L. C. "Harold Bell Wright: Press Agent." *Bookman*, January 1931, 501–2.

"Ministers as Reviewers." *Publishers Weekly*, 8 April 1922, 1040.

Mitchell, Emily, and Margaret Nelson. "Place of the Spirit." *People Weekly*, 14 October 1996, 77–78.

Modern, John Lardas. *Secularism in Antebellum America*. Chicago: University of Chicago Press, 2011.

Montagno, Margaret, with Sylvester Monroe and Pamela Abramson. "Holy Writ." *Newsweek*, 25 July 1977, 58.

Montgomery, Edrene S. "Bruce Barton and the Twentieth Century Menace of Unreality." Ph.D. diss., University of Arkansas, 1984.

———. "Bruce Barton's *The Man Nobody Knows*: A Popular Advertising Illusion." *Journal of Popular Culture* 19, no. 3 (Winter 1985): 21–34.

Moore, R. Laurence. *Selling God: American Religion in the Marketplace of Culture*. New York: Oxford University Press, 1994.

Moore, Thomas. *Care of the Soul: A Guide for Cultivating Depth and Sacredness in Everyday Life*. New York: HarperCollins, 1992.

———. *Soul Mates: Honoring the Mystery of Love and Relationship*. New York: HarperCollins, 1994.

"More Books for Ministers." *Publishers Weekly*, 17 March 1928, 1280.

Moretti, Franco. *Graphs, Maps, Trees: Abstract Models for Literary Theory*. New York: Verso, 2005.

Morgan, David. *Visual Piety: A History and Theory of Popular Religious Images*. Berkeley: University of California Press, 1998.

Moriwaki, Lee. "Filling Deep Spring of Life—Loss of Enchantment 'Killing Us,' Author Says." *Seattle Times*, 6 July 1996, D4.

Morris, Edmund. *Dutch: A Memoir of Ronald Reagan*. New York: Random House, 1999.

Mott, Frank Luther. *Golden Multitudes: The Story of Best Sellers in the United States*. New York: Macmillan, 1947.

"Mr. Barton Makes a Success Story of the Life of Christ." *New York Times Book Review*, 10 May 1925, 11.

Munson, Miriam Ott. "Selling Religious Books." *Publishers Weekly*, 20 February 1926, 589.

Murray, W. H. "The Market for Religious Books." *Publishers Weekly*, 18 February 1928, 671.

Myers, Hope Reynolds. "Inter-Church Reading Program." *Publishers Weekly*, 20 February 1926, 586–88.

Nadel, Alan. *Containment Culture: American Narrative, Postmodernism, and the Atomic Age*. Durham: Duke University Press, 1995.

Neal, Lynn S. *Romancing God: Evangelical Women and Inspirational Fiction*. Chapel Hill: University of North Carolina Press, 2006.

"New Interest in Religious Books." *Publishers Weekly*, 23 February 1924, 596.

Newman, Louise Michelle. *White Women's Rights: The Racial Origins of Feminism in the United States*. New York: Oxford University Press, 1999.

"New Religious Book Poster." *Publishers Weekly*, 19 February 1927, 683.

Newton, J. F. "Religious Books." *Publishers Weekly*, 21 May 1927, 2002–3.

Niebuhr, Reinhold. "Is There a Revival of Religion?" *New York Times*, 19 November 1950, 7.

" 'Nones' on the Rise." *Pew Research Religion and Public Life Project*, 9 October 2012, http://www.pewforum.org/2012/10/09/nones-on-the-rise/. Accessed 31 January 2014.

Nord, David Paul. *Faith in Reading: Religious Publishing and the Birth of Mass Media in America*. New York: Oxford University Press, 2004.

Norris, Kathleen. *The Cloister Walk*. New York: Riverhead Books, 1996.

Nye, Russel. *The Unembarrassed Muse: The Popular Arts in America*. New York: Dial Press, 1970.

O'Bar, Jack. "A History of the Bobbs-Merrill Company, 1850–1940; with a Postlude through the Early 1960s." Ph.D. diss., Indiana University, 1975.

O'Brien, David. *The Renewal of American Catholicism*. New York: Paulist Press, 1972.

O'Reilly, David. "The Man Who Took a Close Look at God: Jack Miles Won a Pulitzer for His Biography of the Deity as Depicted in the Old Testament." *Philadelphia Inquirer*, 16 June 1996, G01.

———. "A 'Pious Agnostic' Puts Love of Neighbor First; after Writing His 'Biography' of God, Jack Miles Realized His Own Doubts." *Philadelphia Inquirer*, 20 July 1997, H07.

Orsi, Robert A. *Between Heaven and Earth: The Religious Worlds People Make and the Scholars Who Study Them*. Princeton: Princeton University Press, 2005.

———. "Everyday Miracles: The Study of Lived Religion." In *Lived Religion in America: Toward a History of Practice*, edited by David D. Hall, 3–21. Princeton: Princeton University Press, 1997.

———. "Sacred Superheroes: What 20th Century U.S. Catholic Children Read." Paper delivered at Literature, Book History, and the Anxiety of Interdisciplinarity Workshop of the Israel Science Foundation, Ben Gurion University, Beersheva, Israel, 1–3 July 2008.

———. *Thank You, St. Jude: Women's Devotion to the Patron Saint of Lost Causes*. New Haven: Yale University Press, 1996.

Osborn, Alex. "Will Dealers Follow the Leader? A Book-Marketing Experience Which Suggests That It All Depends on Who Is Leader." *Advertising and Selling Fortnightly*, 10 March 1926, 40–41.

"Our Unitarian Universalist Principles." http://www.uua.org/beliefs/principles/. Accessed 27 September 2011.

"The Output of Religious Books." *Publishers Weekly*, 17 February 1923, 501.

Overton, Grant. *Authors of the Day*. New York: Doran, 1924.

———. "Twentieth Century Book Buying Habits: Some Notes on Non-fiction, 1900–1920." *Publishers Weekly*, 26 January 1924, 237–39.

Pagels, Elaine. *Beyond Belief: The Secret Gospel of Thomas*. New York: Random House, 2003.

———. *The Gnostic Gospels*. New York: Vintage, 1979.

Patterson, Ronald P. "A Broad-Based Publishing Philosophy." *Publishers Weekly*, 26 September 1977, 65.

Paulson, Michael. "'Words of Reverence' Roil a Church: In Boston, Unitarian Universalists Ponder the Nature of Their Faith." *Boston Globe*, 28 June 2003, A1.

Peale, Norman Vincent. *The Amazing Results of Positive Thinking*. Englewood Cliffs, N.J.: Prentice-Hall, 1959.

———. *The Power of Positive Thinking*. New York: Fawcett, 1996.

———. *The Power of Positive Thinking*. New York: Fireside, 2003.

Pease, Otis. "Bruce Barton." In *Encyclopedia of American Biography*, edited by John A. Garraty, 62–63. New York: Harper, 1974.

Peckham, Stanton. "Retailing: Religion Is Big Business as Christian Booksellers Meet in Denver." *Publishers Weekly*, 16 August 1971, 47.

Peters, William. "The Case against 'Easy' Religion." *Redbook*, September 1955, 22.

Peterson, William S. "Gladstone's Review of *Robert Elsmere*: Some Unpublished Correspondence." *Review of English Studies* 21 (1970): 442–61.

Phelps, William Lyon. "The Why of the Best Seller." *Bookman*, December 1921, 300.

"A Phenomenal Bestseller You Won't Find Listed on the Opposite Page." Advertisement. *Publishers Weekly*, 27 March 1972, 107.

"The Phenomenal Interest in Religious Books." *Publishers Weekly*, 18 February 1950, 1018.

"The Phenomenon of the Religious Best Seller." *Publishers Weekly*, 14 July 1975, 45–47.

Pollock, John. *Billy Graham, Evangelist to the World: An Authorized Biography of the Decisive Years*. New York: Harper and Row, 1979.

Porterfield, Amanda. *The Transformation of American Religion: The Story of a Late Twentieth-Century Awakening*. New York: Oxford University Press, 2001.

Potter, Charles Francis. "Present Day Portraits of Jesus." *Bookman*, 25 July 1925, 590–91.

———. "Spring-Religion-Books." *Publishers Weekly*, 19 February 1927, 687–89.

"President Harding's Letter to the Religious Book Week Committee." *Publishers Weekly*, 1 April 1922, 979.

"A Program for Religious Reading." *Publishers Weekly*, 15 April 1922, 1119.

"A Proper Pulpit Theme." *Publishers Weekly*, 10 March 1923, 806.

Prothero, Stephen. *American Jesus: How the Son of God Became a National Icon*. New York: Farrar, 2003.

Putney, Clifford. *Muscular Christianity: Manhood and Sports in Protestant America, 1880–1920*. Cambridge: Harvard University Press, 2001.

Radway, Janice. *A Feeling for Books: The Book-of-the-Month Club, Literary Taste, and Middle-Class Desire*. Chapel Hill: University of North Carolina Press, 1997.

Ramsey, A. R. "Books and Bookmakers." *Ladies' Home Journal*, June 1889, 11.

R.D. "ABA: The Smoothest Convention Ever: Profitability of Religious Titles." *Publishers Weekly*, 5 July 1976, 48.

"Reaching Out for a Growing Market of Readers, Doubleday Adds an Evangelical Imprint." *Publishers Weekly*, 13 February 1978, 68.

Reagan, Ronald. *Ronald Reagan: An American Life*. New York: Simon and Schuster, 1990.

Reeves, Thomas C. *America's Bishop: The Life and Times of Fulton J. Sheen*. San Francisco: Encounter Books, 2001.

"Religion: The New Rebel Cry: Jesus Is Coming." *Time*, 21 June 1971, online article. Accessed 14 June 2010.

"Religion and the Intellectuals: A Symposium." *Partisan Review* 17, nos. 2, 3, 4, 5 (February, March, April, May–June 1950).

"Religious Best Sellers." *Publishers Weekly*, 13 February 1978, 88.

"Religious Book Clubs 1988." *Publishers Weekly*, 4 March 1988, 46–47.

"Religious Books as Best Sellers." *Publishers Weekly*, 3 April 1926, 1194.

"The Religious Book Season." *Publishers Weekly*, 18 February 1928, 666–68.

" 'The Religious Bookshelf' to Be Published in October." *Publishers Weekly*, 24 July 1920, 223.

"Religious Books in the Mainstream," in "ABA: The Convention Goes West." *Publishers Weekly*, 9 July 1973, 23.

"Religious Books of the Month." *Publishers Weekly*, 29 October 1927, 1641.

"Religious Book Week." *Publishers Weekly*, 15 January 1921, 105.

"Religious Book Week." *Publishers Weekly*, 26 February 1921, 620.

"Religious Book Week and After." *Publishers Weekly*, 2 April 1921, 1048.

"Religious Book Week and the Press." *Publishers Weekly*, 18 March 1922, 851.

"Religious Book Week Plans." *Publishers Weekly*, 4 February 1922, 343.

Religious Book Week poster illustration. *Publishers Weekly*, 17 February 1923, 509.

Religious Book Week poster illustration. *Publishers Weekly*, 5 February 1921, 352.

"Religious Publishers Seek Ways to Meet a Crisis." *Publishers Weekly*, 20 April 1970, 34.

"Religious Publishing and the 'Mainstream.'" *Publishers Weekly*, 10 September 1973, 28.

"Religious Publishing's Second Spring." *Christian Century*, 18 May 1977, 468.

"Religious Publishing's Solomons and Shebas." *Christian Century*, 26 November 1975, 1070.

"The Religious Renaissance." *Publishers Weekly*, 19 February 1927, 684.

Reynolds, David. *Faith in Fiction: The Emergence of Religious Literature in America*. Cambridge: Harvard University Press, 1981.

Ribuffo, Leo P. "Jesus Christ as Business Statesman: Bruce Barton and the Selling of Corporate Capitalism." *American Quarterly* 33, no. 2 (Summer 1981): 206–31.

Riley, Kathleen. *Fulton J. Sheen: An American Catholic Response to the Twentieth Century*. New York: Alba House, 2004.

Ripley, John W. "Another Look at the Rev. Mr. Charles M. Sheldon's Christian Daily Newspaper." *Kansas Historical Quarterly* 21, no. 1 (Spring 1965): 1–40.

———. "The Strange Story of Charles M. Sheldon's *In His Steps*." *Kansas Historical Quarterly* 34, no. 3 (Autumn 1968): 241–65.

Roberts, Jon H. *Darwinism and the Divine in America: Protestant Intellectuals and Organic Evolution, 1859–1900*. Madison: University of Wisconsin Press, 1988.

Robinson, David. *The Unitarians and the Universalists*. Westport, Conn.: Greenwood Press, 1985.

Roof, Wade Clark. *A Generation of Seekers: Spiritual Journeys of the Baby Boom Generation*. San Francisco: Harper, 1993.

———. *Spiritual Marketplace: Baby Boomers and the Remaking of American Religion*. Princeton: Princeton University Press, 1999.

Rose, Jonathan. "Rereading the English Common Reader: A Preface to a History of Audiences." *Journal of the History of Ideas* 53, no. 1 (1992): 47–70.

Roshevsky, Eve. "RPG: What It Is and What It Does." *Publishers Weekly*, 13 February 1978, 86.

Rourke, Mary. "The Intimate Achievement: Thomas Moore, Best-Selling Author and Diviner of the Soul, Meditates on Sex and True Closeness in the Context of a Healthy Spiritual Life." *Los Angeles Times*, 14 July 1998, E2.

Ruark, James E. "Meeting the Evangelical Needs in Religious Publishing: Three Editorial Views." *Publishers Weekly*, 26 September 1977, 66.

Rubin, Joan Shelley. "The Boundaries of American Religious Publishing in the Early Twentieth Century." *Book History* 2 (1999): 207–17.

———. *The Making of Middlebrow Culture*. Chapel Hill: University of North Carolina Press, 1992.

Ryan, Barbara. "Teasing Out Clues, Not Kooks: *The Man Nobody Knows* and *Ben-Hur*." *Reception* 5 (2013): 9–23.

Sanders, Seth L. "Apocalypse Then." Review of *The End of Days: Fundamentalism and the Struggle for the Temple Mount*, by Gershom Gorenberg. *Washington Post*, 24 December 2000, Book World, X05.

Schmidt, Leigh Eric. *Consumer Rites: The Buying and Selling of American Holidays*. Princeton: Princeton University Press, 1995.

———. *Restless Souls: The Making of American Spirituality from Emerson to Oprah*. San Francisco: HarperSanFrancisco, 2005.

Schweber, Howard. "The 'Science' of Legal Science: The Model of the Natural Sciences in Nineteenth-Century American Legal Education." *Law and History Review* 17, no. 3 (Fall 1999): 421–66.

Sedgwick, Eve Kosofsky. *Touching Feeling: Affect, Pedagogy, Performativity*. Durham: Duke University Press, 2003.

See, Lisa. "Speaking for the Evangelical Publishers." *Publishers Weekly*, 30 September 1983, 58–59.

Seldes, Gilbert. "The Living Christ." *New Republic*, 24 June 1925, 127.

———. "Service." *New Republic*, 15 July 1925, 207.

"Selling an Idea." *Publishers Weekly*, 15 January 1921, 105.

Shank, Stanley P. "A Word about Logos," in "Out of the Mainstream: Two Offbeat Religious Bookstore Chains." *Publishers Weekly*, 26 September 1980, 60–61.

Shaw, David. "Lists Flawed: 'Best-Seller' May or May Not Be One." *Los Angeles Times*, 17 September 1976, 1.

Sheen, Fulton J. *Freedom under God*. Milwaukee: Bruce, 1940.

———. *Peace of Soul*. 1949. Liguria, Mo.: Liguria, 1996.

———. *Treasure in Clay: The Autobiography of Fulton J. Sheen*. New York: Doubleday, 1980.

Sheldon, Charles M. *Charles M. Sheldon: His Life Story*. New York: Doran, 1925.

———. "The Ethics of Some Publishers." *Christian Century*, 27 September 1933, 1206–8.

———. "Foreword." In *In His Steps: "What Would Jesus Do?"* New York: Grosset & Dunlop, 1935.

———. *The History of "In His Steps."* Privately printed, 1938.

———. *In His Steps*. New York: Grosset & Dunlap, 1935.

———. "A Plea for a Christian Daily Newspaper." *Kingdom*, 28 June 1895 and 5 July 1895, 164–65, 181–82.

———. "The Topeka Capital This Week." *Topeka Daily Capital*, 13 March 1900, 2.

Shone, Tom. "Holy Unconvincing." *Sunday Times* (London), 7 January 1996, Features, n.p.

Shuck, Glenn. *Marks of the Beast: The Left Behind Novels and the Struggle for Evangelical Identity*. New York: New York University Press, 2005.

Sicherman, Barbara. *Well-Read Lives: How Books Inspired a Generation of American Women*. Chapel Hill: University of North Carolina Press, 2010.

Silk, Mark. "Religious Books: Seven That Made a Difference." *New York Times*, 30 March 1986, section 7, p. 1.

Silverman, Gillian. *Bodies and Books: Reading and the Fantasy of Communion in Nineteenth-Century America*. Philadelphia: University of Pennsylvania Press, 2012.

Singer, Ben. *Melodrama and Modernity: Early Sensational Cinema and Its Contexts*. New York: Columbia University Press, 2001.

Sinkford, William G. "Our Calling: Share the Good News with a World That Badly Needs It." *UU World: The Magazine of the Unitarian Universalist Association* 17, no. 2 (March/April 2003), http://www.uuworld.org/2003/02/calling.html. Accessed 26 August 2006.

Smith, Anthony Burke. *The Look of Catholics: Portrayals in Popular Culture from the Great Depression to the Cold War*. Lawrence: University Press of Kansas, 2010.

Smith, Christian. "Introduction: Rethinking the Secularization of American Public Life." In *The Secular Revolution: Power, Interests, and Conflict in the Secularization of American Public Life*, edited by Christian Smith, 1–96. Berkeley: University of California Press, 2003.

Smith, Erin A. "'Jesus, My Pal': Reading and Religion in Middlebrow America." *Canadian Review of American Studies* 37, no. 2 (2007): 147–81.

———. "Melodrama, Popular Religion, and Literary Value: The Case of Harold Bell Wright." *American Literary History* 17, no. 2 (Summer 2005): 217–43.

———. "The Religious Book Club: Print Culture, Consumerism, and the Spiritual Life of American Protestants between the Wars." In *Religion and the Culture of Print in America*, edited by Charles L. Cohen and Paul S. Boyer, 217–42. Madison: University of Wisconsin Press, 2008.

———. "'What Would Jesus Do?' The Social Gospel and the Literary Marketplace." *Book History* 10 (2007): 193–221.

Smith, Michael Ray. *The Jesus Newspaper: The Christian Experiment of 1900 and Its Lessons for Today*. Lanham, Md.: University Press of America, 2002.

Smith, W. J. "A Progressive Religious Book Store." *Publishers Weekly*, 12 March 1921, 777.

Spangler, Michael W. Review of *The Cloister Walk* by Kathleen Norris. *Christian Century*, 9 October 1996, online article. Accessed 11 October 2001.

Stacey, Judith. *Brave New Families: Stories of Domestic Upheaval in Late Twentieth-Century America*. Berkeley: University of California Press, 1998.

"Starving India: Fifty Million People Affected by the Famine." *Topeka Daily Capital*, 13 March 1900, 1.

Stevens, Jason W. *God-Fearing and Free: A Spiritual History of America's Cold War*. Cambridge: Harvard University Press, 2010.

Stidger, William L. "New Era in Religious Books." *Publishers Weekly*, 25 May 1929, 2462.

Stobbe, Leslie H. "Religious Publishing: More Attention Needed." Letters to the Editor. *Publishers Weekly*, 11 March 1974, 9.

Striphas, Ted. *The Late Age of Print: Everyday Book Culture from Consumerism to Control*. New York: Columbia University Press, 2009.

Stroud, Irene Elizabeth. "Words of Wisdom." Review of *Amazing Grace* by Kathleen Norris. *Women's Review of Books* 16, no. 1 (October 1998): 17–18.

"Suggestions for Booksellers for Religious Book Week." *Publishers Weekly*, 17 February 1923, 511.

Susman, Warren. "Piety, Profits, and Play: The 1920s." In *Men, Women, and Issues in American History*, vol. 2, edited by Howard H. Quint and Milton Cantor, 191–216. Homewood, Ill.: Dorsey, 1975.

Sweeney, Megan. *Reading Is My Window: Books and the Art of Reading in Women's Prisons*. Chapel Hill: University of North Carolina Press, 2010.

Tagg, Lawrence V. *Harold Bell Wright, Storyteller to America*. Tucson, Ariz.: Westernlore, 1986.

Tebbel, John. *Between Covers: The Rise and Transformation of Book Publishing in America*. New York: Oxford University Press, 1987.

———. *The Golden Age between Two Wars, 1920–1940*. Vol. 3 of *A History of Book Publishing in the United States*. New York: Bowker, 1978.

Thatcher, Floyd. "Welcome to a New Breed of Religious Writers (and About Time, Too)." *Publishers Weekly*, 4 March 1983, 46.

Thompson, Clive. "Checking It Twice: Nobody Really Knew Which Books Were Top-Selling—Until Bookscan Came Along, with New Technology for Tracking Sales." *Washington Post Book World*, 5 May 2002, T15.

Tickle, Phyllis A. *God Talk in America*. New York: Crossroad, 1997.

———. *Re-discovering the Sacred: Spirituality in America*. New York: Crossroad, 1995.

Tinder, Daniel. "Future Fact? Future Fiction?" *Christianity Today*, 15 April 1977, 40.

Tompkins, Jane. *Sensational Designs: The Cultural Work of American Fiction, 1790–1860*. New York: Oxford University Press, 1985.

Truitt, Eliza. "Culturebox: Apocalypse Soon: Booksellers' Biggest Nightmare Has Already Come True." Slate.com, 30 July 2001, http://www.slate.com/articles/arts/culturebox/2001/07/apocalypse_soon.html. Accessed 1 March 2011.

Turner, Catherine. *Marketing Modernism between the Two World Wars*. Amherst: University of Massachusetts Press, 2003.

"Two Comments on PW's CBA Convention Coverage." Letters to the Editor. *Publishers Weekly*, 26 September 1977, 49–50.

"Two New Religious Departments." *Publishers Weekly*, 15 January 1927, 195.

"Untangling Novels' Facts from Fiction." *Dallas Morning News*, 16 January 2004, A1.

Untitled review. *Living Church* (Milwaukee, Wis.), 4 November 1933, 11.

Vanderwaal, Cornelius. *Hal Lindsey and Biblical Prophecy*. St. Catherines, Ontario: Paideia Press, 1978.

"Views on Publishing: William R. Barbour, Jr., Revell President, Talks about 'Getting Our Books Out There Where the Unbeliever Action Is.'" *Publishers Weekly*, 14 March 1977, 55.

Wagner, C. Everett. "Religion Rings the Cash Register." *Plain Talk Magazine* 2 (April 1928): 456.

Wald, Alan M. *The New York Intellectuals: The Rise and Decline of the Anti-Stalinist Left from the 1930s to the 1980s*. Chapel Hill: University of North Carolina Press, 1987.

Walkowitz, Judith R. *City of Dreadful Delight: Narratives of Sexual Danger in Late-Victorian London*. Chicago: University of Chicago Press, 1992.

Walters, Ray. "Paperback Talk." *New York Times*, 6 April 1980, 27.

Ward, Hiley H. *The Far-Out Saints of the Jesus Communes: A Firsthand Report and Interpretation of the Jesus People Movement*. New York: Association Press, 1972.

Ward, Mrs. Humphry. "The New Reformation, a Dialogue." *Nineteenth Century* 25 (March 1889): 454–80.

———. *Robert Elsmere*. New York: Macmillan, 1888.

Warner, Michael. *Letters of the Republic: Publication and the Public Sphere in Eighteenth-Century America*. Cambridge: Harvard University Press, 1990.

Weber, William C. "Religious Books Deserve Attention from the Newspapers Every Week." *Publishers Weekly*, 17 February 1923, 517.

Weiss, Jeffrey. "Ripping 'The Da Vinci Code.'" *Dallas Morning News*, 6 May 2006, 1H, 3H.

Wharton, Gary C. "The Continuing Phenomenon of the Religious Best Seller." *Publishers Weekly*, 14 March 1977, 82.

"What Is a Religious Book? (An Editorial in the Rock Island *Argus* April 1, 1922)." *Publishers Weekly*, 17 February 1923, 513.

"What Is a Religious Book?" *Publishers Weekly*, 2 April 1927, 1409.

"What Is a Religious Book?" *Publishers Weekly*, 29 March 1924, 1107.

"What's Selling on the Religious Books Scene." *Publishers Weekly*, 8 March 1971, 55–58.

Whipple, Leon. "Books on the Belt." *Nation*, 13 February 1929, 182.

"Why Harpers Have Entered the Field of Religious Books." *Publishers Weekly*, 19 February 1927, 695.

"Why Is Harold Bell Wright?—Answered by Himself." *New York Times*, 28 August 1921, 15.

"Why the Common People Do Not Buy More Books." *Publishers Weekly*, 24 September 1921, 977.

Wilkinson, Bruce. *The Prayer of Jabez: Breaking Through to the Blessed Life*. New York: Multnomah, 2000.

Winston, Diane. "Gallup Says America Has a Shallow Faith." *Dallas Morning News*, 11 December 1999, 1G.

Winston, Kimberly. "Religion Update: Opening New Pathways to Consumers; Opportunities Arise in E-Commerce, Mass Merchandising, and Specialty Book Clubs." *Publishers Weekly*, 15 March 1999, 56–57.

Wister, Owen. "Quack-Novels and Democracy." *Atlantic Monthly*, June 1915, 721–34.

Witham, Larry. "God Is Now a Celebrity as Humans Seek Answers." *Washington Times*, 29 April 1995, C5.

Wolfe, Alan. *The Transformation of American Religion: How We Actually Live Our Faith*. New York: Free Press, 2003.

Woodward, Kenneth L., with John Barnes and Laurie Lisle. "Born Again!" *Newsweek*, 25 October 1976, 68.

"Wright Confesses He Is 'at Sea' in Literary Circles." *Buffalo (N.Y.) Courier*, 6 September 1921.

Wright, Harold Bell. *The Calling of Dan Matthews*. 1909. Gretna, La.: Pelican Publishing Company, 1995.

———. *The Eyes of the World: A Novel*. Chicago: Book Supply Company, 1914.

———. *God and the Groceryman*. New York: Appleton, 1927.

———. *The Shepherd of the Hills*. 1907. Gretna, La.: Pelican Publishing Company, 2000.

———. *That Printer of Udell's*. 1903. Gretna, La.: Pelican Publishing Company, 1996.

———. *Their Yesterdays*. Chicago: Book Supply Company, 1912.

———. *To My Sons*. New York: Harper, 1934.

———. *When a Man's a Man*. Chicago: Book Supply Company, 1916.

———. *The Winning of Barbara Worth*. 1911. Gretna, La.: Pelican Publishing Company, 1999.

"Writing 'A History of God': Former Nun's Book Traces Development of Religions." *Washington Post*, 4 December 1993, D7.

Wuthnow, Robert. *After Heaven: Spirituality in America since the 1950s*. Berkeley: University of California Press, 1998.

———. *Sharing the Journey: Support Groups and America's New Quest for Community*. New York: Free Press, 1994.

"Year-Round Bookselling Campaign Bulletins." *Publishers Weekly*, 23 February 1924, 598.

Yoffe, Emily. "How the Soul Is Sold." *New York Times*, 23 April 1995, section 6, p. 44.

INDEX

Education, 52, 136, 305, 310, 324–25 (n. 69).
    See also Cultural capital; Social class
End-times prophecy, 2, 16, 201, 222, 231, 233,
    245, 298. See also *Late Great Planet Earth,
    The*; *Left Behind*
Evangelical books and publishing, 43–44, 48,
    201–2, 207–17, 221, 232, 300–302, 368 (n. 64)
Evangelicals, 17, 208, 214, 215, 222–23, 279, 284,
    296, 297, 311, 368 (n. 66). *See also* Conserva-
    tive Christians; Fundamentalism
Evolution, 69, 89, 101, 115
Eyes of the World (Wright), *The*, 14, 48, 52, 57,
    58–59, 65

Feminism, 42, 287–89, 291–93, 300–301, 311,
    364 (n. 16), 365 (nn. 30, 31), 366 (n. 38),
    368 (nn. 61, 62). *See also* Gender; Women
Fosdick, Harry Emerson, 88, 137, 141, 142, 143,
    157–77 passim, 184, 191, 192–98
Frykholm, Amy Johnson, 1, 11–12, 13, 35, 97, 242,
    298–99, 358 (n. 65), 359 (n. 83), 360 (n. 112)
Fundamentalism, 70, 101, 103, 129, 140, 231,
    232, 239, 311; and modernism controversy,
    9, 15, 28, 77, 128; seekers defined in opposi-
    tion to, 259, 260, 262, 263, 269, 284. *See also*
    Conservative Christians; Evangelicals

Gender, 31, 39–43, 67, 71–72, 95–96, 178, 179–83,
    195, 220, 256–58, 310, 323 (n. 40), 324
    (n. 62), 330–31 (n. 112), 331 (n. 113). *See also*
    Feminism; Manliness/Masculinity; Women
Gnostic Gospels (Pagels), *The*, 9, 278, 281, 289,
    290, 295
Gnosticism, 17, 276, 278–79, 281, 285, 286–87,
    288–89, 290, 297, 310, 311, 363–64 (n. 8)
God: A Biography (Miles), 16, 250, 263–67
Graham, Billy, 137, 140, 141–42, 158, 159, 162, 163,
    166, 171, 179, 183–87, 188, 192, 206, 210, 218
Great Books program, 10, 11, 12, 242, 339
    (n. 65), 363 (n. 60)

Hedstrom, Matthew, 13, 86–87, 88, 104–5, 159,
    309, 332 (nn. 13, 22), 333 (n. 36), 334 (n. 61),
    336 (n. 95)
Herberg, Will, 15, 141, 162, 176
Heresy/heretics, 42, 43, 45, 121, 123; and
    Unitarian Universalists and seekers, 16, 17,

274, 276, 277, 278–79, 283, 285, 291, 295. *See
    also* Orthodoxy; Theology
Hinduism, 6, 93, 94, 95, 104, 193, 194, 195, 280
Historical biblical criticism, 24–25, 27, 34, 35,
    41, 89, 94, 102, 103–4, 115
History of God (Armstrong), *A*, 16, 250,
    259–63, 294
History of the book, 3, 360 (n. 111)
Humanities, 9, 17, 46, 307

Individualism, 70–71, 101, 114, 122, 155, 160, 178,
    183, 196–98, 232–34, 245, 251–52, 258–59, 305
In His Steps: What Would Jesus Do? (Sheldon),
    2, 13–14, 22, 23, 30–35, 39, 43, 44, 46, 105, 303
Inside of the Cup (Churchill), 14, 21, 22, 39–43,
    44, 46
Intellectuals, 24–27, 34, 51, 53, 58–59, 67, 108;
    as different kinds of readers than ordinary
    people, 15, 72, 123, 124, 135–36, 138–42, 153,
    155, 305; in *Partisan Review* "Religion and
    the Intellectuals" symposium, 145–52
Intensive reading/traditional literacy, 28, 44,
    132, 322 (n. 24)

Jackson, Gregory, 2, 29–30, 31, 35, 64, 312,
    320 (n. 28), 321 (n. 7), 322–23 (n. 36), 323
    (n. 40), 324 (n. 62), 325 (nn. 80, 82), 329
    (n. 85), 330 (n. 88), 331 (n. 113)
Jesus Movement / People, 210, 211–13, 235
"Jesus Newspaper," 23, 36–38, 324 (nn. 52, 57)
Jewish books and readers, 5, 10, 94, 169–70
Judaism, 95, 104, 146, 158, 166–71, 176, 250,
    259, 261, 263, 280, 293, 346 (n. 42)
Judeo-Christian, 159, 302

Language, sacred, 269, 270–72, 274, 276
Late Great Planet Earth (Lindsey), *The*, 2, 3,
    8, 9, 11, 16, 201–21 passim, 222–46 passim,
    310, 311, 315
Left Behind series, 1, 236, 268, 296, 298–99,
    300, 304, 358 (n. 65), 368 (nn. 58, 64)
Liberal Protestantism, 21, 43, 48, 59, 70, 78, 89,
    236, 249, 276, 311, 312, 329 (n. 65). *See also*
    Religious liberals; Seeker spirituality
Libraries, 23–28, 42, 78
Liebman, Joshua Loth, 137, 141, 144–45, 157–87
    passim, 190–91, 196, 198, 259, 346 (n. 42)

Life-application method. *See* Religious
   reading
Lindsey, Hal, 2, 8, 16, 201–21 passim, 222–46
   passim, 311, 315
Literary canon, 43–46, 47, 57
Literary criticism, 256, 264, 266–67, 294–95,
   321 (n. 32)
Literary studies, 17, 46, 72, 303, 306–7, 325
   (nn. 82, 86)
Lived religion, 3, 4, 107, 108, 121–29, 132, 246,
   308, 311, 312–13. *See also* Religious studies

Manliness/Masculinity, 48–50, 109–13, 179,
   311, 326 (n. 12), 337 (n. 18), 348 (n. 92).
   See also Gender
Man Nobody Knows (Barton), *The*, 2, 4, 9, 14,
   75, 105, 106–32 passim, 303, 311
Marty, Martin, 159, 202, 203, 214–15, 216, 227–28
Marxism, 146, 149, 150, 151, 306
Melodrama, 14, 47, 51, 59–67, 310, 329 (nn. 65,
   72). *See also* Allegory
Mencken, H. L., 48, 51, 213
Middlebrow, 14, 15, 76, 92, 107, 121, 135, 171,
   176, 186, 194, 215, 283, 310, 311, 320 (nn. 23,
   28); historical origins of in religious reading, 10–13, 308; personalism, 98–99, 102,
   118–20, 143–45, 196; religion, 96–100, 123,
   125, 142–45, 152–55, 239–44
Miles, Jack, 16, 250, 263–67
Modernism, 9, 15, 28, 45, 58–59, 77, 97, 101,
   128, 146, 255, 328 (n. 57)
Moore, Thomas, 2, 16, 250, 253–59, 260, 261,
   267, 269, 272
Muslims, 6, 158, 193, 194, 195, 250, 259, 261,
   263, 293
Mysticism, 99, 102, 104, 251, 260, 261, 263, 309,
   311, 334 (n. 61), 363 (n. 7), 366 (n. 37)

Natural theology, 65, 91, 172, 334 (n. 59)
New Age, 16, 224, 225, 226, 245, 249, 250, 254,
   269, 363 (n. 63), 368 (n. 64)
New Criticism, 3, 45, 325 (n. 86)
New York intellectuals, 145–52. *See also* Intel-
   lectuals; *Partisan Review*
Niebuhr, Reinhold, 138, 139, 141, 142, 156, 305,
   342 (n. 33)
Norris, Kathleen, 2, 16, 250, 267–74

On Being a Real Person (Fosdick), 15, 135, 142,
   158, 163–66, 170, 184, 192, 195–98
Orsi, Robert, 4, 117, 217, 308, 312–13,
   368 (n. 66)
Orthodoxy, 24, 25, 27, 39, 40, 41, 285, 287, 289.
   See also Heresy; Theology

Pagels, Elaine, 276, 278, 281, 282, 285, 289,
   290, 298
Paperback books, 16, 205–6, 211, 213, 217, 221, 226
Partisan Review, 9, 15, 136, 145–52, 162
Pastoral counseling, 163–64, 177
Peace of Mind (Liebman), 15, 135, 137, 141, 144,
   157, 158, 161, 166–71, 183, 187, 192, 198
Peace of Soul (Sheen), 15, 136, 137, 158, 161,
   171–76, 183, 189
Peace with God (Graham), 15, 136, 137, 141, 158,
   183–87, 192
Peale, Norman Vincent, 2, 4, 15, 135, 136, 137,
   140, 141, 142, 143, 156, 158, 160, 162, 165,
   176–92 passim, 198, 304, 305
Popular reading, 6–8, 319–20 (n. 15), 320 (n. 18),
   322–23 (n. 36)
Postmodernism, 16, 261, 267, 272, 273, 275
Power of Positive Thinking (Peale), *The*, 2, 4,
   15, 136, 137, 140, 143, 156, 158, 176–92 passim,
   304, 305
Premillennial dispensationalism, 233, 236–39
Protestant-Catholic-Jew (Herberg), 141, 162
Psychoanalysis, 92, 152, 157, 167, 171–73, 306,
   346 (n. 53)
Psychology/psychotherapy, 15, 89, 90, 92–93,
   101, 135, 137, 140, 157, 160–61, 252, 254–56,
   270, 279, 297–98, 302, 309, 311, 367 (n. 50).
   See also Self-help

Race, 5–6, 11, 47, 67–70, 71–72, 95–96, 178,
   205, 252, 256–58, 281, 296, 310, 320 (n. 17),
   330 (n. 108), 331 (n. 119); readers identifying across, 31, 323 (n. 40), 331(n. 113)
Radway, Janice, 10, 96, 97, 98, 120, 121–22, 196
Reagan, Ronald, 47, 56, 222, 351 (n. 53)
Religious Book Club, 13, 14, 75, 76, 87–105,
   107, 113, 120, 129, 143, 159, 163, 167, 249, 311,
   312, 331–32 (n. 4), 333 (nn. 39, 42)
Religious books: definition of, 78–80, 203,
   210–11; distribution of, 14, 53–55, 101, 104,

203, 327 (n. 39); function of, 80–83, 207–9; language in, 3, 16, 96–97, 107, 122–23, 193, 204, 211, 221, 241, 262, 267; marketing of, 85–86, 129–31, 142–43, 203–7, 209–10

Religious Book Week, 14, 76–78, 105, 159

Religious community, 100, 227, 252, 274, 276, 279, 280, 290, 297

Religious identity narratives, 274, 275, 276, 279, 289, 297, 302

Religious liberals, 17, 274, 276, 279, 291, 295, 296, 297, 300, 310. *See also* Liberal Protestantism; Seeker spirituality; Spiritual left

Religious Publishers Group of the American Booksellers Association, 203, 205, 209

Religious publishing, history of, 2, 202–13

Religious reading, 11, 35, 97, 242, 307–13, 367–68 (n. 55).

Religious studies, 17, 312, 313

Robert Elsmere (Ward), 13, 14, 22, 23–27, 34, 35, 38, 39–40, 43, 44, 46

Rubin, Joan Shelley, 10, 12–13, 92

Science and religion, 15, 70, 71, 89, 90–92, 100, 137, 147, 148, 149, 150, 151, 153, 167–68, 185, 261, 291, 309–10, 331 (n. 118), 333 (n. 48), 333–34 (n. 30), 334 (n. 59)

Science fiction, 16, 224, 225, 236, 244

Seeker spirituality, 8, 13, 16, 250–53, 262, 264, 265, 268, 274–75, 276, 279–81, 283, 300, 311, 334 (n. 61), 365 (n. 23). *See also* Religious liberals; Spiritual left

Self-help, 15, 135, 143, 160, 204, 210, 250, 253, 254, 256, 257. *See also* Psychology/ psychotherapy

Sentimental fiction/domestic fiction, 29, 48, 49, 50, 125

Sheen, Fulton, 15, 136, 137, 140, 141, 142, 157, 158, 159, 160, 161, 162, 171–76, 183, 184, 189–90, 198, 346 (n. 53)

Sheldon, Charles, 2, 13, 22, 23, 27–28, 28–30, 43, 44, 45, 48, 105, 303, 310

Shepherd of the Hills (Wright), *The*, 14, 48, 61–68, 70

Social class, 30–31, 54–55, 71–72, 95–96, 136–38, 154, 215, 252, 256–57, 276, 281, 305,

310, 320 (n. 17), 322–23 (n. 36), 323 (n. 40), 330–31 (n. 112), 331 (n. 113), 363 (n. 7). *See also* Cultural capital; Education

Social Gospel, 3, 5, 8, 9, 13, 21–23, 47, 125, 309, 310, 327 (n. 40)

Spiritual left, 275, 280. *See also* Religious liberals; Seeker spirituality

Spiritual practice/discipline, 16, 250, 260, 261, 270, 272, 274, 275, 276, 286, 297

That Printer of Udell's (Wright), 14, 22, 31, 47, 48, 49, 56, 59–60

Theater, 60–61

Theology 14, 16, 28, 42, 76, 102, 103, 115, 120–21, 139, 140, 142, 150, 151, 185, 265–66, 305; lack of importance or interest for readers, 9, 11, 28, 99, 107, 125–29, 166, 193, 203–4, 236–39, 251, 271, 311, 340 (n. 71). *See also* Heresy; Orthodoxy

Unchurched / "the nones," 84, 203, 239, 286, 360 (n. 12)

Unitarian Universalism, 11, 17, 121, 275, 276–302 passim, 309, 310, 311, 363 (nn. 2, 7), 364 (n. 9), 365 (nn. 22, 24, 30), 366 (n. 37)

Ward, Mrs. Humphry, 13, 22, 23–27, 35, 38–39, 40, 44, 45

What Can A Man Believe? (Barton), 14–15, 106, 113, 128

When A Man's A Man (Wright), 48, 49, 52–53

Winning of Barbara Worth (Wright), *The*, 14, 49, 57, 68–70

Women, 17, 39–43, 68–69, 180–82, 252, 276, 281, 286, 297, 311, 324 (n. 63), 330 (nn. 108, 109), 347–48 (n. 82), 364 (n. 11), 365 (nn. 23, 32). *See also* Feminism; Gender

Wright, Harold Bell, 4, 8, 14, 22, 31, 45, 46, 47–72 passim, 113, 130, 310, 326 (n. 24), 328 (n. 45)

Youth readers, 16, 211–13, 221, 233, 311, 352 (n. 72)

Zondervan, 16, 201, 206, 207, 210, 211, 217, 221, 224, 226, 239, 240